D0360421

RICHARD DANBURY read philosophy at Cambridge University and trained as a barrister before practising in criminal law. In a bid for freedom in 1998 he escaped to South America to reinvent himself as a travel writer, spending six months on the continent researching the first edition of this book. He first visited South America in 1992 and has also hiked in North America, Asia, Africa and Europe.

Married to Trailblazer author, Melissa Graham, with whom he wrote *The Rough Guide to Chile*, he now lives in London and works for the BBC.

HENRY STEDMAN researched and updated this second edition of *The Inca Trail*. Born in Chatham in Kent, he didn't learn to walk till the age of two but enjoyed the experience so much that he's been on his feet ever since. Over the past ten years Henry's legs have taken him up and down the Himalaya in Nepal, the Yellow Peak Range in China, the Karakoram in Pakistan, the Chouf in Lebanon, the Cordilleras in the Philippines, the Dolomites in Italy, Gunung Leuser in Sumatra and round the Ramonafana National Park in Madagascar.

Henry is the author of Trailblazer's *Trekking in the Dolomites* and *Istanbul to Cairo Overland*, co-author of *The Rough Guide to Indonesia*, *The Rough Guide to Southeast Asia* and the *Bradt Guide to Palestine*. He is currently working on his next Trailblazer project, *Kilimanjaro – treks and excursions*.

The Inca Trail, Cusco & Machu Picchu
First edition: 1999, this second edition 2002, reprinted with amendments 2004

Publisher
Trailblazer Publications
The Old Manse, Tower Rd, Hindhead, Surrey, GU26 6SU, UK
Fax (+44) 01428-607571
info@trailblazer-guides.com
www.trailblazer-guides.com

British Library Cataloguing in Publication Data
A catalogue record for this book is available from the British Library

ISBN 1-873756-64-X

© Richard Danbury 2002
Text, maps and photographs (unless otherwise credited)

The right of Richard Danbury to be identified as the author of this work has been
asserted by him in accordance with the Copyright, Designs and Patents Act 1988

Editor: Patricia Major
Typesetting: Henry Stedman and Anna Jacomb-Hood
Proof-reading: Anna Jacomb-Hood and Melissa Graham
Layout: Anna Jacomb-Hood and Bryn Thomas
Maps: Jane Thomas (trail maps); Nick Hill (town plans)
Index: Jane Thomas

Warning: mountain walking can be dangerous
Please read the notes on when to go (p19-20) and on mountain safety (pp32-34 and
pp164-170). Every effort has been made by the authors and publisher to ensure that
the information contained herein is as accurate and up to date as possible. However,
they are unable to accept responsibility for any inconvenience, loss or injury
sustained by anyone as a result of the advice and information given in this guide.

Printed on chlorine-free paper from farmed forests by
D²Print (☎ +65-6295 5598), Singapore

THE
INCA TRAIL
CUSCO & MACHU PICCHU

RICHARD DANBURY

SECOND EDITION RESEARCHED AND UPDATED BY
HENRY STEDMAN

TRAILBLAZER PUBLICATIONS

Richard Danbury dedicates this book to the memory of his parents

Acknowledgements

From Richard At the risk of sounding like an Oscar winner, there are many people, both in the UK and in Peru, to whom I owe thanks. For providing help and information in London: Giovanna Salini at the Peruvian Embassy, the DTI and FCO, and Marcia Walker at the Peru Support Group. In Peru I must thank the INC, the SAEC and Infotur. The staff at Humanities 1 in the British Library provided great help with general research, and in more specific fields Samya Beidas Emanuel gave a hand with economics, and doctors Chris Danbury and Gus Gazzard helped with medical stuff. I was also lucky enough that another type of doctor, Dr Ann Kendall, found time to help with information about the Cusichaca. Thanks also to the Arequpia tourist office, and the La Reyna hospedaje in the same town: sorry that we had to cut you out. Thanks to Richard Derham for checking the maps and not getting lost, and to his sister Katie for secretarial work (keep that forehead stiff). An enormous thank you to Bryn for letting down the lifeline, and all at Trailblazer, particularly Patricia Major for sensitive editing, Jane Thomas for the index and all the hard work and inspiration involved in turning my sketches into maps, and Anna JH for typesetting. For this second edition, thanks again to everyone above at Trailblazer and, in addition, thanks to Henry Stedman for researching and updating the text, Nick Hill for the town plans and site maps and Melissa for proof-reading.

For walking with me, Paul Vick, and to Simon (from Wall Street) and Nell (from Sesame Street) for putting up with our bickering. Thanks also to Ladia and Jitka for company, photographs and the invitation to Prague. Gustavo Rivera Basurz, Lima for friendship and a lift (*Defiende a la Republica: Esribe a tus amigos de todo el mundo!*). And thanks again to Melissa, for so much and I'd better stop now or I'll get sloppy.

From Henry I'd like to thank: Nadege Menager, Pascale Delagnes, Miranda Withams, Amy Porter, Max Milligan, Anne-Sophie Melis, Rosa at La Tertulia, Andreas Koehler, Morten Haug, Einar Magelssen, Oyvind Eng, Ronal Cobos, Alberto Silva Palomino, George Robinson, Natasha Epstein, and Maria Melvyn Ladron de Guevara Salas at the INC.

A request

The authors and publisher have tried to ensure that this guide is as accurate and up to date as possible. However things change quickly in this part of the world. Prices rise, new hotels are built and trails are re-routed. If you notice any changes or omissions that should be included in the next edition of this book, please write to Richard Danbury at Trailblazer Publications (address on p2) or email him: richard.danbury@trailblazer-guides.com. A free copy of the next edition will be sent to persons making a significant contribution.

Updated information will shortly be available on the Internet at
www.trailblazer-guides.com

Front cover: Machu Picchu (photo: © Richard Danbury)

CONTENTS

INTRODUCTION

PART 1: PLANNING YOUR TRIP

With a group or on your own
Tours and trekking agencies 12 – Porters, arrieros and guides 15

Getting to Peru
By air 16 – Overland 17

Budgeting
Accommodation, food, transport 18

When to go and for how long?
When to go 19 – For how long? 19

Route options
The classic Inca Trail 20 – Variations on the classic trail 21
Shorter Trails 21 – Chilca (Km77) up the Silque Valley 21
The Mollepata trek 24 – The Vilcabamba Trail 24 – Combining
or altering routes 24

What to take
Boots 25 – Clothes 25 – Equipment 26 – Food 28 – Medical kit 29
Maps 29 – Recommended reading 29 – Internet sites 31

Pre-departure preparations
Fitness 32 – Inoculations 32 – High-altitude travel 33
Insurance 34

PART 2: PERU

Facts about the country
Geographical background 35 – Historical outline 37
The people 45 – Politics and economics 47 – Culture 50

Practical information for the visitor
Documents and visas 52 – Airport tax 52 – Money 52 – Getting
around 53 – Accommodation 54 – Electricity 55 – Time 55
Post and telecommunications 55 – Holidays and festivals 56
Food and drink 57 – Shopping 59 – Safety 60 – Drugs 61

Flora and fauna
Mammals 62 – Reptiles 62 – Birds 63 – Flora 64

PART 3: THE INCAS

Pre-Inca civilizations
In the beginning 62 – Pre-ceramic peoples 67 – The Initial Period 68
Chavín 70 – Mastercraftsmen 71 – Tiahuanaco-Huari 74 – The days
before the Inca 76

Days of the Inca
Piecing together the jigsaw 78 – The origins of the Incas 78 – Oral
history 79 – Class and clans 81 – Inca government 82 – How they
ran the empire 83 – Spiritual life of the Incas 84 – Inca culture 86

The fall of the Incas
Plague and civil war 90 – Pizarro and Almagro 91 – First contact 92
The trap 92 – The great checkmate 93 – The march on Cusco 94
Cusco: capital of the empire 95 – Sow the wind 95 – Reap the
whirlwind 96 – Vilcabamba 96 – Reap another whirlwind 99

PART 4: LIMA
History 100 – Arrival 102 – Getting around 103 – Orientation 104
Services 104 – Where to stay 107 – Where to eat and drink 114
What to see 115 – Shopping 118 – Moving on 119

PART 5: CUSCO AND AROUND

Cusco
History 122 – Arrival 124 – Getting Around 124 – Orientation 125
Services 125 – Where to stay 130 – Where to eat and drink 134
Shopping 138 – What to see 140 – Moving on 146

Around Cusco
Ruins near Cusco (day hike: Sacsayhuaman, Qenko, Salapunco,
Puca Pucara, Tambo Machay) 147 – The Sacred Valley (Pisac, Chinchero,
Urubamba, Ollantaytambo, Aguas Calientes) 151

PART 6: MINIMUM IMPACT AND SAFE TREKKING

Minimum impact trekking
Environmental impact 160 – Economic impact 162 – Cultural
impact 163

Safe trekking
Safety in the hills 164 – Health in the hills 165

PART 7: TRAIL GUIDE AND MAPS

Using this guide
Route descriptions 171 – Route maps 171

Practicalities
Food and water 172 – Tickets and prices 172 – Getting to the trailheads 174

The classic Inca Trail
Km88 to Huayllabamba 175 – **Map 1 177** – Huayllabamba to
Pacamayo camp 178 – **Map 2 179** – Pacamayo camp to the third pass 180
Map 3 181 – Third pass to Machu Picchu 185 – **Map 4 187**

Variations on the classic trail
Starting at Chilca 190 – **Map 5 191** – Starting at Km82 192 – **Map 6 193**

The shorter trail
Km104 to El Camino Segrado del Inca 194 – **Map 7 195**

Chilca up the Silque Valley
Chilca to halfway up 198 – **Map 8 199** – Halfway up to past
Ancascocha 200 – **Map 9 201** – Past Ancascocha to valley turn 200
Map 10 203 – Turn in the valley to Paucarcancha 204 – **Map 11 205**
Options from Paucarcancha 207

The Mollepata trek
Mollepata to above Marcocassa 207 – **Map 12 209** – Above Marcocassa
to Soray 210 – **Map 13 211** – Soray to the pass 210 – **Map 14 213**
The pass to Pampa Cahuana 212 – **Map 15 214** – Pampa Cahuana to
Paucarcancha 216 – **Map 16 215**

Other trails near Machu Picchu
Chilca circuit 216 – The full Mollepata 216 – The Riverside trail 217

The Vilcabamba Trail
Introduction 218 – Preparations 220 – Timing and getting to the
trailhead 220 – The Vitcos walk 223 (**Map 17 224**) – Huancacalle to
Ututo 222 (**Map 18 226**, **Map 19 227**, **Map 20 228**) – Ututo to
Urpipata 229 (**Map 21 230**, **Map 22 231**, **Map 23 233**) – Urpipata to
Espíritu Pampa 234 (**Map 24 235**, **Map 25 236**) – Espíritu Pampa to
Chaunquiri 239 (**Map 26 240**, **Map 27 241**)

PART 8: MACHU PICCHU

The Lost City? 243 – Practicalities 243 – History 245 – A guide to
the ruins 249 – Moving on 258

APPENDICES

A. Quechua and Spanish words and phrases 259
B. Glossary 262   C. Peruvian embassies 264
D. Train timetables 267   E. Bibliography 268
F. Peruvian tour agencies licensed for the Inca Trail 271
G Update – February 2004

INDEX

GOLD BREASTPLATE FROM CUSCO

INTRODUCTION

Declared both a natural and a cultural World Heritage Site by UNESCO, the **Machu Picchu Historical Sanctuary** is truly a rare and wonderful place. Where else in the world can you walk for days through cloud forests and over razor-sharp passes, in country that's been inhabited for thousands of years by civilizations only discovered by Europeans less than five hundred years ago? Where else could you have such a breathtaking goal to your trek: the magical, lost city of Machu Picchu which rises from a high spur of mountain, like a stage set in a green amphitheatre of forest-clad hills?

THE INCA HERITAGE

For thousands of years the people of South America developed separately from the rest of the world. Their culture culminated in the Incas, a people whose empire was centred on Peru and which stretched further than that of the Romans, yet who governed without having discovered iron, the wheel or writing. Like the Romans, the Incas left behind them monumental stone constructions, built for the most part without mortar yet strong enough to withstand centuries of earthquakes that have toppled more modern edifices. Also like the Romans, they left behind them one of the most extensive road networks in the ancient world, for the most part paved and drained, which linked every part of their realm.

Many of these roads have been rediscovered, and some of them have been cleared. The **Inca Trail** is one such road, part of a network that once penetrated the thick rainforest which grows either side of the river Urubamba. Walkers who follow it today pass over high-altitude wind-blown grassland and down to steamy encroaching jungle. At the end of the road is **Machu Picchu**. On these grasslands and in this jungle is a multitude of plant, bird and animal life, and beside this ancient Inca road are recently rediscovered castles and remote fieldstone inns.

The Incas also left their capital, **Cusco**, which for the most part has been spared the complete destruction suffered by Mexico, capital of that other great ancient American people, the Aztecs. It's still possible to wander along Cusco's Inca alleyways which run between walls of perfectly hewn stone and visit the remains of the magnificent Sun Temple, once the religious heart of an empire. And the 'new' buildings such as the Cathedral and the Compañía, built in the sixteenth century by the Spanish colonizers, are beautiful in their own right.

VISITING CUSCO AND MACHU PICCHU

In the days of the Incas, Machu Picchu was a long hard walk from Cusco. *Chasquis*, Inca messengers, ran the roads of the Inca Trail and herders drove llama trains laden with maize and potatoes over the high passes. Today Machu Picchu is only four hours from Cusco by train, along a railway that's been pushed through the jungle along the banks of the Urubamba river.

However, you can still walk. The high tableland around Cusco leads down to the fringes of the Amazon rainforest, and the area is criss-crossed with roads and tracks, ancient and modern, passing through unrivalled natural and ancient beauty. As you walk you'll pass dazzling high glaciers and remote corries, along trails lined with original Inca canals and dotted with remote unvisited ruins where a multitude of orchids grow in the clear Andean air.

ABOUT THIS BOOK

The book is designed to take you from your armchair to these cities of the Incas, Cusco and Machu Picchu, and to guide you along the Incas' trails, stretches of some of the best hiking in the world. The book includes information on getting to Peru, a guide to Peru's capital Lima, background material on modern Peru; there's a chapter devoted to the Incas and their predecessors, and chapters on Cusco and Machu Picchu. Detailed trekking maps are included, as are site plans and descriptions of what's known about the abandoned ruins you'll pass on your way.

For this edition the trekking section of this book has been expanded to include full details of a wonderful walk to the last refuge of the Incas at Vilcabamba. The ruins of this city now lie abandoned and overgrown in a heavily forested valley. The hike to get there includes a stunning variety of scenery, from lofty mountain passes, via pampa, puna, pasture, dwarf forest and cloud forest to thick lowland rainforest, the 'eyebrows of the jungle', that smothers and engulfs the lost, ancient stones of Vilcabamba.

RESPONSIBLE TRAVEL

Sadly, as with many tourist sites, the paradox of tourism means that the trails, ruins and cities of the Sanctuary are at risk, threatened by their own beauty. It's this beauty that draws the tourists who bring much needed money but at certain times of the year the main trails have become overcrowded and the fragile environment and old ruins damaged by thoughtless visitors who fail to behave with sensitivity. Such damage is not inevitable and this book contains a section suggesting how on your visit you can help preserve this beautiful environment.

Peru is full of wonders. Its beauty is breathtaking, and its culture fascinating. If you are sensitive to the place, it can have a greater impact on you than you have on it. So, in the words of Rudyard Kipling:

'Something hidden. Go and Find it. Go and look behind the Ranges
Something lost behind the Ranges. Lost and waiting for you. Go!'

(From *The Explorer*, which inspired the man who rediscovered Machu Picchu, Hiram Bingham).

PART 1: PLANNING YOUR TRIP

With a group or on your own?

So you've decided to take one of the greatest walks on the planet. The first question to ask yourself always used to be, 'Am I going to do this with a tour or on my own?' Sadly, independent trekking in the Machu Picchu Historical Sanctuary isn't an option any more as in 2001 the Peruvian government brought in a new set of rules about who can walk the trail and how they can do it. Briefly, you can now walk the trail only with a tour company or in the company of a guide.

I said 'sadly', but some of the changes are for the best. In the past there were too many people walking the trail, causing too much damage, litter and erosion, and the new regulations will help stop that. This doesn't mean the end of the road for the independent trekker, as you can still walk to Vilcabamba (see p218) on your own – just not any of the Inca Trails.

The good news is that these guided tours are not expensive: from US$140-200 or £100-140 for the four-day trip which is only from about US$35-50/£25-35 a day. These are the lowest prices but there are also discounts for students.

Where to book

Nowadays, your first question is, 'Shall I book my tour at home or in Cusco?' Both are possible. If you're confident about arranging things on spec, and you've time to hang around should a place not be immediately available wait until you get to Peru before you set something up but note that with the new trail regulations, a place may not be available for a week or perhaps even longer in high season. There are lots of operators in Cusco (some decent, some less so: see p130), arranging things there tends to be cheaper, and your money goes more directly into local (rather than Western) pockets. On the other hand, travelling with everything sorted out before you leave is not to be sniffed at, and there are lots of tour companies outside Peru who'll do all the organizing for you, for a price – see p12.

Just the ruins

You can, if you don't want to do the walk, just visit the ruins. Most of the companies mentioned below do straightforward tours to Machu Picchu, and you need never see a pair of hiking boots and a rucksack.

It's as easy to get to the ruins by public transport as it is to get to the trailheads. A passenger train runs regularly between Cusco and the valley floor below Machu Picchu (see p258), and there's also a helicopter. From the valley floor there's a bus up to the ruins.

TOURS AND TREKKING AGENCIES

Agencies in Cusco usually charge from about US$140-200/£100-140 for the standard four-day trek to Machu Picchu, although there are some cheaper options – see p130 for more information. Alternatively, travel companies at home can sort everything out for you; prices are in the region of US$2160-4320/£1500-3000 and tours range from two to three weeks. The Peruvian consulate in your home country (see p264) can supply you with the names and telephone numbers of other operators.

Agencies in the UK and Ireland

● **Andes** (☎ 01556-503929, 🖹 01556-504633, 🖳 john@andes.org.uk, www.andes.org.uk, 37a St Andrew's St, Castle Douglas, Dumfries & Galloway DG7 1EN. Tailor-made treks and climbs.

● **Andean Trails** (☎/🖹 0131-467 7086, 🖳 info@andeantrails.co.uk, www.andeantrails.co.uk, The Clock House, Bonnington Mill Business Centre, 72 Newhaven Rd, Edinburgh EH6 5QG. Organize treks for small groups and also offer tailor-made itineraries.

● **Audley Travel** (☎ 01869-276210, 🖹 01869-276214, 🖳 latina@audleytravel.com, www.audleytravel.com), 6 Willows Gate, Stratton Audley, Oxon OX27 9AU, offers tailor-made tours.

● **Exodus** (☎ 020-8675 5550, 🖹 020-8673 0779, 🖳 info@exodus.co.uk, www.exodus.co.uk), 9 Weir Rd, London SW12 OLT.

● **Explore Worldwide** (☎ 01252-760000, 🖹 01252-760001, 🖳 info@exploreworldwide.co.uk, www.exploreworldwide.co.uk), 1 Frederick St, Aldershot, Hants GU11 1LQ. Also in **Ireland** at Maxwells Travel (☎ 01-677 9479, 🖹 01-679 3948), D'Olier Chambers, 1 Hawkins St, Dublin 2. This is a large company, doing five-day hikes and ruins-only trips.

● **Guerba Expeditions** (☎ 0845-130 1770, 01373-858956, 🖹 01373-858351, 🖳 info@guerba.co.uk, www.guerba.com), Wessex House, 40 Station Rd, Westbury, Wiltshire BA13 3JN. Agents for GAP (see Canada, p14).

● **Hayes and Jarvis** (☎ 0870-898 9890, 🖹 0870-333 1914, 🖳 res@hayesandjarvis.co.uk, www.hayesandjarvis.co.uk), Sandrocks, Rocky Lane, Haywards Heath, West Sussex RH16 4RH. A large, well-established firm.

● **The Imaginative Traveller/Adventure Bound** (☎ 020-8742 8612, 0800-316 1404, 🖳 brochures@imtrav.net, www.tucantravel.com), 14 Barley Mow Passage, Chiswick, London W4 4P. Agents for Tucan, one of the largest operators in the area.

● **Journey Latin America** (☎ 020-8747 8315, 🖹 020-8742 1312, 🖳 journey@latinamerica.co.uk, www.journeylatinamerica.co.uk), 12-13 Heathfield Terrace, Chiswick, London W4 4JE. Also in **Manchester**: 12 St Ann's Square, 2nd Floor, Manchester, M2 7HW (☎ 0161-832 1441, 🖹 0161-832 1551). One of the market leaders for tours to South America.

● **Ramblers Holidays** (☎ 01707-331133, 🖹 01707-333276, 🖳 info@ramblersholidays.co.uk, www.ramblersholidays.co.uk), Box 43, Welwyn Garden, Herts AL8 6PQ, a reliable operator.

● **South American Experience** (☎ 020-7976 5511, 🖷 020-7976 6908, 🖳 info@ southamericanexperience.co.uk, www.southamericanexperience.co.uk), 47 Causton St, Pimlico, London SW1P 4AT. Mainly does flights (see p16) but also arranges tailor-made tours.

● **Travelbag Adventures** (☎ 01420-541007, 🖷 01420-541022, 🖳 sales@travel bag-adventures.com, www.travelbag-adventures.com), 15 Turk Street, Alton, Hants GU34 1AG, offers a variety of tours.

● **World Expeditions** (☎ 0800-074 4135, 020-8870 2600, 🖷 020-8870 2615, 🖳 enquiries@worldexpeditions.co.uk, www.worldexpeditions.co.uk), 3 Northfields Prospect, Putney Bridge Rd, London SW18 1PE. See also p15.

Agencies in Continental Europe

● **Austria** Charisma (☎ 01-585 3680, 🖷 01-585 3680 60, 🖳 abyss@ tauchreisen.at), Hofmuhgasse 20, A-1060 Wien.

● **Belgium** Boundless Adventures (☎ 02-426 40 30, 🖷 02-426 03 60, 🖳 bou ndless.adventures@joker.be), Verdilaan 23/25, 1083 Brussels-Ganshoren; **Divantoura** (☎ 09-223 00 69, 🖷 09-223 04 35, 🖳 info@divantoura.com, www.divantoura.com), Bagattenstraat 176, 9000, Gent; also St Jacobsmarkt 5, 2000 Antwerpen (☎ 03-233 19 16). Agents for Explore Worldwide, see p12.

● **Denmark** Inter-Travel (☎ 33-15 00 77, 🖷 33-15 60 18, 🖳 inter-travel@inter-travel.dk, www.inter-travel.dk), Frederiksholms Kanal 2, DK-1220 Kobenhavn K. Agents for Explore Worldwide, see p12.

● **France** Club Aventure (☎ 08 25 30 60 32, 🖷 04 96 15 10 59, 🖳 info @clubaventure.fr, www.clubaventure.fr), 18 rue Séguier 75006 Paris; also at Le Néréïs, Avenue André Roussin, Saumaty-Séon, 13016 Marseille.

● **Germany** Reise Theke (☎ 351-471 6222, 🖳 info@reisetheke.de), Mensa Reichenstrasse 1, Dresden 1069; **Explorer Fernreisen** (☎ 0211-99 49 02, 🖷 02 11-38 22 88, 🖳 marketing@explorer-fernreisen.com), Huttenstrasse 17, 40215 Dusseldorf.

● **Netherlands** Trotamundos (☎ 043-350 0308, 🖷 043-321 6970, 🖳 info @trotamundos.nl, www.trotamundos.nl), Postbus 1695, 6201 BR Maastricht. Agents for GAP – see Canada p14. **Adventure World** (☎ 023-5382 954, 🖷 023-5384 744, 🖳 atc@euronet.nl), Muiderslotweg 112, Haarlem 2026 AS. Agents for Explore Worldwide, see p12.

Agencies in the USA

● **Adventure Center** (toll free ☎ 800-227-8747, 🖷 510-654-4200, 🖳 ex@ adventurecenter.com), 1311 63rd St, Suite 200, Emeryville, CA 94608. Agents for Explore Worldwide (see p12).

● **Adventure Travel Network** (☎ 619-544-0800, toll-free ☎ 1-800-467-4595, 🖳 info@atntravel.com), 7 Horton Plaza, San Diego 92101. Agents for Tucan, one of the largest operators in the area.

● **GAP (USA)** (☎ 914-666-4417, 🖷 914-666-4839, toll free ☎ 1-800-692-5495, 🖳 adventure@gap.ca, www.gap.ca), 760 North Bedford Rd, Suite #246, Bedford Hills, New York 10507. See GAP (Canada) for a description.

● **Holbrook Travel** (☎ 352-377-7111, toll free ☎ 800-541-7111, 🖷 352-371-

3710, ✉ advisor@holbrooktravel.com, www.holbrooktravel.com), 3540 NW 13th Street, Gainesville, FL 32609-2196. Ruins-only tours, but they do stay in the upmarket Machu Picchu Pueblo Hotel (see p157).

● **Wilderness Travel** (☎ 510-558-2488, toll-free ☎ 1-800-368 2794, 🖹 510-558-2489, ✉ info@wildernesstravel.com, www.wildernesstravel.com), 1102 9th St, Berkeley, California 94710-1211. A very good company.

● **World Expeditions** (☎/🖹 415-989-2212, toll-free ☎ 1-888-464-8735, ✉ contactus@weadventures.com), 6th Floor, 580 Market Street, San Francisco, CA 94104.

Agencies in Canada

● **GAP (Canada)** (☎ 416-260-0999, 🖹 416-260-1888, toll-free ☎ 1-800-465-5600, ✉ adventure@gap.ca, www.gap.ca), 19 Duncan St, Suite 401, Toronto, Ontario M5H 3H1. This is a very large, well-run organization that offers many tours on the Inca Trail – they do the Km77 walk.

● **The Adventure Center** (☎ 416-922 7584, ✉ toronto@theadventurecenter.com, www.theadventurecenter.com), 25 Bellair St, Toronto, Ontario M5R 3L3.

● **Trek Holidays** (☎ 780-439-9118, toll-free ☎ 1-888-4566-3522, 🖹 780-433-1283, ✉ adventure@trekholidays.com), 8412-109th St, Edmonton, Alberta T6G 1E2. Agents for Explore Worldwide – see p12.

● **Westcan Treks** has offices in **Calgary** (☎ 403-283 6115, ✉ calgary@westcantreks.com, www.westcantreks.com, 336 14th St NW, Calgary, Alberta T2N 1Z7), and **Vancouver** (☎ 604-734-1066, ✉ vancouver@westcantreks.com, 2911 West 4th Ave, Vancouver BC V6K 1R3.

Agencies in Peru
See Cusco, p130.

Agencies in South Africa

● **Shiralee Travel** (☎ 028-313 0526 🖹 028-312 4507, ✉ liesel.maree@harveyworld.co.za), 32 Main Road, PO Box 1420, Hermanus, 7200. Agents for Explore Worldwide, see p12.

● **Seekers Travel** (☎ 11-790 0081, ✉ ronels@seekers.co.za), Shop G22 – Fourways Crossing Centre, William Nicoll Road Fourways, Johannesburg.

Agencies in Australia

● **Adventure Associates** (☎ 02-9389 7466, 🖹 02-9369 1853, ✉ www.adventureassociates.com), 197 Oxford Mall, (PO Box 612), Bondi Junction, Sydney NSW 2022. Mainly does long tours, but one of their South American options is the Km88 trek.

● **Adventure World** has branches in **Perth** (☎ 08-9226 4524, 🖹 08-9281 3299, ✉ info@adventureworld.com.au, www.adventureworld.com.au), 4th Floor, 197 St George's Terrace, Perth, WA 6000) and **Sydney** (☎ 02-8913 0755, 🖹 02-9956 7707), 3rd Floor, 73 Walker St, Sydney, NSW 2000). This company is an agent for Tucan, a large operator.

● **Inca Tours** (☎ 02-4351 2133 or toll-free ☎ 1-800 024 955, 🖹 02-4351 2526), 3 Margaret St, Wyong NSW 2259.

● **Peregrine Travel Centre** (☎ 03-9662 2700, 🖹 03-9662 2422, 🖥 web sales@peregrine.net.au, www.peregrine.net.au), 258 Lonsdale St, **Melbourne**, Victoria 3000: also in **Sydney** (☎ 1300-854 444, ☎ 02-9290 2770, 🖹 02-9290 2155, 🖥 enq@peregrine.net.au), 5th floor, 38 York Street, Sydney NSW 2000; **Brisbane** (☎ 07-3854 1022, 🖹 07-3854 1079, 🖥 peregrine@backtrack.com.au), 1st Floor, Scout Outdoor Centre, 132 Wickham St, Fortitude Valley, Queensland 4006 and **Perth** (☎ 08-9321 1259, 🖹 08-9481 7375, 🖥 peregrinewa@tpg.com.au), 1st Floor, 862 Hay St, Perth, WA 6000.

● **World Expeditions** (☎ 02-9279 0188, ☎ 1300 720 0000, 🖹 02-9279 0566, 🖥 enquiries@worldexpeditions.com.au, www.worldexpeditions.com.au), Level 5, 71 York Street, **Sydney** NSW 2000. Also in **Melbourne** (☎ 03-9670 8400, 🖹 03-9670 7474, 🖥 travel@worldexpeditions.com.au), 1st Floor, 393 Little Bourke St, Melbourne, Victoria 3000; **Brisbane** (☎ 07-3216 0823, 🖹 07-3216 0827, 🖥 adventure@worldexpeditions.com.au), Shop 2, 36 Agnes St, Fortitude Valley, Queensland 4006; and **Perth** (☎ 08-9221 8240, 🖹 08-9221 8238, 🖥 holiday@worldexpeditions.com.au), Suite 2, 544 Hay St, Perth, WA 6000.

Agencies in New Zealand

● **Adventure World** (☎ 09-524 5118, 🖹 09-520 6629, 🖥 discover@adventureworld.co.nz), 101 Great South Road, PO Box 74008, Remeura, Auckland.

● **World Expeditions** (☎ 09-522 9161, toll-free ☎ 0800-350354, 🖹 09-522 9162, 🖥 enquiries@worldexpeditions.co.nz), 21 Remuera Road, Newmarket, Auckland.

PORTERS, ARRIEROS (MULETEERS) AND GUIDES

On most of the walks in this book you'll be going with a tour company and they'll provide guides and porters. The exception is the Vilcabamba trek (see p218), where you can go it alone and you can organize your own arriero (muleteer) to carry some of your kit and act as your guide. You can arrange things in

---

Hiring arrieros

It sounds simple enough, but it took no end of argument and persuasion...to convince these worthy arrieros that they were not going to be everlastingly ruined by this bargain. Hiram Bingham, 1922, *Inca Land*

Some things never change. Even today arrieros drive a hard bargain and will convince you that, however much you pay, you're stealing the bread from their children's mouths. If you're hiring an arriero, don't be surprised if he insists on taking two mules. Since the dawn of time, muleteers all over the world have refused to take only one animal. It's not a rip-off, it's an insurance policy should one of the mules go lame or should you become exhausted and need a ride.

Cusco but I prefer finding help in the villages on the trail rather than using a tour agency for a number of reasons: you know you're not exploiting the locals and are paying a fair price for a fair service; also, you're putting your tourist dollars directly into the local economy and not lining the pockets of already flourishing Cusqueños or Limeños. And anyway, it's more personal.

You can pick up a muleteer and mules in Huancacalle (see p222) on your way to Vilcabamba. Remember when negotiating that you'll need to discuss where he's going to sleep; if he has to rely on the villagers en route for accommodation then how far you walk per day will largely be dictated by where he will be able to find lodging. You should also discuss whether you are going to provide food for him, or whether his fee includes an allowance for him to buy his own before departure. Finally, don't forget to factor into his wages a sum for his return journey; he may only be walking with you for four days, but it will probably take another two or three for him to return back home.

The going rate (at the time of writing) for a porter or for an arriero is s/20-30 per day, which is about US$6-9/£4-6. A tip is expected: 5-10% is customary but porters and arrieros are usually very ill-paid so be generous.

Getting to Peru

BY AIR

The following main airlines fly to Lima: Aero Continente, Aeroflot, Aerolíneas Argentinas, Air France, Alitalia, American Airlines, Avianca, British Airways, Continental, Copa, Delta, Ecuatoriana, Iberia, KLM, Lan Chile, Lan Peru, Lloyd Aéreo Boliviano, Lufthansa, Servivensa and Varig. Many of the tour operators mentioned above (pp12-15) can get you tickets. Note that flights connecting Peru and Chile are now subject to a tax of US$50, payable at the airport.

Airpasses covering Peru are available; as the exact details of the offers change regularly, you should check with your travel agent. At the time of writing, a five-coupon Lan Peru airpass costs US$390/£270, and a two-coupon pass US$173/£120.

For a detailed website guide to flights to and from Lima, visit 💻 www.traficoperu.com.

From Europe

The main gateway is Madrid, but there are flights from Paris, London, Amsterdam, Frankfurt and Shannon. The main market for discount flights is the UK, and the cheapest cost from £500 in the low season to £650 in the high season. Check for cheap deals at Internet sites such as 💻 www.opodo.co.uk, www.ebookers.com, www.expedia.co.uk, www.cheapflights.com.

● **Journey Latin America** See p12. As well as organizing tours this company often has good deals on flights.

● **South American Experience** See p13. A specialist in South America, this company mainly offers flights.

● **STA Travel** (☎ 0870-166 7686, ▭ www.statravel.co.uk). One of the largest budget-flight companies in the world with branches all over the place.

● **Trailfinders** (▭ www.trailfinders.com); **London** (☎ 020-7938 3939), 194 Kensington High Street, London W8 6RG; **Birmingham** (☎ 0121-236 1234), 22-24 The Priory, Queensway, Birmingham B4 6BS; **Cambridge** (☎ 01223-461600), 22 Sidney St, Cambridge CB2 3HG; **Manchester** (☎ 0161-839 6969), 58 Deansgate, Manchester M3 2FF; **Glasgow** (☎ 0141-353 2224), 254-284, Sauchiehall St, Glasgow G2 3EH; **Bristol** (☎ 0117-929 9000), 48 Corn St, Bristol BS1 1HQ; **Newcastle** (☎ 0191-261 2345), 7-9 Ridley Place, Newcastle NE1 8JQ. Also in **Belfast** (☎ 028-9027 1888), 42-44 Fountain St, Belfast BT1 5EE and **Dublin** (☎ 01-677 7888), 4-5 Dawson St, Dublin 2.

From the USA and Canada
The main gateways are Miami and New York, though there are flights from Dallas, Los Angeles and Houston. Expect to pay at least US$1300-1500 from the States and C$1000-1500 from Canada.

● **Air Brokers International** (☎ 1-800-883-3273, ▭ sales@airbrokers.com, www.airbrokers.com), 323 Geary St, Suite 411, San Francisco, California 94102.

● **STA Travel** (▭ www.statravel.com). Branches countrywide including: **New York** (☎ 1-212-627-3111), 10 Downing St, New York, NY 10014, and **Los Angeles** (☎ 1-323-934-8722), 7202 Melrose Avenue, CA 90046. Also in **Vancouver** (☎ 1-604-806-4040).

From Australia and New Zealand
There are currently no direct flights to Peru from Australia or New Zealand. From Australia, the cheapest fare is about A$2000. From New Zealand, expect to pay from NZ$2400.

● **Flight Centre** (▭ www.flightcentre.com). Many branches in **Australia**, including Melbourne (☎ 03-9650 2899), 19 Bourke St, Melbourne, and in **New Zealand** (☎ 09-358 4310), 350 Queen St, Auckland.

● **Trailfinders** (▭ www.trailfinders.com.au). Branches in **Brisbane** (☎ 07-3229 0887), 91 Elizabeth St, Brisbane 4000, Queensland; **Sydney** (☎ 02-9247 7666), 8 Spring St, New South Wales, Sydney 2000; **Cairns** (☎ 07-4041 1199), 3 Hides Corner, Lake St, Cairns, Queensland 4870; **Perth** (☎ 08-9226 1222), 840 Hay St, Perth, WA 6000, and **Melbourne** (☎ 03-9600 3022), 372 Lonsdale St, Melbourne, Victoria 3000.

OVERLAND
It's very difficult to get to Peru overland from Central America, because of the swampy region in Columbia known as the **Darien Gap.** The Pan-American highway, which links most of the rest of the two continents, stops either side of this fearsome natural obstacle. It's much easier to get to Peru and Cusco over-

land from neighbouring countries. There are buses from La Paz in **Bolivia** that cross Lake Titicaca on a ferry and reach Cusco via Puno.

From **Brazil**, there's a ten-day ferry ride up the Amazon from Manaus to the Peru's Amazonian port of Iquitos, from which you can fly to Cusco. In times past you could also take a boat up the river to Cusco but it's not safe because of bandits.

From **Ecuador** in the north and **Chile** in the south there are major bus routes into Peru along the Pan-American highway.

Budgeting

The price of a guided tour on the Inca Trail to Machu Picchu is around US$150-200/£100-140 for four days, although if you're a student you may be able to get a cheaper package – see p130. These tours should include the price of a ticket for the trail (US$25-50: see p172). Day-to-day costs will be around US$20-25/£10-15 a day for basic living; on US$35/£25 a day you will have a very comfortable time. To get some perspective on the costs below, a housemaid gets paid on average US$130 a month, and a doctor about US$1800.

ACCOMMODATION

The cheapest hotels cost US$3.50/£2.50 per person per night. At the other end of the scale, the most expensive hotel I found was charging US$300/£230.

FOOD

A local will pay around US$1/£0.50 for a filling lunch and a backpacker will pay about US$4/£3 for a light one in a tourist café. You can easily eat more expensively though not necessarily much better: breakfast at Machu Picchu Sanctuary Lodge costs US$30/£20, and dinner at one of Lima's more flashy restaurants can cost US$60/£40 per person (without wine).

TRANSPORT

A 24-hour luxurious bus ride from Lima to Cusco will set you back about US$30/£22, and a flight to Cusco will cost you up to US$80/£50.

THINGS TO BUY

You're inevitably going to be tempted to buy souvenirs. The cost of these will depend on how good you are at bargaining and the quality of the thing you're buying: cheap Andean pan-pipes cost about US$2.50/£1.60 but prime quality handwoven textiles can cost hundreds of dollars.

When to go and for how long?

WHEN TO GO

The best time to go is in late April or May. The trekking season is April/May to October. In June/July the trails become very, very busy, and it's sometimes difficult to get on a tour, and if you do it'll be difficult to find a spot to pitch your tent. At other times of the year the trails will be less crowded but be prepared for some serious rain and impassable roads: the Vilcabamba Trail may be so washed out at this time that you probably won't find a guide willing to take you.

FOR HOW LONG?

The longest walk in this book takes two weeks and the shortest only two days. The basic Inca Trail from Km88 takes four days – see p20 for more details.

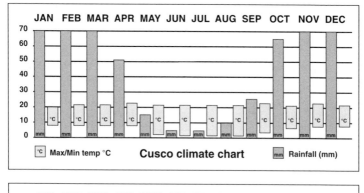

Cusco climate chart

°C Max/Min temp °C   Rainfall (mm)

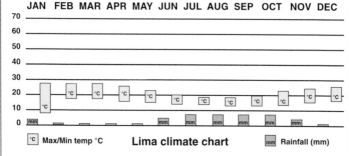

Lima climate chart

°C Max/Min temp °C   Rainfall (mm)

To work out how long your Peruvian trip's going to be, you've got to add five days to the length of the trail you're thinking of walking. This allows a day to fly to Cusco from Lima (more if you're travelling overland), a day to fly back, a day just in case there's a problem with the flights, and a couple of days acclimatizing to the altitude in Cusco. If you're not already booked on a tour you should allow another 2-5 days because there may be a waiting list for places.

Acclimatizing is very important. If you don't spend a little time allowing your body to get used to Cusco's thin air you can expect a thoroughly miserable and exhausting time, and you might also be risking your life. See p165-7 for more information.

Route options

(**See Route Options map on pp22-3**). All but three of the trails in this book end up following the ancient Inca road from the village of Huayllabamba to Machu Picchu, the route trekkers call 'The Inca Trail'. In 1911 the Hiram Bingham expedition began to uncover this route and Dr Paul Fejos discovered more of it in 1944. The trails that don't follow this route are the two-day route to Machu Picchu from Km104, the Riverside Trail from Km88 (for both see 'Shorter trails' opposite) and the Vilcabamba Trail (see p218).

THE CLASSIC INCA TRAIL (3-4 days)   (see p175)

The classic Inca Trail starts at kilometre 88 (Km88) on the railway line that runs from Cusco to the jungle town of Quillabamba – the foot of Machu Picchu mountain is at Km113. The first part of the walk, from Km88 to the village of Huayllabamba, is a relatively gentle stroll taking you through eucalyptus groves and past the extensive ruins of Patallacta. The hike from Huayllabamba is more gruelling but it's a superb walk through varied scenery and vegetation, travelling from barren grassland to encroaching jungle, through stone-hewn tunnels and over 4200m (13,750ft)-high passes. At the end of your journey lies the legendary Machu Picchu, Lost City of the Incas.

> ❑ 'OLD MARTIN: *You call them the Andes. Picture a curtain of stone hung by some giant across your path. Mountains set on mountains: cliffs on cliffs. Hands of rock a hundred yards high, with flashing nails where the snow never moved. Scratching the gashed face of the sun'.* **Peter Shaffer,** *Royal Hunt of the Sun* (Act 1 Scene 7)

The walk's tough: it's only 43km (26.6 miles) long but you walk up 2150m (7000ft) and down 2100m (6880ft). Incidentally, the record time for running, (yes, running), the trail is held by Edgar Rodriguez, the President of the Cusco Athletic League, who is said to have completed the trail in 3 hours 50 minutes.

VARIATIONS ON THE CLASSIC TRAIL

Chilca (Km77) along the Urubamba (4-5 days)   (see p190)

Instead of starting at Km88, you can start further up the Urubamba at a village called Chilca (at kilometre 77 on the railway, so it's also known as Km77). It's a small place – blink and you'll miss it.

The hike from here along the Urubamba to Huayllabamba takes a full day, but it's not really worth it – you'll see nothing along this route that you wouldn't see if you started at Km82. The only reason to do this trek is if you've got time to burn, or if your tour starts from here.

Km82 along the Urubamba (3½-4½ days)   (see p192)

The compromise between starting at Km88 and Chilca is to start at Km82. This walk takes you further along the banks of the Urubamba than the Km88 hike, rewarding you with wonderful views down the valley; it isn't so wearing as starting at Chilca. You'll also pass the Inca hill fort, Inca Raccay, which provides a breathtaking view over Patallacta.

SHORTER TRAILS

Km104 and the Purification Trail (1½-2 days)   (see p194)

The recently-built short path from the Inca site of Chachabamba (at Km104) to Huinay Huayna and the last part of the Inca Trail is an exposed walk across an open hillside, not worth doing if you can afford the time to walk one of the other routes.

Alternatively, from Km104 you could follow the path along the river for 3km to the ruins of Choquesuysuy (see p197) and take the three-hour climb up the 'Purification Trail', a newly-cleared original path up to Huinay Huayna. The trail has been so named because Choquesuysuy is thought to have been a place of ritual cleansing for those approaching Huinay Huayna.

The Riverside Trail from Km88 (2-3 days)   (see p217)

Rather than following the Urubamba river from Km104, you could simply follow it all the way from Km88. Though it avoids the passes involved on the Classic Trail it also misses out on all those dramatic views; it's really just a pleasant hike along the river valley across forest- and grass-clad slopes rather than over mountain passes.

CHILCA (KM77) UP THE SILQUE VALLEY (5-7 days)   (see p198)

This is a very beautiful valley walk on which you're unlikely to meet many gringos. The area around here was once the land of the Bethlemites, the wealthiest religious group in the province, and the walk up the verdant Silque valley takes you through their rich and fertile old farmland. There's a 4700m (15,740ft)-high pass to climb, and if you tell people that you're walking that way they'll think you're mad – it's much quicker to get to Huayllabamba along the Urubamba.

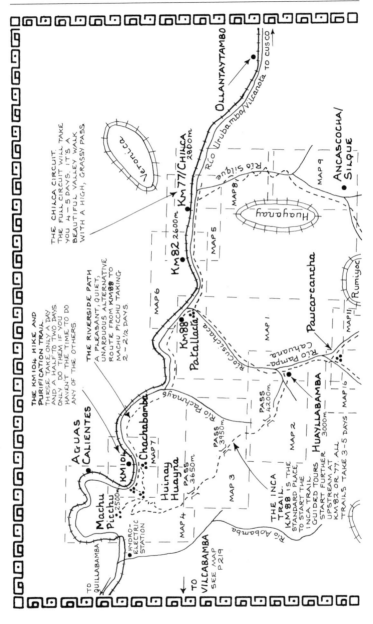

THE KM104 HIKE AND PURIFICATION TRAIL
THESE TAKE ONLY A DAY AND A HALF TO TWO DAYS ONLY. DO THEM IF YOU HAVEN'T THE TIME TO DO ANY OF THE OTHERS.

THE RIVERSIDE PATH
A PLEASANT, QUIET, UNARDUOUS ALTERNATIVE ROUTE FROM KM88 TO MACHU PICCHU TAKING 2 – 2½ DAYS.

THE CHILCA CIRCUIT
THE FULL CIRCUIT WILL TAKE YOU 4–5 DAYS. IT'S A BEAUTIFUL VALLEY WALK WITH A HIGH, GRASSY PASS

THE INCA TRAIL. KM 88 IS THE STANDARD PLACE TO START THE INCA TRAIL. GUIDED TOURS START FURTHER UPSTREAM AT KM82 OR 77. ALL TRAILS TAKE 3–5 DAYS

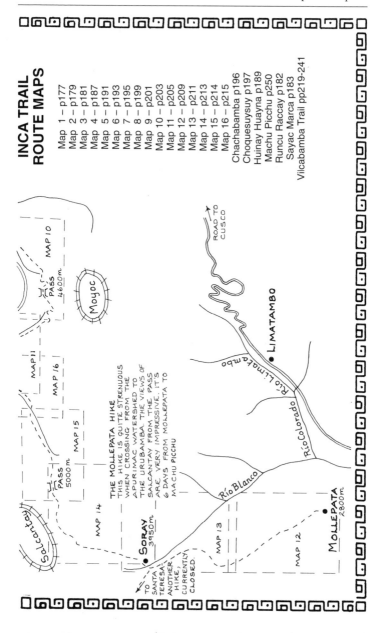

INCA TRAIL ROUTE MAPS

Map 1 – p177
Map 2 – p179
Map 3 – p181
Map 4 – p187
Map 5 – p191
Map 6 – p193
Map 7 – p195
Map 8 – p199
Map 9 – p201
Map 10 – p203
Map 11 – p205
Map 12 – p209
Map 13 – p211
Map 14 – p213
Map 15 – p214
Map 16 – p215

Chachabamba p196
Choquesuysuy p197
Huinay Huayna p189
Machu Picchu p250
Runcu Raccay p182
Sayac Marca p183
Vilcabamba Trail pp219-241

THE MOLLEPATA HIKE
THIS HIKE IS QUITE STRENUOUS
WHEN CROSSING FROM THE
APURIMAC WATERSHED TO
THE URUBAMBA. THE VIEWS OF
SALCANTAY FROM THE PASS
ARE VERY IMPRESSIVE. IT'S
6 DAYS FROM MOLLEPATA TO
MACHU PICCHU

MAP 10
PASS 4600m.
Moyoc

MAP 11
MAP 16
MAP 15
PASS 5000m.

Salcantay
MAP 14
SORAY 3950m.
TO SANTA TERESA, ANOTHER HIKE, CURRENTLY CLOSED.

MAP 13
Río Blanco

MAP 12
MOLLEPATA 2800m.

Río Colorado
Río Limatambo
LIMATAMBO
ROAD TO CUSCO

THE MOLLEPATA TREK (6 or 7 days)   (see p207)

Along with the Vilcabamba Trail (see below), this is the most difficult and most dramatic of the hikes in this book. You start in the village of Mollepata, and walk from the valley of the Apurímac to the valley of the Urubamba, over the shoulder of Mount Salcantay. There's a 5000m (16,400ft)-high pass, and you pass within touching distance of the glacier that gives birth to the river Cusichaca. If you're a glutton for punishment, you can start in the desert heat down by the river Apurímac and add another day to this hike.

THE VILCABAMBA TRAIL (9 days in all; 4 days walking)   (see p218)

This trail takes you between the remote villages of Huancacalle and Chaunquiri via the ruins of Espíritu Pampa, once believed to have been the site of Vilcabamba, the legendary last capital of the Incas.

This is a much tougher challenge than the classic Inca Trail: there are no designated campsites, the path is often very muddy in places and can be overgrown and the ruins themselves are nowhere near as spectacular as Machu Picchu. It's the trek itself that makes this route really worthwhile, a remote and beautiful hike through many of Peru's vegetation zones. Much of the trek is low-lying: altitudes range from 3800m down to 1000m.

While there are only three to four days of actual walking involved, once you've added on the time it takes to get to and from the trail, plus a couple of days in Quillabamba and Huancacalle, you can probably count on the entire expedition taking roughly nine days.

COMBINING OR ALTERING ROUTES

With the exception of the Vilcabamba trail, there's scope for linking together these routes, or doing different bits of them, or doing them in a different order. See the map on p22-3. There are many other hikes you could take in these hills and many other places to explore. However, you should bear in mind that the park authorities don't allow you to start at Machu Picchu and walk in the direction of Huayllabamba.

Two obvious alternative hikes are a **Chilca circuit**, and a hike from **Mollepata to Machu Picchu via Chilca** (see p216).

What to take

The golden rule is to travel light. If you're in doubt, leave it out and take more money with you. The more that's in your bag, the more weight you'll have to carry and the more you'll curse yourself. Wherever you go in Peru, don't wear military clothes or carry military-style equipment as people might mistake you for a soldier or a terrorist. For hiking it's still a good idea to travel light but if you want to be fully equipped you're going to have to carry much more. What follows is a list of what you'll need for safe and comfortable hiking.

BOOTS

Good boots, well broken in, are essential. Don't skimp on them – the more you pay, the better quality you'll get. There are two main types on the market. **Fabric boots** are generally lined with Gore-tex (if they're not, don't even look at them) and are waterproof and immediately comfortable. They're not as tough as leather boots and don't last as long. **Leather boots** are tough and last ages, but to keep them water-resistant you have to keep rubbing in dubbin or some other waterproofing agent.

Plastic boots for mountaineers are not necessary or suitable for the hikes in this book.

CLOTHES

Back in 1922, to avoid frostbite Bingham had to order each man in his party to put on four pairs of thick woollen socks and three pairs of longjohns. Modern fabrics, however, are light and keep you warm and dry without being too bulky.

Most hikers wear several layers of clothing, rather than just a thick jumper or an enormous jacket. The advantage of doing this is that you can peel off layers as you walk and still keep comfortable, or you can combine the layers to prepare yourself for all kinds of weather from damp heat to dry cold.

● **Jacket** If you can afford it, buy a waterproof jacket made from Gore-tex, a material that is breathable (ie it lets your sweat out) and highly waterproof. It's effective but not quite the all-purpose fabric the advertisements would have you believe. There are other similar fabrics on the market that are similar, such as Sympatex, but I don't find them quite as good.

● **Down jacket/fleece top** Under your waterproof you should wear a warmth layer. Some people wear fleeces (tightly woven nylon) because they're light and

---

The bare necessities?
From here to the top, we were to carry only such things as were absolutely necessary. They included the Mummery tent with pegs and poles, the mountain-mercurial barometer, the two Watkins aneriods, the hypsometer, a pair of Zeiss glasses, two 3A Kodaks, six films, a sling psychrometer, a prismatic compass and clinometer, a Stanley pocket level, an eighty-foot red-strand mountain rope, three ice axes, a seven-foot flagpole, and American flag and a Yale flag. In order to avoid disaster in case of storm, we also carried four of Silver's self-heating cans of Irish Stew and mock-turtle soup, a cake of chocolate, and eight hard-tack, besides raisins and cubes of sugar in our pockets. **Hiram Bingham, 1922, Inca Land**

warm, but I find them bulky. The alternative is a down (feather-stuffed) jacket, very light, very warm, very compact but also very expensive.

● **Jersey** I'm not convinced that there's anything better than a woollen jumper and a cotton shirt, although there are some good micro-fleeces around.

● **Shirts** Light cotton shirts with long sleeves and collars are best. Many people take T-shirts and end up with burnt necks in the fierce sun. Two or three shirts should be enough.

● **Trousers/pants and skirts** Poly-cotton travellers' clothing of the sort sold by Rohan is good since it dries quickly but it's expensive. Don't take jeans. They absorb water and sweat like a sponge, and take ages to dry. They're heavy and bulky and for the same weight you can pack both a pair of warm and a pair of light trousers. Women should not wear shorts or short skirts.

● **Inner layer/underwear** The important thing about a skin layer is that it draws away sweat from your body and dries quickly. Cotton isn't very good: T-shirts get sopping wet and then cling to you, and the moment you stop walking you freeze. I recommend thermal underwear – silk thermals are warmest but most expensive.

For normal underwear, three changes of whatever you usually wear is fine.

● **Socks** Three pairs of thick socks is enough.

● **Hat** A sun hat with a wide brim is important protection against the heat during the day. A woolly hat (the locally-knitted hat is known as a *chullo*) is essential at altitude and on cold evenings.

● **Gloves or mittens** Cheap woollen gloves are available in the tourist shops in Cusco and are essential.

● **Swimsuit** Useful when you're washing in the open.

EQUIPMENT

Backpack
This is another thing that you shouldn't skimp on. You'll be wearing it for days on end so make sure it fits your back well, is tough and has the right capacity for you.

There are two types of rucksack, **internal frame** (the bag incorporates a rigid back-piece) and **external frame** (with the bag hung from a frame). You hardly ever see external frame rucksacks in Europe anymore, but they're still common in the US. Leading makes are Karrimor, Berghaus and Lowe.

It's vital to line your backpack with at least one strong plastic bag to keep everything dry, and a good idea to pack everything inside it in plastic bags, too.

Sleeping bag and mat
Down **sleeping bags** are lighter and pack up tighter than foam-filled ones but they're more expensive and difficult to dry if they get wet. You'll need at least a

three-season bag, possibly a four-season if you feel the cold. Some people bring a **sleeping bag liner**, made from a folded sheet sewn up on two sides. This can be easily washed and so helps keep the sleeping bag clean; it also makes it warmer.

Sleeping-mats do two things: obviously they cushion you, but more importantly they insulate you from the chilly ground. A **foam sleeping-mat** is OK, but the self-inflating air-mats made by **Therma-rest** are much more comfortable. They do tend to puncture, however, so take a repair kit, too. You can hire mats and bags in Cusco.

Tent

Don't bother with anything but a free-standing tent – the ones with metal poles that you can pitch anywhere. These are so much better than old A-frame tents which are a waste of money these days. Make sure you buy one that packs up tightly and is light, and don't forget to seal the seams before your first night out in the rain.

Tents are expensive, and if you're not planning many other trekking holidays it's not really worth buying one. You can hire them in Cusco.

Stoves, pans and crockery

Although **butane gas stoves** like the camping-gaz ones that run on the little blue cylinders don't normally work at altitude, you can buy cylinders for them containing a butane-propane mix which is completely satisfactory. They sell these cylinders in Cusco.

Unless they're able to run on a wide range of fuels, **liquid fuel stoves** are next to useless in Peru, because the proprietary fuel on which they run is unobtainable and they get clogged up on Peru's filthy petrol. If you bring a liquid fuel stove it must be able to run on as many fuels as possible, and be easy to clean.

Bring a couple of **aluminium pans** that can be stored nestling inside each other. Some people don't bother with plates, as you can eat out of the pans. Do bring **cups** and **cutlery**, and a wire scrubber for cleaning off your burnt-on porridge. You can hire or buy these things in Cusco.

General equipment

Other essential items include **matches** and a couple of **lighters**, **sunglasses** (mountain or skiing sunglasses are good because they enclose your eyes and reduce glare), a **torch** (a head torch is recommended because it leaves your hands free), **spare batteries** (easy to forget, impossible to do without), a **whistle** (to summon help), a **small sewing kit**, **plastic bags**, a **penknife** (with scissors and a tin opener), **water bottles** (carry two litres capacity per person; the Platypus Hoser system, a water bottle connected to a tube from which you can drink as you walk along, is becoming popular with trekkers everywhere and recommended because it encourages you to drink more), **water purifying tablets** (chlorine doesn't kill all the bugs, iodine's much better – see p169) a **sun hat**, **toothpaste**, **toothbrush**, **loo paper**, **sanitary towels** (for what they're designed for, and to deal with any serious bleeding injury), **sun block**, **lip balm**, **soap** and a **medical kit** (see p29). All toiletries are readily available in Cusco.

If you're planning to walk the Mollepata trek or from Chilca up the Silque valley, or the Vilcabamba trail a **compass** is essential.

Useful items include **spare bootlaces**, **spare buckles** for your rucksack, **candles** (for when your spare batteries run out), **string** (for a clothes line), **compact binoculars**, **paper and pen** (many hikers bring a **diary**), **insect repellent** (particularly if you're heading to Vilcabamba), a **small trowel** for burying your turds, and a small, thin **towel**. You could bring **biodegradeable washing liquid** although you can clean just about anything from your pans with a wire scouring pad. Some people find a **collapsible plastic bucket** useful for washing thereby not polluting the water source.

Some people like taking a walking stick or ski pole, useful for stiff descents, but sticks have now been banned on the Inca Trail from Huayllabamba to Machu Picchu since they damage the path.

You don't need mountaineering equipment (ice-axes, ropes, crampons) on these treks.

Cameras and photography

Some people don't carry cameras, feeling that carrying a camera turns them from a participant into a mere observer, but whenever I've left my camera at home I've regretted it. A slim **compact camera** will be fine for snapshots, but if you're more ambitious you should take an **SLR** with a polarizing filter and a wide-angle lens. It'd be good to take a portrait lens too but you shouldn't weigh yourself down too much. If you take a **digital camera** or any camera with rechargable batteries you'll need to take spares as there's nowhere to recharge batteries on the trails.

As for **film**, because the light's so strong you needn't bother with anything faster than 200ASA unless you're travelling in the wet season. It's best to bring all the film you need from home. Although print and slide film can be bought in Cusco and Lima, you can't be sure that it hasn't been left lying around in the sun (which degrades the chemicals in the film). When flying never put film in baggage that goes in the hold as this may be X-rayed (or even lost). Remove film from your hand luggage before it is X-rayed. The official may simply point to a label on the machine that says 'Film Safe' but you should not believe this and request a hand search.

Because of the strong light, the best time to take photos is in the early morning or late afternoon. If you want to take someone's picture always ask them first. Like you they value their privacy (see p163).

If you're buying videos in Peru note that the system used is NTSC not PAL. This is used in USA, and not compatible with the UK's system.

FOOD

Bring some dehydrated or vacuum-packed trekkers' food from home and use it as emergency rations or a treat, but don't load yourself up as you'll be able to buy all the main food you need in Cusco. When you're off up the mountains, take food that doesn't weigh much but which provides large amounts of carbohydrate, sugary food and little treats to raise your spirits. Examples of good food to take, all of which you can buy out there are dehydrated potato, polenta, *quinoa* (an Andean grain), porridge, milk powder, dried noodles and packet soup. Also take some dried fruit and nuts, chocolate, boiled sweets, sugar, stock cubes, salt, pepper (keep them in used film canisters), dried sausage or tinned meat. Ground cinnamon and cloves go well in the porridge. All of this is light and nutritious. It helps greatly if you divide the food into a separate plastic bag for each day, and then you won't have to empty your whole rucksack looking for the last packet of soup.

MEDICAL KIT

Mine contains: assorted **plasters**, different sizes of **sterile gauze**, a **triangular bandage**, a **crepe bandage**, **elastic knee supports** (essential, particularly if you've had knee problems in the past as the steep descents place enormous strain on knees), some **moleskin** or **compeed** (for blisters), **antiseptic** cream and wipes, **antihistamine cream** and **antihistamine tablets**, **ibuprofen**, soluble **aspirin** tablets (for sore throats), a **spare lighter**, **spare needle and thread**. You might also want to take **acetozelomide** (Diamox) for altitude sickness (see p165) and for diarrhoea **loperamide** (Imodium) and **re-hydrating powders**.

Some people carry a course of antibiotics which they get from their doctor at home. Note that overuse of antibiotics can create super bugs that are resistant to treatment so you should use them only if it's really necessary.

MAPS

The IGN (Instituto Geográfico Nacional) in Lima sell good maps of the region, which you can also buy from the South American Explorers' Club (see p106). The maps you want, which are on a scale of 1:100,000, are: 2444 (27-r) and 2344 (27-q), while for Vilcabamba you'll also need the north-western corner of map 2344 (27-q), as well as 2244 (27-p) and 2245 (26-p). Watch out for old editions of 27-q since the bottom of the map is incomplete and does not include Mollepata, the starting point for one of the treks; it is on the new edition of this map. There's also a 1:200,000 map of the region to the north of Cusco that's of no use for hiking because the scale's too great and it's inaccurate. However, it does give a general overview of the region.

These maps are now available at some specialized map shops outside Peru. Stanfords has them and takes mail orders (☎ 020-7836 1321, 🖹 020-7836 0189, 🖳 www.stanfords.co.uk, 12-14 Long Acre, London WC2).

RECOMMENDED READING
Guidebooks
My favourite guidebook is *The Rough Guide to Peru* but *Peru Handbook* (Footprint) and the Lonely Planet's *Peru* are both excellent. Hilary Bradt's *Backpacking and Trekking in Peru and Bolivia* (Bradt Travel Guides in the UK,

Globe Pequot Press in USA) is the classic guide to trekking in these two countries. Charles Brod's *Apus & Incas* (Inca Expeditions, 1989) is a very good guide to hiking in the area around Cusco but difficult to obtain. There's also Peter Frost's *Exploring Cusco*. The only widely available phrase book in Quechua is published by Lonely Planet.

General books on Peru

The Peru Reader (Duke University Press 1995), edited by Orin Starn and others, is an interesting introduction to all of Peru, past and present. For analyses of modern Peru, read *Fujimori's Peru* edited by John Crabtree and Jim Thomas (Institute of Latin American Studies 1998), and *Shining Path,* Simon Strong (HarperCollins 1992). *A Fish in the Water* by Mario Vargas Llosa (English translation Faber & Faber 1994) is a description of his 1990 election campaign.

The Incas and their ancestors

Richard Burger's lavishly illustrated *Chavín and the Origins of Andean Civilisation* (Thames and Hudson 1992) is the seminal book on how it all started. *The Incas and their Ancestors* by Michael Moseley (Thames and Hudson 1992) is a good survey of where it went from there.

In the nineteenth century, Prescott and Markham wrote famous histories of the Incas but the best book on the subject is John Hemming's *The Conquest of the Incas*, (Penguin 1983, Papermac 1993). This book is excellent reading and a thorough piece of scholarship. *The Incas* by Terence D'Altroy, Blackwell 2002, is the most recent survey of Incan culture.

There are hundreds of other books on the Incas, ranging from children's pop-up books to academic tomes. The best place to start looking for a reading list is in the bibliography of Rebecca Stone-Miller's art history book *Art in the Andes*, (Thames and Hudson 1993). *The Cities of the Ancient Andes* by Adriana von Hagen and Craig Thomas (Thames and Hudson 1998) also has a good reading list.

Machu Picchu

Machupicchu, Devenir Histórico y Cultural, Efrain Chevarria Huarcaya, (UNSAAC 1992) is a guide to Machu Picchu and its position in Peru's history and culture (available only in Spanish). *Machu Picchu* by John Hemming (Readers' Digest *Wonders of Man Series* 1981) is the best book in English on the subject. *The Machu Picchu Guidebook*, Ruth Wright and Alfredo Zegarra, Johnson Books, 2001, is a good modern guide to the site.

Worth a read are *The Sacred Centre,* Johan Reinhard (Nuevas Imágenes 1991), which gives an alternative view of what Machu Picchu's about, and Jim Bartle's and Peter Frost's attractive coffee-table book, *The Machu Picchu Historical Sanctuary* (Nuevas Imágenes 1995). An even more delightful coffee-table book is *Realm of the Incas* (HarperCollins) by Max Milligan, former owner of the Cross Keys pub in Cusco. The book should now be out; I saw the proofs of this mighty tome, and the photos are simply gorgeous. *Lost City of the Incas*, Hiram Bingham, (Weidenfeld & Nicholson, 2002), is a reprint of Bingham's classic account of the discovery of Machu Picchu including his original photographs and some beautiful modern ones.

Vilcabamba

A copy of Vincent R Lee's *Forgotten Vilcabamba – Final Stronghold of the Incas* is by far the best and most comprehensive on the subject. If you're planning on walking the Vilcabamba trail, it will enhance the pleasure of your walk tenfold; Benjamin Cobos at the Sixpac Manco Hostal in Huancacalle has a copy that he sometimes lends out. Lee's first book, the much shorter *Sixpac Manco – Travels among the Incas*, is also a good read and contains a lot of the same information. Both of these books contain detailed diagrams of the ruins. Gene Savoy, the man who finally established the location of the ancient capital of the rebel Incas (see p96) wrote up his explorations in *Antisuyu* (Simon and Schuster 1970). The last few chapters of John Hemming's classic *Conquest of the Incas* are also very relevant to this trail.

Travelogues and expedition reports

Early descriptions of Peru include *Peregrinations of a Pariah* by Flora Tristan and the beautifully illustrated 1877 book *Peru. Travel and Exploration in the Land of the Incas* by E George Squier (Macmillan). Hiram Bingham's most accessible account of his travels is *Inca Land* (Constable & Co, 1922) and of

---

INTERNET SITES

Peru
🖥 www.peru-explorer.com (a good travel website for Peru) and 🖥 www.travel-library.com (an excellent travel site with listings and links for Peru).

Cusco
www.cuscoperu.com is a listings site for Cusco in English, and another good site in Spanish is www.cuscoonline.com. Also worth a browse is www.unsaac.edu.pe/cusco/, run by the local university.

There are a number of good sites on Machu Picchu and the Inca Trail. One, with links all over the web, is 🖥 www.ex.ac.uk/~RDavies/inca. A personal favourite is the ultra-informative Andean travel web, 🖥 www.andeantravelweb.com. The site of Gene Savoy, one of the discoverers of Vilcabamba, is at 🖥 www.genesavoy.org/, and Vincent R Lee, another Vilcabamba traveller, can be found on-line at 🖥 www.blissnet.com/~sixpacmanco/books.htm. Also worth a look is 🖥 www.pacaritambo.com, an informative (if a little odd) site specializing in ancient South American cultures.

Finally, 🖥 www.machupicchuperu.com, is the official site of the nearby town of Aguas Calientes (see p157).

General information
🖥 www.traficoperu.com (detailed information on as diverse things as flights and restaurants, lodging and car hire), 🖥 www.paginasamarillas.telefonica.com.pe (Peru's yellow pages online). 🖥 www.saexplorers.org is the website of the South American Explorers' Club (see p106). A good general Latin-American travel site is 🖥 www.amerispan.com/lata.

the discovery of Machu Picchu is *The Lost City of the Incas* (Duell, Sloan and Pearce 1948). This last book is now available in a reprint all over Cusco, and there's also a new larger format edition (see books on Machu Piccu, p30). Dr Paul Fejos explored what's now called the Inca Trail and published the results in *Publications in Anthropology #3: Archaeological Explorations in the Cordillera Vilcabamba* (The Werner Gren Foundation, The Viking Fund 1944).

Cut Stones and Crossroads (Penguin 1984) is a good modern travelogue written by Ronald Wright (sadly now out of print); and Matthew Parris has published a characteristically well-written book called *Inca Cola* (Weidenfeld & Nicholson, 1990).

Other books

The *Royal Hunt of the Sun*, Peter Shaffer, is a play about the fall of the last Inca Atahualpa (see p93). *The Heights of Machu Picchu,* Pablo Neruda, (Jonathan Cape 1966) is an extended piece inspired by the ruins by the Nobel Prize-winning Chilean poet.

Two good books on keeping yourself healthy are *Bugs, bites and bowels,* Dr Jane Wilson Howarth (Cadogan Books 1995) and *Medical Handbook for Mountaineers,* Peter Steele (Constable 1988).

For more information on the effects of high altitude, there's an accessible guide aimed at non-medics: *Altitude Illness, Prevention & Treatment* by Stephen Bezruchka MD (Cordee 1994).

Pre-departure health preparations

FITNESS

Obviously it shouldn't need saying but one of the most important health preparations is to get reasonably fit. You don't have to be a marathon runner, but you'll enjoy yourself much more if you're in good shape.

INOCULATIONS

Before you travel you should make sure that you've been immunized against the following diseases: **tetanus**, **polio** and **diphtheria**, **tuberculosis**, **yellow fever**, **hepatitis A** and **typhoid.** Check that the shot you had is still effective and that you do not need a booster. There was a serious outbreak of cholera in Peru in 1991 but there's not much point being inoculated against it as the cholera germ has become resistant to the vaccine. If you're going to the jungle (below 2000m) or on the Vilcabamba trek you should take a course of anti-**malaria** tablets.

Opposite: Quechua women, Ollantaytambo. (Photo © Henry Stedman).

If you're walking the longer trails, consider having a **rabies** inoculation too. It's expensive and you need to leave a month between injections, but as you will be a couple of days' walk from the nearest transport to the nearest hospital and the locals' dogs aren't usually friendly, it's wise to have one. The inoculation won't, however, prevent the disease, it'll only buy you more time to get to hospital.

> ❏ **Dealing with dogs**
> It's worth noting that if a dog does run up to you barking you should do as the locals do: pick up a stone and throw it in the dog's direction. If there's no stone nearby simply making as if to pick up a stone will usually scare off the dog.

To check on the latest requirements, look at the **US Center for Disease Control** 🖥 www.cdc.gov, or ask a doctor. Travel clinics, however, are usually better informed than your local doctor. Up-to-the-minute health information and an on-the-spot vaccination service is available in London at **Nomad Travellers Store & Medical Centre** (☎ 020-8833 4114, STA Travel, 40 Bernard St, WC1N 1LJ). There are also clinics run by **Trailfinders** (see p17) and **British Airways** (☎ 020-7606 2977 to find one near you). Note that while some inoculations are available on the NHS in the UK, you'll have to pay for all inoculations at travel clinics.

HIGH-ALTITUDE TRAVEL

The effects of high altitude

You should be aware of the possible ill effects of high altitude before you go, and people with heart and lung problems or high blood pressure should get advice from their doctor before travelling. Children are more susceptible to altitude sickness than adults so should not be taken above 3000m or 10,000ft. Young adults (in their teens or early twenties) are also more susceptible and extra days should be allowed for acclimatization. Cusco is at 3360m (11,000 ft) above sea level, and the highest pass described in this book is 5000m (16,400ft).

The altitude can do funny things to you. The first thing you'll notice is that you're always short of breath, but you may also lose your appetite, have difficulty sleeping and sometimes wake up feeling as if you've been slightly smothered. You might also notice your companions' breathing becoming increasingly shallow as they sleep, before an enormous grunting breath reassures you they're still alive. Don't worry, all this is normal. It's caused by your body having to deal with less oxygen at a lower pressure than it's used to at lower elevations. Almost everyone who comes to Cusco notices some of these things, and it's so common that the better restaurants and hotels have oxygen available.

You might notice several other things happening, too, in your first days up there with the gods. Your hands, face and ankles may swell up, and you may

---

Opposite: Below Salcantay on the Mollepata trek. The pass is at about 5000m (16,400ft) so you need to be well acclimatized before taking this trek. (Photo © Bryn Thomas).

fart and burp more than usual. You're most likely to get a headache. Rarely, some people suffer from fainting fits, but these aren't serious on their own.

Having given you all the bad news, I should reassure you that the most obvious effect of altitude you'll notice, once you're acclimatized, is a feeling of clearness and health.

Acclimatization

Altitude sickness can be fatal but is entirely preventable. The key to avoiding problems is to acclimatize (see p165). The biggest mistake to make is to belt up from Lima (which is at sea level) and then expect your body to do everything that it normally does when you're breathing richer air. Take a couple of days lazing around Cusco while your system catches up with you. After two weeks, you'll hardly notice the altitude.

For more information on health and safety while trekking see p164.

INSURANCE

You should take out travel insurance before you leave or check you're covered by your domestic policies. In the US and Canada, your domestic health insurance, home owners insurance or rental insurance may cover you on this trip; check with your insurer.

Many travel insurance policies will cover you for trekking the routes described in this book but some won't. Check the small print before you sign up. For added safety, take out insurance specially tailored for trekkers or mountaineers. The British Mountaineering Council (☎ 0870-0104878, 🖹 0161-445 4500, 🖳 www.thebmc.co.uk), 177-179 Burton Rd, Manchester M20 2BB, does this type of insurance for members.

PART 2: PERU

Facts about the country

Peru is an amazing country. Within its borders there's part of the largest jungle on earth, the planet's driest desert and a large section of the world's second highest mountain range. The seas around Peru are no less impressive – there's a thousand times more food in Peru's coastal waters than in the average ocean. Because it's a land of such extremes, Peru has an immense range of life forms: you can find 20 out of the planet's 34 life zones in Peru, more than any other country in the world.

Peru's attractions are not only geographical: it possesses a rich cultural tradition, both ancient (Peru is the source of ethereal Andean music) and modern (exemplified by the novelist, Mario Vargas Llosa, and the poet César Vallejo).

But Peru's not just a place of fascinating geography, natural history and cultural interest: it's also a country that's emblematic of modern South America. Climbing out of the pit of hyperinflation and attempting to establish economic stability, Peru is trying to live with the atrocities of a past conflict while struggling to entrench democracy.

GEOGRAPHICAL BACKGROUND

Peru covers 1,280,000 square kilometres and is divided into three basic zones: *costa* (coast), *sierra* (highlands) and *selva* (jungle).

Geographical regions

The Pacific Ocean is circled with a ring of fire of soaring mountains and active volcanoes, caused by the massive plates that form the skin on the earth's core of molten rock ramming into each other. These plates can rise into the air and form mountains or can sink deep into the planet's crust and melt. When this melted rock rises to the surface again it causes volcanoes to form. This is how the Andes, the mountain range that separates Peru's Amazon rainforest from the Pacific coast, were formed and this is the cause of Peru's frequent earthquakes.

Costa The geography of Peru's coast is dominated by the **Humboldt (or Peru) current**. This is a cold stream of water, so cold that it creates above itself a wide mass of chill coastal air. This air forms a barrier that the warm moist winds of the Pacific can't penetrate, and so scarcely any rain falls on the coast. Because the coast's so parched, the **Atacama desert** has formed – a long thin strip of scorched land that extends far down into Chile. The Humboldt current is also rich in nutrients and supports a vast amount of sea life.

Sierra   There are two branches of the Andes in Peru, the *Cordillera Blanca* (White Range) fronting the Amazon and the *Cordillera Negra* (Black Range) which parallels the coast. Between the two ranges is the *altiplano* (high plateau), an enclosed plain 800km long, which is characterized by high grasslands called puna whose fertile topsoil has been scraped off by glaciers. It's too cold up here for this soil to be replaced naturally, and so it's pretty barren land.

Selva   The eastern slopes of the Andes are covered by the edge of the Amazonian rainforest, which the locals call the *cejas de la selva* or eyebrows of the jungle. The selva itself is largely unexplored.

Climate
Peru carries the curse of El Niño. Usually the country's climate is predictable; it's always dry on the coast and there's regular rainfall in the mountains but a couple of times in a decade El Niño hits.

El Niño is a change in the weather brought on by a change in the currents of the Pacific Ocean. What happens is that the coast becomes bathed in warmer waters that have made their way across the Pacific. The Humboldt current disappears, and the fish that bless Peru's coast swim south to colder waters. Damp winds roll from the sea over the desert, causing heavy rains that drench the land and cause serious flooding. Many people die or are made homeless. The effects aren't limited to South America. On the other side of the world, El Niño inverts usual weather patterns and causes devastation. Whilst the mechanics of this scourge are understood, the cause isn't. It seems to come in seven-year cycles but until we know why El Niño happens, there's no way of predicting exactly when it will come back.

The phenomenon was first noticed to occur around Christmas, and so called *El Niño* (the boy) after Jesus. El Niño has an opposite called *La Niña* (the girl), when the seas are unusually cold. El Niño shows that Peru's climate isn't static, but there's more to it than just these short term disturbances. About 12,000 years

---

El Niño and the fall of the Moche and Tiahuanaco
The periodic climatic upheaval of El Niño causes great damage. The last major one, in 1998, killed at least 900 people, destroyed hundreds of thousands of domestic animals and caused an estimated US$90 billion worth of damage across the world. In the past, however, El Niño's done worse. It's probable that it finished off two ancient Peruvian civilizations and prompted the expansion of a third.

Samples of ice taken from a Peruvian glacier suggest that there was an El Niño about the time of the decline of the Moche civilization (see p72), which supports theories that the Moche were wiped out by massive climatic change. It's also likely that the same phenomenon caused the fall of the greatest of pre-Inca civilizations, the Tiahuanaco, and a similar environmental catastrophe destroyed the fertile lands of Chimú and spurred them on to conquer their neighbours (see p76).

ago most of Peru was covered by massive ice sheets, and even within the past 4000 years there have been cycles of heating and cooling; just 300 years ago Peruvians were growing plants at 4200m that you can only grow today at 3700m. The one thing that's static about Peru's climate is the fact that it changes.

● **Costa** Summer is from December to April. The temperature ranges from 25°C to 35°C, and rainfall is extremely rare. Winter comes from May to November, when the temperature drops by about 10°C and there's lots of fog and cloud and a little rain too.

● **Sierra** There isn't really a summer and winter in the sierra, more like a rainy and a dry season. April or May to October is the dry season, when temperatures range from 25°C by day to -20°C by night. November to March is the wet season; the temperature's pretty much the same by day, but it's much warmer at night.

● **Selva** The wet and dry seasons are the same as the Sierra, but it's hot just about all the time.

HISTORICAL OUTLINE

For Peru before the Spanish see Part 3, pp66-99.

Peru under the Spanish

In 1542, after the Spanish authorities consolidated their power by mopping up a brief revolt by some rebellious *conquistadors* (the name given to the Spanish conquerors of the Americas), they created the Viceroyalty of Peru. It was a massive, immensely rich place, governing all of South America except Venezuela and Brazil. Peru was the jewel in the crown of Spanish South America, the centre of law, administration and commerce for a whole continent. Lima became one of the most important cities in the hemisphere; the highest court in the continent was in Lima, and if you were a trader anywhere between Quito and Chile your goods could only leave the continent through Lima's port, Callao. Things only got better for the Spanish Peruvians with the discovery in 1545 of a mountain of silver called Potosí, in what's now Bolivia.

Spanish rule in theory The Spanish Crown tried to rule humanely, protecting the Indians from the excesses of the settlers. The principles of rule were fiercely Roman Catholic and profoundly nationalistic, not surprising considering that Spain had just emerged from under the heel of the Moors. The theory was that the Crown was supreme, and no government should be left to the locals, be they conquistadors or *cabil-*

❑ Bishop la Casa, a contemporary supporter of the Indians, wrote: '...long before they [the Indians] had heard the word Spaniard they had properly organized states, wisely ordered by excellent laws, religion and custom... [they were ruled by] laws that at very many points surpass ours, and could have won the admiration of the sages of Athens... Now what belief will be placed in the Spaniards – greedy, violent, and cruel men who put unarmed and harmless Indians to the sword and rob them with extraordinary avarice?'

dos (town councils). Everything was owned by the Crown and was supposed to revert to the Crown. Spaniards were permitted to hold *encomiendas* (land, and with it the benefit of the labour of any Indians who lived on it) only if they spread Christianity, and they were not permitted to live on their property, nor could they leave it to their children. Indians were not slaves; they were equals who simply hadn't learnt of the Gospels, and they should be treated as such. Crown agents called *corregidors* were appointed as supervisors.

Spanish rule in practice It didn't, of course, work like that on the ground. Spain was making too much money really to want to emancipate the Indians, and even if Spanish intentions had been uncompromised by greed, it was too far away to supervise the implementation of the laws. In any case, the *encomenderos* (owners of encomiendas) were out for all they could get, wouldn't have obeyed laws that deprived them of their labour force. Consequently many Indians were worked to the bone (the silver mines at Potosí – see boxed text below – were particularly horrific places), and much of the glory of Imperial Spain was built from the sweat and blood of the children of the Incas.

La Leyenda Negra

The stories of the great atrocities inflicted by the Spanish on the Incas are called by some *La Leyenda Negra* (The Black Legend). Anglo-Saxons, looking south with envious eyes, have always been prepared to believe the worst about the Spanish Empire, and stories of great evils perpetrated on the noble Peruvians have been frequently told by historians such as Markham and Prescott. In the nineteenth century, the Inca civilization became for many in the Romantic movement a golden age of harmony, violated by the conquistadors.

The truth is more complicated, of course. The Incas didn't run a perfect society: they were ferocious and merciless in war, and Atahualpa (see p93) admitted that if he'd captured the Spaniards he would have enslaved them and had them castrated. But the bottom line has to take account of the horrors of Spanish rule, especially the horrors associated with the silver mines of Potosí, Bolivia. It was there that hundreds of thousands of Indians met their deaths, suffocated in the depths of the mountain or maddened by the chemicals used to extract the silver itself.

Spaniards maltreating Incas
FELIPE HUAMÁN POMA DE AYALA

Convoys of pressed labour made their way here from all over the old Inca Empire, men separated from their families, and tied together by the neck. If these poor sufferers were too weary to continue, or if they fell, the Spaniards didn't waste time loosening their bonds, they simply cut their bodies from the yoke with swords. These were days of great suffering.

However, it wasn't simply a case of the European power raping Peru and Peruvians (though there's no doubt they did both), and from Don Cristóbal Paullu Inca onwards some Indians did very well out of the conquest.

The empire in decline The flower of Peru's and Lima's glory held the seeds of the decline of the Viceroyalty, and Peru's pre-eminence was one of the causes of the decline of the Spanish Empire. For example, it was incredibly inefficient to have the continent's only port in Callao; this caused smuggling to become commonplace and Spain's laws to be flouted. Disregard for the mother country extended further: the colonists did not like the benevolent attitude of the Crown to Indians or the fact that locally born Spaniards (Creoles) were denied any power – such positions were reserved for newcomers from Spain. It didn't help matters that less money was coming in from mining and that pirates were scourging the coast.

The empire rallies and Peru declines A historian has described the eighteenth century, when the Bourbons replaced the Hapsburgs on the Spanish throne, as a second conquest. The colonies were once again ruled with vigour, and South America was transformed. Power was consolidated by the tightening of the regulations prohibiting Creoles from holding public office, and the Jesuits were expelled. Peru ceased to be the only Viceroyalty in the continent, and became just one of many: the Viceroy of new Granada deprived Peru of its northern territory in 1718, the Viceroyalty of Río de la Plata (Argentina, Paraguay and Uruguay) cut off its eastern provinces in 1776 and Chile became a virtually autonomous captaincy general. The trade system was reformed removing Lima's monopoly as a port, and old taxes were put up and new ones imposed.

Days of rebellion This caused problems. In 1780 a prosperous Indian called José Gabriel Condorcanqui took the name of the last Inca Tupac Amaru (see p142), and revolted against the authorities. He said – to start with at least – that he was loyal to the Spanish Crown and Church, and was rebelling against increased taxation and oppressive labour. Then his movement began to mean something more: it began to be an attempt to recreate the rule of the Incas. He was captured and executed in 1781 (his execution took seven hours), but his revolt carried on till 1783.

These events were seen amongst Europeans (for example Baron von Humboldt, the German naturalist after whom the sea current was named) as a war waged by the forces of civilization against those of barbarism. It's now seen rather differently as the stalking horse of Peruvian Independence.

Liberation
The turn of the eighteenth century was a time of revolution in America and France – something that wouldn't have escaped the notice of the Spanish colonies in South America. Then, in 1808, Napoleon invaded Spain who, desperate to resist the French, asked for help from its empire, and the price of Spanish American support was more recognition of the rights of Creoles. And

so, partly because of the revolutionary atmosphere of the time, and partly because of the abasement of Spain, Spanish America began to taste independence.

Peru was very loyal to the Crown, because it had done very well out of the empire. It's no surprise then, that it was liberated by outsiders rather than being the seat of sedition. What is surprising is that in the wars of liberation there were more Peruvians in the monarchist army of Spain than in the liberating army of South America.

Peru was freed by the two great South American liberators: **San Martín** and **Simon Bolívar**. Two more different men it's difficult to imagine. San Martín was a refined, cautious, cold Argentinian; Bolívar was a heated, hairy, impulsive Venezuelan but both were equally brilliant generals. San Martín started the ball rolling by kicking the Spanish out of Argentina and Chile, but he needed to secure his victory by denying Spain the wealth of Potosí and access to the port of Callao. In other words, he needed to liberate Peru. He landed in Pisco from Chile in 1818 and fought his way up to Lima, entering the city and declaring Independence in 1820 just as the Viceroy was escaping with the remains of the royalist army.

San Martín travelled north to meet Bolívar, from whom he sought help in defeating the Viceroy. Bolívar refused, wanting all the glory for himself, and so San Martín abandoned the country to his northern colleague. Bolívar finished off the royalists at the battles of Junín (6 August 1824) and Ayacucho (9 December 1824).

First steps in independence

Bolívar was made political supreme chief in 1824 but the Peruvians feared absorption into his 'greater Colombia' and abandoned him soon thereafter. Sadly there was a reluctance by civilians to take power because there was no tradition of self-government in the country and so, in a coup that was to mark a pattern in the rest of Peru's history, the *caudillos* (military leaders) seized control. A soldier called **Gamarra** became president, and the die of Peru's history was cast.

In 1835-6, Peru was promptly invaded by the dictator of Bolivia, Santa Cruz, who planned to create a confederation with Bolivia. Chile and Argentina put a stop to these plans at the battle of Yungay in 1839, and recreated Peru's independence. Gamarra became president again, and retaliated by invading Bolivia; his army was defeated and he was killed at Yngavi in 1841.

One revolt later an honest and tolerant man, **Ramón Castilla**, became president. His presidency coincided with the exploitation of *guano* (bird excrement fertilizer) in the Chincha islands and the nitrate of Tarapacá, so he had wealth to play with. He built railways and invested in the education of the Indians, abolished the system of tribute, and emancipated black slaves. Prosperity and stability weren't to last, and the next president, **Balta** (1868-72), encouraged by Castilla's example, spent vast sums on the Andean railways, money the country could ill afford. He hung the albatross of Peru's national debt around its neck.

War with Spain

Then in 1864 came war with Spain, which had never formally let go of the colonies. A Spanish squadron seized the valuable Chincha islands. The Peruvian president, Pezet, would have been happy to pay a ransom to get them back, but he was quickly replaced as leader by a man called Prado, who went to war against the Spanish in alliance with Chile, Ecuador and Bolivia. The Spanish bombarded Callao and the Chilean port of Valparaíso in 1866, then slunk off home, but it wasn't until 1871 that an armistice was signed. Not till 1879 did Spain finally acknowledge Peruvian independence.

War of the Pacific

Having beaten off the Spanish, Peru didn't have much time to enjoy peace. The price of guano, a main Peruvian export, fell after the invention of chemical fertilizers and so Peru's finances got worse. Prado decided to make the sale of nitrates a government monopoly and he arranged compensation for the mine owners; the Chileans who owned the mines didn't think he paid them enough.

Their government was spoiling for a fight anyway, and Prado's action antagonized them. Bolivia and Peru, aware of this, had entered into a half-secret alliance against the Chileans in 1873.

War broke out between Chile and Bolivia in 1879, and surprisingly, when Peru offered to mediate between the two, the Chileans declared war on Peru. To start with, all went well for the Peruvians. They won the battle of Iquique sinking the Chilean ship, the *Independencia*, but then it all went wrong and they lost Arica. By 1881 the Chileans had occupied Lima, and a humiliating peace treaty was signed at Ancón in 1883, which ultimately resulted in Peru losing its southern provinces.

Picking up the pieces

If Peru was in a bad way before the War of the Pacific it was desperate after and by 1890 couldn't pay its foreign debt. The British bondholders who held this debt formed the **Peruvian Corporation**, an organization which undertook to pay it off in return for annual payments, a 66-year lease of the railways and guano concessions. The Peruvians hated this arrangement but despite the humiliation, relative peace followed, and the country was buoyed up by rising copper production. Reforms were introduced such as direct suffrage, public education programmes and municipal elections. One of the main presidents of this time was **Leguía**, who ruled from 1908-12 and then from 1919-30. He began well, but when he was conciliatory to Chilean claims for Peruvian land in the south and Ecuadorian claims in the north he lost the sympathy of his people.

The dance of APRA and the army

The Depression finished off Leguía, and he was ousted in a coup in 1931, but a more interesting fish was being fried far from the centre stage of Peruvian politics. This was the **APRA party** (*Alianza Popular Revolucionaria Americana*) formed by Victor Raul Haya de la Torre. APRA was to dominate Peru right through to the 1980s, either through being in power or being suppressed by the army.

APRA started off Marxist and was bent on integrating the oppressed minorities of Peru, resisting what they called the economic imperialism of the US, and founding a union of Latin American states. Haya de la Torre first stood for president in 1931 and lost. APRA cried foul, and in 1932 staged an **uprising in Trujillo**, during which they killed 50 army hostages. Up to 5000 people were then taken out into the desert by the army and shot. APRA retaliated by assassinating the president in 1933.

Banned by the authorities, APRA continued to operate covertly and endorsed a presidential candidate in the 1936 elections. However, just as their candidate was about to win, Congress annulled the elections and gave General Benavides dictatorial powers. He was followed by Dr Manuel Prado Ugarteche who, except in his relations with Ecuador, was a pan-Americanist: Peru followed the USA and belatedly declared war on Germany and Japan in February 1945.

In 1941 Ecuador and Peru had a **border war** which Peru won, causing Ecuador to cede parts of its southern territory. The war still festers: it last erupted in 1995 but a deal in 1998 brought the two countries to peace.

In the 1945 election, APRA was legalized and got a majority of the seats in the lower house and half of the seats in the upper house. However, shortly after the election, President Bustamente (elected on an APRA ticket) went independent and so APRA staged an uprising in Callao. They were banned again and suppressed so fiercely that Haya de la Torre had to seek sanctuary in the Colombian embassy for the next five years.

Land reform – 1963
In the fifties, the power of APRA declined. In a bizarre marriage of convenience, they sided with their old enemies, the army, in support of Manuel Prado in the 1956 election. About this time the pressures from landless *campesinos* (peasants) increased, and there was a bloody revolt in the Cusco area led by Hugo Blanco.

After the inconclusive 1962 election, a military junta rather predictably seized power but they permitted another election in 1963 that was won by **Belaúnde Terry**. By this stage everyone was worried by the campesinos' volatility, and so agrarian reform was implemented, 500,000 acres of land being distributed. This was an important step, and the campesinos of Peru, who had from time immemorial worked the land for a distant landlord – the Incas, the encomenderos, the hacienda owners – finally worked the land for themselves. Whether you think they have thrived or withered since depends on your politics.

The military take control
The military didn't hold back for long, and in 1968 they forced the resignation of Belaúnde, imprisoned politicians and suspended rights. It was a time of friendship with Soviet Russia and of censorship. Nationalization of industry followed and with the agrarian, mining, and industrial laws the government seized control of Peru's industries. More land was given to the campesinos and in 1973

Terrorism in Peru

The two main terrorist groups in Peru are the Communist party of Peru, (Sendero Luminoso or Partido Comunista de Peru) and the Tupac Amaru Revolutionary Movement (MRTA).

The **Sendero Luminoso**, founded in the 1970s by philosophy professor Abimael Guzmán Reynoso (aka 'Comrade' or 'Presidente Gonzalo'), are Maoists intolerant of global capitalism and the Peruvian government. They draw their support from dissatisfied campesinos (of which there are many), particularly those who live in the highlands around Ayacucho. The Sendero ruthlessly persecute those who don't support their ideology. If you're not with them, you're against them, and any other group is a target: in 1991, for example, they killed four mothers and their children because they were distributing free milk to children. Today they're much less active than they were, though they've not completely gone: in March 2002 a car-bomb exploded in Lima which was attributed to them. They still garner support abroad from some quarters, and they have an old website ⌨ www.blythe.org/peru-pcp, and ⌨ www.csrp.org. Guzmán has been in prison since 1992; Nicholas Shakespeare's novel, *The Dancer Upstairs*, is based on his arrest.

The other Peruvian terrorist organization, the **MRTA**, was little-known abroad until they took over the residence of the Japanese ambassador in December 1996, having got in disguised as waiters. (It was only by chance that the then Peruvian president, Alberto Fujimori, himself of Japanese ancestry, wasn't there.) The MRTA are a more moderate left-wing terrorist group, but they've never been as strong as the Sendero. The Japanese ambassador's siege gained them notoriety, and then won Fujimori support when in April 1998 he sent in the military. The building was stormed and all but one of the hostages were released unharmed. All the terrorists were killed, as were two soldiers. The MRTA are today a spent force.

---

the government reformed the education system, recognized the equality of women, built rural schools (permitting children to be taught in Quechua and Aymara) and gave autonomy to the University. The national debt grew, increased by the cost of agrarian reform and a decline in the price of fishmeal and copper.

Things fall apart

The army allowed elections again in 1978 and after a new constitution was drafted, Haya de la Torre was finally elected President. However, he didn't last long, beaten in the 1980 elections by Belaúnde Terry who reorganized the economy along free-market lines.

It was about now that things started to go seriously wrong. In 1982-3, an El Niño hit the fishing industry, and the terrorist movements **Sendero Luminoso** (The Shining Path) and the **MRTA** (*Movimiento Revolucionario Tupac Amaru*, Tupac Amaru Revolutionary Movement) built up a head of steam. Peru's currency, the sol, collapsed, and inflation ran riot. In 1983 APRA were elected and **President García** tried to remedy the situation by not paying more than 10% of

Peru's foreign debt, a move that caused the international banks to refuse to make any further loans to Peru. The situation got steadily worse. García's administration became increasingly characterized by graft and human rights abuses, which peaked when the *Rodrigo Franco Commando* (a right-wing death squad) started fighting the terrorists with extreme violence. The people who suffered were those caught in the middle, the campesinos.

The economy got steadily worse, and in 1987 García moved to nationalize the banks, a move that caused strikes and inflation. The country descended into a spiral of misery.

1990s – Peru under Fujimori

The 1990 election was, therefore, one of the most important for a century. With the economy and society in tatters, the novelist **Mario Vargas Llosa** (see p50) stood for President as a moderate right-wing candidate against APRA. Hardly anyone noticed another contender, a provincial agricultural engineer of Japanese ancestry, called **Alberto Fujimori**. Against the odds, Llosa lost, and Fujimori won.

In 1992 Fujimori shut down the Congress and dismissed the Supreme Court, and in 1993 the constitution of Peru was rewritten. Fujimori then embarked on economic and legal reform which he claimed would enable the country's economy to grow and assist in the crushing of the Sendero Luminoso. It also allowed him to stand for another term in office.

It's been called the **President's coup**, for that's what it was: a bloodless coup d'état. However, it did bear some good fruit when in 1992 Abimael Guzmán, the leader of the Sendero, was arrested by the police and the economy was brought under control. The Peruvian people obviously thought that Fujimori's actions were justified since nearly two out of three of them voted for him in the 1995 elections, when he beat the former head of the United Nations, Javier Perez de Cuellar. A negotiated peace with Ecuador followed, and Fujimori managed the economy to the satisfaction of the IMF and USA but at considerable cost in terms of human rights.

Then Fujimori tempted fate. He re-wrote the constitution yet again to allow him a further term. His opponent this time was a man called Toledo, a former shoe-shine boy and one time economist with the World Bank. After an election of dubious fairness, Fujimori won. But just as he was settling in to his unprecedented third term in office, the wheel of fortune turned and his past caught up with him. His shadowy right-hand man, Vladimiro Montesinos, who had been his eyes and ears as the head of the state intelligence agency ('Servicio de Inteligencia Nacional', or SIN), fell from grace.

A video tape of Montesinos bribing a member of Congress was leaked to the press. The tape led to the revelation that Montesinos had bribed or threatened most of the Peruvian establishment to garner support for Fujimori. Montesinos fled abroad, and it was only when he'd left that it was discovered he'd salted away some US$48 million in various foreign banks.

Fujimori held onto power for a couple of months, declaring he intended to track Montesinos down. But then he left the country on a run-of-the-mill tour, and stopped off in Japan. He's never left. Much to the irritation of Peruvians, he said that he'd always been a Japanese national. Only a Peruvian national can be president of Peru – this revelation meant that he'd been an illegal president for 10 years.

Toledo comes to power
Fresh elections were called. Alan García, the man who had caused such economic chaos in the late eighties, stood against Fujimori's challenger, Alejandro Toledo. The centrist Toledo narrowly won, standing on a manifesto that promised to create a million new jobs while keeping a prudent hold of the country's purse strings. He also vowed to bring Fujimori back to Peru to face charges of corruption, human rights' violations and murder.

Toledo is of Andean Indian ancestry, a fact that he exploited skilfully throughout the campaign, even adopting the nickname 'Pachacutec' after the great Inca emperor. There are those in Peru who believe that it would take a ruler of the Inca Pachacutec's capability to solve the country's many problems; whether Toledo, the first president of Indian descent, proves to be just such a leader remains to be seen.

Clearing up the mess
Fujimori now faces an international arrest warrant. Peru's asking the Japanese to extradite him to face charges of bribery, corruption, involvement in death-squad massacres and being an illegal president. There are also allegations that he set up a campaign of forced sterilization of campesino women. The Japanese are unlikely to let him go, but Montesinos, Fujimori's Rasputin, was tracked down to Venezuela and brought back to Peru. At the time of writing he's languishing in a Limeño jail, refusing to cooperate with the courts.

THE PEOPLE

Most (70%) of Peru's 26.2 million people live in modern cities, but the society is deeply rooted in its past; about half the population is **Quechua,** the descendants of the Incas. The blood of the Incas was mixed with that of the Spanish from the first days of the conquest, and a third of the people are the products of these unions: **mestizo**; a fifth are **Caucasian**.

The others that make up Peru include the significant minority of **Aymara** around Lake Titicaca, and about 250,000 indigenous **jungle tribespeople**. There's also a small **black** population, based south of Lima, who are the descendants of those unfortunates brought to Peru as slaves (in the first century alone after the conquest as many as 10,000 were brought to Peru).

The Quechua who farm the highlands prefer to be called campesinos (rural labourers) and not *indios* (Indians), which they consider an insult.

Education and literacy
About one in ten adult Peruvians is illiterate. Over a third of Peru's population is under 14 and education's now free and compulsory up to the age of 16. It's difficult to enforce this in rural areas, but the government estimates that most of Peru's children have primary education, two thirds of children go to secondary

school and a quarter are in tertiary education. The government spends 9.3% of its budget on education, but publicly-funded schooling doesn't have a good reputation and those who can afford it send their children to private schools.

Language
(For useful words and phrases see p259). Spanish is the main language today, but **Quechua** (or *Runasimi*, 'the people's mouth') is spoken by about 10 million people concentrated around Cusco and southern Peru, two million of whom don't speak anything but Quechua. In the main tourist areas in Lima and Cusco English is understood by some people. Around Lake Titicaca, the ancient language *Aymara* survives; it dates from before the Incas.

Quechua, the language of the Incas, was not written down till the sixteenth century so there are many different ways of transcribing it. It's difficult to be consistent, as different words have become familiar in different spellings: Inca can be written Inka, Sacsayhuaman as Saq'saywaman, and Cusco as Cuzco or Q'osqo. I've tried to be consistent in my spelling of Quechua words, using Dr Ann Kendall's work as a guide, except where a particular spelling of a word has become so familiar that spelling it another way looks bizarre.

Religion
Ninety-five per cent of the population are **Roman Catholic**, and the Peruvian church is the cradle of 'liberation theology', a socialist interpretation of Christianity. However, in more rural areas the people have been better described by the anthropologist, Robert Randall, as **'Pagan Catholics'** whose Catholicism is mixed with indigenous beliefs, placing a veneer of Christianity on ancient ceremonies and substituting saints for local spirits. There are various **Protestant** churches active in Peru, and they're considered predatory by some Catholics: you'll often see stickers in people's front windows telling Protestant canvassers to go away. Some of these churches are the charmless North American imports that have spread all over the world, but some are indigenous, such as the IEP (Evangelical Church of Peru) which has been in the country for a hundred years.

Pilgrimage to Qoyllor Riti
This pilgrimage is a good example of what has been called Pagan Catholicism. Qoyllor Riti is a village in the *Nevado* (snow-capped peak) Ausangate near Cusco, and once a year in early June many people climb the hills on a pilgrimage there. The Christian basis for the festival is that Christ appeared here to a young shepherd called Marianito in the eighteenth century but the festival dates back to the days before Christianity arrived in Peru, back to the days when pilgrimages were made to the *Apus* or spirits of the mountains who needed to be placated with human sacrifice. Some say that to this day there's always a death on the pilgrimage: a baby freezes to death on the glacier, or a campesino falls from a precipice and the Apu is satisfied.

POLITICS AND ECONOMICS

Politics

The president hires and fires ministers and is elected every five years with the 120 members of congress. The country is divided into 25 departments, governed by prefects who are also appointed by the president. Departments are divided into provinces, which are sub-divided into districts, each governed by a mayor elected every five years.

Current politics

Toledo, leader of the centrist party *Peru Posible*, won just 52% of the final vote in the 2001 elections against García's 48% – one of the narrowest victories ever, and one that ensures that García will continue to have a strong voice in parliament as leader of the opposition party *Alianza Popular Revolucionaria Americana* (APRA), which was originally a revolutionary left-wing party. Even though he lost, the election and his return to the heart of Peruvian politics still represent quite a comeback for García following nine years in exile in Colombia waiting for corruption charges dating back to his tenure as president to expire.

Other political parties are: *Acción Popular* (AP) – centre right; Fujimori's old party, *Cambio 90*, that has all but ceased to exist; *Izquierda Unida* (IU) – a left-wing umbrella group, now split by internal division and the *Partido Popular Cristiano* (PPC) – a right-wing, pro-business party centred around Lima. There is widespread disillusionment with traditional political parties in Peru.

Human rights

In the late 1980s and 1990s, there were some very unpleasant things going on in Peru. Both the Shining Path (see p43) and the government were responsible for methodical campaigns of killing, maiming and intimidation. Around 30,000 people died, and 6000 suffered the dreadful fate for themselves and their families of 'being disappeared'. And as late as 1998 there were reports of forced sterilizations being carried out on campesino women.

With the new government, there is some new hope. A Truth and Reconciliation Commission has been set up, and in April 2002 began hearings in an attempt to close the door on the country's horrific past. A spokesman summed up the Commission's task, when he said: 'What is absolute, what is definitive is that people were unjustly killed and human rights were violated. We are not trying to open Pandora's box, we are trying to air things that have been forgotten and stink.' But the Commission has an uphill struggle as it has no legal powers.

The economy

Peru is blessed with abundant mineral resources, seas teeming with fish and a wide range of climates that means just about anything can be grown there, but in the past hyperinflation and political instability practically ruined the country. The situation's better now and the economy is thriving, but there are still enormous differences in wealth and opportunity between the richest and poorest Peruvians.

Coca and cocaine

It's been said that coca leaf has as much to do with cocaine as elephants have to do with ivory – it's the raw material from which the refined product comes, nothing more. Coca leaf has been chewed in the Andes for thousands of years, and it's as central to Andean culture as coffee is to the Arabs and tea is to people from the Indian subcontinent. Once, coca leaf was reserved for the Incas themselves, but in the days of the Spanish Empire it was chewed almost incessantly by overworked labourers.

The quid of leaves is chewed with a mixture of lime or quinoa and potash called *llipta*, releasing a natural anaesthetic which relieves hunger, and, in some way that's not understood, relieves the effect of altitude. Coca leaf has a long history in Andean culture, and you can see the characteristic quid in the cheeks of some portrait pots from the days of the Nazca (see p73), and implements associated with its use have been found from the Moche culture (see p72).

But the coca leaf is most famous around the world today because of its derivative, cocaine. This alkaloid was first isolated by a scientist called Gaedake in the nineteenth century, and when it was discovered it seemed an unalloyed benefit to humanity – a pain-relieving drug of great potency. However, over the years its abuse and restriction have created the demon that cocaine is today. In Peru, the main problem is the enormous profits that cocaine production can bring, and the growing of coca leaf to produce cocaine is organized by largely Colombian gangs of narco-terrorists, whose anarchic rule subjugates swathes of Peru's remote jungle.

The United Nations, and the USA's Drug Enforcement Agency (DEA), seem set to try to solve the world's cocaine problem by eradicating all coca leaf growing in the Andes. Sadly, this ignores both the traditional nature of the leaf in Andean society and the poverty that drives campesinos to try to make money from growing it. When the DEA torch remote fields that campesinos have spent months cultivating, they create hatred. The campesinos see cocaine as a problem of the urban West rather than rural Peru, and believe that the US's 'War On Drugs' is cynically fought in the highlands of Peru rather than where it could have more effect – in the USA itself – because there are no votes to lose in Peru.

The Fujimori administration privatized large chunks of state-owned industry, reforming the tax system and eliminating many price controls and import tariffs. Toledo, too, is following a pro-market agenda. The economy is now largely free market and, following the reforms, the growth rate for real GDP was as high as 13%; it was a more realistic 7.4% in 1997. However, with the catastrophes of 1998 – El Niño and the Asian economic crisis – this halved. In 2000 the growth rate for real GDP stood at 3.6% and the uncertainty that characterized the end of Fujimori's reign further damaged the outlook. The goal for GDP for 2002 was 3.5-4%.

Peru's chief exports are minerals and metals; it's traditionally been a mining economy but fishmeal and agricultural products are also important. The

---

De Soto's diagnosis

One of Peru's most eminent economists, Hernando de Soto, has suggested that there is a structural problem at the heart of Peru's (and the rest of the developing world's) economic troubles. In *The Mystery of Capital: Why capitalism triumphs in the West and fails everywhere else* (London, Bantam Press 2000), he suggests that capitalism succeeds in the West because people can liquidate the value of the land they occupy, by mortgages, for example. They can do this because they can prove they own the land. In other countries where it's difficult to prove title to land, the wealth bound up in your property is frozen and inaccessible. He estimates that in the developing world as a whole, US$29,000 billion of wealth is tied up. This figure has come in for criticism as being too high, and the book itself has come in for criticism for not suggesting a practical way of registering land claims.

---

largest proportion of Peru's trade is done with the United States (29%) and the EU (25%), but Japan is heavily involved.

Domestically, manufacturing makes up the biggest individual slice (21%) of GDP, followed by trade and agriculture. Other significant activities are mining and construction. Annual inflation is around 3.7%.

Continuing economic problems Under-employment is a serious problem in Peru: estimates suggest that a staggering 94% of Peruvians don't have a proper job, and Peru's wealth and income are still highly concentrated in the hands of a few old families, a source of festering discontent. According to the Peru Support Group (a NGO), just under half the population earn less than a dollar a day. A little under half the population is under the poverty line, and the richest 10% hold a third of the country's wealth.

On the international side of things, Peru's national debt is still large at five times the annual income from exports – a fifth of all the money Peru makes from its exports is spent on paying the interest on this debt.

The environment

Peru has its share of environmental problems as the country tries to balance the need for economic growth with ecological sensitivity.

The current hot potatoes are proposed oil developments in the jungle. The largest one of these is the Camisea Project: in 1998 Shell considered the exploitation of oil reserves in the selva to the north of Quillabamba, and this caused concern amongst environmental NGOs. There's 11 trillion cubic feet of oil and gas under the forest, and exploiting it would create US$500 million to US$1 billion. However, the area is rich in bio-diversity and is populated by indigenous people who have little or no contact with the outside world. Shell, stung by international reaction to their Nigerian activities, abandoned the project but the government is still keen to develop the region.

CULTURE

Writing

Peru has a vibrant and powerful literary tradition, from the days of the conquest on. Many of the conquistadors left records of their battles, and on the Inca side there's the work of **El Inca Garcilasco de la Vega**, and **Felipe Huamán Poma de Ayala**. Today **Mario Vargas Llosa** is Peru's most famous writer, a man whose books can stand up against the South American Titan, Gabriel García Márquez. Vargas Llosa was born into a middle-class family and is related to an ex-president of Peru. He writes narratives woven with the complexity of Andean fabric: try *Conversación en la Catedral* (Conversation in the Cathedral), or *La casa verde* (The Green House). **César Vallejo** (1892-1938) is one of the Spanish language's greatest modern poets. Vallejo broke linguistic rules to write poetry that appears rough but has magnificent imaginative power.

Visual arts

The most significant form of **painting** to come out of Peru is the **Cusco school**, which flourished in the seventeenth and eighteenth centuries. The Cusco school consists of paintings of formal European subjects, such as religious themes, which have been re-interpreted by indigenous artists. There is a lot of decorative flower and bird patterns, and the use of applied gold on the canvas pre-empts Klimt, but the things that most tourists notice are the bizarre details such as angels armed with muskets. These paintings are still made and sold in the San Blas district of Cusco (see p144). Christopher Isherwood came across these pictures and commented in *The Condor and the Cows* (1948): 'In the lounge, there are some beautiful and absurd Colonial religious paintings. My favourite represents an angel, a fairylike little girl with a sword and golden butterfly skirts, who has her foot coquettishly planted on a sprawling demon. The demon, who is old enough to be her father, is obviously loving it. He is leering and caressing her foot with the enthusiasm of a boot-fetishist'.

Peruvian **cinema** has never reached the heights of other Latin American countries such as Mexico or Brazil, but in Cusco in 1955 Manuel Chambi set up a pioneering film club. The name Chambi is also famous in **photography** – Martín Chambi was a pioneering Cusqueño photographer, who took, in 1920, the first iconic shot of Machu Picchu. A collection of his photographs was recently published (Phaidon, 2002).

Music and dance

Music and dance are a breathing part of everyday campesino culture. The music's going to be familiar to you, either from Andean buskers who play in shopping malls all over the world, or from songs like Simon and Garfunkel's hit *El Condor Pasa*. Many people think that they composed the tune, but it's in fact a traditional Andean melody that was written in the eighteenth century to mark the execution of the rebel Tupac Amaru II (see p39).

The basic instruments played are the *queña*, a simple flute with a notched end, and the *charango*, a mandolin originally made from the shell of an armadillo. You'll also see panpipes, drums, guitars and – occasionally – harps. Pipes of old didn't have the full scale, so tunes jumped from one player to another, but today they're made with a full complement of notes. The most widely available modern version of traditional Andean music is the Chilean group Inti Illimani.

More traditional musical styles come in different forms, such as the almost waltz-like *huayno* from the highlands or the *crillo* from the coast; a song called *La flor de la canela* sung by Chabuca Granda used to be the soul of Lima. Today they play **chicha** in the *pueblos jóvenes* (shanty towns), a music that's a fusion of Colombian dance with Andean music. Also watch out for brass bands pumping out oompa-oompa music at any major festival; it's usually an unforgettable cacophony of a dozen or so different bands blasting away at different tunes in different tempos all at the same time.

Media

The main **newspapers** are *El Commercio* and *La República*, and there are numerous tabloids that decorate their front pages with bare-bottomed women and fill their insides with gruesome stories of car crashes (with pictures) and horrific murders.

The airwaves are packed with **radio** stations, and in the mountains they're the only way people can get the news.

In Lima and Cusco there is a wide range of cable **TV** stations including the predictable CNN and BBC World. There are five domestic TV stations: Television Nacional de Peru (Canal 7; the state broadcaster), America TV, Panamericana, Andina TV and Frecuencia Latina (Canal 2). The airwaves are stuffed with Mexican soaps and US movies. The press is now relatively free, though in Fujimori's day journalists who were critical of the government were at best harassed, and at worst killed. Seven lost their lives.

Sport

This is South America, so **football** (soccer) is all that matters. The main teams are Alianza, Universitario and Sporting Cristal. Don't mention the World Cup: Peru missed out in 1994, 1998 and again in 2002. The 1998 campaign was particularly gutting for Peruvians, as Chile squeezed into the finals ahead of Peru by the smallest of margins and in 2002 they lost out once more to another old enemy, Ecuador. Learn the names of a couple of Peruvian footballers (their star striker, Claudio Pizaro, plays in Germany, and Nortberto Solano plays for Newcastle in the UK) and you'll never be at a loss for conversation. If you want more on Peruvian football, visit 🖳 www.FutbolPeruano.com.

Practical information for the visitor

DOCUMENTS AND VISAS

To stay in Peru for up to 90 days no tourist visa is needed by citizens of EU countries, the US, Canada, Australia, and New Zealand. Nevertheless, check with a Peruvian embassy (see p264) that this is still the case.

You should have proof that you've got enough money to finance your stay in Peru and a return ticket to show you're going to leave again, though you're not likely to be asked for these. You'll be given an Embarkation and Disembarkation card (TED) when you arrive, valid for 60 to 90 days. Always keep it, or a copy of it, on you and don't lose it or you'll be fined s/12 (US$3.40/£2.30). You can extend your stay by applying at the Immigration and Naturalization Department (DIGEMIN, see p107 and p129), or by leaving and re-entering the country. They'll give you another 30 or 60 days, and charge US$20 (£14.20).

For those that need a tourist visa, it will cost around US$15 (prices vary according to your nationality), and two passport photos, a return ticket, and 'proof of economic solvency' are required.

AIRPORT TAX

When you leave Peru, you'll have to pay US$25 (about £18), though to Chile it is now a whopping US$50, payable at the airport. On some internal flights (like Lima–Cusco) there's an airport tax of s/12 (US$3.40/£2.30).

MONEY

Currency

The currency is the *nuevo sol*, often just called the sol, whose symbol is **s/**. A nuevo sol is divided into 100 *céntimos* (or cents), and is pretty stable: as a guide, it was s/3.59 = US$1 in May 2002, s/3.32 = US$1 in May 1999, s/2.85 = US$1 in May 1998 and s/2.52 = US$1 in December 1996.

Notes in circulation are s/200, s/100, s/50, s/20, s/10. Coins in circulation are s/5, s/2, s/1, s/0.50, s/0.20 and s/0.10.

Hoard your s/10 and s/20 notes and avoid any with a value of over s/50 as you'll have difficulty getting change, but don't accept 'no change' as an excuse to rip you off. Don't get landed with damaged notes, as no one else will take them off your

❏ Rates of exchange Peru Nuevo Sol	
Aus$1	s/1.94
Can$1	s/2.29
Euro€1	s/3.30
NZ$1	s/1.60
UK£1	s/5.27
US$1	s/3.59

For up-to-the-minute rates of exchange check the Internet: **www.oanda.com/convert/classic**

hands. You can often use US dollars instead of soles but watch out for forgeries; there are many in circulation.

There was horrendous inflation in the early 1990s (7600% in 1990), and the currency was twice devalued. Be careful that you don't get handed these worthless old notes when you exchange money. They are called *intis* and, rather confusingly, *soles*; there's no need to worry because they look completely different from nuevos soles – and nuevos soles have 'nuevos soles' written on them. All mentions of 'soles' in this book mean nuevos soles.

Other forms of money

There are many **ATM**s (cash machines) in Lima and Cusco where you can get money on your Visa or MasterCard, and many shops where you can use them as **credit cards**. Visa is the more useful. Using your **bank/debit card** through an ATM linked to the Cirrus, Maestro or Plus systems it should be possible to get cash advances direct from your bank account. Check the logos on your card and the logos on the ATM. And to avoid nasty surprises when you return home, it's a good idea to know what interest rate your bank charges on cash withdrawals.

It's much safer to carry **travellers' cheques** than cash but avoid the less well-known brands and take only US dollars – the number of soles you can buy for one pound sterling is sometimes half the amount you can buy for one US dollar because of high commission charged on foreign currencies other than US$. American Express dollar travellers' cheques are by far the most commonly accepted.

Banks and cambios

Exchanging money and travellers' cheques is easy; there are many **banks** (opening times vary, but are generally weekdays 9am-12pm, 4-6pm) and **cambios.** Take your passport with you when you change money as you will need to prove your identity. There are often *cambistas* (money changers) on street corners, some of them wearing waistcoats that say they're regulated by the municipality. They seldom provide a better rate of exchange than the banks and cambios, and they're more likely to short-change you.

GETTING AROUND

Travelling between cities

The main way of travelling overland is by **bus**, and they're very cheap. Buses range from Chilean-style comfort wagons, the most luxurious road transport I've ever used, to broken old rattletraps. Always check where the departure terminal is, as it's often in a different place from the ticket office. There are hundreds of different bus lines competing with each other, but the main ones are **Cruz del Sur** and **Ormeño**.

Where no buses run you can often **hitch** on a truck, but payment is often expected. It's wiser not to hitch alone.

There are some passenger **trains** still operating, notably the run from Arequipa and Puno to Cusco (called the Southern Railway) and the run from

Cusco to Machu Picchu. But following privatization of the railways in the late 1990s, trains are no longer the cheap option they used to be, particularly as tourists are now forbidden from taking the local trains. There are also remains of a railway from Lima to the highlands (the Central Railway) which doesn't run at the moment, though has done so intermittently over the past couple of years. For details of times and prices see p267.

Planes run regularly between Cusco, Lima and other towns (see p119 and p146), and there's a **helicopter** that connects Cusco with Machu Picchu (see p146). The main domestic airline is AeroContinente (☎ 242 4242 or 241 4816, 📄 241 3074, 🖥 www.aerocontinente.com, Av Pardo 651, Miraflores, Lima), and an airline called LanPeru (☎ 446 6995, 📄 215 1818, 🖥 www.lanperu.com, Paz Soldan 225, San Isidro, Lima) started operations in late 1999. It stopped trading in November 2000 but was up and flying again at the time of writing.

You can sometimes cadge a lift with Groupo Ocho – the Air Force – but their schedules aren't reliable.

Local transport
In Peru **taxis** don't use meters and will normally charge what they can get away with, so fix the price before you step into the cab. If you're not sure what the price should be, either ask a passer-by or offer to pay one half to three quarters of the price the *taxista* is asking. Tipping isn't usual or expected.

Buses in cities tend to be beaten-up old crocks, but they're cheap; they charge flat fares. Disorganized though the system may appear, they'll cover just about every part of a city, and travelling by bus is a great way of meeting people, but beware of pickpockets and bag-slashers.

You can also travel by **colectivo** – enormous, chuntering old Dodges or spanking new Japanese minibuses that speed along set routes filled to the gunwales with paying passengers. They have their routes written on the windscreen.

Hiring a car
Don't drive in Lima unless you've got a strong stomach and a forceful personality, and if you drive outside Lima expect bad roads and aggressive drivers. For car hire companies and rates, see p104 (Lima) and p125 (Cusco). You need an international driving licence valid for 30 days; you can get one from your country's automobile association.

ACCOMMODATION

Price
The hotels listed in this book are divided into three classes: **budget**, **mid-range** and **expensive**. All prices change, and hotel prices change particularly quickly, so the chances are they'll be higher when you visit than they were when this book was researched. However, you'll still be able to make comparisons between the relative expense of different hotels. When giving prices in the text, **sgl/dbl/tpl** refers to single, double and triple rooms. The hotel price is always followed by information in brackets: '**att**' means there is an attached bathroom

and '**com**' means there is a shared or communal bathroom. If breakfast is included in the cost of the room, that's mentioned too, although in Peru it's normal for breakfast to be extra.

In the **budget** class are hotels that charge up to s/30 for a room. **Mid-range** hotels are those that charge from s/30 (US$8.50) to US$60. The class is wide, so hotels of a similar price are listed together within the class. **Expensive** hotels charge more than US$60, and sometimes add another 10% for service and 18% for tax on top of the price of the room (prices in this book include this extra charge). The cost of a room is usually negotiable, and you should get a bargain if the hotel is empty. Try saying '*tiene usted algo un poco más económico*' (have you got one a little cheaper)?

Standards
A Peruvian hotel can call itself a *residencial*, a *hostal*, a *hotel*, a *pensión* or a *hospedaje* – it makes no difference to the standard of what's on offer. The cheapest hotels offer a plank bed in a dirty room in a dangerous part of town run by a threatening manager, or they may provide a sunny room in an old colonial mansion, so ask to see a room before you part with your money. You won't get plank beds in any hotels listed in this book and expensive hotels will be up to the international standard you'd expect.

Availability
You'll have no problem finding somewhere to stay unless you turn up on a major holiday or festival (see p56), and even then you'll probably find somewhere, it'll just be more expensive.

ELECTRICITY

220 volts AC, 60 cycles. Expect power cuts and power surges, and don't touch the bare wiring you'll see in your shower!

TIME

Peru is five hours behind GMT (UK winter time).

POST AND TELECOMMUNICATIONS
Telephone and fax
You can dial international calls directly from public phones in the street, but you'll need a phonecard to pay, which you can buy from women who hang around phones selling them or in shops that display a sign saying *tarjeta telefónica* (telephone card). There are two sorts: the regular phonecards and the increasingly popular and better-value 147 cards, where you dial 147 and follow the instructions given by the operator. You can also make a call from telephone company offices but this will be more expensive. The number to dial for the operator is 100; for information it's 103 and for the international operator it's 108. However, the cheapest way to dial abroad from Peru is to use a computer

and dial through the Internet. Internet cafés in both Cusco and Lima can help you out with this, and the cost should be no more than a couple of soles per hour.

To phone Peru from abroad dial your international access code, then 51. Add 1 for Lima, or 84 for Cusco. To dial home from Peru, first dial the international access code 00, then add your country code (UK 44, USA and Canada 1, Australia 61, New Zealand 64), then your STD and number required.

You can send and receive faxes from hotels and telephone company offices.

Email

Email is rapidly replacing other forms of communication for travellers. Cybercafés spring up like mushrooms and die like mayflies, so check websites such as 🖳 **www.cybercafes.com** for the latest picture. If you don't already have a free address with one of the companies such as hotmail or yahoo you can easily set up an account at a cybercafé.

HOLIDAYS AND FESTIVALS

1 January	New Year (all Peru)
6 January	*Fiesta de Ollantaytambo* (Cusco)
14 January	*Feria de Pampamarca* (Cusco): a large agricultural fair
April	Maundy Thursday, Good Friday and Easter (all Peru)
1 May	Labour Day (all Peru)
7-9 June	*Qoyllur Riti* (Cusco): an Apollonian pilgrimage to the glaciers of the high Andes
June	Corpus Christi (all Peru, but especially Cusco): statues of saints are paraded around Cusco's packed streets; it takes place on the Thursday after Trinity Sunday (ninth Thursday after Easter)
24 June	*Inti Raymi* (Cusco): the old Inca festival of the winter solstice, which was suppressed by the Spanish and recreated in 1944; elsewhere the celebration is called Peasants' Day
29 June	St Peter and St Paul (all Peru)
15-17 July	*Fiesta de Paucartambo* (Cusco): a Dionysiac festival to honour the Virgin of Carmen of Paucartambo (a village near Cusco) with masked dancers
28/29 July	Independence Day (all Peru)
30 August	*Santa Rosa de Lima* (all Peru)
7 October	Battle of Angamos (all Peru)
18 October	*El Señor de los Milagros* (Lima): a day of religious processions
1 November	All Saints' Day: (all Peru): the day when Peruvians remember their dead
8 December	Immaculate Conception (all Peru)
24 December	*Santorantikuy* (Cusco): originally a market which sold objects for Nativity Scenes, this is now a large market for practically anything; elsewhere, the day is a pre-Christmas holiday
25 December	Christmas (all Peru)

Post

Post is slow but generally reliable, and stamps for a postcard outside the Americas will cost about s/3.80; they're usually available where you purchase your post-cards. Main *correos* (post offices) have **poste restante**, and American Express offices also hold letters addressed to their clients. It helps if the people who are sending you letters underline your surname, and when looking for your letters you should check under *all* the names on the envelope; they're often misfiled.

FOOD AND DRINK

Peruvian food can be excellent. There's a tradition of good eating and drinking that goes back to the days of the Incas. Pedro Pizarro reported that when the Inca Atahualpa ate: 'Ladies brought in his meal and placed it before him on tender thin green rushes. … They placed before him all his vessels of gold, silver and pottery on these rushes. He pointed to whatever he fancied and it was brought. One of his ladies took it and held it in her hand while he ate.'

Meat

You will get bored with *lomo* (beef loin steak) cooked *cordon bleu* (stuffed with cheese and ham), *milanesa* (beaten into a thin steak, rolled in bread-crumbs and fried), and *a lo pobre* (fried with an egg on top). Chicken is often cooked in these ways too, or just plain roasted. *Parilladas* (a mixed grill and a restaurant that sells grilled meat) are generally very good and filling, if lacking in imagination.

More interesting dishes are *lomo saltado* (strips of beef cooked in onions, peppers, tomatoes and soy sauce, served with rice), *anticucho* (beef-heart kebabs), *causa rellena* (a very slightly spiced potato cake mixed with tuna or chicken) and *aji de gallina* (shredded chicken stewed in a gently spiced cream sauce).

Fish

The coast of Peru has truly excellent fish: *congrio* (a pacific conger eel), *lenguado* (sole), *corvina* (sea bass) and shellfish. Try *jalea* (fried whitebait), *chupe de camarones* (special prawn chowder), and especially the traditional Peruvian dish *ceviche* (raw white fish marinated in lemon and onion and served with two types of maize). Ceviche originated when coastal slaves weren't allowed to cook food on fires and had to prepare their fish in another way – they invented cold cooking with lemon juice.

Other dishes

The potato was first cultivated in Peru as long as 10,000 years ago so not surprisingly there are hundreds of different varieties and many ways of cooking them. Some of the waxy, firm beauties you eat out here will put to shame the humble spuds you get at home.

> ❏ **Pet food**
> In the Cusco area, you'll see *cuy* (guinea pig) on offer – it tastes a bit like duck and has a tough skin. Cuy is laid flat on your plate, as if it had been run over by a bus then peeled off the wheel. They say it's cooked in one piece to prevent someone trying to dish you up cat.

You could also try *chuño*, which is potato that's been freeze-dried. Freeze-drying is a traditional way of preserving potatoes for leaner times by leaving them out in the bitterly cold Andean nights.

Peruvians are good at replicating other country's cuisines: pasta is often freshly made and first-class (Cusco is famous for its pizzerias) and Chinese food (*Chifa*) is also good.

Dessert

For dessert, there are *picarones* (light fried doughnuts on a plate of honey) and *mazamorra morada* (a sweet-tasting dish derived from purple maize) which looks like jelly.

Drink

Non-alcoholic Tea is usually served without milk but with sugar and lemon. **Herb teas** are often available. In Cusco you should try *maté de coca*, which is made from coca leaves and said to help alleviate the symptoms of altitude sickness. It's available in most restaurants. **Coffee** is usually served as coffee essence that you add to hot water; instant coffee is better. In some places you can now get a cappuccino or espresso.

> ❏ **Maté de coca**
> Coca leaf, even in tea bags, is a prohibited drug in most countries, and if you try to take some home you risk jail (in the UK coca leaf is a Class A drug, the importation of which carries a long prison sentence).

Don't drink **water** from taps or streams without first purifying it (see p169). Alternatively you can buy bottled mineral water. Coke, Pepsi, Fanta and Sprite are widely available. You're going to have to try the ubiquitous home-grown soft drink, **Inca Cola**, at least once – the name's too intriguing to miss. It tastes like bubblegum.

Alcoholic Avoid Peruvian **wine**, it's not very good, and drink Chilean or Argentinian wine instead. However, the Peruvian spirit **Pisco** (distilled from grapes) is a gift from the gods. Be prepared: it's strong though usually drunk diluted in the refreshing cocktail Pisco Sour. The Chileans claim that they were the ones who invented Pisco, but it's probably Peruvian.

> ❏ **Pisco Sour**
> 2 fl oz Pisco
> $^1/_2$ lemon (Peruvian lemons are very small so make this $^1/_4$ of a normal one)
> 1 egg white (whisked)
> 2 dessertspoons of sugar
> The spirit, egg and lemon juice are shaken together then served over crushed ice with a dash of Angostura bitters.

The **beer** is watery lager and it all seems to taste the same; brands include Cristal, Cusqueña, and Arequipeña.

Chicha (see p59) is a **maize wine/beer** that dates back to the time of the Incas – you can identify houses that have chicha for sale because they fly red flags or bin-bags from sticks. The historian Prescott described it as sparkling champagne, but then he'd never tasted it. Another historian, John Hemming, more realistically describes it as murky pale cider.

Chicha

The 'champagne of the Incas' is still widely drunk today. Different areas of Peru make chicha in different ways, and the chicha from the Cusco region is made as follows:

Maize grains are soaked overnight, and then put in the sun to germinate. When they are part-germinated, they are boiled up, and then strained through a sieve. The liquid produced is called *upi*, and it's put to one side. The maize grains left in the sieve are boiled once more, and then sieved again, which produces a liquid called *seque*. The seque and the upi are then mixed to produce chicha, and the residue is fed to animals. Chicha is often flavoured with cinnamon and cloves, and sweetened with molasses.

Health

(See pp165-170) Drink only purified or bottled water and avoid ice in drinks. If you can't peel it, wash it in purified water, cook it or shell it, then don't eat it, otherwise you run the risk of getting diarrhoea. Avoid things like salads, raw vegetables, unpeeled fruit, ice cream, unpasteurized dairy products and anything that's not been freshly cooked. You can make a solution for washing vegetables by putting 12 drops of iodine in a litre of water.

Tax and tipping

Expensive restaurants sometimes add another 10% for service and 18% for tax to the bill. The service element in this should make its way to the waiter, so theoretically there's no need to tip, although the reality is that the money will go straight into the manager's pocket.

SHOPPING

Fabrics

Fabrics are profoundly important to Andean peoples, and they always have been. The Inca wore clothes made from the most delicate and beautiful fabrics possible. Pedro Pizarro described Atahualpa's clothes: 'He was ... wearing a dark brown tunic and cloak. I approached him and felt the cloak, which was softer than silk. I asked him "Inca, of what is a robe as soft as this made?" He explained that it was from the skins of [vampire] bats that fly at night.'

You can't get bat skin anymore, but woollens made from **alpaca** (a relative of the llama, domesticated for its beautiful wool) are widely available. The quality varies greatly: if you burn a couple of fibres and it smells of plastic, it's not made from alpaca but acrylic, and if it stinks when slightly wet, it's not alpaca, it's **llama**. You might also find fabrics made from **vicuña** wool, a beautiful, fine silken fibre that used to be reserved for the Inca himself. This stuff is incredibly expensive (the poor beasts are rare and were almost hunted to

PRIMER·CAPÍTVLO·DELASMÖÏAS
ACLLACOÏAS

The highest-quality cloth in Inca times was produced by the weavers of the Acclawasi (House of the Chosen Women)
FELIPE HUAMÁN POMA DE AYALA (c1590)

extinction), but very beautiful. If you do buy vicuña make sure it's come from a reputable source, as the animals are endangered.

Fabrics dyed using traditional techniques tend to be more expensive and more subtle than those that use modern dyes. You can pick them up at one of the tourist markets, such as Chinchero (see p154), Pisac (p152) and Ollantaytambo (p155).

Arts and crafts

You can buy other traditional Peruvian crafts such as Andean pipes and cheap copies of Moche erotic pots (see p72). Never be tempted to buy the framed insects and stuffed animals you'll be offered in Cusco, as the trade in them depletes the resources of the forest. Many of them are protected species anyway, and either Peruvian Customs or your own will confiscate them. Any 'Inca' artefacts you're offered are probably fake, and if they're not it's illegal to try to export them.

Rip offs

Peru's not, as a character said in Peter Shaffer's play *The Royal Hunt of the Sun*: 'a silent country, frozen in avarice', but if you feel you've been taken for a ride contact the **Tourist Protection Service** (☎ 0800 4 2579, and it's a free call, not available from pay phones). This organization is run by the government to deal with tourists' complaints.

SAFETY

'The Prefect had been very solicitous about our welfare, and, although we assured him that we preferred to travel without a military escort, he insisted that a sergeant and at least one soldier should accompany us as long as we were in his Department…. There was no danger, and highway robbery is unheard of in Peru.' *The Lost City of the Incas*, by Hiram Bingham, 1948. Whatever it was like in Bingham's day, Peru now has a crime problem, so you need to be careful. But being careful doesn't mean being paranoid, and most of the guide books to Peru are so liberally spiced with warnings that it seems you're entering a war zone. You're not, and you will have no trouble provided you take sensible precautions:

● **Don't flaunt your valuables** It's wisest not to travel with anything you might be upset to lose. Leave expensive jewellery at home and bring a wrist watch that looks obviously cheap. Leave your passport and wads of money in your hotel safe.

● **Be aware** Don't go to dodgy areas, take care when travelling at night. Be aware of people around you and beware of any who are paying you undue attention. It helps to walk around in groups, at least until you've got your bearings and feel secure. Take taxis when you arrive in a new place.

● **Take precautions** Wear a money belt and carry your money in a couple of different places on your body. Some people stick a US$100 bill under the insole in their shoe for emergencies, or put one in an elastic bandage on their leg. Make sure your luggage is secure – you could put chicken wire inside your bag to prevent slashing razors, or buy a flour sack and sew your rucksack into it to secure easily opened pockets. (Don't use a fishmeal sack for this, as they stink.)

● **Don't fall for tricks** Common scams involve catching your attention and then picking your pocket; someone might spit on you or stick chewing gum on your shirt, or an old lady might collapse under your feet. There'll be an accomplice who's standing behind you, and when you're not on your guard they will whip out your wallet and that'll be the last you see of it. Also be on your guard against fake policemen; always ask to see an ID. Whilst on the subject of the police, be careful of corrupt policemen as they might try to plant drugs on you, and never get into a police car if you can avoid it, but insist on walking to the police station.

In Cusco they've taken the art of distracting you to the limit. Be on your guard. As in all countries there is the occasional mugging.

● **If the worst happens** Remember, they're probably after your money, so stay calm and hand it over – it's worth much less than your health. If you are unlucky enough to be a victim of crime, go to the **Tourist Police** (see p106 and p128) who speak English and are helpful. Get a police report for insurance.

Having said all that, you should remember that hundreds and thousands of people visit Peru each year without any problems at all. Nothing's likely to happen to you if you take care.

As for the risk from **terrorism**, as the SAEC (see p106) say, you're more likely to be run down by Lima's mad traffic than come to grief from the Sendero Luminoso or the MRTA.

DRUGS

For many people, there's nothing that needs to be said about this. But for others, you should know that buying or using drugs can land you in prison for the next 15 years, and the person you're thinking of buying them from may be a police informant. Think long and hard about it – is it really worth the risk?

Flora and fauna

FAUNA

Mammals

The star of the Sanctuary, but an animal you'll be extremely lucky to see, is the **Andean (or Spectacled) bear** (*Tremarctus ornatus*). These bears pose no threat to hikers as they are both shy and herbivorous; and on the contrary they are the ones who are threatened by the inroads we make into their habitat. See p159 for more on this bear.

Whilst on the subject of large, frightening animals, don't expect to see any **puma** (*Felis concolor*), the fanged cat of Peru, because they are very, very rare. You're more likely to see the **Colpeo fox**, a scavenger that lives in these hills and preys on the ill and the dying, or an Andean **skunk**, a **weasel**, or if you're lucky a **White-tailed deer**. The Sanctuary also boasts **pudú** (pigmy deer), timid little nocturnal beasts which are rarely seen during the day.

Keep a look out for **mountain viscachas** – there are hundreds of these rabbit-like rodents living in the Machu Picchu ruins, and you'll see their pellet-like droppings everywhere, even if you can't see the viscachas themselves.

The animals (apart from horses) which you'll see most frequently are **llamas** and **alpacas**, cousins of the camel that have been domesticated for thousands of years for their meat, wool and ability to carry cargo. They have two wild relatives, **guanacos** (big with a white belly) and **vicuña** (gentle-looking with inquisitive eyes and a furry chest), both of which are rarely seen in the Machu Picchu Sanctuary but are more common in the south.

Reptiles

Also keep a lookout for snakes: **coral snakes** and **bushmasters** are both reasonably common in the selva and are poisonous.

The Peruvian Paso

Horses were native to South America, but they died out many thousands of years ago. They were re-introduced by the Spanish, who used them to great effect in battles against the natives.

Some of the descendants of the mounts of the conquistadors have been developed into a breed of horse called the Peruvian Paso, or Peruvian Stepping Horse. It's famous for its characteristic way of walking, with high-stepping forelegs and powerful hind legs, which makes it comfortable to ride. It has great stamina, being able to maintain a regular speed of about 11mph (18kmph) over rough country.

Birds

The Incas considered birds to be the messengers of the apus, the spirits of the cordillera (mountain range), and the mighty condor represented the great snow peaks while the lesser birds represented lesser mountains.

ANDEAN CONDOR

● **Andean condor** The Andean Condor (*Vultur gryphus*) is enormous, averaging over a metre from bill to the tip of the tail and much more across the wings. In the air, apart from by its sheer size, a condor is identifiable by the characteristic forward-pointed finger-feathers at the end of its wings, its white ruff and bald head. Despite its reputation as a mountain bird it's not common here and is more usually found on the coast where it can find more carrion. It's had a bad press over the years, and stories have been told of its attacking travellers, carrying away goats and killing small children. The great writer and traveller Bruce Chatwin relates in his book, *In Patagonia*, an unlikely story about being harried by a condor, and George Squier (*Peru – Travel and Exploration in the Land of the Incas*, 1877) includes a picture of himself almost being attacked by one of these massive birds, just managing to see it off with a shot from his pistol. One glance at the feet of a condor (usually only possible when you come across a stuffed one) tells you this is impossible, as instead of sharp, evil talons condors have what look like over-sized chicken feet. They couldn't grasp anything, let alone carry away a struggling small child up into the air.

GEORGE SQUIER FENDS OFF A CONDOR

● **Birds of prey** The large birds that you'll see are more often than not birds of prey. You're likely to catch a glimpse of an **American Kestrel** (*Falco sparverius*), an **Aplomado Falcon** (*Falco femoralis*) or a **Mountain Caracara**

MOUNTAIN CARACARA

(*Phalco-boenus megalopterus*). The kestrel is quite a small bird, averaging just under 30cm from beak to tail, with grey wings, a grey head, white cheeks and a brownish breast and tail. The falcon is about 10cm longer and has light brown wings and tail and a paler breast. The caracara is larger still, 50cm from beak to tail, and has characteristic black, white and grey wings and a black and white tail.

BLACK-CHESTED
BUZZARD EAGLE

You might also see the **Black-chested Buzzard Eagle** (*Geranoaetus melanoleucus*) and various different types of **hawk**. The buzzard eagle is big, 70cm from beak to tail, and is predominantly a grey colour, with black edges to its wings and a black neck and head. The feathers on the tips of its wings do not spread forward as much as those of the condor. Hawks generally range from 40 to 50cm long and in colour from grey and white to brown and beige.

● **Waterfowl** If you're interested in birds, you shouldn't only be looking upwards, as the Sanctuary also boasts many different types of birds in the trees and on the water and ground. In streams, lakes and ponds you can find the famous **Torrent Duck** (*Merganetta armata*) of Matthew Parris's book *Inca Cola*. Male torrent ducks are a stripy black and white with red beaks, and females have reddish-brown chests and grey backs. You can also see **Andean (or Ruddy) Ducks**, red with a spiky black tail, dark head and wide bill, and the **Crested Duck**, a sleek grey with a touch of red on the wings. **Andean Geese**, with a rather menacing grey stripe around the eye, can sometimes be seen, while black and white **Giant Coots** are common.

● **Humming birds** Of the smaller birds, the ones that cause the greatest excitement are the various types of beautifully-named humming birds: **Sunangels** (*Heliangelus amethysticollis*), **Great Sapphirewings** and the world's largest, the **Giant Hummingbird** (*Patagonia gigas*), a surprisingly dull brown bird but a massive (for a hummingbird) 24cm from the tip of its bill to the end of its tail.

● **Other birds** One of the most famous birds in the Sanctuary is the **Cock of the Rock**, with its stunning head-dress of red feathers that reminds some of the red fringe that the Inca used to wear as a badge of his rank. This is Peru's national bird. On the ground you can see **partridges**, which at one stage were so common that they gave their name to a town (Pisac, the name of a town in the Sacred Valley, means partridge). In the skies, keep a watch for **swifts** and **swallows** with their characteristic swept-back wings and pointed tails. In woodland look out for **woodpeckers**. You're more likely to hear than to see a woodpecker called the **Andean Flicker**, a largish bird (33cm from beak to tail) with a beige head, grey and dark brown body and a yellow breast.

FLORA

Many of the plants you'll see in the Sanctuary have relatives that are commonly grown in Europe and North America.

There are **begonias**, **lupins**, **fuchsias**, **daisies**, **elders**, **buttercups**, **lilies**, and **cacti**. You'll also see **calceolaria** (ladies' slipper), which is very common and has bright yellow flowers. **Salvia** is quite common in some areas, and you may see **kantu**: Peru's national flower (see photo opposite).

Epidendrum
Orchid

Leguminosae
Lupin

Calceolaria engleriana
Ladies' slipper

Bromeliaceae
Flowering bromeliad

Masdevallia veitchiana
Huakanki orchid

Labiateae
Salvia

Datura arborea
Moonflower

Begoniaceae
Begonia

Cantua buxifolia
Kantu

Centre photo © Bryn Thomas. Top left, top centre and middle right © Henry Stedman
All other photos © South American Pictures/Tony Morrison

Lythraceae cuplea   *Lantana*   *Culcitium*

Arum Lily   *Puya*   *Dahlia*

Veronica   *Commelina*   *Trimezia*

All photos © Henry Stedman

Bromeliads, relatives of the pineapple, can be seen in the Sanctuary. One of the most impressive Peruvian plants (sadly not native to the Sanctuary) is the puya Raimondi, that lives for a hundred years, grows ten metres high and flowers just once before it dies.

Orchids

One type of plant that you will come across in the Sanctuary is the orchid. The place is blessed with about 200 different varieties, and there are said to be up to 3000 orchid species just in Peru. New species are discovered each year.

You may see the **Huinay Huayna** (the name means 'forever young') orchid or *Epidendrum secundum* a small pink star-burst of a flower, which gave its name to the Inca ruins just near the Trekkers' Hotel. Also in this area, keep your eyes peeled for *Masdevallia veitchiana*, locally called **Huakanki** (the name means 'you'll cry') which has extremely beautiful purple-and-orange coloured flowers with three delicately pointed petals (see photo opposite p64).

Orchids are, however, in danger in the Sanctuary. They are at risk from plant hunters and also from the destruction of their habitat. Fires in the mid-1990s destroyed large areas of virgin forest.

Medicinal plants

Some plants have medicinal uses. For example, a tea from the leaves of a plant from the *Labiateae* family (a shrubby family that includes sage) called **muña** (*Minthostachyys glabrescens*) relieves the effect of altitude. However, be careful about playing around with plants which you may not recognize – the tea made from the seeds of a lupin known as **Q'era tarwis** (*lupinus mutabilis*) is used as fish poison. Datura, the moonflower, is also poisonous.

Forests

The forests are an important part of the ecology of the Sanctuary, in particular the **cloud forests**. These, as you would guess from their name, get most of their moisture from fog and clouds rather than the rain: look for stumpy trees (such as the *polylepis* species) and shrubs loaded down with moisture-absorbing moss and lichen. There's one of these forests on the section of the trail between Huayllabamba and the first pass.

FIELD GUIDES

It's difficult to find a good but compact field guide for Peru. For birds there's John Dunning's *South American Birds*, or the comprehensive *Birds of the High Andes* (Jon Fjeldsa and Niels Krabbe).

There's a good section on orchids and birds in Peter Frost's and Jim Bartle's *Machu Picchu Historical Sanctuary*, (part-written by the expert birder, Barry Walker, who runs the Cross Keys bar in Cusco).

PART 3: THE INCAS

Pre-Inca civilizations

Peru is a place of great antiquity. The Incas were only the third empire to dominate the Andes. Before they built their roads and terraces, before they counted on their *quipus* (string used for record-keeping – see p83) and before they worshipped the sun, other cultures had flourished in the barren deserts and soaring mountains of this part of South America. The first pan-Andean civilization, the **Chavín**, thrived about 2500 years ago, the second, the **Huari-Tiahuanaco**, about 1000 years ago, and between these times of cultural unity many smaller peoples rose and fell. The glories of the Incan state, the architecture, the textiles, the roads, the agriculture, the social organization were developed out of the foundations of these more ancient civilizations of Peru.

IN THE BEGINNING

Paleo-Indians, the first settlers of the Americas, walked over the tundra some 20,000 years ago, chasing their migrating food across the land bridge that joined the continents of Asia and North America. This was possible because in those days the world was much colder than it is today, and massive ice sheets froze the oceans into glaciers, making the sea level much lower. The waters have now risen again, and the land bridge is lost beneath the Bering Straits.

Early days in South America

How long it took for humans to work their way down to South America is something about which archaeologists don't agree, but the generally accepted view is that we've been on the continent for between 9000 and 11,000 years. It has been suggested that the first settlers arrived in South America about the same time as they arrived in North America, making a pretty swift migration down the two continents, though this view is disputed.

There's more agreement about what the first people were like: they hunted to survive, eating ancient American horses, which are now extinct, mastodons and the wild relations of the llama. After about 2000 years, differences developed between people on the coast and those living in the highlands.

The highland people

Digging in the floor of a deserted old cave in the Callejón de Huaylas called the Guitarrero Cave, archaeologists have discovered that agriculture began here in the highlands in about 8500BC. By 4000BC animals were being domesticated, and by 3000BC highlanders were planting and eating a wide variety of foods such as maize, gourds, squash, some tubers and grains. As well as telling us about the foundations of agriculture, the Guitarrero Cave has also unveiled what may be the first example of Andean art: a small rock wrapped in textile in about 5500BC. It's from these humble beginnings that the glory of South American cloth arose.

The coastal people

The coastal settlers had the benefit of the lush pastures of the Pacific Ocean (one archaeologist has suggested that as many as 6,500,000 people could have been fed by the anchovy schools swimming in the chill Pacific), so they didn't need to develop agriculture or domesticate animals until much later than the people living in the highlands. At first the coastal dwellers caught their food by angling and scavenging for shellfish but in time they fished with a spear headed by a delicate stone point. This spearhead, which was carved like a slender willow leaf, is called a Paijan point.

Chinchorros About 5000BC an interesting people, the Chinchorros, lived on the desert coast around Tacna and Arica. They were quite sophisticated, inventing bone fishhooks and living in stable communities. About 7000 years ago, long before the ancient Egyptians, they started to mummify their dead.

❏ **Earliest mummies**
The custom of mummifying the dead to prepare them for the after life goes back at least 7000 years in South America. Bodies were usually placed in a foetal position, seated in a basket and wrapped in many layers of embroidered textiles.

The mummies have been preserved, partly because they were buried in the dry sands of the Atacama desert, but partly because of the preservation techniques used by the Chinchorros. The bodies of the dead were wrapped in fabric, bound with reeds and a face mask of clay was placed over their skulls. Some of these mummies, the oldest in the world, are on display in the museum near Arica in northern Chile. The Chinchorros' mummies started a Peruvian tradition, continued by the Incas some 6500 years later.

PRE-CERAMIC PEOPLES (3000 TO 1800BC)

Unlike the rest of the world, civilization evolved in Peru before the invention of pottery. This wasn't realized at first. There are many large temples on the coast in which archaeologists couldn't find any ceramic remains, and these temples were dated by other pottery that was found nearby, pottery that was scattered around by much later inhabitants. Carbon dating, however, such as was performed in 2002 at the site of Caral, shows that the old temple complexes were far more ancient than these ceramics, and the civilizations that built them must have existed without pottery. We now think these are the oldest complex sites in the Americas.

The oldest temples were built about the time of the Old Kingdom of ancient Egypt (about 3000BC), many years before the rise of the other most ancient American civilization, the Olmecs of Mexico. Some of these structures are almost as huge as the Egyptian Pyramids; it's estimated that 2,000,000 work-days were needed to use 100,000 tons of stone in constructing the nine vast complexes at El Paraíso by the river Chancay to the north of Lima.

Kotosh

Most of the decoration of these temples hasn't survived but at one site, Kotosh, by the headwaters of the river Marañon, you can still see the type of thing that adorned these places. Kotosh dates from 1000 to 2000BC and consists of two mounds, in one of which there's the **Temple of the Crossed Hands**. This is an adobe room with trapezoidal niches, a design that was to become so character-istic of the Incas. Under one of the niches there's a sculpture of a pair of crossed arms. The decoration has survived because, for a reason that's not understood, at some stage in the past the sculptures were carefully protected with sandbags before the whole complex was buried.

What were these people like?

That these people were traders and travellers is evident from the finding of Ecuadorian shells in a grave at a site called Aspero, between the rivers Chancay and Huarmey. They had reasonably advanced techniques for dealing with their environments: in the highlands a 4000-year-old irrigation canal has been found, and on the coast archaeologists have dug up the remains of fine cotton fishnets and floats made from gourds.

Delicate textiles have been reconstructed from debris found at Huaca Prieta, north of the river Moche, with painstaking work recreating complicat-ed patterns showing birds of prey with snakes on their breasts and crabs that dissolve into smiling snakes.

All this is informative but it's the imposing temples that tell us most about these people. To build the temples, these cultures must have been sophisticated enough to have developed a system of division of labour that provided enough surplus food to supply the workers; but archaeologists disagree as to whether the enormous temples indicate centralized, authoritarian regimes or a loose con-federation of peoples performing communal labour. Perhaps there was a mix-ture of both systems as with the Incas themselves.

THE INITIAL PERIOD (1800 TO 1000BC)

The years from 1800BC to 1000BC are called the 'Initial Period' because it used to be thought that this was when Peru's cultures started becoming more sophis-ticated; the rise of sophisticated cultures always being linked with the develop-ment of pottery and these were the days in Peru's history when pottery was being invented. The ball of civilization actually started rolling long before but the name's stuck.

The invention of pottery

The coastal people cracked the problem of pottery at a different time from those who lived inland, but both were quite late considering that people had been firing clay dolls for hundreds of years (one was found above the niche of the crossed hands in Kotosh, see p68) and the Ecuadorians had been making pottery for a thousand years or so.

Pottery styles of the coast On the coast the first pots were fired at places like La Florida in Rímac but they're pretty basic as ceramics go, thin-walled and with a mottled finish, their shape based on the gourds that they replaced. In time they became more sophisticated, and the northern Cupisnique culture developed the stirrup-spout pot (two arms leading to a single spout, which prevents the pot making a glugging noise). The Cupisnique are also famous for their hallucinogenic-inspired portrait pots, psychotropic drugs derived from the San Pedro cactus being very important in ancient Peru.

The making of pottery coincided with the development of coastal agriculture, metalwork and smelting (small bits of beaten copper dating from before 1000BC have been found at Mina Perdida, just south of Gargay), and the construction of even larger public buildings than had hitherto been built. The largest such as the La Florida complex would have taken one man about seven million days to build, and the structure at Moxeke is thirty metres high and has a base that covers the same area as three and a half football pitches. There are two basic designs of building – those south of the Chancay river were built with 'U' shaped courtyards, and north of the river they have sunken circular courtyards. They're all grey-brown mounds now, but originally all these buildings were painted with bright dazzling colours: reds, pinks, yellows, white and greyish-blue, which illuminated the clay sculptures that were moulded onto the walls. These buildings were either tombs of important people, centres of religion, or sites of oracles.

Inland pottery styles Highland pottery was influenced by the styles and techniques of the jungle where the standard was apparently quite advanced; as an early example of ceramics the highland style at Kotosh is relatively sophisticated. Shards of these early pots (indicating a trade connection) have been found in the jungle in a place called the Cave of the Owls, which makes archaeologists suspect that there's a lost jungle civilization from which the highland people learnt the art of pottery. This suspicion is strengthened by the fact that these pots are often decorated with jungle animals like jaguars, spider monkeys and snakes.

The technique of working gold was being discovered inland at the same time as that of making pots. At Waywaka, in the south-central highlands, the body of a man who lived sometime between 1900BC to 1450BC has been found holding in his hands foils of beaten gold. In the same way as the coastal people, the inlanders left significant footprints, both literal (two footprints were carved into a boulder at a place called Pacopama during this period) and metaphorical, such as a 9km-long irrigation canal cut into the bedrock.

The people

These were pretty violent times. In the Río Casma valley, north and east of Huanuco, there's a site called **Cerro Sechín** that consists of over 300 carvings of mauled soldiers: heads lie on the ground, bleeding from their eye-sockets, and severed torsos try to stop their guts from spilling on the ground. In the **Huaca de los Reyes** mound at a place called Caballero Muerto (Dead Horseman) in the lower Moche valley, there are the remains of a two-metre (six-foot) high clay head of a snarling catman.

However, it was not all blood and gore. On the south coast, the **Paracas** left behind some of the most beautiful fabrics ever to be discovered in Peru. These people wrapped their dead in layers of cloth, and the dry sands of the Atacama desert preserved both the dead and the textile. The fabric is amazing, made from alpaca wool and rich in colour and intricate pattern.

CHAVÍN (1000 TO 200BC)

The Chavín were the first pan-Peruvian civilization, unparalleled in their unification of the multitude of peoples of Peru. They lived in a society that venerated gold, used llamas for cargo carriers, had highly developed textiles and built enormous public buildings in dressed stone. Their influence lasted about 800 years, and it was from this source that the Incas grew.

The cult of Chavín

The Chavín extended their influence over an area twice the size of modern Portugal, but they probably weren't a trading empire or a military power. They were a cult group. Characteristic Chavín iconography, such as the Chavín fanged cat, spread out from the centre of the culture, an oracle called Chavín de Huantar. What sort of cult were they?

Some have suggested they were evangelists and say that the icons of Chavín made their way into many different places in the same way as the cross

The role of hallucinogenic drugs in Chavín religious life

Hallucinogenic drugs, from the San Pedro cactus or the Vilca seed, have been used in Andean religion since the earliest times. In the capital of the Chavín civilization, there's a fascinating representation of their use.

The walls of the sunken courtyard of **Chavín de Huantar** were decorated with carved heads, set deep into stone, resembling gargoyles that are found on European cathedrals. These carvings, fixed onto a wall in tiers, are three dimensional carvings of men and beasts, showing the transformation of a man into a snarling feline. Some of the carved heads have mucus pouring from the nose, something that happens when hallucinogenic snuff is snorted. This has led Chavín scholar, Richard Burger, to suggest that these heads represent a drug-taking shaman transmuting from man to possessed prophet.

of Christianity makes its way today into places as different as the Vatican and small altiplano villages in Bolivia. However, Richard Burger (the author of a beautiful book on the Chavín, see p30) thinks that the cult was rather like the Pachacamac cult in Inca times: it was an organization superior to but also complementary to domestic religions just as the Oracle of Delphi in ancient Greece did not supplant other pagan faiths.

The essence of the Chavín style of carving is found on objects at **Chavín de Huántar** such as *El Lanzon*, the Tello Obelisk and the Raimondi Stela, all of which can be seen today in museums in Lima (see p117). The Chavín style may be adapted by local cultures, but it's all essentially the same and can be found in various guises on pottery, goldwork and textiles across Peru.

Skilled engineers

The spread of the Chavín influence indicates that trade was becoming more common and people were moving around. Rare Ecuadorian shells are often found in tombs of the Chavín era, as is precious lapis lazuli from the Atacama desert in Chile. There were other developments too. The construction of the Castillo (castle), the central building at Chavín de Huantar, shows not only that the people of this time could organize labour forces, but also that they had engineers.

The Castillo is a high structure that is honeycombed with water courses, which would make the whole building resonate and rumble with sound when water flowed in them. Designing a building that could 'speak' like this would have needed well-developed engineering skills.

The **Raimondi Stela** depicts the duality of the Chavín god of agriculture and fertility. Here he stands with his feet firmly placed on the ground. Turn the picture upside down to view the god as a many-faced animal figure descending from heaven to earth.

MASTERCRAFTSMEN (200BC TO 700AD)

From about 200BC the time of the Chavín peace was over. A village was built on the site of the Castillo at Chavín de Huántar, whose stones were reused as hut walls, fortifications were built where previously none had been needed, and trade diminished. These were days of violence, made manifest in the discovery of headless and armless bodies buried during this period. Chaos reigned.

But these weren't entirely black days. Between 200BC and AD700 some of the most impressive civilizations in Peruvian history thrived, creating some of the country's finest art, hence the name 'Mastercraftsmen period'. In the south, the **Huarpa** built sophisticated clay-lined irrigation canals, metres wide and kilometres long. In the Callejón de Huaylas the Recuay made fine polychrome pots and squat statues, and on the coast the oracle of Pachacamac was founded by people of the Rímac river. However, the high-water marks of this period were left by two of the most significant of Peru's civilizations who created some of the finest and most intriguing works of art: the Moche and the Nazca.

The Moche
The Moche conquered the territory from the Piura river in the north of Peru to the Huarmey in the south. They were a bloodthirsty lot: there are many representations on their ceramics of prisoners and battles, but the lack of defensive buildings within the Moche empire suggests that once they conquered a race there was peace. Judging from the structures they left behind, they organized their empire in quite a complex way. In the north they ruled through local puppet lords leaving very few large buildings of their own while in the south they ruled directly, building monumental administrative centres in each valley. The Moche state lasted about 1000 years, but their legacies lasted longer still: they were great craftsmen in metallurgy, in architecture but most importantly in clay.

Moche ceramics One of the great highlights of pre-Hispanic Andean art is Moche portrait pots, the naturalism of which is breathtaking. The high points are the portraits of men: looking on the finest of these is like looking into the eyes of a still breathing Moche noble. However, Moche artists could represent many other things: from buildings to demons, from human pregnancy to a llama with her young, and in the fired clay you can read things like happiness, serenity, surprise and even disease and disfigurement: there is a pot of a woman with leishmaniasis (a disease that rots the nose and lips) and a pot of a man with a cleft palate.

The Moche also made pornographic ceramics, quite astounding in their graphic representation of various sexual acts, small copies of which can be found in just about all the tourist markets of Peru. Scholars are divided as to why the Moche took such pains to represent such diversity of sexual acts (including bestiality and sex with skeletons), and theories range from the suggestion that these are a celebration of life to the idea that they may be religious artefacts.

Moche buildings The Moche's main temple was the huge **Huaca del Sol** (Sun Temple) complex which, in its time, was the largest adobe structure in the Americas. It was massive. What remains is a mere fragment of what was built because of the greed of the Spaniards who developed a novel way of pillaging these old tombs. Tunnels were dug under the structure and then a nearby river diverted to wash away the adobe. With the temple dissolved, gold and treasure could be either picked from the ruins or fished out of the river.

El Señor de Sípan – a hoard missed by the Spaniards

As well as producing portrait pots, the Moche also decorated their ceramics with line drawings in a style rather like that of the ancient Greeks. It's thought that these line drawings illustrate about 25 different stories from the mythology of the Moche. In one scene captives are paraded before an important person, then killed with their fresh spurting blood being caught in a cup. The cup is then handed to the VIP, who wears quite unmistakable clothing. Archaeologists call this person the Warrior Priest. He was the subject of one of the most amazing archaeological finds of the century.

In 1987, the body of a Warrior Priest was discovered, encrusted and surrounded by his unmistakable ornaments of office. *El Señor de Sípan* (Lord of Sípan), as he's been called, had evaded the greed of the Spaniards. Before his body was found, he'd been known only through representations on thousand-year-old pottery. The story of the discovery is fascinating in itself. A local man, Ernil Bernal, and his friends dug a small tunnel into an adobe pyramid of Huaca Rajada. After a night of pillaging the tomb, they were looking for a way out. Bernal's walking stick went into the roof above him. He pulled it out, and the roof began to give way. First some dust fell on him, then some clods of earth. And then, suddenly, a torrent of gold collapsed through the roof and he was buried in treasure. Sadly, it was a week before the curator of the local museum was told of the find, and by then much of value had been lost, ultimately to find its way into the hands of rich collectors in the USA. Only 123 objects from the tombs were ever returned to Peru.

The Nazca

The barren desert pampa by the Nazca river was the workplace of German mathematician, Maria Reiche, for many decades. The whole pampa is crisscrossed by a multitude of lines, patterns, polygons and designs, discovered when the area was first surveyed from the air in 1926. There is a hummingbird that is five times the length of a jumbo jet, an enormous monkey with a whirl of a tail, a killer whale and a bird the size of a house. How? Why?

'How' is the easy question. The dry dusty surface is a natural blackboard – the dark surface conceals a light sandy base, and clearing the dark surface reveals the lighter sand underneath. By removing the dark surface, the Nazca created their patterns, and the desert is so stable that these have lasted through the centuries.

'Why' is more difficult. Theories range from the frankly bonkers (Erich von Däniken in his book, *Chariots of the Gods,* said that the Nazca lines are runways for extraterrestrial spacecraft) to the sensible (Maria Reiche thought that there were astronomical and calendrical reasons for the lines). The current favourite comes from the observation that many of the lines are orientated towards water sources, suggesting that they are likely to be processional routes designed to be walked upon as part of the ritual worship of water.

Nazca pottery The Nazca did not leave only their perplexing lines behind them. They also created some very fine polychrome pottery, drawing on pots with a palette of 13 slip colours, sometimes using the same icons as appear in the lines. The pots themselves are beautiful in their combination of colours and, in a similar way to the Moche portrait pots, appeal to today's aesthetic tastes.

TIAHUANACO-HUARI (AD700 TO 1000)

The coast of Peru was again united at the end of the first millennium. Two related but distinct peoples dominated the Andes: the Tiahuanaco (or Tiwanaku) and the Huari (or Wari). The two were united by an icon that has been called the Gateway God, the Staff God or Viracocha.

Legendary Tiahuanaco

Tiahuanaco has been the site of legend for centuries. In some Incan myths, it was the place of giants, and Viracocha came here to make humanity out of mud. For today's mystics it's still a place of enduring mystery: HS Bellamy in *Built before the Flood* insisted that Tiahuanaco was built thousands of years ago and destroyed when one of earth's moons (he thought we had more than one) hit the surface of the earth. In early 1998 John Bashford-Snell, accompanied by a team from the Explorers' Club of New York, began searching in the area around Titicaca for Plato's lost city of Atlantis. More recently it was suggested that Tiahuanaco was the capital of a sophisticated worldwide civilization that was destroyed over 10,000 years ago.

The **Gateway God** (or Staff God), fundamental icon of the Huari and the Tiahuanaco people. The figure was carved on the Gateway of the Sun, a monumental doorway that's still standing at the extensive site of Tiahuanaco, now in Bolivia.

The site of Tiahuanaco

Tiahuanaco is on the south side of Lake Titicaca, in Bolivia. It was first settled from 400BC, but it wasn't until about AD500 that stone buildings and high pyramids were constructed.

The whole site is very reminiscent of the Inca (with its giant blocks linked together without mortar), but it was built by people who flourished just under 1000 years before their rise. Old accounts say that Pachacutec (see p79) modelled Cusco on this site, which was already ancient by the time of the Incas.

The empire of Tiahuanaco Like the Inca empire, at its peak Tiahuanaco spread its wings over vast tracts of what is now Chile and Bolivia. The Tiahuanaco traded with peoples as far to the south as the oasis of San Pedro de Atacama and the peoples of the Azapa valley, both of which are now in Chile. In cemeteries in these areas, amongst the dead buried in the local style, there are the graves of people buried surrounded by Tiahuanaco finery: wood carvings, gold, textiles. These artefacts are sufficiently small and light to be portable over long distances, and it's likely that they were carried by llama caravans across the desert, sent from Tiahuanaco to reward local agents of the Tiahuanaco empire, or perhaps local regents who ruled in the name of the faraway capital.

Closer to home, the Tiahuanaco ruled more directly. The major colony was a very large site called Omo in the Moquegua valley. Omo was occupied quite early on before it was suddenly abandoned, only to be re-inhabited later. This odd pattern might be explained by the fact that the Tiahuanaco felt threatened by the sudden establishment of the Huari citadel of Cerro Baul, just 20km away.

Tiahuanaco life Like most great Andean peoples, the Tiahuanaco were skilled farmers. They developed a way of preparing the land that produced twice the yield of crops as the techniques of today. They built ridged fields: a field in which trenches are dug and the earth excavated is piled in a ridge between the channels, which are then filled with water. Tiahuanaco ridged fields have imported rock bases and have high-quality imported soil on top, indicating that much work was involved in their construction. They are more fertile than other fields, but they're difficult to build and maintain. When the Tiahuanaco culture declined, these field systems declined and were ultimately replaced by the terraced hillsides of the Inca, but the land around Titicaca has never again been as productive as it was in the days of the Tiahuanaco.

In AD562 there was a great drought in the whole of Peru which lasted thirty years. We know this from analysing samples taken from glaciers, samples that indicate the weather patterns of Peru throughout the centuries. This drought was a contributory factor to the decline of the Moche – about this time the Huaca del Sol was abandoned. (Moche civilization was dealt a double blow by the drought killing crops and then the advance of sand dunes burying the ancient capital.) However, the Tiahuanaco survived and even thrived; an icon of the Gateway God has been found painted on a Moche pyramid, indicating that the Tiahuanaco cult stretched as far to the north as the river Piura.

The demise of the Tiahuanaco Eventually the great civilization of Tiahuanaco suffered the fate of all peoples, and by AD1000 the fields lay fallow, the distribution of high grade Tiahuanaco pottery had stopped, and the empire had fragmented. Why this happened isn't known – like so many things in Andean pre-history it is a mystery – but the creators of the earliest great

Andean stone city lived on, spiritually in the myths of the Incas, and physically in the silent remains of their architecture.

The Huari

The Huari and Tiahuanaco knew of each other but it seems they didn't like each other. Near the river Moquegua the Huari built the fort of Cerro Baul within a short distance of the Tiahuanaco settlement of Omo, in what looks like a directly confrontational act. Nevertheless there's no doubt that the Huari were influenced by them: the Gateway God and other Tiahuanaco icons appear painted in many pieces of Huari pottery and tapestry. However, the way the Huari depicted the Gateway God illustrates that there were differences between the two cultures: the Tiahuanaco representations of the god has sun rays emanating from behind his head, while those of the Huari can be more abstract and often appear with different accoutrements, for example, sometimes bearing cobs of maize, not wielding rods of power.

Who the Huari were is one of these things about which scholars can't agree. Some say that they were an empire that expanded by force, but there is little evidence of military conquest about the time of their expansion. Others say that their style and icons were present in client states because of the influences of trade. Still others suggest the icon was dispersed throughout Peru because the Gateway God was a religious symbol of their shared Peruvian religion like the fanged cat of the Chavín.

The heritage of the Huari In a similar way to the Tiahuanaco, it's likely that the Huari survived so long and were so successful because of their agricultural technology: in their case a system of irrigation that involved long canals, high-altitude water sources and extensive irrigated terraces (probably derived from the Huarpa see p72). This was a labour-intensive technique but it was fruitful so they survived the days of drought. Their methods were later adopted by the Incas.

THE DAYS BEFORE THE INCA (AD1000 TO 1450)

The Chimú (Chimor) culture from the northern coast dominated the period before the rise of the Incas. Other civilizations also flourished, such as the Aymara kingdoms who stepped into the void left by the decline of Tiahuanaco (the Aymara still thrive today).

Around Cusco, the Killke replaced the Huari and were probably descended from the Huari who lived in a settlement called Pikillacta, and on the south coast the Ica carried on the ceramic and textile traditions of the Nazca and the Paracas. To the north of the Rímac, where Lima is now, the Chancay thrived. The Rímac itself was inhabited by the Ichma.

The Chimú

The great rival of the Inca empire was the northern empire of Chimú. At its height, this nation encompassed two-thirds of the Peruvian coast, stretching from Tumbes in the north to just above Lima in the south. It was not conquered by the

Incas until AD1470, and when the Spanish arrived there were still people alive who remembered the old traditions.

The Chimú were not the only people on the north coast. At first, it seems they lived peacefully with their neighbours, irrigating the barren desert with extensive canal systems, but in about AD1100 there was a great flood caused by El Niño which altered the water system. No amount of careful rebuilding could repair the canals, so the Chimú began to take other peoples' agricultural land by conquest.

Chimú stirrup-spout vessel

Chimú and Sican One of their more significant northern neighbours were the Sican, who lived near the site of the modern city of Lambayeque. The Chimú conquered the Sican in about AD1370.

The Sican had an ancient history and are responsible for the production of much beautiful art, one of their main sites called Batan Grande yielding up thousands of golden artefacts. (Interestingly, the Sican manufactured a type of money in the form of small copper axes, which they buried with their dead.)

The origin myths of the Chimú and Sican are remarkably similar, and consequently there have been attempts to link these with archaeological discoveries. Sadly it's not really been possible. In both traditions, society was begun by a man who arrived from the sea saying that he had been sent to take control. In the Sican tradition this man was called Naymlap. On his death, his court and 12 children spread the story that he had sprouted wings and flown away, and then each founded one of the 12 cities of the Sican people. For the Chimú, the man was called Taycanamu, and he settled in the lower Moche valley. When he died, his children did not found cities but extended the territory of his people by conquest, including, in the end, the Sican.

Chan-Chan The centre of the culture was the great Chimú city, Chan-Chan which covers six square km and consists of 12 great palaces or *ciadadelas* built by communal (*mit'a*) labour (see p82). Ciadadelas are enclosures surrounded by a large wall, inside which there are labyrinths of storage rooms, a large platform (which doubles as a burial place) and audience rooms called *audiencias*. The outsides of the audiencias are decorated with adobe friezes of the sea, and they are often U-shaped – an architectural feature dating back to the Initial Period (see p68).

The ciadadelas were probably a ruler's residence and, when he died, his tomb. It's likely that as with the Incas (see p84), a ruler's estate was preserved for his living relatives and his successors had to make their own way in the world. Chan-Chan has been responsible for some of the greatest treasure found in Peru, and at one stage the Spanish formed a mining company to exploit these ruins. Chimú metalwork is some of the most sophisticated in ancient Peru, and if the Chimú were such craftsmen imagine what wonders the Incas must have produced.

Conquest of the Chimú   The last Chimú ruler was Minchancamon. According to oral history, he was single-handedly responsible for the extension of the Chimú empire from the river Chillon to the river Tumbes in the far north. According to archaeology, which has dated the Chimú settlements in these regions, this is unlikely; more probably he took the credit for the victories of his forefathers. When he was conquered by the Inca he was taken to Cusco with his best artisans, a puppet monarch was left to rule in his place and the Chimú empire was broken up. Loyal Inca settlers took over Chimú land, and the Chimú themselves were exiled to other places within the Incas' territory. So ended the last great empire before the Incas.

Days of the Inca

PIECING TOGETHER THE JIGSAW

The Incas did not have writing, and so a caste of oral historians (*amautas*) arose to keep alive the legends and stories of the past. Much of the information that these people carried died with them but some was recorded by early Spanish writers. Fitting together these oral histories with the facts that can be deduced from archaeology is one way we can get a picture of what life was like under the Incas.

Oral history is inevitably unreliable: the Incas simply air-brushed awkward or embarrassing facts from their past. However, the nearer to the Spanish conquest you get, the clearer the picture becomes because there are other sources of information. The conquistadors wrote accounts which they published on their return to Europe, and some of the Incas left their side of the story; a mestizo called Garcilasco de la Vega wrote an early history of Peru, and an account dictated by the rebel Inca Titu Cusi himself (see p97) has survived the years.

There are many other documents too, and new discoveries are still being made. The historians, Luis Miguel Glave, María Remy and John Rowe recently uncovered in the library of a Cusco monastery some papers which cast light on the mystery of Machu Picchu (see p245). Our knowledge of what life was like under the Incas, and what happened during their fall has been pieced together like a jigsaw.

THE ORIGINS OF THE INCAS

Myth
There are two different myths about the creation of the Incas. According to the first, the primordial Inca called Manco Capac emerged from the depths of Lake Titicaca and travelled underground with his brothers and their sister-wives to a place near Cusco called Pacaritambo. There they all emerged from the ground and made their way to Cusco. Manco's three brothers were either turned to

stone or grew wings and flew away, while Manco himself pressed on. When he arrived in the Cusco valley he thrust his golden staff into the fertile soil and it disappeared. This he took as a sign from his father, the Sun, that the valley was good and there he stayed, naming the place Qosqo, which meant 'navel of the earth'. There, too, he built the first *Coricancha* (Sun Temple).

The second myth is also set near Lake Titicaca. In Tiahuanaco, the creator god, Viracocha, ruled over a shadowy people whose name has been forgotten (see p74). They angered him and so he arose from the waters of the lake and turned them all to stone, replacing them with the sun, the moon and with humanity. These new people were sent out from Titicaca to the four corners of the earth, and the Incas were sent to Cusco.

Archaeology

The myths might be true when they say that the Incas aren't native to the Cusco region: there's archaeological evidence that a people called the Killke inhabited the area before the Incas (see p122) and were displaced by them. But there's also a lot of archaeological evidence suggesting that the Incas were a local people whose ceramics and architecture evolved from the arts of local populations like the Killke.

ORAL HISTORY

Inca is properly the title of the monarch (often called the Sapa Inca) and according to the chronicler Bernabe Cobo, writing 100 years after the conquest, the first eight Incas were Manco Capac, Cinchi Roca, Lloque Yupanqui, Mayta Capac, Capac Yupanqui, Inca Roca, Yahuar Huaca and Viracocha Inca. Little is known about any of them apart from Viracocha Inca. Stories exist about him because he was the father of one of the great folk heroes of Inca history, Pachacutec.

Pachacutec (c1438-1463)

Viracocha Inca's bitter enemy were the Canchas, a tribe who attacked Cusco. He and his anointed heir, Urco, fled but his younger son, Pachacutec, remained to destroy the Canchas. It was said that such was the support for him that even the stones of the field grew legs to fight on his side. Once his victory was complete he allowed his father back to Cusco, but usurped the throne for himself and exiled his brother, erasing him from the roll of history.

Pachacutec rebuilt Cusco and transformed it from a much more meagre settlement into a stone city based on the ruins he'd seen at Tiahuanaco. He also ordered Sacsayhuaman to be built, (although the size of this place makes one suspect that it was the product of more than one Inca's rule) and he began the expansion of the Inca empire. Pachacutec was an important figure in Inca history, but it may be that he usurped not only the throne but also the glories of his forefathers. The stories about his taking power differ; some leave out Urco, some credit Viracocha Inca with a much more dynamic rule – but also such great feats are attributed to him that doubt is cast on his historicity. Was he superhuman or a composite man?

The Inca and his wife. An attendant holds a feather sunshade. This is one of a series of somewhat fanciful engravings by the 19th century traveller, Paul Marcoy.

Tupac Yupanqui (or Topa Inca: c1463-1493)

Pachacutec may have shared the latter days of his rule with his son, Tupac Yupanqui, as there may have been a greater and a lesser Inca ruling at the same time (see 'Clans' below). When Pachacutec died, Tupac Yupanqui succeeded him. He was a great conqueror and has been called the Alexander the Great of the Americas. He extended the empire so that the Incas ruled a territory that ran from Ecuador to the river Maule in Chile, extending from the shores of the Pacific into modern-day Argentina. This was an empire that stretched the same distance as Cyprus is from London or Minneapolis from New York.

One of Tupac Yupanqui's greatest achievements was the conquest of Chimú, the desert empire that at one stage rivalled the Inca's own in size and sophistication (see p78). Sadly the Incas themselves left very little information about this conquest, even though it must have been a significant undertaking – an example, perhaps, of the Incas airbrushing their rivals from the record of history. The oral history we do have comes from accounts collected by the Spanish from old Chimú people who remembered the days before the coming of the Incas.

Tupac Yupanqui didn't do quite as well in the east. The Incas never extended their empire far into the Amazon, finding the heat, humidity and disease too much for their mountain troops.

Huayna Capac (c1493-1525)

Huayna Capac was Tupac Yupanqui's chosen successor, but he almost never made it to be Inca when his brother challenged the succession. However Huayna Capac managed to beat off his sibling and took over the empire.

He started his rule by campaigning in the south, in Chile. After a year, he moved to the north of the empire where he spent the rest of his life fighting. He died shortly before the arrival of the first Europeans on Peru's shores, and was the last in the line of the great independent Incas.

CLASS AND CLANS

The Inca was the sovereign, the head of the state religion and the son of the Sun. He was a general too, and he led his forces into battle. He was the distillation of all power, the focus of all respect and the icon of his people. The state was governed by the Inca, supported by his nobles who were called *orejones* (big ears) by the Spanish because they extended their earlobes as a mark of rank. Positions of greatest responsibility were reserved for Incas true by blood, people of the same royal family or tribe as the Inca. In time the empire grew too large for these positions to be filled solely by his relatives so the Inca created a caste of Incas by privilege from the people who lived around Cusco in the Sacred Valley of the river Urubamba and allowed them to hold office.

Clans An important facet of Inca society was its division into two clans: *Hanan* and *Hurin*, which roughly mean upper and lower. You can see the physical expression of this division in the way that the Incas divided their cities into two parts: in Machu Picchu, for example, and in old Cusco.

Scholars disagree over the significance of this division. Some think it was simply tribal town planning, a way of making sure that there was a fundamental rift within Inca society, which reduced any risk of united opposition to central rule – on the principle of divide and rule. Others believe that these were two great clan groups that divided the whole of Inca society from top to bottom, even to the extent of having a greater and lesser Inca ruling at the same time. The monarch, drawn from the Hanan, was called the Sapa Inca.

INCA GOVERNMENT

Administration

At its height, the Inca empire – Tahuantinsuyu – was 5500km (3400 miles) long, longer than the full extent of the Roman empire. Tahuantinsuyu means place of the four quarters, (or *suyu*). The four suyu were: Collasuyu (to the far south), Cuntisuyu (to the south-west), Chinchaysuyu (the northern quarter), and Antisuyu (generally to the east: the forested lower slopes of the Andes). The word Andes is a derivation of this Quechua word Antisuyu. Four principal roads led from the centre of Cusco to these provinces.

Tahuantinsuyu was profoundly hierarchical – the Inca himself at the top, with his orejones below him, and below them men who were in charge of successively smaller clan groups called *ayllus*.

Land and labour

The lands of each ayllu were divided into three parts: the produce of one part went to the community, the priests had the rights to a second part and the produce of the last third was the state's. This maintained the state religion, the administration and fed the people. The members of the ayllu were also subject

August – a time of planting
FELIPE HUAMÁN POMA DE AYALA (c1590)

to a tax called *mit'a*, payable in food, cloth or labour. Mit'a labour built canals, walls, road and cities, and Sacsayhuaman, for example, the great fortress temple that overlooks Cusco.

When the Spanish came they greedily incorporated this system of taxation to their own ends, stating that a vast proportion of each Indian's yearly labour was to be for the benefit of the Spaniard who owned the encomienda on which the Indian lived. The Spanish argued that they were simply continuing the ancient system but changing the beneficiary from heathen to Christian. This was, of course, complete cant. In the days of the Incas, the people could expect to benefit from mit'a labour by being fed from the state's storehouses (*qollqa*) in times of famine, or being protected by a fort (*pucara*) in times of war.

The burden of mit'a labour was relieved by the benefit of shared wealth and responsibility, but in the days of the Spanish mit'a labour was nothing more than exploitation.

The system wasn't bad for all the Indians, and the native middlemen, called *caciques* (originally a Caribbean word) or *curacas* (the Quechua word), generally did rather well. Some Incas went so far as to become Hispanicized, most importantly Don Cristóbal Paullu Inca, Atahualpa's brother. Paullu was baptized, took a Spanish name, built a church in Cusco (see p146) and led armies against the independent Inca state of Vilcabamba (see p96).

The system of ayllus survives to this day, and campesino society is founded on the notion of reciprocal obligations. If you need a roof on your house, then your neighbours are obliged to come and help but in return you must help them with their harvest, say, next year. The ayllu structure is a pan-Andean thing, with the Aymara who live in Bolivia and northern Chile having the same basic attitude to communal work.

Expansion

The Incas were well versed in conquest by many means, from ethnic-cleansing and resettlement, to indoctrination, to the menace of total war; but they preferred to conquer by threat rather than use of force.

When the Incas conquered a new nation they sent a group of loyal settlers (*mitimaes*) to the occupied territories. By planting loyal citizens the Inca could ensure a concentration of local support as the isolated settlers banded together in a hostile country. In the meantime the leaders and chiefs of the newly conquered people were taken to Cusco, educated and indoctrinated into Inca civilization. The idols of the conquered were brought to Cusco, too, and were placed in minor shrines in the Coricancha (see p142). Should there be a revolt, despite all these precautions, the idols were brought out, befouled and thrown into the sewers, and the Incas would attack with ruthless violence.

HOW THEY RAN THE EMPIRE

Record keeping

The Incas never invented writing. Yet without writing, they managed to govern a vast territory and make provision to feed and provide work for the population who lived there. They had to keep records to be able to achieve this – records of how much food they had in storage, of how many people there were in this village, of how long it would take to get from that place to the next on the road. To record this information, the Incas used a system of knots on strings, called *quipus*. The secrets of reading quipus were entrusted to a class called the *quipucamayoc*, but the basic prin-

Quipucamayoc (record keeper)
FELIPE HUAMÁN POMA DE AYALA (c1590)

ciples of quipu reading are still known. The Incas counted in base ten, as we do, and they placed knots in different places on the string to indicate whether they were counting one unit, ten units, a hundred units and so on. Different coloured strings signified different things, and so a roll of strings with knots could contain a large amount of information about provisions, populations and wealth. Many of these rolls of knotted string survive and you can see them in museums today.

Some people think that this wasn't the only form of record-keeping that the Incas devised and that there's a lost form of communication hidden in Inca cloth. Many of the designs you'll see woven into Quechua fabrics today have a significance: this one represents a condor, that represents a llama. The theory suggests that in the days of the Incas similar cloth designs were a system of communication.

Inca roads

The Incas had a famous system of roads that led to every corner of the empire. It was said that the Inca in Cusco could breakfast on fresh sea-fish every morning, so efficient were the roads and the system of relay-runners (*chasquis*) that ran on them.

The road network was extensive; there were two main north-south trunk roads, one following the cordillera, one the coast, with numerous east-west link roads. Within this framework there were many smaller roads leading to sacred or important places: the Inca Trail to Machu Picchu is one of these. In total there were about 33,000km (20,000 miles) of roads covering the empire, which if laid end to end would be enough to take you two-thirds of the way around the earth.

Travel was permitted only on official business, and the average campesino was not allowed to travel unless, for example, he was required for mit'a labour. Guardians of the roads were appointed to check on traffic, and overseers of royal bridges looked after the many twine suspension bridges traversing the deep canyons that fracture the Andes. Messages were carried by runners in relays, and there were *tambos* (inns, or way-stations) where travellers could rest and expect to find food and a place to sleep for the night.

Many roads still exist today, and if you visit Chile's Atacama desert to the east of Chañaral, for example, or the nearby Parque National Tres Cruces, you'll still see the faint outlines of implausibly straight roads heading off into the dust and heat, leading now to nowhere.

SPIRITUAL LIFE OF THE INCAS

The Incas worshipped a wide variety of gods. The main deities were Inti the sun, thunder, lightning, the rainbow, the Pleiades, Viracocha (the creator) and Pachamama (the earth-mother).

The Inca – Son of the Sun

The Inca was the son of the Sun, and therefore was a living emanation of a god. Religion and the state were so closely entwined that our separation of the two would have been incomprehensible to the Incas. As a living god the Inca was the head of the state religion but he was more than just a figurehead. His religious standing was the wellspring from which he drew his political power.

He wasn't an abstract figure. He was linked to everyday life by a complicated system of festivals and ceremonies. For example, no one was allowed to sow seed until they had been told that the Inca had broken the ground in Cusco (the information was sent out from Cusco by chasquis). Some of these festivals, such as Inti Raymi are still celebrated.

The Inca's power after death

The Inca's importance didn't end with his death. His estate was maintained (a system called *panaca*), and at every important ceremony his mummified body was brought out and placed on a sacred dais (*usno*) to participate with the living Inca and all the other dead ones. The dead were ritually fed and given drink, which was burnt on an altar beside them, before they were returned to the darkness of their living palaces.

A special class of people looked after his lands and preserved his wealth. Machu Picchu itself may have been such an estate, once owned by Pachacutec, and maintained for the benefit of his mummy. This system of fossilizing an Inca's possessions forced each new Inca to forge his own way and create his own heritage from newly-conquered lands. It was a spur to conquest.

Priests and spiritual places

The state religion had a caste of priests, the chief of which was the *Villac Umu*. He was a very powerful man in the empire: he acted as a military adviser in the days of the Spanish conquest. The centre of religion was Cusco, the capital of the state. The centre of the centre was the Coricancha, the Sun Temple, from which sacred lines (*ceques*) radiated to sacred places (*huacas*), rather like the physical roads that ran from the main square to the four suyus. Modern scholars think that this is no accident, and that the huacas and ceques were orientated along the same sacred axes as the geographical quarters.

Despite the centre being in Cusco, religion wasn't centralized and each place had its own spirits and huacas that were worshipped. Some huacas were carved stones, like the Yurac-Rumi, a carved white stone near Vitcos (see p223), or Qenko near Cusco (see p150). Others were simply geographical features like waterfalls or springs, and some were shrines like the Intihuatana at Machu Picchu (see p254). Still others were supposed to be the fossilized remains of the magnificent dead, the hill overlooking Cusco's airport being those of one of Manco Capac's brothers. As the Inca empire expanded, it absorbed new gods, spirits and huacas, some of which – like Pachacamac on the coast – became major shrines for the Incas themselves.

The Spanish destroyed huacas when they found them, and prohibited their worship, claiming that they were possessed by the devil. Intihuatanas were smashed, and places like the Yurac-Rumi were exorcized. It didn't work. To this day the Quechua find such places sacred, believing mountains, for example, to be inhabited by spirits called *apus*. Old huacas are still worshipped, and cere-

LAON3ENACOIA
RAVAOCLLO

The Coya, the Inca's wife
FELIPE HUAMÁN POMA DE AYALA (c1590)

monies like Qoyllur Riti (see p46) incorporate elements of the old religion into Christianity.

Sacred women

Women were very important to Inca spirituality. One of the major deities was the female Pachamama (who inevitably got confused with the Virgin Mary); and the Inca's wife, the *coya* (who, as with the Pharaohs of ancient Egypt, was also his sister) was a person of high status and nobility.

Women were tightly bound into religious and profane life. There were convents of Inca nuns (*acllas*), drawn from the most beautiful maidens in the empire. They were headed by mother superiors (*mamaconas*), and their mission in life was to serve the Inca. They wove his fabric and looked after him, brewing his sacred *chicha* (maize beer) and preparing his food. The most beautiful acllas were awarded to high-status men as rewards for distinguished acts, whilst other acllas confined themselves to a life in his service. Some, indeed, confined themselves to a death in his service on the rare occasions when a situation demanded human sacrifice.

INCA CULTURE

Architecture

The Incas are of course most famous for their architecture. They built in a number of different styles, all of which seem to be characteristically Inca. Some of these characteristics are in fact Andean rather than Inca, such as mortarless walls derived from the Tiahuanaco, the trapezoidal arch (first seen in Kotosh) and terracing (derived from the Huari). Others are strikingly Inca, such as the way that their architecture incorporates a natural form, perhaps as a rock outcrop or a hillside, and enhances it with the structures that are built around it. Machu Picchu itself is a classic and perfect example of this, situated as it is astride a ridge and emphasizing the outcrop that is the Intihuatana, and surrounded by the terracing that forms and reflects the shape of the living rock.

Types of Inca building One type of Inca building is the imposing stone fortress-like Sacsayhuaman (see p148), whose walls are made from blocks the size of large cars, locked together without mortar but immovable because of the perfect fit.

Another type is the regular fine-bricked buildings such as Coricancha (see p142), whose delicate brickwork was reserved for the highest status buildings. Again these walls have no mortar, just accurately carved blocks in walls that taper inwards as they get higher to resist earth movements. In the famous circular wall in Coricancha you can see that these bricks aren't really rectangular blocks but are carved so their inside faces fit together in a three-dimensional jigsaw.

The Incas also built using simpler techniques. A method of fitting rough stone together with adobe (mud) was called *pirka*, and some pirka structures still remain. The most basic construction technique was to build a simple adobe wall on a fieldstone foundation, but most of these haven't survived the passage of time.

How did they do it? It isn't known how the Incas managed to achieve such a snug fit in their ceremonial structures using the few tools they had – river stones and small bronze crowbars (they hadn't discovered iron).

Inca stonemasons
FELIPE HUAMÁN POMA DE AYALA (c1590)

There are many theories. One suggests that after one row of stones was laid it was dusted with a small film of fine sand, and when a new course was placed on top and removed, marks in the sand would indicate where the base layer needed to be carved. The top layer was then hoisted up on wooden props, the lower level was carved, and then the new course was lowered into its newly-made slots. However, this theory doesn't explain how the Incas managed to get their vertical joints as good as their horizontal ones. Another plausible theory suggests that the Incas used a tool a little like a builder's scribe to score a guideline on the rock to be cut.

Inca technology in modern use

After the conquest, the highlands became depopulated as the Spanish removed its inhabitants to purpose-built villages. The terraces and canals fell into decline and the land has never again been as fertile as it was in the days of the Incas.

But recently, a project run by the Inca expert, Dr Ann Kendall, has started to reverse that. Dr Kendall is an archaeologist who excavated in the Cusichaca valley (see p176), paying close attention to the old Inca canals that transect these hills. She realized that, using only ancient technology, these old watercourses could be repaired and irrigate the dry terraces of the Cusichaca valley, thus increasing the area's agricultural productivity and benefiting the impoverished local community. So, in a practical spin-off from her archaeological excavations, she began to help the campesinos to repair the old Inca water channels. The project worked, and the fertility of the area increased massively.

Dr Kendall is now bringing these skills to other parts of Peru, breathing life into the dead old water channels. If you'd like more information about this fascinating blending of archaeology and development visit 🖳 www.cusichaca.woden.com.

Predictably, this question has attracted the usual outlandish theories: it's been seriously suggested that the Incas achieved their masterful masonry by melting the rocks, focusing the sun's rays into the corners using parabolic mirrors.

Textiles

It's difficult to overstate how important woven cloth was to the Incas. It was a statement of rank, an object of value and even a medium of exchange. It's said that when the Spanish first arrived they were handed not gold and silver but fabric. What you wore was an indication of your rank. The acllas wove the finest fabric for the Inca, called *qompi,* some of which he gave away as an honour to the most worthy of his subjects. The tunics he wore were of magnificent patterning and were made from such varied fabric as vicuña wool and vampire-bat skin (see Fabrics, p60). Soldiers had their own uniforms, and the reports of the first sight the Spanish had of the Incas describe the royal vanguard being dressed in black and white checked cloth. Everyday cloth was also made, called *awaska*, and was worn by the vast majority of people.

Ceramics

The Incas made pottery, but they never reached the aesthetic heights of their ancestors, the Moche and the Nazca. The characteristic Inca pot form is the large *urpu*, which has a fat belly, a curved base and long spout. It was generally a vessel for storage and transport of food: chicha, maize and chuño (freeze-dried potato).

It was carried slung over the back, tied to the body by a band of cloth that passed through the little eyes on the pot's side. Porters on the Inca Trail today still carry baggage in this way.

Metalwork

The melting down of Inca metalwork is one of the Spaniards' greatest crimes. Hardly any gold or silver escaped the furnaces; most of it reduced from dazzlingly-worked artefacts to lump-gold. A few objects remain but they're only things that were small enough to escape the flames of Spanish greed. We can only dream about what Inca metalwork must have been like, prompted by descriptions left by the conquistadors.

Hunting

Royal Hunts (*chacos*) were a great sacred event. Beaters encircled a large area and started to walk inwards; and

> ❏ **Inca gold**
> 'In one cave they discovered twelve sentries of gold and silver, of the size and appearance of those of this country, extraordinarily realistic. There were pitchers half of pottery and half gold, with the gold so well set into the pottery that no drop of water escaped when they were filled, and beautifully made. A golden effigy was also discovered. This greatly distressed the Indians, for they said that it was a figure of the first lord who conquered this land. They found shoes made of gold, of the type that women wore, like half-boots. They found golden crayfish such as live in the sea, and many vases, on which were sculpted in relief all the birds and snakes that they knew, even down to spiders, caterpillars and other insects.'
> **Pedro Pizarro** *Discovery and Conquest of the Kingdoms of Peru,* 1571.

inside the circle, the animals would be herded closer and closer together. Such was the scale of the hunt that it would take many days for the circle to tighten. When the beaters stood almost shoulder to shoulder, hunters entered the circle and killed or sheared the animals it contained: guanaco and vicuña (types of llama), puma, foxes, deer and bears. The hunt provided the locals with much meat and wool, and the nobles with sport.

Warfare

The Spaniards weren't very impressed with the Incas' weapons, and that's not surprising since the Incas hadn't progressed beyond the slings, clubs (*chambis* and *macanas*) and bronze-headed javelins that the Moche had used centuries before. At close quarters a Spaniard's lightning-fast rapier would usually make short work of an Inca armed only with a club or javelin. Despite its effectiveness the rapier wasn't the greatest advantage the Spaniards had over the Incas nor, given the amount of time it took to load and fire, was the arquebus (gun): it was the horse.

The Incas had never seen horses before and didn't know how to fight them. They must have felt rather like the Romans when faced with the elephants of Hannibal. The Spanish were, of course, excellent fighters, renowned in Europe for their prowess in war but it's unlikely that this alone would have been sufficient to take the Inca empire. Just the sight of an armoured Spaniard on the back of his beast, thundering towards the massed ranks of Inca warriors would have

The Incas and Easter Island

Thor Heyerdahl, the Norwegian explorer and writer, was convinced for many years that the ancient Peruvians colonized Easter Island, the tiny speck of land 3700km west of Peru in the Pacific Ocean. He based his theory on a number of things: a wall on Easter Island which bears a striking resemblance to Inca masonry; the fact that the dominant tribe of Easter Island had elongated ears like the Inca Orejones (see p81); and the discovery of the sweet potato on Easter Island, a plant that's a species native to South America. Heyerdahl also pointed out that the predominant currents in the Pacific Ocean lead from Peru to Easter Island, a fact which, he said, makes the colonization of Easter Island from Peru likely. (Heyerdahl spectacularly proved that it is possible to float from Peru to Easter Island on a raft when in 1948 he did just that aboard his reed raft, *Kon Tiki*.)

It's a seductive idea, and it's backed up by oral history. On the coast of Peru, there's a myth that a king, called Kon Tiki, defeated in battle, sailed off into the sunset and was never seen again. There's a complementary myth that both Easter Island and its near neighbour, the Marquesas Islands, were colonized by a man from a country far away to the east who arrived by sea, and this man is called Tiki in some myths.

Sadly for Heyerdahl, his theories have never been accepted by the academic community, not least because there's no evidence of any Peruvian language, ceramics or textiles on these islands. Still, it's an intriguing possibility.

sent fear into the hearts of the bravest. Only by avoiding confrontations on flat ground were the Incas successful against the invaders. The native Americans who mastered the horse themselves, such as the Mapuches of southern Chile and the Apaches of North America, managed to check the Spanish advance.

How, then, were the Incas so successful in building their empire before the arrival of the Europeans? This is one of those questions to which there's no easy answer, but it's likely that the efficient road network was the key, allowing reinforcements to be brought up to support an Inca fighting column in times of need. The Incas could then overwhelm their adversaries by sheer force of numbers.

This fits with the fact that the Incas found it extremely difficult to subdue the peoples in the extreme north and south of their empire. The Chronicles tell how hard pressed the Incas were in the north, against local tribes who protected themselves with strings of forts, and in the south, the Incas never managed to conquer the Mapuche. Their lines of communication were stretched too far, and they couldn't bring up their support easily – they had literally reached the end of the road, even for their extremely efficient infrastructure.

The fall of the Incas

On 24 September 1532 Francisco Pizarro marched into the lands of the Inca empire with 62 horsemen and 106 infantry. How he managed to subdue and rape the greatest empire of its day is a fascinating story of greed and cunning.

PLAGUE AND CIVIL WAR

Some years before Pizarro marched out, the old Inca Huayna Capac had retired to Quito, the northern city of the Inca empire. Huayna Capac was in the north subduing local tribes. One of his legitimate sons, Huascar, had remained in the imperial capital Cusco. The bastard son, Atahualpa, was with Huayna Capac in Quito.

Generally, these were times of peace, the empire was secure and life was luxurious. But it was not to last. Disaster struck in the form of a plague of biblical proportions which spread over the land, and Huayna Capac himself died as did his heir, Ninan Cuyuchi. Modern historians think that the plague was smallpox, or some other disease brought to the New World by the Europeans, freshly arrived in the hemisphere. The vanguard of conquest, it killed off the Inca, his heir and many of his court and brought the country to civil war.

Huascar coveted the throne, as did his natural brother Atahualpa. Huascar had the support of the Cusco nobility and the trappings of traditional empire. Atahualpa was in the north, with the seasoned, battle-hardened generals of the Ecuadorian campaign. Civil war erupted. After a long, bitter struggle Atahualpa was the victor.

And so the scene was set for the arrival of Pizarro and his Spanish adventurers. Had they arrived two years before or two years later they would have discovered a stronger, united empire with armies well able to push them back into the sea. As it is, when they arrived they were lucky enough to march into a country ravaged by disease and broken by civil war.

Pizarro and Almagro set sail
FELIPE HUAMÁN POMA DE AYALA (c1590)

PIZARRO AND ALMAGRO

Pizarro was born in Extremadura in rural Spain. He knew hardship in his youth: he was a swineherd in the poorest part of a country still recovering from centuries-long occupation by the Moors. He was illiterate, a poor horseman but a machiavellian judge of human character and a ruthless military genius.

By middle age he found himself a prosperous burgher in the new Spanish colony of Panama. This would have been enough for many: he had climbed far from his lowly beginnings. But it wasn't enough. He wanted more.

The search for El Dorado

Rumours reached Panama of a great, rich country to the south, a country where there were vast treasures of gold and hoards of silver. There had been attempts to reach it – one man had got as far as a river called the Biru (one explanation for the country's name), but had to turn back. Pizarro and his partner, Diego de Almagro, decided to fit out an expedition and go and see for themselves. News was breaking of how dashing Cortés had defeated the infidel Aztecs and secured Mexico for Spain, and these stories confirmed the possibility that there was another great kingdom filled with riches hidden in the undiscovered lands to the south.

First expeditions

Pizarro's and Almagro's first expeditions weren't successful. It's true that they met an ocean-going raft, filled with Inca cloth, which indicated that there was some truth in the rumours of developed lands, but Pizarro and his men became near-shipwrecked on a desert island in the bitter winter of 1527. The conquest of Peru almost foundered at that point, and would have done had Pizarro not drawn a line in the sand with his sword and challenged his men to cross the line to greatness and riches. Thirteen crossed, and thirteen became the richest and most powerful men in all the Americas. Of that thirteen, how many died in their beds? Pizarro was murdered. Almagro was murdered. All but one of Pizarro's brothers met gruesome ends. Such is the price of greed.

In 1528 Pizarro returned to Spain to beg the indulgence of the crown. He got it, and with it the title of Governor and Captain-General of Peru. He secured for Almagro the title of Commandant of Tumbes, a little port on the coast. Almagro was to prove unhappy with this. He agreed to continue with the venture only if he was given all the land beyond Pizarro's claim. Pizarro then returned to Peru at the head of a small army. They landed on the coast at Tumbes, and found a ruined town, a result of the civil war that had been raging in the old Inca empire.

FIRST CONTACT

Pizarro and his men marched up into the hills. They were impressed with what they saw: well-maintained roads, stone towns, orderly people, warehouses filled with food. One contemporary Spaniard wrote of: 'herds of sheep, large fields, and many irrigation channels, green and so beautiful, and the land appeared so cheerful that there was nothing to compare it with...it was undoubtably the best and richest in the world'. This was obviously no land of barbarians. They, on the other hand, could not earn such praise. When they saw food they ate it and when they saw women, they took them.

News of the strange new arrivals reached the Inca's ear. Atahualpa was resting near Cajamarca taking his time over his triumphal return to Cusco, seeking to heal the country of the wounds inflicted by a fratricidal civil war. He heard mention from his chasquis that a group of men, accompanied by strange beasts a little like llamas, had landed on the coast and were walking on the roads without imperial permission. They were breaching all of the Incas' laws: stealing from imperial storehouses and even taking acllas, the sacred nuns, for their pleasure.

The Inca was with an army, numbered in tens of thousands. These weren't just any old soldiers; they were used to battle and were strong, fit and fierce. The Inca could have wiped away the Spanish with a flick of his wrist. Why he didn't is a fascinating question that has been asked and asked again over the years.

Fatally the Inca allowed the Spaniards to advance. They came to Cajamarca, and were stunned when they saw the hills alight with the camp-fires of the Inca's army, and they were afraid. A Spaniard described the sight: 'The Indians' camp looked like a very beautiful city … So many tents were visible that we were truly filled with great apprehension. We never thought that Indians could maintain such a proud estate nor have so many tents in good order'. The Spanish sent emissaries to the Inca, asking him to come and meet them in the main square of the town, to talk. That night, they laid a trap.

THE TRAP

The main square had one exit only and was surrounded by buildings. The small cannon that the Spaniards possessed was set up on a high point. At a certain sign, it was to be fired and the Spanish cavalry was to pour out of its hiding places around the square and attack the natives, who had never seen horses or guns. This would give the Spanish a chance. Despite the plan, and despite their horses and their guns, the Spaniards spent a fearful night.

The next day it looked as if the Inca wasn't going to come. The Spaniards posted as lookouts could see his camp and could see that there was no movement. Things got even more tense in the Spanish camp. Then, in the afternoon, the Inca and his army moved. The chroniclers described the scene: the Incas wore gold and silver crowns, dressed in fine clothing and sang 'graceful' songs. The townspeople swept the road before the procession, which was led by a squadron of men in chequered tunics. Seventy thousand warriors followed. The Spanish urinated out of pure terror.

Atahualpa made his way into the main square. The Spaniards' priest, Vicente de Valverde, approached the monarch as he sat on his litter, and said 'I have come to teach you the word of God'. Atahualpa seized the priest's breviary, and leafed through it, admiring the writing. He then, so the story goes, put it to his ear, then threw it to the ground in irritation. The priest cried out, cursing the Indian devils and letting slip the dogs of war.

It was a massacre. The Indians who bore the Inca's litter were his nobles and not his fighting men. They were amongst the first to fall. The cavalry butchered the rest of the Inca's escort, riding them down through the small, orderly streets or slaughtering them where they stood, dumb-founded by these strange charging half-beasts. It did not last long. A chronicler describes Pizarro's reaching Atuhualpa's litter and grabbing at the unarmed Inca 'with great bravery'. Atahualpa was captured. As John Hemming has said in *The Conquest of the Incas*, the conquest of Peru began with a great checkmate.

THE GREAT CHECKMATE

Atahualpa's troops, still for the most part massed outside the town gates, didn't mount a rescue attempt. The Inca sent word that they were to disband. Why?

Atahualpa had attempted a bargain for his life. He expected to be killed, and when he saw the Spaniards' lust for precious metal offered to fill a room with gold and two more rooms with silver for good measure in exchange for his life. (The Spanish could speak to him because they'd trained up an interpreter whom they'd captured from the ocean-going raft, see p91). The Spanish agreed to the bargain, and as a gesture of good faith, Atahualpa sent word that his army should disband. Power in the Inca state was so distilled in the Inca himself, that without him at their head the people could not act. He was a god, a king, and a general. When he ordered something, they obeyed. So when he ordered that they should not attack the Spanish, they did not. There has seldom been a more crucial and catastrophic misjudgment by one man in the history of his race, or a less trustworthy set of people in whom a captive has placed his faith. The Spaniards were after the Inca's whole country, nothing less, and by ordering his people not to destroy them he destroyed his country.

Messengers were sent to the four suyus of the empire, and told to bring back gold and silver. In time the llama trains arrived – first little by little, then in small bands, then in floods. The room began to fill with gold.

A king's murder

The Spaniards became jumpy. What would happen when the room was full? Wouldn't the Inca go off and raise an army to return and annihilate every last foreigner in his land? They couldn't let him go. Happily enough for them, there

CONQVISTA
CORTALE:LACAVESA:A
ATAGVALPA·INGA·VMA·TA·CVCHV

The death of Atahualpa
FELIPE HUAMÁN POMA DE AYALA (c1590)

were reports that a large Indian army was massing a couple of days' march from Cajarmarca. Charges were laid against Atahualpa that he was planning a rebellion, and he was tried, found guilty and sentenced to death by burning. As an Inca, it was crucially important to him that his body should survive intact so it could be mummified and partake of future rituals, as tradition dictated. Burning was literally a fate worse than death. The Spanish told him that he could avoid the fire by converting to Christianity. So this he did.

Atahualpa, the last undisputed Inca, was garroted on 26 July 1533. In a particularly cynical piece of treachery, even for the Spanish, they burnt his body anyway. He was buried a Christian, and they say that Pizarro, in an act of superhuman hypocrisy, cried at his funeral.

The first puppet Inca

Pizarro realized the importance of maintaining a puppet monarch, through whom he could exercise power with the minimum of force. He therefore selected an Inca to succeed Atahualpa from one of the princelings in Atahualpa's retinue; he chose Huascar's brother, Tupac Huallpa (Huascar had died mysteriously, probably murdered on Atahualpa's orders, during the time of Atahualpa's imprisonment.) This was a masterstroke. Pizarro set himself and the Spanish up as protectors of Huascar's line, and thus bought themselves support from the defeated side in the recent civil war.

Then the Spaniards began the march on Cusco.

THE MARCH ON CUSCO

The march on Cusco was long and hard, and each step of the way the Spanish were fearful of their own shadows and of an Inca army waiting to bar their way.

The army that awaited them consisted of the remains of the army of the north, the army of Quito. However, as the Spanish marched they found friends: many tribes, only recently come under the Incas' yoke, gave them support and encouragement and the Huascar faction inevitably preferred the foreigners to the Quitan army. So the Spanish weren't as entirely bereft of support as their more vainglorious accounts would have us believe, and on their march on Cusco they picked up supplies, willing helpers and auxiliaries.

About half-way to Cusco the young Tupac Huallpa died, probably of natural causes but there were many in Atahualpa's camp who wished him dead. Pizarro exploited the situation by playing off those who wanted the successor to be of Atahualpa's line against those who preferred Huascar's children. When the Spaniards were nearing Cusco, Manco Inca, a young prince of Huascar's line, came forward. With Pizarro's approval he was made Inca.

A desperate defence

The Quitan army did oppose the march on Cusco – but they had neither the weapons nor the tactics to oppose the full force of the Spanish cavalry. Every encounter save one resulted in a crushing rout of the Incas. The glorious exception was partly brought on by the arrogance of a dashing Spanish conquistador, Hernando de Soto.

De Soto wanted to be the first into Cusco, wanted the glory and the money, and he was leading the advance guard of the Spanish column. He came to the Apurímac river. The Indians had burnt the bridge, but the Spanish were lucky enough to find the river at low water and they forded it. As they were making their way up the other side, the horizon blackened with Inca soldiers. The Spanish tried to form up into a defensive line, but the Incas had let loose the mountainside at them, and stones, rocks and boulders crashed into their unprotected ranks, followed by a tidal wave of warriors.

The Spanish made for the top, but their horses were exhausted and five conquistadors fell from the saddle. Once off their horses, they were quickly despatched by the Incas that surrounded them. The remaining Spaniards then retreated and camped for the night, a night that they feared would be their last. However, with the morning light came reinforcements presciently sent forward by Pizarro, and the disheartened Incas faded into the morning mist.

CUSCO – CAPITAL OF THE EMPIRE

The Spanish rode into Cusco, and set up Manco Inca as their puppet. They took control of the city in an arrogant re-founding ceremony on 23 March 1534, and ruled the empire for a couple of years, in relative harmony, Manco was satisfied because he had status, the Spanish were satisfied because they had power. Many conquistadors went home and published accounts of the expedition, but others stayed on and were awarded plots of land, encomiendas, from which they could derive an income. All Spaniards had to live in Cusco, however, to establish a firm, secure and defensible concentration of men.

The northern part of the empire, of course, had yet to be subdued, and the Quitan army still posed a threat to the Spanish, but it was just a matter of time now before that fell. The Spaniards now had a power base, access to the sea, and the loyalty of many of the subjects of the old empire. The Inca generals, Rumñavi, Zope-Zopahua and Quisquis deserve more of a mention than I can give them in these pages, but they were all conquered by 1535.

SOW THE WIND

That could have been the end of the story but it was just the start of another chapter. The first seed of discontent which was sowed related to Diego de Almagro, the short-changed partner of Pizarro. In 1535 he rather grumpily set off to inspect the territory he'd been awarded, and he discovered northern Chile, a vast tract of land as barren as the Sahara. Almagro was to come back, a cloud on his brow and envy in his heart at the riches of Cusco.

That was to prove a problem but a more immediate problem was caused by Francisco Pizarro's brothers. Francisco Pizarro had gone to the coast to found Lima, and the city of Cusco was left under the control of hot-headed and vulgar Juan and Gonzalo Pizarro. They began to insult Manco Inca and abuse his subjects.

REAP THE WHIRLWIND

At Easter in 1536, the announcement was made to the citizens of Cusco that Manco Inca had rebelled and headed for the hills. The conquistadors did what conquistadors do best – they rode out to meet the rebellion head-on. In the valley of Yucay, they came across it: 100,000 to 200,000 Inca soldiers bent on their death. The Spaniards only just made it back to Cusco alive.

The siege of Cusco

And so began the siege of Cusco. These were grim times for the Spanish, all 180 of them, only a half of whom had horses. On an early foray the Mayor had his head cut off. On 6 May the Incas entered Cusco and beat back the Spanish who holed up in buildings, so the Incas set fire to the city.

Manco Inca himself was directing the siege from Sacsayhuaman (see p148), a site that overlooks Cusco. The Spanish realized that dislodging him from this fortress-temple was the only solution. They rode out, around the obstacles that had been placed to trip up their horses, and took possession of the Rodadero. There they faced the massive, three-tiered walls of Sacsayhuaman, which in those days were topped by three castles.

It was a long, savage fight. Juan Pizarro was hit on the head by a sling-shot and killed, but Gonzalo Pizarro and the Spanish, fighting with a desperation borne of terror and a courage that was their wont, took the citadel. They say that in the days that followed condors feasted on the piles of the dead Incas lying around the walls of Sacsayhuaman. The arms of the city of Cusco, granted in 1540, show a castle surrounded by condors that represents this terrible day.

Vilcabamba – the last refuge of the Incas

Manco Inca escaped. He was pursued, and retreated – from Pisac, from Ollantaytambo, and then deep into the jungle where he founded a new city called Vilcabamba. It was here that he carved out a new Inca state, a mere rump of the glories of the past but a state where there were no Spanish.

Manco Inca was attracted to Vilcabamba by its inaccessibility. This, after all, is a region choked with cloud forest, a land of vertical terrain, wild rivers, hazardous bogs and rain. To the Incas this area was known as Antisuyo, one of the four quarters of their once-mighty empire and the only one that had yet to be conquered by the Spanish.

Opposite: On the trail to Vilcabamba. (Photo © Henry Stedman).

Manco Inca founded his new city in 1538, one year after his decision to retreat from Ollantaytambo (see p155). His first attempts at establishing a new capital proved decidedly ineffectual: Vitcos, on the hill of Rosaspata between the Río Vilcabamba and the Andenes stream, was too exposed and vulnerable as was proved when Diego de Almagro's General Orgóñez stormed it. Only the Spaniards' lust for gold saved Manco: while they ransacked the palace, he managed to lose his pursuers and disappear into the jungle.

Manco only escaped with the help of 20 of the fastest runners from the Lucana tribe, who spirited him away. He had to leave almost everything behind, including his son Titu Cusi, who was taken to Cusco and placed in the house of a noble. (Cusi describes being treated well by his captor, Pedro de Oñate, so well that Manco sent Oñate a message thanking him for his conduct). At this point Manco must have been at his lowest ebb, as he realized his remaining people needed somewhere more secure to hide from the Spaniards. And so the site of Vilcabamba was found, a small enclave hidden beneath an almost impenetrable cloak of rain-forest, at the northern end of a wide, low valley.

Yet as it transpired even this secluded hideaway proved insufficient, for just two years later Vilcabamba was attacked by Francisco Pizarro's half-brother Gonzalo and 300 Spanish soldiers. Once again, however, Manco managed to flee in time and the Spanish, though they caused chaos in Vilcabamba, were unable to find him.

After two unsuccessful attempts at catching the Inca, the Spanish authorities decided to embark upon less aggressive means to flush him out and switched to diplomacy. The strategy had started while Manco was on the throne, but as a man well used to Spanish duplicity, he gave these initiatives short shrift. Following his brutal death (see p223) in 1541, however, his successor, Sayri Tupac, proved to be more receptive to the Spaniards' friendly overtures, and in 1557 Tupac was lured out of his forest redoubt with sizeable rewards of property and money and went on to live a life of comfort in Cusco.

Titu Cusi

But if the Spanish thought this was the end of resistance in Vilcabamba, they were mistaken. Instead, the native empire continued much as it had done before, overcoming the loss of their leader by the simple expedient of replacing him with somebody else.

That somebody was Titu Cusi, the half-brother of Sayri Tupac. Captured at the battle of Vitcos and educated by the Spanish in Cusco, Titu Cusi was a wise and capable ruler. He was also one of the great chroniclers of the last years of the Inca empire, towards the end of his life dictating his memoirs which were later made into a book, *Relación*. His reign coincided with a period of relative peace and prosperity for the inhabitants of Vilcabamba, thanks in no small part

---

Opposite: Top: The ruins of Runcu Raccay (see p182), now thought to be a tambo, a rest-house for passing travellers. (Photo © Henry Stedman). **Bottom:** Impressive mortarless Inca walls can still be seen in parts of Cusco. (Photo © Richard Danbury).

to his skill as a negotiator and peacemaker, keeping the Spaniards off his territory by the simple method of ensuring that they never had a pretext to invade. Guerrilla raids on Spanish encomenidas and churches were discontinued under his rule, and by forbidding Spanish settlement in his territory, he thus prevented any arguments occurring between his people and the Spaniards that could escalate into something more serious. He also allowed two Spanish missionaries into Vilcabamba to preach to his people and was himself baptized into the Christian faith (though the traditional pagan rituals continued unabated).

Titu Cusi's policy of appeasement was vindicated on 24 August 1566 with the signing of a peace treaty with the Spaniards that allowed him to remain as ruler in Vilcabamba. But while Titu Cusi had opted for peaceful coexistence, his successor, Tupac Amaru, a legitimate son of Manco Inca, preferred confrontation. Not long after his accession the Spanish priests in Vilcabamba were killed in retaliation for the death of Titu Cusi (see p234), the borders of his kingdom were closed and all correspondence between the two sides came to an abrupt end.

The end of Vilcabamba

For the Spanish and their brutally efficient viceroy, Francisco de Toledo, the final straw came with the murder of one of their envoys to Vilcabamba, Atilano de Anaya, in 1572. An army of 250 Spaniards, along with two thousand friendly natives, was hastily mustered and on 14 April Toledo officially declared war on the state of Vilcabamba. The very next day an élite advance party set out on the long march from Cusco, and were soon occupying the strategically important bridge over the Urubamba at Chuquichaca (in modern-day Chaullay).

As was so often the case throughout the conquest, resistance to Spanish rule was extinguished with more of a whimper than a bang. Tupac Amaru had at his disposal only 1000 fighting men, nearly all of whom were still using the same weapons – stones, slings and axes – as their forefathers two centuries ago. The advancing army met with only one concerted defence on their march, and by the time Hurtado de Arbieto arrived to plant the Spanish flag in the middle of the plaza at Vilcabamba, on 24 June 1572, most of the inhabitants had already fled, having razed the city by fire before they departed.

Over the course of the next two months they were rounded up. Tupac Amaru had sought refuge in the jungle, taking with him the Punchao, the Sacred Idol of the Sun, the icon which in happier days had stood at the heart of the Coricancha in Cusco; the Inca himself was the last to be caught. Tupac Amaru preferred to trust in his Spanish pursuers rather than in the jungle tribes that were his native bodyguards. It was trust that was yet again to prove misplaced, and he was publicly executed in Cusco's Plaza de Armas after a sham trial.

His last words, likely testament to the tortures that had been inflicted on him, amounted to a betrayal of his Inca past. He said: 'Lords, you are here from all the four suyus. Be it known to you that I am a Christian, they have baptized me and I wish to die under the law of God. And I have to die. All that I and my ancestors the Incas told you up to now – that you should worship the sun Punchao and the huacas, idols, stones, rivers, mountains and vilcas – is completely false. When we told you that we were entering in to speak to the sun that it advised you to do what we told you, and that it spoke, this was false. It did not speak, we alone did; for it is an object of gold and cannot speak.'

Punchao, a gold figure the size of a small boy, was recovered by the Spanish but has never been seen again.

REAP ANOTHER WHIRLWIND

The other seed that was sown, that of Almagro's discontent, also grew and blossomed. Almagro returned from his gruelling Chilean venture in 1537, disappointed at the thin pickings of the place. He marched on Cusco, and took it, but his victory was short lived as the Pizarrists would not let go that easily. In 1538 when the Almagrists controlled the sierra and Pizarrists controlled the coast, confrontation was inevitable, and the matter was finally settled at the battle of Las Salinas in April. Diego de Almagro was captured, put on trial and executed.

He had his revenge from beyond the grave. On 26 June 1541 Francisco Pizarro was murdered by supporters of the dead Almagro. One story says that with his dying breath, Pizarro drew the sign of the cross on the floor with his blood. Another story says that his murderers crushed his hands as he was trying to make absolution and cried that he would have to confess his sins in Hell. So died the conqueror of Peru, murderer of Atahualpa and scourge of the Incas.

Epitaph
'OLD MARTIN: So fell Peru. We gave her greed, hunger and the Cross: three gifts for the civilised life. The family groups that sang on the terraces are gone. In their place slaves shuffle underground and they don't sing there. Peru is a silent country, frozen in avarice. So fell Spain, gorged with gold; distended; now dying'.
Peter Shaffer *Royal Hunt of the Sun*, Act 2 Scene 12.

Lima

'Lima the Horrible' was the rallying cry of a band of 1950s Peruvian intellectuals, and after a day or two in this smog-smothered city you may well end up agreeing with them. Certainly the noise, pollution and chaos, added to the need to be on constant alert against muggings, make Peru's capital a stressful place. But it would be harsh to write it off completely, and while it's unlikely anyone would come to Peru just to see Lima, there's enough here to keep you entertained as you prepare to head up to Cusco and Machu Picchu.

Cloaked in the thick, grey *garúa* (sea fog) that engulfs the city for most of the year are still some fine colonial buildings, informative, well laid-out museums and excellent seafood restaurants. The Limeños themselves are a good advertisement for their city – most are wonderfully welcoming.

HISTORY

Origins
People have lived here at the mouth of the Rímac river for the past 7000 years. When you fly into Jorge Chávez airport, you'll see from the aeroplane window some of the large adobe pyramids that these early Limeños built, now surrounded by Lima's urban sprawl. These date from about 3000BC, long before the arrival of the Spanish, long before even the Incas. They were built in the U-shaped style that's characteristic of the temples on this part of the Peruvian coast (see p69).

By the fifteenth century when the Incas arrived, the local shrine and oracle called Pachacamac was already ancient, having been established about 900 years earlier. The Incas absorbed it into their religion, building an *acllahuasi* (convent) at the site. They then occupied the district, and by the time the Spanish arrived there were about 400 temples along the river supported by a network of peaceful communities.

The days of conquest
In 1535 the city of Lima was founded on the banks of the Rímac by Francisco Pizarro, shortly after he'd captured Cusco. He wanted to build his capital close to the sea because this provided the Spaniards with contact to the motherland, and here was a good harbour with a reliable water supply. The city was called *Ciudad de los Reyes* (City of the Kings) after the Magi and the kings of Spain but the name didn't stick, and by the late sixteenth century the place was known as Lima, a corruption of Rímac.

Only a year after it was founded, the city was almost destroyed and the Spaniards pitched into the ocean during the revolt of Manco Inca (see p96). The Inca general, Quizo Yupanqui, besieged Lima but was destroyed by the power of the Spanish cavalry riding on flat ground. The failure to take Lima meant that the Incas could not cut the Spanish off from their lifeline to the sea, and the whole Inca rebellion was doomed.

Capital of Spanish Peru

The viceroy of Spanish South America lived in Lima, and the city attracted the trappings of power. It became a rich place. The University of San Marcos, the continent's oldest, was founded in 1551, and in 1569 the city became the seat of the Spanish Inquisition. An account survives of the entry of a new viceroy into the city in the eighteenth century that illustrates the wealth of the municipality. It describes streets hung with tapestries, local officials decked out in crimson velvet and brocade, and celebrations involving days of bullfights and banquets. This evidence of riches attracted the attentions of less welcome visitors, and Sir Francis Drake was the first of many privateers (pirates) to raid Lima when he attacked the port in 1579. The city walls were built as a result.

In 1746 there was a catastrophic earthquake, one of the many from which Peru has suffered. Most of the glorious old colonial buildings were reduced to dust; 16,000 people died from the quake and its ensuing plagues. A vivid eye-witness account runs: 'Monday 31st [three days later] there was a suffocating smell coming, not only from the countless corpses, but also from the dead horses, dogs and donkeys. The bodies were taken in cartloads to the cemetery where they were buried in large trenches.'

Capital of independent Peru

San Martín liberated Lima from the Spanish in 1821. He was criticized for delaying but said that he felt that the Limeños didn't want to be liberated: they were so plump with the opulence of Spain. San Martín waited until the locals discovered that there was to be no help from the mother country, at which they turned their loyalty to him. The viceroy escaped to the mountains with an army (see p40).

Charles Darwin visited in 1830 on his voyage aboard *The Beagle*, and provided a description of Lima post-independence: 'The city of Lima is now in a wretched state of decay: the streets are nearly unpaved, and heaps of filth are piled up in all directions; where the black gallinazos [vultures], tame as poultry, pick up bits of carrion. The houses have generally an upper story [sic], built, on account of the earthquakes, of plastered woodwork; but some of the old ones, which are now used by several families, are immensely large, and would rival in suites of apartments the most magnificent in any place. Lima, the City of the Kings, must formerly have been a splendid town.' (*The Voyage of the Beagle*).

The city walls were torn down in 1870 as Lima expanded. Although the land was needed for houses, the demolition of the walls was a mistake because in 1881 the city was occupied by the Chileans during the War of the Pacific (see p41). They didn't leave for two years.

More recent times

In 1920 there was a huge influx of poor, unskilled labour and the city's population grew to 170,000. President Leguía worked hard to rejuvenate the city, constructing sewers and building open places such as Plaza San Martín, but the sheer number of people here has been a problem ever since. The population is now over 8,000,000.

Many live in *pueblos jóvenes* (shanty towns) which aren't as bad as others in South America but are still pretty dismal places; unemployment and underemployment are rife. You'll no doubt be driven around by university graduates who work as *taxistas* because it's the only work there is, and for many from the pueblos jóvenes, the only work is on the street.

As with other capitals, there is another side to Lima, a face decorated with the wealth and opulence of the wealthy neighbourhoods of San Isidro and Miraflores, inhabited by people who can afford to shop for groceries in Miami.

ARRIVAL

A note of caution

Lima has a crime problem, and you need to be careful – see p60.

By air

There's a cambio in the arrivals terminal, a glass box of a building, and ATMs (for both soles and dollars) in the departures area. To get to the departures area, go through the doors at the end of the arrivals' hall, try to brush away the touts you will inevitably attract, turn left into the next door building. The cambio is on the right and the ATMs a little further on.

The centre of town is to the east of the airport. Most people stay in either **Lima Centro** or **Miraflores**, and to take you there the taxistas will ask for half as much again as you should be paying – they quote around s/25 to take you the 12km to Lima Centro but you should pay only about s/15 to s/20. A taxi to Miraflores should cost about s/5 more. Walk through the car park and hail a cab from the road and it's even cheaper, for taxi drivers have to pay a fee every time they enter the airport.

Incidentally, you may be accosted at the airport by people falsely claiming to work for the tourist board. They're mostly harmless, and indeed they can be positively helpful on occasions, though if you agree to take one of their taxis expect to pay double the going rate.

By bus

Many buses (s/1.20 from the airport) come in near to the Hotel Sheraton near the Parque Universitario, very near Lima Centro, but there isn't a central bus terminal in Lima, so the place at which you'll arrive will depend on which company you're travelling with and from where. It's best to take a taxi from the terminus to your hotel, as bus stops are a magnet for thieves.

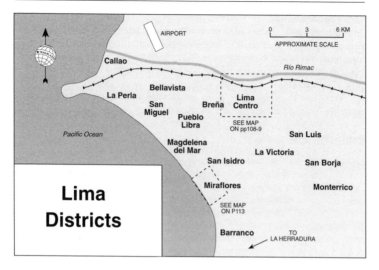

GETTING AROUND

Taxi

Most taxis in Lima are currently unregulated: they're just private cars displaying a 'Taxi' sticker but this is changing. If you see a cab with a number painted on the side of the door it's been registered with the authorities. Yellow cabs with numbers on the door are one stage further on; they're regulated. Both are less likely to try to cheat you.

Bus

The bus network in Lima is a mess. Apparently it all used to be better: buses that ran on particular routes were painted the same colour and there were timetables but nowadays the colours mean nothing and there's no real timetable. They do have their route number and destination written on their front and sides; your hotel will tell you which bus you need to get and from where. **Beware of pickpockets and bag-slashers**.

The main bus thoroughfares in Lima Centro are Av Alfonso Ugarte and Av Tacna, and in Miraflores it's Av Arequipa. The fare is s/1.20 to anywhere in town, or s/2 for outlying districts such as Barranco or Pachacamac.

Tours

Lima Vision (☎ 447 0482, 📄 446 9969 🖥 www.peruvision.com), Jr Chiclayo 444, Miraflores, offer half-day tours of the museums and the city for US$20-35, and a separate half-day tour out to Pachacamac for US$35. **Expediciones Viento Sur** (☎ 429 1414), Av Grau, La Punta, Callao, do cruises around the bay of Lima out towards San Lorenzo Island for US$35. (Abimael Guzman (see p44) is imprisoned on San Lorenzo Island). There are many other companies.

Car rental
Alamo (☎ 444 7000), Benavides 1180, Miraflores; **Budget** (☎ 442 8703, 🖹 441 4174), Canaval y Moreyra 569, Miraflores, and at the airport (☎ 575 1674); **Dollar** (☎ 444 3050, 444 4920), Cantuarias 341, Miraflores, and at the airport (☎ 575 1719); **Localiza** (☎ 242 3939), Av Benavides 735, Miraflores (☎ 242 3939). Prices are variable but range from US$30 to US$50 a day.

ORIENTATION

Lima is built on a flat plain above a large arc of a bay. It's a big place with many different neighbourhoods, and the distances between them are too great for walking.

Lima Centro is the ancient centre of the city on the banks of the Rímac, a good few miles inland from the sea. Plaza de Armas is here, as is the cathedral, the statues of Bolívar and San Martín, a pedestrian zone and many cheap hotels. To the south-west, close by, is the more residential district of **Breña**. To the north are the poorer suburbs. To the south-east is the industrial-commercial area of **La Victoria** and the suburbs of **San Luís** and **San Borja** where the Museo de la Nacíon is (see p117). Further out is the plusher **Monterrico** and the Museo de Oro del Peru (see p117).

Driving west from Lima Centro, you'll come to **Bellavista**, the sea and **Callao**, the port of Lima. There's a fort, a good view of the sea and some excellent cheap *cevicherías* (seafood restaurants selling the dish ceviche). Callao is really not as dangerous as some guidebooks make out, although it's wiser to be out of here by night.

Down the coast from Callao you'll pass through **San Miguel** where the zoo is; **Magdalena del Mar**, the posh embassy district of **San Isidro**; residential **Miraflores** with its more expensive hotels and North American airs, and bohemian **Barranco** with bars and night-life. You'll end up climbing El Morro, the hill which provides a first-class view of the coast and the city. Beyond El Morro is **La Herradura** – the name means 'horseshoe' because that's what the bay looks like.

Unless otherwise noted, addresses in this chapter are for Lima Centro.

SERVICES

Banks and cambios
The following banks have branches all over Lima: **Banco Latino** (MasterCard), Av Paseo de la Republica 3505; **Telebanco** (Visa), Jr de la Unión 790; **Banco Mercantil** (AMEX), Carabaya and Ucayali, **Citibank** (Citicorp), Ribeira Naearrete 857, San Isidro. For cambios try **Boulevard Tarata** at 248 Miraflores (☎ 444 3381), and many others, for example **Interbank**, Jr de la Unión 600, which is quick and gives good rates. **Western Unión** (☎ 422 0014), is at Miró Quesada 198 and Petit Thouars 3595, San Isidro.

```
◧◩◪◩◧◩◫◩◧◩◫◩◫◩◫◩◫◩◫◩◫◩◫◩◫◩◫◩◫◩◫◩◩
```

Embassies and consulates
Argentina (☎ 433 5704), Pablo Bermudez 143, 2nd Floor; **Austria** (☎ 442 0503, 442 1807), Av Central 643, 5th Floor, San Isidro; **Australia** (☎ 221 7020); **Bolivia** (☎ 422 8231), Los Castaños 235, San Isidro; **Brazil** (☎ 421 5650), José Pardo 850, Miraflores; **Canada** (☎ 444 4015), Jr F Gerdes (or Libertad) 130, Miraflores; **Chile** (☎ 221 2818), Javier Prado Oeste 790, San Isidro; **Colombia** (☎ 441 0530), Av Jorge Basadre 1580, San Isidro; **Ecuador** (☎ 442 4184), Las Palmeras 356, San Isidro; **France** (☎ 221 7598), Arequipa 3415, San Isidro; **Germany** (☎ 422 4919), Arequipa 4210, Miraflores; **Ireland** (☎ 446 3878), Angamos Oeste 340, Miraflores; **Israel** (☎ 433 4431) Natalio Sánchez 125, 6th Floor; **Italy** (☎ 463 2727), Gregorio Escobedo 298, Jesus María; **New Zealand** (☎ 221 2833); **Spain** (☎ 212 2155), Jorge Basadre 498, San Isidro; **United Kingdom** (☎ 433 8923), Natalio Sánchez 125, 4th Floor; **USA** (☎ 434 3000), Av la Encalada Cda 17, Monterrico.

```
◧◩◪◩◧◩◫◩◧◩◫◩◫◩◫◩◫◩◫◩◫◩◫◩◫◩◫◩◫◩◩
```

Books (English)
For books in English try **Ibero Librerias**, Benavides 500, Miraflores; or the **British Cultural Library** (☎ 221 7550), Av Arequipa 3495, San Isidro. The **SAEC** (see box p106) has a book exchange for members.

Communications
● **Telephone and fax** The code for Lima is ☎ 01. **Telefónica del Peru** (☎ 433 1616) is at Jr Carabaya 933, Plaza San Martín, but it's expensive and you'd be better off direct dialling from a pay phone in the street. Or, cheaper still, you can phone over the Internet. Check out **Cybersandeg** at 853 de la Unión near San Martín Square; they're welcoming and the staff will help you if you are unsure what to do.

● **Post** The main **post office** (*correo*), is on the block on the north-west corner of Plaza de Armas, open Monday to Saturday 8am-8pm, Sunday 9am-1pm. There's a poste restante here. For **American Express** client mail go to **Lima Tours** (☎ 222 2525, ▤ 222 5700), Pardo y Aliaga 698, San Isidro. The **SAEC** also holds mail for members.

● **Email** All Internet cafés charge approximately s/2.50 per hour. In Lima Centro there's **Carabaya@net**, Jr Carabaya 376 (2nd floor), or the **Internet café** underneath Hostel Espana, or you can try **Cybersandeg** (see above). In Miraflores there's the massive **Studio 2** at the corner of Prado and Ovalo, and **Cyberclub** at 455 Schell. The **SAEC** (see p106) allows members to use its computers to send and receive email.

Emergencies and medical services
● **Ambulance** Alerta Médica (☎ 225 4040); Cruz Roja (☎ 265 8783, 222 0222), or take a taxi.
● **Doctor** Dr Alejandro Rivera (☎ 471 2238) at Instiuto Médico Lince, León Velarde 221, speaks English.

```
□ 🔲🔲 🔲🔲 🔲🔲🔲🔲 🔲🔲 🔲🔲 🔲🔲🔲🔲🔲🔲🔲
```

South American Explorers' Club (SAEC)

This useful club for travellers in South America provides a wide range of assistance to members – everything from storing equipment to helping to find a trekking partner; from reconfirming flights to holding mail, faxes and email. There's a good library of books in English and reports, written by other travellers, on just about every corner of Peru. The people who run the place are a fount of helpful information on everything from train times to more complex issues such as the current political situation in the highlands. There's a comfortable lounge where you can escape Lima's bustle, and the place contains what is probably the only Arsenal football club shirt in the whole of the continent.

SAEC (☎ 445 3306, 🖳 limaclub@saexplorers.org, www.saexplorers.org) is at Calle Piura 135 in Miraflores. They're open Monday to Friday, 9.30am-5pm (to 8pm on Wednesday), and on Saturday, 9.30am to 1pm. Membership costs US$50 per year (US$75 for couples). There's a branch in Cusco, now at Choquechaca 188, ☎ 84-245484, 🖳 cuscoclub@saexplorers.org). There are also other branches in Quito, Ecuador, and in the USA.

```
□ 🔲🔲 🔲🔲 🔲🔲🔲🔲🔲🔲 🔲🔲 🔲🔲 🔲🔲🔲🔲🔲🔲🔲
```

● **Hospitals** Anglo-American (☎ 221 3656), Alfredo Salazar, Cda 3, San Isidro; Maison de Santé (☎ 467 0753), Chorrillos.
● **Pharmacy** Botica Inglés, Jr Cailloma 336, is well stocked.
● **Rabies** Anti-rabies centre (☎ 425 6313).

Laundry

There aren't many laundries in Lima Centro, but most hotels will do laundry for a price. In Miraflores, try **Servrap**, Schell 601.

Maps

● **Lima** Maps of the city can be bought at kiosks and tourist shops, but there's a full map with index of streets in the back of the *Páginas Amarillas* (Yellow Pages) which you'll find at your hotel.
● **Hiking maps** The **Instituto Geográfico Nacional** (☎ 475 9960, 475 3090, 🖹 475 9810), Av Aramburú 1198, Surquillo (take a taxi there), open Monday to Friday 8am-12pm, 1-5.30pm sells good 1:100,000 maps of the hikes in this book. You can also pick these up at the **SAEC** (see above).

Police

Tourist police (☎ 460 0844 and 460 1003) or toll free from a private phone (☎ 0800-42579).

Tourist information

The official tourist information office is one block west of Plaza de Armas at Paseo de los Escribanos 125 (☎ 427 4848), though they proved to be less than helpful whenever I called in. Your best bet is to visit **InfoPeru** (☎ 431 0117, 🖳 infoperu@qnet.com.pe, Mon-Fri 9.30am-6pm, Saturday 9.30am-2pm), Jr de la Unión (Belén) 1066, almost opposite Hostal La Estrella de Belén; it's not the office that faces onto the street, but go through the archway and it's on your right. Privately owned, the office is genuinely helpful, the staff knowledgeable and English-speaking, and there's a refreshing lack of any hard-sell tactics too.

There are lots of other places offering tourist information but they're generally trying to sell you something.

Visa extension
Direccion General de Migraciones y Naturalizacion (DIGEMIN) (☎ 330 4020), Av España 700-734, Breña. They charge s/12 for every extension.

WHERE TO STAY

The districts of Lima Centro and Miraflores have the highest concentration of hotels and services for tourists. Of the two, Lima Centro is dirtier, noisier and has greater crime problem but is more central and cheaper. In the following list I have also included a couple of hotels in the exclusive district of San Isidro, home to many of the consulates and big businesses. Note that the more expensive hotels will add 28% tax to their rates.

Incidentally, if you're staying in Lima's lower-budget accommodation, here are two bathroom tips that will improve your holiday no end: firstly, throw your toilet paper in the bin provided rather than down the toilet, or you'll block it; and secondly, if you're struggling to get hot water in the shower, try turning the tap just slightly rather than all the way.

Note: the following abbreviations are used here: **com = room with common bathroom; att = bathroom attached; sgl/dbl/tpl = single/double/triple**.

Lima Centro
● **Budget accommodation** The first mention has to be *Hostal España* (☎ 427 9196/428 5546), Azangaro 105, close to the Church of San Francisco. Top of the list of places to stay in some guidebooks, this has inevitably become gringo central. It's an old building with an interior courtyard; it has lockers, an Internet café, an information service and a rooftop restaurant that doubles as a kind of mini-zoo. Beds in the dorm cost US$3, singles/doubles are US$6/9 and there are even a few triples at US$12 each. If it's full, there's *Hostal Europa* (☎ 427 3351), Ancash 376, around the corner which costs the same and offers a similar package but not to the same standard.

I prefer *Pensión Ibarra* (☎ 427 8603/427 1035, ✉ pension_Ibarra@letera.net), Av Tacna 359, 14th and 15th floors, Flat Nos 1402 and 1502, a place where your mother would be happy for you to stay. There's no sign outside, and it's in a tower block, but it's safe, has a fridge and cooker and good views. The women who run it are helpful and do laundry, and if you book ahead they'll

---

Lima area code: ☎ 01. If phoning from outside Peru dial ☎ +51-1.

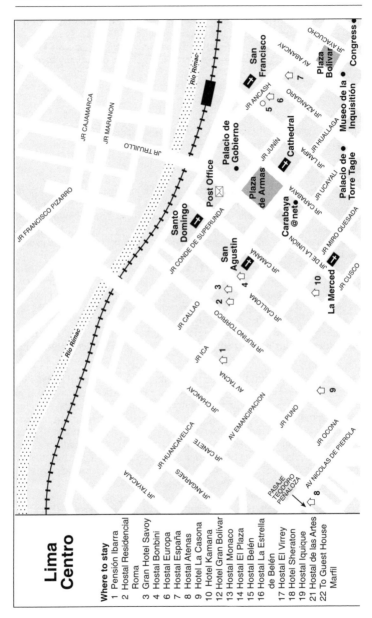

Lima Centro

Where to stay
1 Pensión Ibarra
2 Hostal Residencial Roma
3 Gran Hotel Savoy
4 Hostal Bonbini
6 Hostal Europa
7 Hostal España
8 Hostal Atenas
9 Hotel La Casona
10 Hotel Kamana
12 Hotel Gran Bolívar
13 Hostal Monaco
14 Hostal El Plaza
15 Hostal Belén
16 Hostal La Estrella de Belén
17 Hostal El Virrey
18 Hotel Sheraton
19 Hostal Iquique
21 Hostal de las Artes
22 To Guest House Marfil

11 JR ANDAHUAYLAS

JR PARURO

JR CUSCO

JR AYACUCHO

Central Market

JR UCAYALI

JR MIRO QUESADA

AV ABANCAY

JR PUNO

JR CUSCO

JR AZANGARO

JR LAMPA

JR CARABAYA

JR DE LA UNION

Plaza San Martin

12

JR OCOÑA

15

16

AV NICOLAS DE PIEROLA

14

Parque Universitario

AV ROOSEVELT

JR PACHITA

JR BELEN

17

AV NICOLAS DE PIEROLA

JR LETICIA

AV GRAU

JR MONTEVIDEO

JR COTABAMBAS

MIGUEL **Palacio de Justicia**

AV GRAU

Plaza Grau

18

PASEO DE LA REPUBLICA

Museo de Arte Italiano

Museo de Arte

AV GARCILASO DE LA VEGA

JR QUILCA

JR DAVALOS

13

JR LISSON

AV WASHINGTON

AV URUGUAY

AV BOLIVIA

AV ESPAÑA

AV 9 DE DICIEMBRE

Where to eat
5 Machu Picchu
11 Chinese Restaurants (both sides of street)
20 La Choza Nautica

300m
APPROXIMATE SCALE
330 yards

0

0

ALFONSO UGARTE

21

Plaza Bolognesi

22

AV PORTUGAL

BREÑA

20

19

IQUIQUE

VISA EXTENSIONS

even pick you up from the airport. Rooms cost s/15/30-35 (sgl/dbl, com), though the singles are a little grubby. If tower blocks turn you off, try **Hotel La Casona** (☎ 426 6552, 🖳 casonahotel@latinmail.com), Moquega 289, a wonderful old tiled building. The beds are a bit soft and the rooms a bit tatty, but it's well priced at s/20 per room (sgl/dbl), or s/30 with attached bathroom. It is, however, less secure than other hotels.

Hostal Iquique (☎ 433 4724, 🖺 423 3699, 🖳 barrioperu.terra.com.pe/hiquique), Jr Iquique 758, Breña, is recommended as it's safe, very helpful, friendly and light and clean – though the ground floor rooms smell musty. It costs s/25-32/40-52 (double com/att), and there are discounts if you're a member of the SAEC.

If you're after the **lowest prices**, there's a road of cheap hostals in Pasaje Teodoro Peñaloza (off Nicolas de Pierola), charging s/8 a night (single, com). Don't expect much, and be careful. Around the corner, there's **Hostal Atenas** (☎ 330 5149), Nicolas de Pierola 370, which is s/12/22 (sgl/dbl, com), gringo-free, pretty clean with a lovely painted lobby, and a little less sleazy than the others around here; while just to the north of Jr Lisson is **Hostal Monaco** (☎ 330 3861), Washington 949 – the same kind of thing without the interior decoration at s/12/18 (sgl/dbl, com).

The best value hotel in this price range, however, is the wonderful **Hostal de las Artes** (☎ 433 0031, 🖳 www.arteswelcome.tripod.com) at Jr Chota 1460, just to the north of Plaza Bolognesi. From the beautiful tiled lobby to the comfy rooms, this Dutch-owned place oozes class, and is very affordable too at s/22/32 (sgl/dbl, com), s/27/40 (sgl/dbl, att). Not far behind in terms of quality, though unfortunately in an inconvenient location to the south of Centro in Pueblo Libre, is **Guest House Marfil** (☎ 463 3161, 🖳 yma25@yahoo.com) at Parque Ayacucho 126, between the third and fourth blocks of Av Bolivar. Rooms cost just US$6 per person per night, English is spoken, kitchen and laundry facilities are provided and the owners even offer Spanish classes.

● **Mid-range hotels** A similar type of place to Hostal Iquique, though in a building with more character, is the good **Hostal Residencial Roma** (☎ 427 7576, 🖺 427 7572, 🖳 resroma@terra.com.pe, www.itete.com.pe/resroma), Jr Ica 326. The people who run the Roma are helpful and polyglot, and charge US$10/15 (sgl/dbl, com), US$13/20 (sgl/dbl, att, cable TV extra), which is a little too much.

Hostal Belén (☎ 427 8995, 🖳 artobel@computextos.net), Jr Unión/Bélen 1049, is also in a rambling old building, and has clean lavatories but soft beds in rooms that some people will find poky. The communal areas are light and airy, and there's a wonderful old marble staircase. It costs s/22/35/50 (sgl/dbl/tpl, all com). Next door is the not very friendly **Hostal La Estrella de Belén** (☎ 428 6462), Jr Unión/Bélen 1051. It is, nevertheless, clean and modern and charges s/40/50/80 (sgl/dbl/tpl, att).

At the more expensive end is the recommended, business-orientated **Hotel Kamana** (☎ 426 7204, 🖺 426 0790, 🖳 kamana@amauta.rcp.net.pe), Jr Camana 547, used by tour companies. It's well run if a little antiseptic; sgl/dbls cost

US$37/46. *Hostal El Virrey* (☎ 426 8305, 🖳 www.perutravelnet.com/elvirrey), Av F Roosevelt 115 – don't confuse it with Hostal los Virreyes – is also good at US$/20/25-35 (sgl/dbl, att), and you're getting the same views as you get at the Sheraton. You could try *Gran Hotel Savoy* (☎ 428 3520, 🖺 426 0840, 🖳 reser vas@hotelsavoyperu.com, www.hotelsavoyperu.com), Jr Cailloma 224, where a stay in a genuine 1950s hotel room will cost you US$/3045 (sgl/dbl, att, includes breakfast), or the smart and stylish *Hostal Bonbini* (☎ 427 6492, 🖺 427 3027), opposite at No 209, where their spacious rooms go for s/106/142 (sgl/dbl, att with cable TV). Finally, there's *Hostal El Plaza* (☎ 428 6274, 🖳 hp laza@ddm.co.pe), Nicolás de Piérola 850, which is better decorated than its neighbours and charges US$25/30 (sgl/dbl, att).

● **Expensive hotels** If you're going to splurge on an expensive hotel don't stay in Lima Centro, go to Miraflores. If you must be based here the best hotel is the *Lima Sheraton* (☎ 315 5000/5022, 🖺 315 5024), Paseo de la Republica 170, where you can stay in a standard Sheraton room tinged with Lima shabbiness for US$170 plus tax (double, att).

Hotel Gran Bolívar (☎ 426 7438, 428 7672/3, 🖺 428 7675, 🖳 Bolivar @terra.com.pe), Jr de La Uníon 958, just off Plaza San Martín, has a beautiful lobby – check out the glass ceiling – and it's much more classy than the Sheraton; it's considerably cheaper at US$102/115 (sgl/dbl, att, breakfast), but the rooms are disappointing and there seems to be a shortage of staff.

Miraflores and San Isidro
● **Budget accommodation** A few youth hostels have opened up in Miraflores recently. *Albergue Juvenil* (Youth Hostel; ☎ 446 5488, 🖺 444 8187, 🖳 www.limahostell.com.pe), Av Casimiro Ulloa 328, Miraflores, is the best known and longest established, with clean, spacious rooms, lockers, and a travel agency, though the staff can be a little trying at times; it costs US$10 (discount for members). More friendly is *Hiker's House* (☎ 445 9763, 🖳 hik ers@hikershouse.com), in a very central location at Calle Frederíco Recavarren 427, to the north of Av Benavides; rates are the same as at the youth hostel. Also charging the same is *Albergue Juvenil Kusi Wasi* (☎ 444 1983, 🖳 kusiwasi @terra.com.pe), at Av José Pardo 991, with two-, three- and four-bed rooms, hot water round the clock and kitchen and laundry facilities; rates include breakfast. Better value at US$5 per person is the cut-price *Albergue Juvenil Malka* (☎ 222 5589, 🖳 hostelmalka@terra.com.pe), at Los Lirios 165; it's friendly and comfortable enough, but unfortunately rather inconveniently located in San Isidro, though it is close to Av Arequipa from where you can catch buses to Miraflores and Lima Centro.

● **Mid-range hotels** Most of these hotels have cable TV, fan and phone in the room. At the lower end of the scale is *Hostal Bellavista de Miraflores* (☎ 445 7834, 🖺 444 2938), Jr Bellavista 215, Miraflores, centrally located with a pleasant courtyard at US$40/45 (sgl/dbl, com, breakfast, att extra). *Hostal el Carmelo* (☎ 4460575, 🖳 carmelo@amautoa.rcp.net.pe), Bolognesi 749, Miraflores, is trying hard, and has a good location close to the sea-front Parque

KEY TO MIRAFLORES MAP (OPPOSITE)

Where to stay
1 Albergue Juvenil Kusi Wasi
3 Hiker's House
4 Hostal El Carmelo
5 Residencial Las Americas
6 Hotel Las Palmas
7 Hostal Bellavista de Miraflores
9 Aparthotel Sol de Oro
10 Hotel Las Americas

11 Suites Eucalyptus
12 Hostal Señorial
13 Hostal Lucerna
14 Albergue Juvenil (Youth Hostel)
15 Hotel San Antonio Abad

Where to eat
2 Brujas de Cachiche
8 Café Café

al Amor. Singles/doubles (att) with breakfast are US$35/45 but you can probably bargain them down.

Hostal Lucerna (☎ 445 7321, 🖷 446 6050, 🖳 lucerna@junin.itete.com.pe), Las Dalias 276, Miraflores, is a good, clean hotel with a lovely garden and costs US$50/58 (sgl/dbl, att). The recommended *Suites Eucalyptus* (☎ 445 8594, 🖷 444 3071, 🖳 www.tsi.com.pe/eucaliptus), San Martín 511, is more imaginative, with studies of famous artworks in the rooms. There's no garden here. Rates start at US$33/41 (sgl/dbl, all att).

At the top end of this price bracket is *Hostal Señorial* (☎ 444 5755/445 9724), José Gonzáles 567, Miraflores, a colonial house with a lovely courtyard, good rooms and parking, and a gym, Jacuzzi and sauna. They charge US$40/50/60 (sgl/dbl/tpl, att, breakfast included).

Worth considering is *Hotel las Palmas* (☎ 444 6033, 🖷 444 6036, 🖳 hpalmas@mail.macrostudio.net, www.macrostudio.net/laspalmas), Bellavista 320, Miraflores. It's central, adequate but lacks charm; rooms are inexpensive, however, at US$20/28 (sgl/dbl, att). *Hotel San Antonio Abad* (☎ 447 6766, 🖷 446 4208, 🖳 hotelsanantonioabad@mail.com, www.ascinsa.co m/sanantonioabad), Ramón Ribeyro 301, Miraflores, is recommended. Run by a helpful, polyglot manager (he even speaks Japanese), this is a good, safe, clean place costing US$45/55 (sg/dbl, att, breakfast).

● **Expensive hotels** If you want something flashy stay at *Hotel Las Americas* (☎ 241 2820, 444 7272, 🖷 444 1137, 🖳 www.hoteleslasamericas.com), Benavides 415, a five-star hotel with everything you'd expect for US$180 plus tax. If you haven't got that sort of money, you could try their other establishment the *Residencial Las Americas* (☎ 242 6600, 🖷 242 5976, 🖳 www.hoteleslasamericas.com), Bellavista 216. Suites here begin at US$70 plus tax. Also worth a splurge is *Sol de Oro* (☎ 446 9876, 🖷 447 0967, 🖳 www.soldeoro.com.pe), San Martín 305, an aparthotel, where suites start at US$130 plus tax. Be warned, however, that I have had a report of stuff being taken from rooms here. Finally, there's *Swissotel* (☎ 421 4400, 🖷 421 4422, 🖳 reservations@swisslim.com.pe), Via Central 150, Centro Empresarial Real. They charge from US$195 a night; unfortunately, once again the hotel is located out in San Isidro.

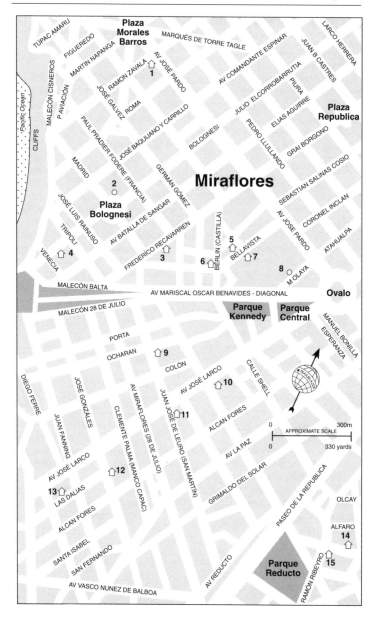

WHERE TO EAT AND DRINK
Lima caters for every palate and pocket. You may not be here for long, but there's no reason to suffer at mealtimes.

Budget food
There are lots of cheap eating places in **Lima Centro**. The restaurant without a name under Hostal Europa (see p107) is fine for breakfasts; try the Americano (egg, bread, jam, tea/coffee, juice) at s/4.50. Just along the road are some good places for lunch: *Bar-Restaurant Machu Picchu* (Ancash 312), which seems overpriced until you see the size of the portions, and *Restaurant Chessman* (Ancash 273). At Av Breña 204-209 you'll find a good cevichería, *La Choza Nautica*.

There's a string of cevicherías by La Puenta in **Callao**. It'd be a shame to pick any one of them out; they're all excellent, and the fish is so light it almost floats off the plate but try *Chifa Marina*. There are other good cheap cevicherías by the fish market on the south of the bay near the Playa Aqua Dulce, underneath El Morro.

In **Miraflores** you can still get a good s/3.50 lunch in the restaurants in the side roads around Larco and Benavides: try the *causa rellena* (spiced potato cake) if you see it. In **Barranco** you can get an excellent traditional dinner in the restaurants under the Puente de Sospiros; walk down towards the sea, they're on your left. Try the *jalea* (fried whitebait) or the *chupe de camarones* (prawn chowder). If you're brave have *anticucho* (beef heart kebabs), which are surprisingly tender and taste a little like roast liver.

Mid-priced restaurants
For a traditional meal with a song, try *Brisas del Titicaca*, Jr Walkuski 168, or *Manos Morenas*, Av Pedro de Osma 409, Barranco. Shows generally start at about 10pm.

There's decent, if a little overpriced, international food (sea bass, filet mignon) with a Peruvian touch in a relaxing dining-room, at *La Ermita*, Bajada de Baños 340, Barranco. If you're a confirmed carnivore and fancy a challenge, try to get through the *parilladas* (mixed grill) at *La Carreta,* Av Rivera Navarrete 740, San Isidro.

There are **pizza restaurants** around Parque Kennedy by the Diagonal, particularly on Berlin (Castilla); they're overpriced, boring and safe. *McDonald's* and *Burger King* are also on Parque Kennedy.

Finally, there's Lima's **Chinese restaurants**. Lima has the largest Chinese community in South America, and the Chinese food here is said to be the best on the continent. The best place to head to for Oriental fare is Capon, to the east of Jr Abancay.

Expensive restaurants
Though it's not cheap, the restaurant at Hotel Gran Bolívar (see p111) is good value; for a lot less than other, flashier restaurants in the city, you can sample some of the best cuisine in Lima. The food at *Brujas de Cachiche*, Bolognesi

460, Miraflores, who specialize in preparing traditional dishes, is excellent – try *ceviche* here if you're not going to risk it anywhere else.

Another top-rate restaurant is **La Rosa Nautica** at Costa Verde, on the end of the pier off the beach below Miraflores. Its location is unrivalled in the whole of Lima, and the food's good.

Cafés and bars

In Lima Centro, two good bars popular with ex-pats are **El Rincón Cervecero**, Jr de la Unión 1045, and the football-mad **Estadio F.C.** at Jr Nicolás de Piérola 926; if you're desperate for a fix of European football, this is the place to come. If neither of these appeal, go to Sentarosa, immediately to the west of Plaza de Armas, which has a number of cosmopolitan bars; they're all overpriced, but they do have the advantage of being within staggering distance of the cheaper hostels.

Café Café, Matir Olaya 250, Miraflores, serves large portions of well-cooked, unchallenging dishes (lomo cordon bleu and milanesa) in a jazzy café with good music, and claims to have a hundred different blends of coffee. If you're after a French-style café there's the French-run **Café de Paris** (Jr Diez Canseco 180, Miraflores – near Larco, just south of Parque Kennedy), where the brasserie-style food is good.

A good place to sit and watch the sun set over the Pacific is **La Posada del Mirador**, Calle Ermita 104, Barranco. Cross the Puente de los Suspiros from the plaza, turn left and walk towards the viewpoint. Pick up some *picarones* (doughnuts with honey) from one of the small cafés on the way. If you want live music, **La Estación**, Av Pedro de Osma 112, Barranco, usually has a Latin singer accompanied on a guitar. For dancing, there's **Break Club** at 1551 Arequipa (Thurs to Sat only), or **Sargento Pimienta** (Sgt Pepper) at Bolognesi 755, Barranco. There are also many discos in the Diagonal in Miraflores.

WHAT TO SEE

You'll probably want to spend as little time in Lima as possible while you sort out your transport to Cusco, but there's lots you could see and do here. Some of it you may not consider seeing unless you are really interested in pre-Hispanic South American ceramics or eighteenth-century colonial Spanish church architecture, so what follows is a short guide to the best of Lima's sights tailored for the person heading out to Machu Picchu.

Lima Centro

● **Plaza de Armas** Plaza de Armas is a nobly proportioned plaza built on the site of an ancient Inca square. Behind high metal railings, the **Palacio de Gobierno** (Government Palace: irregular opening hours, free) takes up the whole of one side of the plaza, and red and purple-uniformed guards parade in the courtyard every morning, usually at 8am. On the right of this building is the **Cathedral** (variable opening hours Monday to Saturday, 10am-4.30pm, entrance s/4, s/3 students), the construction of which first began in 1535. It's been rebuilt a number of times since, and was completely flattened in the 1746 earthquake. The structure you see dates from 1758. Francisco Pizarro's remains lie to the right of the entrance, surrounded by colourful mosaics. Set between the Government Palace and the cathedral is the **Archbishop's Palace**, with its delicate carved wooden balcony.

On the opposite side of the square, running away from the Rímac is **Jíron de la Unión**, a pedestrian precinct lined with cheap shops and fried chicken restaurants.

● **Palacio de Torre Tagle** Now occupied by the Foreign Ministry, this eighteenth-century mansion is one of Lima's colonial pearls. You can poke your head into the patio during office hours and relish the fine balcony and intricate carvings. There's a sixteenth-century carriage in the main courtyard with a built-in commode.

● **Church of San Francisco** (7am-12pm and 4.30-8pm, entrance s/5) One of the few large buildings to survive Lima's earthquakes, this church was consecrated in 1673. It's a very pretty building, but the main attractions are the **catacombs** of the monastery, still piled with the bones of 70,000 of the city's dead (entrance another s/5).

● **La Merced** (8am-12.30pm, 4-9pm, free). There's been a church here since Lima's first mass was celebrated on this spot. It's such an important place that the Virgin of La Merced, the patroness of the religious order that lives here, has been made a marshal in the Peruvian military. The building itself has a façade of dauntingly ornate baroque, a frontage worthy of its importance, constructed from white Panamanian granite which made its way to Lima as ballast in cargo galleons. It's been rebuilt several times.

Other districts

Callao La Puenta (the Point) is refreshingly exposed to the sea breeze and can make a pleasant change from the claustrophobic atmosphere of Lima Centro.

Nearby there's **Castle of Real Felipe** (open daily, 8am-12pm, 1-6pm, s/5, s/3 students), a squat, solid piece of military architecture, completed in 1767. Inside you'll find the **Military Museum** (same hours, no further charge) and around the corner is the **Naval Museum** (Av Jorge Chavez 121, Monday to Friday 9am-5pm, Saturday and Sunday 9am-4pm, entrance s/5, s/3 students). Both of these museums yield an interesting insight into the minds of the Peruvian military, and a lot of space is devoted to explaining why they lost the War of the Pacific to Chile (see p41).

Barranco Definitely worth a visit, this is a great place to relax over a chilled beer while you watch the sunset over the Pacific. Barranco is where Lima's artists and musicians gather, and during the day the pace of life is more gentle here than in the rest of the city. Courting couples frequent the Puente de los Suspiros (Bridge of Sighs). At night, this is a place for dancing and drinking. Catch a bus from Av Tacna in Lima Centro or Av Arequipa in Miraflores.

Miraflores Miraflores is Lima's modern suburb with good views over the sea, North American franchise restaurants and high-rise hotels. It's a pleasant enough place if you like these kinds of things, but it's rather characterless. It gets a bit more lively in the evenings, and the place has a thriving night-life. The central Parque Kennedy (also called 7 de Junio – the name changes often but it's the same park) has a very good weekend **art and craft market** at lunchtime, especially on Sundays. The standard of work for sale is, on the whole, very high, not your usual tacky water-colours; it's expensive though. To reach here from Lima Centro, jump on any bus from Av Tacna that's heading down Av Arequipa (listen out for the conductor's cries of 'Todo Arequipa').

San Miguel San Miguel contains the zoo (☎ 464 4282, usually 9am-5pm, s/6) in the **Parque de las Leyendas**. Even if you don't like zoos, this is a better place to catch up on your Peruvian wildlife than the **Natural History Museum** (Arenales 1256, Jesús María; Mon-Fri 9am-4pm, Sat 9am-5pm, Sun 9am-1pm, s/2.50, s/1.50 students) – at least the animals are alive. There's also an ancient adobe pyramid in the grounds.

Recommended museums
● **Museo de la Nación** (☎ 476 9875; Av Javier Prado Este 2465, San Borja) open Tuesday to Sunday, 9am-6pm, entrance s/6, students s/3. A splendid museum, well laid out and informative. This is an ideal place to put in context all the ancient things you're going to see in Peru, and includes scale models of many of the Inca sights around Cusco. They also have folk dancing exhibitions on Sundays at 5pm. To get here, catch a bus to Javier Prado from Av Tacna in Lima Centro, or from Av Arequipa in Miraflores, and a second along Javier Prado to the museum.
● **Museo Nacional de Antropología y Arqueología** (☎ 463 5070, Place Bolívar, Pueblo Libre) open Monday to Saturday 9am-5pm, Sunday and holidays 10am-5pm, entrance s/10, s/3 students. This is a bit of a prim maiden aunt compared to the flashy Museo de la Nación, but it's a good place: it contains the original objects of which the Nación only has copies. Look for the icons of Chavín (see p70): the Raimondi Stela (if you look at it upside down the image reads completely differently, see p71) and the Tello Obelisk (a sculpture of a male and female cayman), and the Paracas mummies looking rather shocked at having been dug up after centuries under the sands. The model of Machu Picchu will clarify the lay-out of the original when you get there. On the corner of the square you can quench your thirst at the friendly café. From Centro, catch a bus to Av Brasil from Tacna, jump out at block 22 and go west along Av Vivanca. The bus to Av Brazil from Miraflores leaves from Av Pardo.
● **Museo de Oro del Peru** The Gold Museum (☎ 435 2917; Calle Alonso de Molina 1100, Monterrico) is open daily, 11.30am-7pm, entrance s/20. This private collection contains a staggering display of pre-Hispanic gold (though many of the gold pieces on display are copies), Paracas textiles and ceramics including Moche erotic pots. It's wise to have some idea about Peru's pre-history before you come here – go to the Mueso de la Nación first as the Museo de Oro won't teach you much: everything is just stuffed in cupboards or laid on tables without explanation. There's also an excellent bookshop, and a large display of military objects

connected with important people from South American history. From Lima Centro catch a bus to Av Angamos in Miraflores and from there to Monterrico.

● **Museo del Tribunal de la Santa Inquisición** (Plaza Bolívar, Calle Junín 548, open Monday to Friday 9am-8pm, Saturday 9am-5pm). The headquarters of the South American Spanish Inquisition. The tribunal room is beautiful with its carved wooden ceiling, and the dungeons show the unbelievable tortures that went on downstairs.

Pachacamac

Thirty kilometres south of Lima is the ancient shrine and oracle of Pachacamac (daily 9am-4pm s/5, s/2 students); you can get here on one of the buses which leave every couple of hours from Av Abancay or Av Grau in Centro (look for Lurin-Pachacamac s/2; 1hr 20mins). The pyramids are on the whole badly pre-served, and to the untrained eye tend to look like piles of dry mud but some, like the acllahuasi (see p101), have been reconstructed.

The Spaniards would have looted Pachacamac to collect Atahualpa's ran-som (see p93) but it had been stripped by the priests before they arrived. There's a description of what the main shrine looked like in those times, written by the conquistador, Miguel de Estete: 'Its locked door was closely studded with a variety of objects – corals, turquoises, crystals and other things. This was even-tually opened, and we were certain that the interior would be as curious as the door. But it was quite the contrary. It certainly seemed to be the devil's cham-ber, for he always lives in filthy places... It was very dark and did not smell very pleasant'.

SHOPPING

Centro Artesenal, Camino Real 485, San Isidro, is a rather bland Peruvian crafts market. For a more challenging experience and a larger choice, go to the massive **Artesanaria** between 600 and 1000 on Av de la Marina out towards Pueblo Libre. A taxi here from Lima Centro will cost you around s/6. There's also a weekend arts market in **Parque Kennedy** in Miraflores.

There are dozens of overpriced shops to the west of Plaza de Armas; most of the stuff on offer is rather naff, but if you're at the end of your holiday it's your last chance to purchase that life-sized cuddly llama you've been promis-ing yourself.

MOVING ON

By air to Cusco

Lima to Cusco takes about an hour and a one-way ticket costs US$69. Currently, AeroContinente (three early morning flights daily) and Lan Peru (three flights per day) both make the flight.

Overland to Cusco (see map p121)

Travelling overland by bus (or by bus and train) is by far the more scenic way to get to Cusco, even if it does take a lot longer. There are two main routes, via

---

AIRLINE INFORMATION

Airline offices in Lima
AeroContinente (☎ 242 4242), Av Pardo 651, Miraflores; **Aerolineas Argentinas** (☎ 444 0810), José Pardo 805, 3rd Floor, Miraflores; **Air France** (☎ 444 9285), Av José Pardo 601, Miraflores; **Alitalia** (☎ 442 8507), Martir Oláya 129 off 1703, Miraflores; **American Airlines** (☎ 211 7000), Canaval y Moreyra 390, San Isidro; **British Airways** (☎ 422 6600), Andalucía 174 (between 42 and 43 Av Arequipa); **Continental** (☎ 221 4340), Victor Andrés Belaúnde 147, V Principal 110, Office 101, San Isidro; **Iberia** (☎ 421 4616), Av Camino Real No 390, Central Tower, 9th Floor, Office 902, San Isidro; **KLM** (☎ 242 1240), José Pardo 805, 6th Floor, Miraflores; **Lan Chile** (☎ 241 5522), José Pardo 805, 5th Floor, Miraflores; **Lan Peru** (☎ 446 6995, 🖹 215 1818), Paz Soldan 225, San Isidro; **Lloyd Aereo Boliviana** (☎ 241 5510), José Pardo 231, 1st and 7th Floors, Miraflores; **Lufthansa** (☎ 442 4455), Av Jorge Basadre 1330, San Isidro; **Varig** (☎ 442 4361), Camino Real 456, Office 803-804, San Isidro.

Lima airport
General enquiries (☎ 575 1434, 575 0912), **national flights** (☎ 574 5529), **international flights** (☎ 575 1712).

---

the highlands and via **Arequipa**. The most travelled route is via Arequipa because it's shorter and the roads are better; in the rainy season the highland roads can become completely washed away.

For details of bus companies, see p120.

Highland routes The **northern** route goes from Lima inland to La Oroya, turns south-east to Huancayo and Ayacucho, and then heads to Abancay and Cusco. There's no direct **bus** – you take one from Lima to Huancayo and then change. It takes about 50 hours and costs about US$30. There is a railway from Lima to Huancayo but at the time of writing no trains were running on it.

The **southern** route follows the coast, visiting Pisco before heading inland to Ayacucho and then passing through Abancay to reach Cusco. This takes about 35 to 40 hours and costs about US$25. Catch the bus from Lima to Ayacucho where you change to the Abancay or Cusco bus.

There is a third route via Nazca and Abancay; for years this was shut because of banditry, and although it has now reopened, few companies use this road even though it is the quickest at about 24 hours. The Molina bus company at Jr Ayacucho 114 was promising to start a service on this route soon; check with the SAEC (see p106).

All these routes were closed to travellers for many years, but are now opening up again. Don't, as I did, read Mario Vargas Llosa's novel *Death in the Andes* on the bus to Cusco, as it starts with a description of two French tourists taking the highland bus and getting held up and murdered by the Sendero Luminoso.

Arequipa route The other way to travel to Cusco is via Arequipa. It looks like a terrible detour on the map, but in fact it's one of the quickest overland routes at about 30 hours for the entire trip. Anyway, Arequipa is a very pretty city and you might be able to fit in a climb up the volcano El Misti or a trek down the Colca Canyon. There are direct buses from Lima to Arequipa. To get from Arequipa to Cusco, you can take a bus or the train.

● **Lima to Arequipa (bus)** Direct buses on this route cost s/30-55; the journey time is about 16 hours.

● **Arequipa to Cusco (bus)** The bus can either go via Juliaca (a reasonable road) or straight to Sicuani (a less good/terrible road); both take about 12 to 15 hours and cost around s/30. Travelling by night is not really recommended because you'll miss the view.

● **Arequipa to Cusco (train)** The privatization of Peru's rail network means all the routes and schedules are subject to change and some routes may be discontinued. The Arequipa–Puno route was scheduled to be suspended in June 2002, so check the situation with the SAEC or 🖳 www.perurail.com.

If the Arequipa–Puno train is still running it should take 25 to 30 hours to get from Arequipa to Cusco. It's more comfortable and reliable than the bus but it's also a lot more expensive; check the timetable, too, before you leave or you'll risk being stuck in Arequipa for a couple of days. Puno is an hour down the railway from Juliaca, 8 hours 45 minutes from Cusco, at the end of the line. If you want to break your journey between Arequipa and Cusco, this is a reasonable place to do it. Puno is a bit of a dive but it's beautifully sited on the shores of Lake Titicaca. On all the trains, you'll probably meet touts selling rooms in some of Cusco's cheap hotels and tickets for travel agencies – don't part with your money until you've seen what they're offering.

See p267 for details of current timetables and prices.

Bus companies

There are many companies, including:

● **Cruz del Sur** (☎ 424 1005), Jr Quilca 531, the biggest company, recommended for most destinations

● **Carhuamayo** (☎ 426 0785), Montevideo 766 and Av 28 de Julio 1758, have a 'direct' service (via Arequipa), to Cusco

● **Civa** (☎ 428 5649), Esquina Zavala y Montevideo 217, good for the Lima–Arequipa–Cusco route

● **Tepsa** (☎ 427 5642) good for northerly destinations

● **Leon de Huanuco** (☎ 423 3429), Av 28 de Julio 1520, Victoria, specialize in travel to Ica, Nazca and all points south

● **Empresa Paz S.A.** (☎ 428 5095), Montevideo 106, also cover routes to Ica, Nazca and all points south

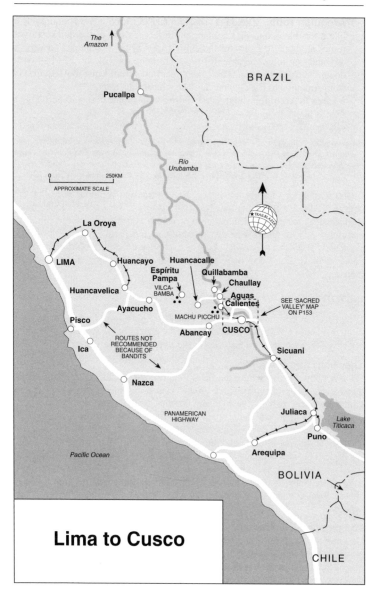

The Amazon

BRAZIL

Pucallpa

Río Urubamba

0   250KM
APPROXIMATE SCALE

TRAILBLAZER

La Oroya

LIMA
Huancayo   Huancacalle
Espíritu   Quillabamba
Pampa   Chaullay
Huancavelica   VILCA-   Aguas
BAMBA   Calientes
Ayacucho   SEE 'SACRED
VALLEY' MAP
MACHU PICCHU   ON P153
Pisco   CUSCO
Abancay
ROUTES NOT
Ica   RECOMMENDED   Sicuani
BECAUSE OF
BANDITS

Nazca
PANAMERICAN
HIGHWAY   Juliaca
Lake
Titicaca
Puno
Pacific Ocean   Arequipa

BOLIVIA

Lima to Cusco

CHILE

PART 5: CUSCO

Cusco
(Qosqo, Cuzco)

What remains with you is the sense of a great outrage, magnificent but unforgivable. The Spaniards tore down the Inca temples and grafted splendid churches and mansions onto their foundations. This is one of the most beautiful monuments to bigotry and sheer stupid brutality in the whole world. **Christopher Isherwood**, *The Condor and the Cows*, 1948.

Cusco was the capital of the Incas, the cultural and religious focus of the empire. Today it's the focus for almost all visitors to Peru but it's much more than a tourist town. With a population of almost 300,000 it's a large commercial centre and the administrative capital of Cusco department.

Cusco is 3360m (11,000ft) above sea level, and the air is thin here. When you first arrive, don't do anything too energetic: take a couple of days to acclimatize.

HISTORY

It's difficult to know much for certain about Cusco's origins because there is no written record of Peruvian history before the arrival of the Spanish, and there are very few recorded oral histories of the times before the rise of the Incas.

The Huari and the Killke
What *is* known is that before the Incas the great culture known as Huari dominated the Cusco valley. The area around Cusco and the sacred valley of the Urubamba were part of the highland frontier of the Huari state. The Huari declined and withdrew to their capital west of Cusco. The local people, the Killke, were left to their own devices, building hilltop defences throughout the area.

One place where the Killke did not build their forts was in the Cusco valley itself. This makes archaeologists think that it wasn't necessary to build fortifications around Cusco, suggesting that by about the twelfth century there were settlements in Cusco already stable, secure and strong enough to deter attacks from outsiders. The Incas had taken them over by about the thirteenth century.

The capital of the Incas
Cusco in the days of its glory as the capital of the Incas must have been a magnificent sight. The seat of the god-king, the Inca, it was a city constructed to reflect the might of the empire. Walls were sheathed in gold, something which was imposing enough to impress even the Spanish thugs sent by Pizarro to search for loot for Atahualpa's ransom (see p93). One was sufficiently moved

to write to the king: 'The city is the greatest and finest seen in either this country or anywhere in the Indies. We can assure Your Majesty that it is so beautiful and has such fine buildings that it would be worthy of notice even in Spain.'

Cusco was impressive not only because it was built from fine dressed stone and covered in precious metals. It had also been built with an understanding of the infrastructure a city needs and boasted channels providing running water and sewerage making it cleaner and more healthy than any European city. Such cleanliness did not survive the conquest, and another Spaniard wrote: 'now there are large piles of garbage on the banks [of the river Huatanay]. It is full of dung and filth. It was not like this in the days of the Incas, when it was clean and the water ran over stones. The Incas sometimes went there to bathe with their women.'

The city was not only the seat of political power, but also the cultural and religious centre of the empire. The cardinal roads to each *suyu* of the Inca empire led out from the main square, and sacred religious lines from spiritual places converged on the Coricancha. All roads led to Cusco, and the *ceques* pointed towards Cusco.

Construction and destruction

Despite the vast amount of work that clearly went into Cusco's construction, legend has it that the city was built on the orders of one man alone: the Inca Pachacutec (see p79). He tore down Cusco's old humble buildings shortly after seizing power and ordered them to be replaced with a stone city. Some say that Pachacutec designed Cusco to look like a puma, a sacred animal of the Incas. The river Tullumayo formed the spine of the puma, the river Huatanay the belly, and the fortress or temple mound of Sacsayhuaman made the puma's head.

But the Cusco of Pachacutec has been lost to us although you can still make out the puma, and we see only a pale imitation of past splendours. The magnificent gold was torn off by the greedy hands of the Spanish, and in the siege of Cusco the whole city was burnt when rebel Incas put it to the torch in a desperate attempt to smoke out the Spanish invaders (see p96).

Cusco after the conquest

After the conquistadors secured Peru for the king of Spain, they needed to found a capital. They were dependent on the sea for communications and reinforcements so Cusco was not a suitable place to set up government. Francisco Pizarro therefore founded his capital on the coast, in 1535. From this point, Cusco's influence began to wane.

The town itself was largely rebuilt by the Spanish on old Inca foundations, re-using the snug Inca stonework pillaged from many sites including the massive Sacsayhuaman. The Spanish work is less strong than that of the Incas, as shown by the occasional serious earthquake that shakes colonial buildings to the ground leaving their Inca foundations standing. The monastery of Santo Domingo (which is built over Coricancha) has pictures showing that exactly this happened in the 1950 earthquake.

Throughout the following centuries Cusco was overshadowed by Lima, but it did enjoy brief flashes of its former importance. It was the centre of rebellion in 1780 when José Gabriel Condorcanqui, also called Tupac Amaru II, rose against the Spanish, and again in 1825 when Bolívar himself arrived and set up camp. The royal oath of independence was sworn by Peru's first Prefect, Garmarra, before the cathedral's *Señor de los Tremblores* (see p141), and in the seventeenth and eighteenth centuries, the city's artists distinguished themselves in creating the famous Cusco School of painting.

With the rebirth of interest in the ancient civilizations of Peru, the discovery of Machu Picchu in 1911 and the development of the subsequent tourist trade Cusco re-emerged as one of Peru's principal cities.

ARRIVAL

Take a couple of days to acclimatize when you first arrive. Acclimatization is easier if you don't overeat and avoid smoking and alcohol.

A note of caution

Cusco has a bad but deserved reputation for robbery, and the area around San Pedro station and the market can be a hot spot, as is the San Blas district. Be careful when you walk around, especially when arriving and leaving. See p60 for more details.

By air

The airport is about a five-minute taxi ride from Plaza de Armas. A taxi to the plaza will cost about s/5 from the airport car park, and s/3 from the road outside, because there is a fee *taxistas* (taxi drivers) have to pay to get into the compound. Walking to the plaza would take you about 40 minutes, but I wouldn't recommend it (see 'A note of caution' above).

By rail

The train from Puno arrives at **Huanchac station**, which is at the south-eastern end of Av El Sol, 20 minutes' walk from the centre of town. The train from Machu Picchu and Ollantaytambo arrives at **San Pedro station** (also called Machu Picchu station) which is just by the church of San Pedro, 10 minutes' walk from the south-west of the plaza.

By bus

Long-distance buses will bring you to the bus terminal, which is close to the statue of Pachacutec to the south-east of town, near the airport. Take a taxi to the centre – it'll cost about US$2-3/£1.50-2.

GETTING AROUND

Taxis in Cusco are much better than those in other Peruvian cities, and they should charge a flat fare of s/2 for a trip anywhere in the centre (except the airport), though if they see you've just arrived, they might just forget this. You can flag them down on almost any street, or find them around Plaza de Armas.

There have, however, been reports of taxi drivers robbing people; the safest thing would be to arrange a taxi through your hotel so that they know who you're going off with. Other forms of transport are the communal **colectivos** which are cheaper if much less comfortable than taxis.

If you're on a bigger budget you may want to hire a **car**. Try **Avis** (☎ 248 800) at Av El Sol 808, with cars from US$25 per day, or **Localiza** (☎ 242285/ 263448, 🖳 localiz@mail.cosapidata.com.pe), Av El Sol 1089. You've got to be over 25 to drive a hire car, and the daily rates vary from company to company. Petrol's extra.

ORIENTATION

Central Cusco is small and set out almost on a grid, with Plaza de Armas pretty much in the middle. If you stand by the fountain in the plaza and look up at the figure of Jesus (north), the hill to Jesus' right is the hill of Sacsayhuaman (north-west). Between Sacsayhuaman and the plaza is a district of steep streets and cheap hotels. Between Jesus and you is the cathedral and the district of San Blas, while behind you (east and south) is the Compañía and Av El Sol which leads to Huanchac station, the indoor souvenir market (see p138) and the airport. Jesus is looking almost to the south-west, towards the market and San Pedro station.

Wandering around Cusco, you'll notice a rainbow flag hanging from houses, shops and bars. It looks very much like the gay and lesbian banner but the flag's actually the emblem of the Quechua and is a different design, though only slightly, bearing as it does an extra blue line.

SERVICES

Banks and cambios

Banco de Crédito (Visa), Av El Sol 189; **Banco Latino** (MasterCard), Av Almagro 125–127, but there is an ATM in the wall of El Dorado Inn on Av El Sol 395; **Banco Wiese**, Calle Maruri 315, charges the lowest bank commission when changing travellers' cheques but is slow. The ATMs at Interbank, above the Telefonica offices on Av El Sol, accept Cirrus, Visa and Maestro cards.

There are **cambios** all over Cusco, and it's difficult to pick out any one over the other, but **Multitours**, Av El Sol 314 (☎ 236946), exchange Visa, Thomas Cook and AMEX travellers' cheques. The AMEX agent in Cusco, Lima Tours (see Tour Agencies, p131), does not deal with travellers' cheques. **DHL/Western Union** (☎ 224167) is at Av El Sol 627A and Santa Catalina Ancha 165 TDA 311 (☎ 248028).

Save up your **small-denomination notes and coins** before leaving Cusco: the towns and villages in the mountains seem to suffer from even more of a shortage of small change than the rest of Peru.

Bookshops

Many of the tourist shops on Portal de Comercio and Portal de Confituría sell books, and **Los Andes** (☎ 234231), Portal Comercio 125 specializes in them,

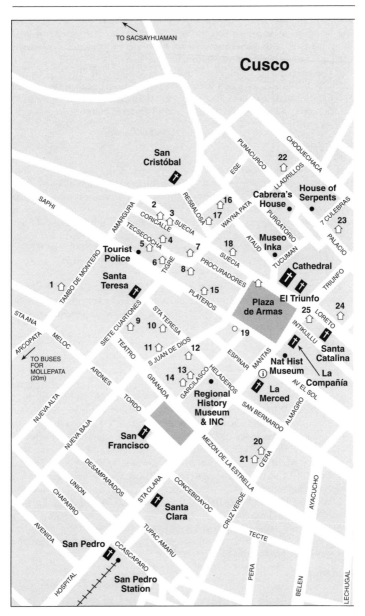

Cusco

TO SACSAYHUAMAN

San Cristóbal

TO SACSAYHUAMAN

PUNACURCO

CHOQUECHACA

ESE

LLADRILLOS

22

Cabrera's House

House of Serpents

SAPHI

AMARGURA

CORICALLE

SUECIA

RESBALOSA

WAYNA PATA

PURGATORIO

7 CULEBRAS

23

2

3

16

17

PALACIO

TECSECOCHA

4

18

ATAUD

Museo Inka

TIGRE

5

7

SUECIA

TUCUMAN

Cathedral

Tourist Police

6

8

PROCURADORES

Santa Teresa

TAMBO DE MONTERO

El Triunfo

TRIUNFO

STA ANA

1

15

PLATEROS

LORETO

24

25

ARCOPATA

MELOC

SIETE CUARTONES

STA TERESA

Plaza de Armas

INTIKULLU

9

TEATRO

10

19

Santa Catalina

TO BUSES FOR MOLLEPATA (20m)

S. JUAN DE DIOS

11

12

ESPINAR

MANTAS

La Compañía

ARDNES

13

Nat Hist Museum

NUEVA ALTA

TORDO

GRANADA

14

GARCILASCO

HELADEROS

AV EL SOL

La Merced

NUEVA BAJA

Regional History Museum & INC

SAN BERNARDO

ALMAGRO

20

DESAMPARADOS

MEZON DE LA ESTRELLA

21

Q ERA

San Francisco

UNION

STA CLARA

CONCEBIDAYOC

CHAPARRO

Santa Clara

CRUZ VERDE

AYACUCHO

AVENIDA

TUPAC AMARU

TECTE

San Pedro

CCASCAPARO

San Pedro Station

HOSPITAL

PERA

BELEN

LECHUGAL

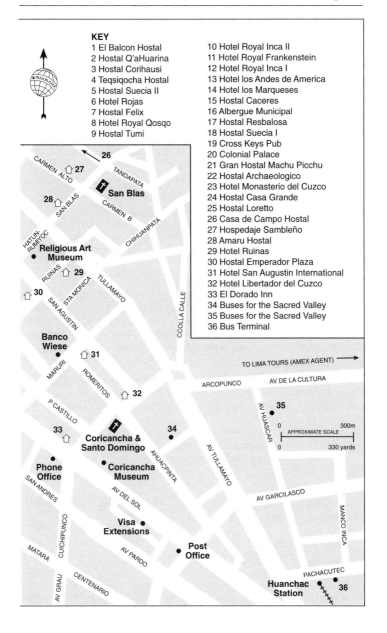

KEY
1 El Balcon Hostal
2 Hostal Q'aHuarina
3 Hostal Corihausi
4 Teqsiqocha Hostal
5 Hostal Suecia II
6 Hotel Rojas
7 Hostal Felix
8 Hotel Royal Qosqo
9 Hostal Tumi
10 Hotel Royal Inca II
11 Hotel Royal Frankenstein
12 Hotel Royal Inca I
13 Hotel los Andes de America
14 Hotel los Marqueses
15 Hostal Caceres
16 Albergue Municipal
17 Hostal Resbalosa
18 Hostal Suecia I
19 Cross Keys Pub
20 Colonial Palace
21 Gran Hostal Machu Picchu
22 Hostal Archaeologico
23 Hotel Monasterio del Cuzco
24 Hostal Casa Grande
25 Hostal Loretto
26 Casa de Campo Hostal
27 Hospedaje Sambleño
28 Amaru Hostal
29 Hotel Ruinas
30 Hostal Emperador Plaza
31 Hotel San Augustin International
32 Hotel Libertador del Cuzco
33 El Dorado Inn
34 Buses for the Sacred Valley
35 Buses for the Sacred Valley
36 Bus Terminal

CARMEN ALTO
27
26
TANDAPATA
San Blas
28
SAN BLAS
CARMEN B
HATUN-RUMIYOC
CHIHUANPATA
Religious Art Museum
RUINAS
29
TULLAMAYO
STA MONICA
30
SAN AGUSTIN
CCOLLA CALLE
Banco Wiese
31
MARURI
ROMERITOS
32
P CASTILLO
TO LIMA TOURS (AMEX AGENT)
ARCOPUNCO
AV DE LA CULTURA
AV HUASCAR
35
0   300m
APPROXIMATE SCALE
0   330 yards
33
Coricancha & Santo Domingo
34
AHUACPINTA
AV TULLAMAYO
Phone Office
Coricancha Museum
SAN ANDRES
AV DEL SOL
AV GARCILASCO
CUICHIPUNCO
Visa Extensions
MATARA
AV PARDO
Post Office
MANCO INCA
AV GRAU
CENTENARIO
PACHACUTEC
Huanchac Station
36

but the best bookshops are the **Libreria Jerusalen**, Heladeros 143, and the **Special Book Service** opposite the post office on Av El Sol.

Communications

● **Telephone and fax** Cusco's telephone code is ☎ 84. There are public pay phones everywhere, and it's easy to ring abroad, or you can get someone else to do it for you at **Telser** (☎ 242424; they also send and receive faxes), Calle de Medio 117, or the central **Telefonica del Peru** on Av El Sol 382. Remember that you can also phone via the Internet – see Email below.

● **Post** For letters, the **correo** (daily 8am-8pm), is on the west side of Av El Sol, on the sixth block downhill from Plaza de Armas, and **AMEX** client mail is at Lima Tours (see Tour Agencies, p131).

● **Email** You won't have any trouble finding an Internet café – they're everywhere and they all charge about s/2.50 per hour. All of them are pretty good, but three to recommend are: **Tambo Lodge**, on Plaza de Armas, which offers Internet phone capabilities (s/1 per minute); **Internet Station Speed X** at Tecsecocha 400, which is one of the fastest; and best of all, **Inkanet**, Carmen Alto 113 in San Blas, which is also very quick and charges just s/3 per hour for Internet phone calls.

Emergencies and medical services

Fire ☎ 103; **Police**: ☎ 105; **Tourist Police**: ☎ 321961 (24 hours), Saphi 510, and an office on Plaza de Armas at Portal carrizos 250, near the Compañía (9am-6pm), very helpful; **Hospitals**: Regional ☎ 231131, IPSS ☎ 221581, Lorena ☎ 226511; **Tourist Medical Assistance** ☎ 222644/621838 (24 hours). **Pharmacy** (☎ 245351), Calle Heladeros 109, (24 hours).

Equipment rental

Camping equipment can be hired at most of the tour agencies on Plateros and Procuradores, but do check the quality because some of it is pretty ropy. Butane and butane-propane gas cylinders can also be obtained at these places, or at one of the tourist shops on Portal de Comercio. However, the best place for all of this is **Soqllaq'asa** (☎ 252560), Calle Plateros 365, on the second floor, where they will also buy equipment you no longer need.

For **shoe repair**, try Elmer at 270 Matara, down the hill to the south-east of Plaza de San Francisco.

Hiking provisions

There's a good supermarket on the corner of Almagro and Av El Sol, another at Plateros 346, and the market opposite San Pedro station.

Opposite: Top: The Coricancha in Cusco (see p142) was the Incas' Temple of the Sun. The Dominicans grafted their monastery, Santo Domingo, onto its foundations. (Photo © Richard Danbury). Bottom: Parade of the Señor de los Tremblores – see p141. (Photo © Henry Stedman). (Following pages): Across Cusco's Plaza de Armas. (Photo © Richard Danbury).

Film and camera shops

Film and camera shops are not recommended. It would be much wiser to bring your films home to be developed. If you can't wait there is a string of film shops that also do developing on the first block of Av El Sol down from Plaza de Armas, on the west side of the road. If you have to buy, check the use-by date and avoid film that looks as if it might have been kept in the sun.

Laundry

You won't have any trouble finding someone willing to take in your laundry for a small consideration. The cheapest (s/2 per kg) is the anonymous shop opposite the northern end of Av El Sol. Then there's Laundry Flash (7am-8pm) at Saphy 675, which will deliver your laundry back to your hotel.

Language courses

Of all the language schools in Cusco, the best is probably **Academia Latinoamericana de Espanol** (☎ 690293, 🖹 225235, 🖳 www.latinschools .com) at Av El Sol 590, which can also arrange for you to stay with a host family. Also try **Amauta** (☎ 241422), Procuradores 50, Casilla Postal 1164 and **Excel** (☎ 232272, 🖳 www.rcp.net.pe/excel), Calle Cruz Verde 336.

Tourist information

There is one very helpful tourist office in the arrivals hall of the airport, and one less helpful and reliable one at Portal Mantas 117 in the arcade next to the Merced (☎ 252974/263176). They both hand out free maps and provide information.

The SAEC (☎ 245485, 🖳 cuscoclub@saexplorers.org), two blocks from Plaza de Armas at Choquechaca 188 Apt. 4, is also a veritable treasure trove of information, and members receive discounts at many of the hotels, sights and entertainments in Cusco (including 10% off drinks at the Cross Keys, see p137).

Visa extension

Ministerio del Interior, Av El Sol 620 (☎ 222741), open Monday to Friday, 9am-1pm, 3-6pm.

Embassies and consulates

Belgium and Holland (☎ 221146/098), Av El Sol 954 (under the Savoy Hotel); **France** (☎ 233610), Av Micaela Bastidas 101, Edif, Diagonal, 4th Floor, Huanchac; **Germany** (☎ 235459), San Augustin 307; **Italy** (☎ 233192), Av Garcilasco 700, Huanchac; **UK** (☎ 226671, 🖹 236706), Barry Walker (landlord of the Cross Keys Pub), find him at the pub or Casillo 606; **USA** (☎ 224112), Instituto Cultural Peruano Nort Americano (ICPNA), Calle Tullumayo 127.

Opposite: Impressive examples of Inca stonework: the Inca Trail (top) and the massive stones of Sacsayhuaman (bottom, see p148). (Photos: top © Richard Danbury; bottom © Henry Stedman).

Tour agencies

Since 2000 the Peruvian government has been bringing in new rules to cover access to the Inca Trail. The rules are designed to reduce the environmental impact of thousands of trekkers yet maximize the amount of money that's derived from tourism. To trek in the Machu Picchu Historical Sanctuary you must now take a tour with a licensed tour operator. Apart from the Vilcabamba Trail, most of the trails in this book are through the Sanctuary and so must be organized through a licensed operator but theoretically you can still hike the first parts of the Mollepata walk or the Chilca walk as long as you don't end up at Machu Picchu.

The UGM (Unidad Gestion Machu Picchu, the government agency responsible for all this) has been slow both in outlining the rules and in appointing companies licensed to lead tours in the Sanctuary but just as we were going to press they finally revealed the **full list of licensed tour operators – see p271**. There were originally supposed to be only 23, but that rose to 50 and was supposed to sink to 34. There are now 54. If past history's anything to go by, this number's likely to change, so before you hand over any money, ask to see the company's paperwork.

The prices for hiking the Inca Trails run from US$140 (US$90 students with ISIC card) to whatever you're willing to pay. A lot of operators are currently saying their prices are 'estimates': don't fall for that. Get a fixed price.

Remember that the cheaper deals aren't necessarily the best value, as cut-price operators will bus you in and out of an area, leaving you with half-a-dozen other groups and an ill-informed guide who hardly speaks Spanish, let alone English. They also have a reputation for not clearing away their litter, not caring a fig about the environment and treating their porters appallingly. And their equipment's likely to be dodgy. And the food's likely to be terrible. And transfers are probably not included in the price.

To book, you'll have to give the tour company a photocopy of your passport, signed in blue (to prevent it being further photocopied), who'll pass it on to the UGM. The days of just pitching up in Cusco and walking the trail are gone. Now the average wait is two days, and as demand increases the wait will increase too, so if you're turning up in Cusco on spec you ought to allow a good week. That'll be no great torment, as there's lots to do in Cusco, and many operators offer tours other than the Inca Trail: walking the Ausangate circuit, white-water rafting and trips down into the jungle in the Manu National Park, for example. *(cont'd opposite)*

WHERE TO STAY

Hot water is a problem in Cusco, whatever the people at the hotel may tell you. Water supply is unpredictable and vanishes completely at certain times of day. Try to talk to someone already staying in the hotel to get an idea of whether you are going to get a shower for your money. As for the cost of your room, Cusco prices are highly negotiable and depend on the usual laws of supply and demand. If you find yourself in Cusco in low season, you'll be able to find plenty of bargains.

□ ⌐ᄂ⌐ ⌐ᄂ⌐ ⌐ᄂ⌐ ⌐ᄂ⌐ ⌐ᄂ⌐ ⌐ᄂ⌐ ⌐ᄂ⌐ ⌐ᄂ⌐ ⌐ᄂ⌐ ⌐ᄂ⌐ ⌐ᄂ⌐

Tour agencies (cont'd)

At the upper end of the price scale are the professionally-run **Andean Life** (☎ 221491, 🖳 www.andeanlife.com) at Plateros 341; **Q'ente Tours** (☎ 238245, 🖹 222535; 🖳 www.qente.com), Calle Plateros 325, a very costly 'luxury' operator (their tours even have tables and chairs and a full dinner service) with fees starting at around US$300; and the long-established and even more expensive **Explorandes**, (☎ 238380; 🖳 www.explorandes.com), Av Garcilasco 316A. All of these offer top-quality tours, although you pay through the nose for them. Slightly less extortionate, **SAS** (☎ 237292, 🖹 225757, 🖳 info@sastravelperu.com, www.sastravel.com), on Plaza de Armas at Portal de Panes 143, is a thoroughly well-organized outfit. They even employ an SAS flag bearer to accompany the walk, an indication of their attention to detail and the pride they take in what they are doing – though it can make trekkers feel like they're part of a scout troop on a yomp. Their four-day trek is not the cheapest in town, at about US$190, but they take groups of as few as four people, and they also promise that they won't combine with groups from other agencies. I've heard consistently good reports about them.

At the cheaper end of the market, **United Mice** (☎ 221139), Plateros 351, is one of the more popular agencies licensed for the Inca Trail with the four-day walk starting at around US$120. Other trekkers have recommended **Wayki Trek**, (☎ 224092, 🖳 waykitrek@hotmail.com), Procuradores 44, (below La Tertulia) and **Inti Kuntur** (☎ 246235, 🖳 www.geocities.com/intikunturpe/cusco.htm), 265 Portal de Confituria on Plaza de Armas. **Plaza Tours** (☎ 690368), Portal Confituria 241, Plaza de Armas, and **Top Vacations** (☎ 263278, 🖳 topvacations@terra.com.pe), Portal Confituria 265, Plaza de Armas, have also been recommended though they're not currently on the Inca Trail licensee list. Surprisingly, neither is the ever-popular **Lima Tours** (☎ 228431, 🖹 221266), Calle Machu Picchu D-24, Urb Manuel Prado, Av Cultura, though that may be a short-term omission.

For the jungle, **Manu Nature Tours** (☎ 252721, 🖹 234793, 🖳 mnt@amat-ua.rcp.pet.pe), Av Pardo 1046, have a good reputation. For horse-riding around the archaeological sites near Cusco choose **The Corcel Ranch** (☎ 245878, ask for Hernan), Procuradores 351; it's s/20 for a trip that takes about four hours.

Disabled travellers should contact **Apumayo Expeditions** (☎ 246018, 🖳 apumayo@mail.cosapidata.com.pe), Calle Garcilasco 265, Interior 3, who run special tours.

□ ⌐ᄂ⌐ ⌐ᄂ⌐ ⌐ᄂ⌐ ⌐ᄂ⌐ ⌐ᄂ⌐ ⌐ᄂ⌐ ⌐ᄂ⌐ ⌐ᄂ⌐ ⌐ᄂ⌐ ⌐ᄂ⌐ ⌐ᄂ⌐

An organization has been set up to help find rooms for visitors with a traditional Cusqueño family. Contact **Asociacion de Micro y Pequeñas Empresas de Establecimientos de Hospedaje** (Small Business Association of Family Lodgings), Portal de Panes 123, Office 109 (☎ 242710, 🖳 ititoss@terr.com.pe).

Note: the following abbreviations are used here: **com = room with common bathroom; att = bathroom attached, sgl/dbl/tpl = single/double/triple**.

Budget accommodation

The best place to find cheap hotels is in the hilly streets that lead from Plaza de Armas up to Sacsayhuaman. Recommended are *Hostal Resbalosa* (☎ 224839/

240461), Calle Resbalosa 494, which has a bright friendly courtyard, beautiful 180° views over the town towards Mount Ausangate, and costs just s10/15/20 (dorm/sgl/dbl com). Avoid the rooms around the entrance, which are older and noisier. Another good value place is *Hotel Rojas* (☎ 228184), Tigre 129, with a pleasant green courtyard behind enormous front doors, s/25/35/45 (sgl/dbl/tpl com), s/50/70 (sgl/dbl att). Try to get the top floor rooms, which have a view.

Worth looking at are *Hotel Royal Qosqo* (☎ 226221), Tecsecocha 2, which is well maintained and costs s/15/30/40 (sgl/dbl/tpl, com), and *Hostal Felix* (☎ 241949), Tecsecocha 171, a real gringo dive s/20 (double, com) – as is *Hostal Tumi*, Siete Cuartones 245, s/10/20 (sgl/dbl, com), s/20/25 (sgl/dbl, att). Also worth considering is *Hostal Caceres* (☎ 232616/228012), Plateros 368, an old house with blue creaking woodwork and a friendly welcome; s/15/25/36 (sgl/dbl/tpl, com), and one double with attached bathroom for s/40.

In other areas, there are the highly recommended *Gran Hostal Machu Picchu* (☎ 231111), Calle Q'era 282, with its two colonial courtyards and talkative parrots ('¡Hola gringo!'), s/40/70 (sgl/dbl, com), or at the other end of town in San Blas the recommended *Hospedaje Sambleño* (☎ 262979, 🖹 221452), Carmen Alto 114, which has cable TV in the lobby and is a bargain at s/15 per person for a room with attached lavatory, though prices are bound to go up. There are many other little hospedajes tucked away around here in Calle Tarapata.

South of San Blas there is the recommended *Hostal Casa Grande* (☎ 264 156, 🖹 243784), Santa Catalina Ancha 353, an old house and good value at s/15/30 (sgl/dbl, com), or s/20/40 (sgl/dbl, att).

Other places worth looking at are the two Hostals Suecia run by the same people who are friendly and popular with foreigners. *Hostal Suecia I* (☎ 233 282), is at Calle Suecia 332, and *Hostal Suecia II* (☎ 239757) at Tecescocha 465. Both cost s/20/30/45 (sgl/dbl/tpl, com), and Suecia II has some doubles with attached bathroom for s/45.

Also recommended but is the youth hostel: *Albergue Municipal* (☎ 252 506), Kiskapata 240, which is spanking clean, has a café and good views from a sunny concrete balcony. It costs s/15 a person with a discount for members and is a great place to stay if you're in a group. Finally, the *Hotel Royal Frankenstein* (☎ 236999), at San Juan de Dios 260, deserves a mention for sheer weirdness if nothing else. With a sales pitch that advertises 'Cold dark gloomy rooms' with 'spiders on request' it's a wonder they receive any guests at all. To be fair they're selling themselves a bit short and it's not that bad, with cooking and laundry facilities for guests to use but it is rather overpriced at US$5 for a dorm bed, US$17/20 sgl/dbl.

Incidentally, there are cheap hotels around both train stations (the *El Imperio* by San Pedro has been recommended), but they are a little out of the way and in unsavoury areas.

Cusco area code: ☎ 84. If phoning from outside Peru dial ☎ +51-84.

Mid-range hotels

Hotels in this category are spread throughout Cusco, and usually set their rates in US dollars, but be careful to check whether the price includes taxes and service. Budget hotels tend to forget about taxes and service, and expensive hotels slap the extra percentage on top but you can never be sure with the mid-range places.

A little expensive for what you get but with great character is the recommended *Hotel los Marqueses* (☎ 232512, 🖷 227028, 🖳 marqueseshotel@hot mail.com), Calle Garcilasco 256, an old house with ancient carved doors, antique chairs, old paintings in the lobby and a very pretty courtyard. They charge US$25/35 (sgl/dbl, att, breakfast).

Closer to Sacsayhuaman than the Albergue Municipal are two other recommended hotels which are on the same street as each other. The first is *Hostal Q'aHuarina* (☎ 228130), Calle Suecia 575, which is efficient, clean, modern and friendly and offers free coca tea throughout the day. It has only six rooms and is good value for Cusco at US$18/28 (sgl/dbl, att, breakfast). Just down from Q'aHuarina is *Hostal Corihausi* (☎ 232233, 🖳 www.corihausi.com), Calle Suecia 561, Casilla Postal 157, which charges US$30/40/50 (sgl/dbl/tpl, att, breakfast), a larger hotel favoured by some adventure tour companies. Try to get the room directly above reception which has the best view in all Cusco.

If you fancy something a little more central there's *Hostal Emperador Plaza* (☎ 261733/227412, 🖷 263581, 🖳 www.emperador@nexopera.com), Santa Catalina Ancha 377. It's as clean as a new pin, has cable TV in the rooms and costs from US$48/53/68 (sgl/dbl/tpl, att, breakfast); the balcony rooms are best. Also central but much older is the aptly named and rather splendid *Colonial Palace* (☎ 232151), Calle Q'era 270, US$18/25 (sgl/dbl, att, breakfast) and *Teqsiqocha Hostal* (☎ 248600), Calle Tecsecocha 474, where all the rooms are en suite and piping hot water is usually available on tap around the clock; this quiet little place is reasonably priced at US$15/25/32 sgl/dbl/tpl and deservedly growing in popularity.

Hostal Loretto (☎ 226352), Loretto 115, deserves a mention because some rooms have genuine Inca walls, but it's overpriced at US$25/40/50 (sgl/dbl/tpl, att, costs more in high season). If you want to stay in San Blas, try *Amaru Hostal* (☎/🖷 225933, 🖳 www.cusco.net/amaru), Cuesta San Blas 541, an old house with a green courtyard filled with geraniums in rusty cans. It also has a book exchange and piano, and they charge US$8/12 (sgl/dbl, com), US$15/22 (sgl/dbl, att). Finally, *Hostal Archaeologico* (☎ 232569, 🖷 235126), Lladrillos 405, is a favourite with the French. It's pleasant enough but at US$25/36 (sgl/dbl, com, breakfast) you can do better for the money. For those who want to get away from it all, *Casa de Campo Hostal* (☎ 244404, 🖷 243069, 🖳 www .telser.cm.pe/amauta), at the very northern end of Tandapata in San Blas at number 296B is just delightful. Built on a slope overlooking the town, the rooms and terrace are simply gorgeous, the location so peaceful, and they'll even throw in an airport pickup if you book in advance. Rooms start at US$25/40 (sgl/dbl), though bargaining is distinctly possible, and there's a 10% discount for SAEC members.

The most impressive hotel in this category, however, is *El Balcon Hostal* (☎ 236738, 🖹 225352, 🖳 www.el-balcon-hostal-cusco.com), Tambo de Montero 222, housed in a restored pre-colonial house dating back to 1630. All 16 rooms are en suite, many with magnificent views of the city, and the staff are incredibly friendly, as is the office cat. It's a bit of a climb to get here, but it's worth every step: room prices are US$35/45/65 (sgl/dbl/tpl).

Expensive hotels

More than others, these hotels jack up their prices in high season and are willing to give away bargains when the rooms are empty. The prices quoted can go up by about 20% in June/July.

The two best hotels in Cusco are the Hotel Monasterio del Cuzco and the Hotel Libertador del Cuzco. *Hotel Monasterio del Cuzco* (☎ 246419, 🖹 246 983, 🖳 www.orient-express.com), Calle Palacio 136, is a sensitive conversion of the old Seminary of San Antonio Abad, and along with everything you'd expect from an international five-star hotel it also has a gilded chapel and a Michelin-starred chef. It's not cheap at US$184/194 (sgl/dbl, att, breakfast), but you can knock the prices down. *Hotel Libertador del Cuzco* (☎ 231961, 🖹 233 152, 🖳 www.libertador.com.pe), Plazoleta Santo Domingo 259, is a converted colonial building, once a palace called the Casa de Los Cuatro Bustos. Again this hotel has the full five-star package but is a little more welcoming to dirty trekkers than the Monasterio. It costs US$203.52 (single or double, att, breakfast).

Down from the first rank but still very good is *Hotel Ruinas* (☎ 260644/ 245920, 🖹 236391, 🖳 ruinas@mail.interplace.com.pe), Calle Ruinas 472. This place has character and the rooms with outside views are the best. It is well run and costs US$90/125 (sgl/dbl, att).

Hotel San Augustin International (☎ 221169/231001, 🖹 221174), Calle Maruri 390 deserves a mention because of its adobe-style interior decoration; it costs US$102 (double, att, breakfast). If you can't afford the San Augustin International, *El Dorado Inn* (☎ 231232/231135, 🖹 240993, 🖳 www.cosapidata .com.pe/empressa/doratur/doratur.htm), Av El Sol 395, has a similar quirky interior with aerial walkways. Rooms are US$89.68/102.66 (sgl/dbl, att, breakfast).

Hotel Royal Inca I (☎ 231067), Plaza Regocijo 299, US$54/78 (sgl/dbl, att, breakfast), is built on the foundations of Pachacutec's palace. It's slightly better than its more expensive sister, *Hotel Royal Inca II,* which is just up the road. Also good is the efficient *Hotel los Andes de America* (☎ 222253, 🖹 223058; 🖳 losandes@telser.com), Garcilasco 234-236, US$110/130/160 (sgl/dbl/tpl, att, breakfast).

WHERE TO EAT AND DRINK

Cusco is overflowing with places to eat and drink, from cheap steaming antic-ucho barrows on the street to exclusive restaurants; from back-street bars with sticky plastic tablecloths to loud, brash, young clubs where the music hits you like a fist. If you're looking for food or drink, just wander around Calle Procuradores or Calle Plateros and you are bound to find something that takes your fancy. If you can't afford many of Cusco's culinary pleasures, there are any number of the usual **cheap** s/3 menu places, particularly on Pampa del Castillo, near the Coricancha, or south of Plaza de Armas on Mantas and around Plaza San Francisco, including my favourite, the *Ccoyllor* café at 291 Garcilasco.

The following is only a small selection of what's on offer:

Best food in Cusco The competition for this prestigious award has been rather blown away by the arrival of Cusco's first ever Michelin-starred chef at *Hotel Monasterio* (see opposite). With food this exquisite being served in suitably sumptuous surroundings, you could be in any one of the finer restaurants in Europe – an illusion that the bill will do nothing to dispel. Back in the real world, honourable mentions must go to the *Inka Grill* (see below); *Los Perros*, on Tecsecocha 238, for its magnificent salads and *wontons* to die for; and *Macondo*, at Cuesta San Blas 571, which is simply the coolest and campest restaurant in Cusco, and one run by of its most flamboyant citizens. *El Truco*, Plaza Regocijo, is stylish and has good service and if you're lucky they'll put a flag on your table to remind you of your nationality. *La Retama*, Portal de Panes 123, can cook fish meunière and steak béarnaise (dinner for two s/115 with wine) but it's often booked up.

Don't forget by the way that expensive restaurants will add 28% tax and service on to your bill.

Best Peruvian My favourite restaurant in Cusco is *Inka Grill* on Plaza de Armas at Portal de Panes 115, which is more modern and imaginative than its competitors as regards food and décor. They try to give Peruvian dishes a contemporary twist, so you could have *pollo relleno prosciutto* (chicken stuffed with prosciutto ham), or a good (but very expensive at s/28) *aji de gallina*. A meal for two with wine will cost about s/170. A close second, however, and a little cheaper, is *Pacha Papa* on Plaza San Blas at No 120. With dishes ranging from commonplace roast *cuy* (guinea pig) to the more exotic *alpaca* steaks, a very pleasant evening can be had munching on the native wildlife; the outdoor seating is a bonus too. *Paititi*, Portal de Carrizos 270 (on Plaza de Armas has decent Peruvian dishes and folk music; around s/50 for two people. *Mesón de Espaderos,* Espaderos 105, has a wider range which includes cuy, anticucho, trout, and fine *parilladas*. *Café Restaurant Roma*, Portal de Panes 105, is pretty much the same as the rest, but it does extend to ceviche. It has Inca walls inside.

Best pizza An honourable mention must go to the two homely little places on Tecsecocha, *Les Cyranos* and *Pizzeria Urpi*, both of which are equipped with proper ovens which they use to churn out pizzas every bit as good as those you'd find in Italy. But the queen of pizzerias remains *Chez Maggy's*. With no fewer than three establishments on Procuradores (at Nos 344, 365 and 374), another on Plateros (No 348), and a further outpost in Aguas Calientes, Maggy's has come to dominate the city's pizza industry – though the bases are a bit crispy for me. They also run a delivery service (☎ 246316).

Best vegetarian For something very different, why not try *Tercer Mundo*, 346A Matara, to the east of Plaza San Francisco, which has a limited if imaginative three-course menu that changes daily (their banana tortillas are a treat) and all for just s/3.

Best Mexican While their portions are sometimes on the small side, *El Cuate*, at Procuradores 385, has fought off the competition to snaffle this particular award, thanks to the helpfulness of the staff, the charmingly rustic interior and some mighty fine dishes, including a lava-hot stuffed pepper that will blow your socks off. Expect to pay about s/10-15 for a main course.

Best all-you-can-eat buffet breakfast Two candidates here: *Amaru* on Plateros is proving very popular, not least because of its balcony seating and the variety of breakfasts on offer. A good place but the award for this particular category goes to *La Tertulia* at Procuradores 44, thanks to the classical music that accompanies every breakfast, the efficient service provided by its adorable waitresses and the superior quality of its scrambled eggs.

Best bakery Streets ahead of any rivals in Cusco, *El Buen Pastor*, at 579 Cuesta San Blas, has everything you could ask from a bakery: great, great bread, fantastic *empanadas*, drool-inducing gateaux and low prices. What's more, this place is a charitable concern, helping to finance a home for girls from disadvantaged backgrounds.

Best place to hang out *Trotamundos*, Portal de Comercio 177 (overlooks Plaza de Armas), has a laid-back atmosphere, board games, good breakfasts and real toast. If the views from the balconies overlooking the plaza are starting to bore, *Los Perros* on Tecsecocha, with its comfy armchairs, book exchange and six-year old *Rolling Stone* magazines is as good a place as any to wile away an afternoon.

The Dutch-owned *La Bodega*, 146 Carmen Alto in San Blas, is another laid-back and friendly place with magazines and they do some great snacks too – their chicken sandwich was the best I tasted in the city.

Best Chinese Sadly I found that none of the Chinese restaurants in Cusco could match their rivals in Lima, but if you're desperate for a plate of fried rice try the restaurant on Calle Q'era on the other side of the road from the Colonial Palace.

Best Middle Eastern food To be honest, the Peruvians have yet to master the art of Middle Eastern cooking, though there are a few places that are trying pretty hard. *Nafiz*, for example, at Choquechaca 132 in San Blas, tries gamely at *falafel*: the results are rather scrawny but they're no worse than any other in Cusco. *Narguila*, on the bend of Tecsecocha, is more authentic, the food's big and the waiter speaks Hebrew but *Victor Victoria*, nearby on Tigre, wins this category. Don't take my word for it – ask the vast number of Israelis who hang out here.

Best British Sunday roast *Greens*, round the back of the church at San Blas at Tandapata 700, wins this award by virtue of there being no competition. Their Sunday lunch is just fine, though you do have to let them know you're coming at least one day in advance. The s/30 bill is a bit pricy, though, all things considered.

Best coffee There are many places that *claim* to brew the best coffee in Cusco, from the achingly trendy *Los Perros* on Tecsecocha (top of the best cappuccino category) to *Planeta Sur* in San Blas – winner of the award for most stylish coffee machine if nothing else. But for my money the best coffee in the city, or at least the best-value coffee, can be found at *Cross Keys*: OK, so you have to plunge the filter yourself, but two cups for s/3 is marvellous value.

Best juices While a couple of swanky juice bars have opened up on Procuradores, none can compete in terms of price, atmosphere or taste with the juices on offer at the **market** in San Pedro. Around s/2 will get you glass after glass of your favourite fruity concoction.

Best hot chocolate This category was invented specifically to honour the Swiss-run *Granja Heidi*, at Cuesta San Blas 525, which serves up half-litre jugs of piping-hot, authentic chocolate for just s/2.5. If there were awards for best natural food, best yoghurt or best crêpes, they'd probably win those too.

Bars and clubs

The *Cross Keys,* Portal Confiturías 233, is almost a British pub (and is therefore your best bet for showing premier league football) just as *Paddy O'Flaherty's* at Triunfo 124 and *Rosy O'Grady's* at Santa Catalina Ancha 360) are almost Irish pubs (the former being far superior), and *Norton's Tavern* is almost a North American bar (but with a conspicuous absence of customers, though this may be because the entrance is hidden away in the Hostal Loreto courtyard). *Los Perros* (see p135) remains the most popular watering hole, despite the art exhibitions they put on the wall. A possible rival, *Mystique*, has opened on Calle Suecia. Many of these places have happy hours (Cross Keys 9-9.30pm. Norton's 7-9pm, Paddy's 10-10.30pm) when spirits are half price.

You will have no trouble finding a club in Cusco; the difficult part is trying to avoid them. Touts swarm around Plaza de Armas handing out flyers and free drink tokens, so it is now possible to spend an entire evening touring around the clubs without once paying for your drink. The clubs themselves tend to be located on the corners of the plaza. The two busiest, *Excess* and *Uptown*, next to each other on Calle Suecia, are a little too crowded for some tastes, and there have been a few robberies in the latter recently; *Midland* plays the widest variety of music, is one of the friendlier, more unpretentious places and is deservedly growing in popularity; *Eko*, at Plateros 334, plays solid dance music throughout the night and attracts younger travellers as does *Mama Africa* on the south-eastern corner of the plaza. The cellar-like *Kamikase* on Plaza Regocijo is slightly less loud and has the occasional live band. Best of the lot, however, is *Ukuku's*, at Plateros 316, with fewer gringos and some fantastic live music.

Cusco shopping – a guide

As well as its other, more enduring claims to fame, Cusco enjoys a reputation as the souvenir capital of Peru. Souvenirs here are more varied and a good deal cheaper than elsewhere in the country.

The first place you should look — just to get an idea of prices if not actually to buy — is the **Centro Artesanal**. In May 2001 the street sellers who used to occupy the arcades between Plaza de Armas and Plaza Regocijo, and who imbued the centre of Cusco with so much colour and character, were removed by the city authorities overnight and banned from returning. Those who could afford the rent made their way to the *mercado*, a purpose-built but rather anaemic indoor market by Huanchac station at the southern end of Av El Sol. Few tourists actually bother to make it this far down Av El Sol – bad news for the vendors, but good news for those after a bargain and willing to haggle. Those vendors who couldn't afford to hire a kiosk at the indoor market have set up shop in other locations in the city, in particular the Plazoleta Nazarenas, above Plaza de Armas to the east.

Three other Cusqueñan markets you should know about: the plaza in San Blas is the venue for a cute little **Saturday craft fair**, while on Plateros 334 is the daily **Tresors del Inca market**. On the way to the airport (catch a cab from the centre of town) is the **Centro Comercial el Molino**, commonly known as **Contrabandas**. As the name suggests, many of the vendors here deal in smuggled goods and designer rip-offs and as such the market does a good line in cheap cigarettes (half the normal price) and compact discs (s/9 a throw). The quality of the goods cannot be guaranteed, of course, nor should you expect a refund if things go wrong, so shop carefully. Watch your bags and wallets here too. Other places to buy traditional goods are the markets at Pisac (see p152) and Chinchero (p154).

Then there are Cusco's souvenir shops, most of which look the same, sell the same sort of stuff, and charge roughly the same amount for it too. The following, therefore, may not be a list of the best, but at least it contains some of the more interesting souvenir shops in Cusco.

● **General souvenirs** Four worth mentioning are: the **Galeria Latina**, San Augustin 427, which is hugely expensive and a bit too flash for some but which has just about the best of everything, from antique blankets and carpets to cotton shirts and Panama hats, via Alpaca jumpers and gold jewellery.

Jatum Maqui, next to Los Perros at Tecsecocha 432, manages to be a good deal cheaper without suffering a commensurate drop in quality.

La Mamita, on Plaza de Armas at Portal de Carnes 244, has a small but exquisite selection of pottery (see opposite), jewellery, baskets and blankets.

Minka, San Blas 525-529, is a charitable concern which has been set up to help people with special needs.

● **Jewellery Carlos Chaquiras** at Triunfo 375 is perhaps the finest jewellers in Cusco, though there are a few around Plaza de Armas that aren't far behind.

Leo's Fancy at Procuradores 372 has some interesting necklaces, and there are some inexpensive beads-and-bangles places further up the alley. *(cont'd opposite)*

Cusco shopping – a guide (cont'd)

No summary of Cusco's jewellery shops would be complete without mentioning **Magic Hands** on San Blas. The owner, a mystical sort of fellow, is very selective about whom he lets into his establishment: only those with auras of a benign colour, apparently, are permitted to enter. Pass this test and you'll find yourself in a dimly-lit store contemplating some fine and highly individual necklaces and earrings, while the owner advises which particular pieces will be good for your chakras. It's all rather bizarre. (Those with the wrong shade of aura, incidentally, may find that walking up to the door with a big bag of money causes the owner to suffer from temporary colour blindness.)

● **Leather** Take a trip down San Augustin, below San Blas, and you'll come across three shops — **Sumac Tika** at No 216, **Miguel Angel** at No 327 and **El Tumi** at No 345 — specializing in leatherwear, their stock including hats, shoes, wallets, belts and bags.

● **Alpaca and llama woollens Alpaca III**, Plaza Regocijo, has good quality alpaca woollens in Frank Bough designs but note that there's a cheaper branch of the same shop in the departure lounge of the airport and **Etno Artesania**, Triunfo 118, has more modern styles.

● **T-shirts** For something a bit different from the common-or-garden Peruvian football shirt or the awful 'I love Cusco' numbers, check out **Hecho en Cusco** at 340 Procuradores, with psychedelic handmade designs starting at about s/30 (bargaining possible).

● **Footwear** Not everybody's cup of tea it has to be said, but those brightly coloured shoes and boots made out of a combination of leather and thick woven cloth enjoy a small but intensely loyal following among travellers. Buy a pair at **Away**, Procuradores 361, which also has a fine collection of blankets for sale.

● **Ponchos and textiles Trendas Museo**, just down from the Cross Keys pub on Plaza de Armas, has the widest range of antique and new ponchos in Central Cusco. A little expensive but it's worth coming here to see some of the fabulous old blankets and ponchos they have in the store even if you don't want to buy.

● **Ceramics and pottery Maky** at Carme Alto 101 has a fine collection of tea sets, incense holders and other pottery.

Slightly superior, and much more expensive too, is **La Mamita** on Plaza de Armas at Portal de Carnes 244, the stockists for Seminario Ceramicas of Urubamba (see p154).

● **Instruments** Half museum, half shop, **Takinuna** at Carmen Alto 110 has a wide variety of instruments both great and small, weird and wonderful — though it's difficult to distinguish between what is on sale and what is an exhibit.

Instrumentos Qosco at Cabracancha 455, the narrow alley to the south of the Religious Art Museum, is the place to head to for locally-made guitars.

● **Andean music** Try **Flutes of Peru** at 230 Av El Sol, which has a fair selection of traditional and modern Peruvian music on tape and CD, and the owner is both knowledgeable and helpful.

Other entertainment and things to do

Peliclub, at Tecsecocha 458, is a small independent **cinema** that shows some classic old movies (s/5, s/2 students). Just down the road is Sunset Café – part of the Hotel Royal Qosqo – which shows three recent releases per day (s/2 per film), and many of the pubs and nightclubs (Bernie's on Saphy, Mama Africa's, Ukuku's, Excess) also show movies in the afternoon. If none of the films on offer grabs you, you can always visit the video store at Portal de Panes 123, where you can choose any video you want and watch it in the comfort of one of their private video booths (s/6).

If you fancy doing something a little more active, Mama Africa's (see p137) has **salsa lessons** starting at 9pm, followed by **samba lessons** at 10pm.

Finally, if you've just back from the trail there's no better way to pamper yourself than to visit Siluet at Calle Quera 253, down an alley by the Chinese restaurant, a **health spa** with a sauna (s/25), Jacuzzi (s/12) and masseur/se (s/25). It's open every day from 10am to 10pm.

WHAT TO SEE

Plaza de Armas

Just as it is today, the main square was a focal point for the people of Cusco in the time of the Incas, but it used to be twice as big. Plaza de Armas was once called Aucaypata and was a ceremonial area enclosed on three sides by the

---

Boleto Turístico Unico (BTU) – Visitor's Ticket

There's an entrance fee of about US$2 at most of Cusco's museums and archaeological sites. Many of these can also be visited using the Boleto Turístico Unico (BTU or Visitor's Ticket), which costs US$10 (half price for students), is valid for ten days and is sold at the **Instituto Nacional de Cultura** (INC) on the corner of Garcilasco and Plaza Regocijo, at the Centro Artesanal by Huanchac Station, and at some of the sites. The ticket allows only one entrance to each of the sites it covers – tiresome if you want to go back – but if you paid entrance fees for all the sites separately it would cost much more than US$10. Note that the ticket does not cover the Coricancha-Santo Domingo complex, merely the small (and rather dull) museum in the grounds whose entrance is on Av El Sol. The Visitor's Ticket allows you entry to these sites:

Sacsayhuaman	Cusco Cathedral
Pikillacta	Religious Art Museum
Tipón	Church of San Blas
Ollantaytambo	Regional History Museum
Pisac	Chinchero ruins
Qenko	Santa Catalina Museum
Puca Pucara	Palacio Museum
Tambo Machay	Coricancha Museum (not the complex)

❏ **The Virgin saves the Spanish**

During the siege of Cusco, the Spanish were at one stage cornered in the Suntur Huasi or round house (where the Triunfo church is now). The roof of this building was thatched, and the Incas aimed a hail of red-hot stones from their slings at the straw until the roof caught fire.

What happened next depends on who you want to believe. The Spanish said that they were protected by divine intervention. The Virgin Mary appeared, joined by Saint James (the patron saint of the Spanish Army) and sprinkled water on the flames to douse the fire, and save the Spaniards. The Incas, on the other hand, remarked that the Spanish had positioned some of their auxiliaries on the roof to beat out the fire.

Mary douses the flames
FELIPE HUAMÁN POMA DE AYALA (c1590)

imposing mansions of the Inca. The other side of the river Huatanay, which ran down one side of Aucaypata in a stone ditch, was Cusipata where Plaza Regocijo and its surrounding buildings now stand. Cusipata was the square of celebration, and a Spaniard described being there on a feast day when so much chicha (corn beer) was drunk that the drainage ditch overflowed with pure urine; to this day, the gutters and flagstones of Plaza de Armas are regularly awash on festival days.

Cathedral

(Monday to Saturday 2-6pm, entrance with Visitor's Ticket through the church of Jesús María.) Built between 1556 and 1669 in the Renaissance style, the cathedral nestles between the church of **Jesús María** (1733) on its right and on its left **El Triunfo** (1536), the site of Cusco's first church and the resting place of the historian, El Inca Garcilasco de la Vega. All three buildings are currently undergoing restoration, and for this reason certain sections may be closed off, and paintings removed when you visit. The cathedral is probably built on the site of Inca Viracocha's palace, and the next-door Triunfo is built on the site of the Suntur Huasi, where the Spaniards hid during the siege of Cusco.

The floor plan of the cathedral is a Latin cross with added processional aisles and ambulatories. It's filled with wonders, from the carvings of alder and cedarwood by Martin Torres and Melchor Huamán (don't miss the minute detail on the choir), to the sacristy, filled with portraits of past bishops of Cusco. The blackened crucifix, generally kept halfway down on the right, is the *Señor de los Tremblores* (Lord of the Earthquakes, currently in the Triunfo), which was paraded around Cusco to stop the 1650 quake. It worked and this example of particularly Andean religiosity is commemorated in a painting that currently stands facing the entrance to the Triunfo. There's also a very famous painting in here of the Last Supper at which Christ and his disciples are shown feasting on cuy (guinea pig). Sadly it's not often on view these days, as the building renovations mean it's kept in storage.

The Compañía (Jesuits' Church)

(No set opening hours; admission free). This is the other massive church on Plaza de Armas. The Jesuits wanted it to be more imposing than the cathedral,

Loyala captures Tupac Amaru
FELIPE HUAMÁN POMA DE AYALA (c1590)

but the Pope stopped them just before they finished, and the two buildings are so very similar it's a close-run thing.

Work began in 1578, but the structure was practically demolished by the 1650 earthquake, and the church wasn't finished until 1668. It is a single nave design and was built on the palace of the Inca Huayna Capac, described by chronicler Pedro Sancho as the greatest of the Incas' palaces on the square with its red and white gateway ornamented with precious metal.

One of its most interesting paintings, which hangs by the door, represents the marriage of Martín García de Loyola to Ñusta (Princess) Beatriz. Loyola was the nephew of the Jesuits' founder, St Ignatius, but he was also the gallant captain who hunted down the last Inca Tupac Amaru. Beatriz was of royal Inca blood, and the marriage of the two was highly significant for the Jesuits because it associated them with this symbolic union of Spain and Peru, so Loyola's and Beatriz's noble forbears look on approvingly at the union.

Other sights around Plaza de Armas

● **Museum of Natural History** (Monday to Friday 8am-1pm, 3-6pm, s/1). The museum is housed in a little building to the right of the Compañía. It's not very informative but is worth a visit if only to see the horrors it contains: a two-headed alpaca, a two-headed guinea pig, a six-legged goat and a frog the size of two clenched fists.

● **Inca walls** The wall on the north-western side of the plaza is probably the remains of the Inca Pachacutec's palace, and the northern corner of the square is the site of the palace of the Inca Sinchi Roca.

Coricancha (Temple of the Sun) and Santo Domingo

(About 500m south-east of Plaza de Armas; open Monday to Saturday 8am-5pm, Sunday 2-4pm s/4, s/2 students). The Coricancha was the centre of Incan religion. It was lavishly decorated, even by the standards of ancient Cusco. The Inca historian Garcilasco de la Vega, writing 50 years after the fall of the Inca Empire, described the interior: 'In the walls of the rooms giving on to the cloister, four tabernacles were hollowed out in each of the outside walls.... They had moldings round the edges and in the hollows of the tabernacles, and as these moldings were worked in the stone they were inlaid with gold plates not only at the top and sides, but also the floors of the tabernacles. The edges of the moldings were encrusted with fine stones, emeralds and turquoises, for diamonds and rubies were unknown there. The Inca sat in these tabernacles when there were festivals in honour of the Sun.' The Spaniards stole the lot.

The Corincancha consisted of a number of chapels dedicated to different deities: the Rainbow, Thunder and, of course, the Sun himself. The kidnapped idols of subdued tribes were kept hostage in the temple and if the tribe stepped out of line the idols were ridiculed and then destroyed.

Outside the temple was the garden, in which the Incas displayed some of the most astounding of their goldwork. Garcilasco describes what it contained: 'That garden, which now serves the monastery with vegetables, was in Inca times a garden of gold and silver such as existed in the royal palaces. It contained many herbs and flowers of various kinds, small plants, large trees, animals great and small, tame and wild, and creeping things such as snakes and lizards, and snails, butterflies and birds, each placed in an imitation of its natural surroundings.' He goes on to describe a field of golden maize and statues of men, women and children. Most, of course, did not escape the greedy Spanish furnaces.

After the Spaniards' triumphant entry into Cusco, Coricancha was given to Juan Pizarro but he didn't have long to enjoy it. He was mortally wounded at the siege of Sacsayhuaman and on his deathbed gave it to the Dominicans (the priest, Vincente Valverde, who accompanied the Pizarros was a Dominican), who built the monastery of Santo Domingo in its stead as a symbolic gesture of Christianity's superiority over the native religion. In 1950, however, an earthquake flattened the monastery, leaving the fantastic Inca masonry unmoved.

The monastery of Santo Domingo is worth a visit too, with a splendid carving of Santo Domingo by Melchor Huamán and the graves of the rebel Incas Sayri Tupac and Tupac Amaru and of Juan Pizarro himself. There is an underground Coricancha **museum** in the grounds (entrance via Av El Sol, Visitor's Ticket).

West and south of Plaza de Armas
This is the area south of Plateros, and north of Av El Sol behind the Portales de Comercio and Confituría.
● **La Merced** (daily except Sundays, 8am-12pm, 2-5pm s/3, s/2 students). Built in 1534 and then rebuilt after the 1650 earthquake, La Merced rivals the cathedral in its riches and has particularly beautiful cloisters. It faces the old Indian market, which allowed the clergy inside the church to preach to the milling crowds outside. Both Almagros are buried here, as is Gonzalo Pizarro. This is another monument that's currently undergoing restoration.
● **San Francisco Church** (daily 6.30-8am, 6-8pm). Austere and with rather bloodthirsty decoration, this church and monastery dominates the square outside.
● **Santa Clara Church** (free). The church isn't often open, but if you're lucky enough to get inside you'll find wall-to-ceiling angled mirrors which multiply a

hundredfold the candlelight. When I visited, a woman was singing in a mournful, high-pitched, mesmeric wail which made the whole place feel like another world.

● **Regional History Museum and House of Garcilasco** (8am-6pm, entrance by Visitor's Ticket). The museum has an overview of Peruvian history with some interesting exhibits such as a Nazca mummy, and a collection of paintings of the Cusco School. Look for St Michael armed with a gun. The house itself was rebuilt by the famous Peruvian architect, Víctor Pimentel, after it almost collapsed in the 1986 earthquake.

● **Market** Bustling, smelly, noisy, and filled with fat women in large hats carving dripping hunks of meat or spooning multi-coloured beans from huge sacks. All the world's goods are here, such as living frogs and skinned dead ones being sold amongst the piles of fresh fruit. A must – but be careful of your wallet and watch out for bag slashers.

● **Santa Teresa** (unpredictable opening hours, free). A pleasant church with illustrations of Saint Teresa's life inside, but the outside of the building gets used as a public toilet, so hold your nose. The square in front of the church is pretty, and the wall bordering Calle Sapphi is a marvellous example of polygonal field-stone masonry.

East of Plaza de Armas

This is the arc of streets south of Triunfo and north of Av El Sol, behind the Compañía.

● **Calle Loreto** Another famous Inca alley, leading off Plaza de Armas, the left-hand wall of which used to be the Acllahuasi (see p86).

● **Banco Wiese**, Calle Maruri (free, open when the bank is). The bank occupies the palace of Tupac Inca Yupanqui, with its wonderful Inca walls. There's a little museum inside telling you about the history of the building and exhibiting some of the artifacts found here.

● **Religious Art Museum and Archbishop's Palace** (Monday to Saturday 8.30am-12pm, 3-5.30pm, entrance with Visitor's Ticket). This building is in **Hatun Rumiyoc,** an alley which was originally the side of the palace of the Inca Roca. The wall contains the famous twelve-angled stone which you can see on every bottle of Cusqueña beer. The museum has a fine collection of religious paintings with accurate period detail, and the colonial building founded on Inca remains is impressive.

● **Convent and Museum of Santa Catalina** (Monday to Thursday, Saturday 9am-5pm, Friday 9am-3.30pm, Visitor's Ticket). The museum is small and uninspiring, filled with some religious art and a couple of fairly interesting models. However, the proportions of the interior of the building are quite beautiful, especially by the stairs up to the first floor internal balcony.

● **San Blas** (Monday to Wednesday, Friday and Saturday 10-11.30am, Monday to Sunday 2-6pm) is a simple church, but it contains a breathtaking carved cedar wood pulpit. At the top stands St Paul, his foot resting on a human skull, believed to belong to the craftsman who made the pulpit. The area around is the ancient district of Cusco's artisans.

CUSCO – WALKING TOURS

West

Start your tour in **Plaza de Armas**, and face south-west. Walk down the small alley (Medio) towards Plaza Regocijo. To your right is the **Town Hall**, and the road which leads uphill (north or right) from the square leads to the church of **Santa Teresa** (see opposite), while on the other side of the square (downhill, left and south) there's the **Regional History Museum** (see opposite) in the reconstructed house of Garcilasco de la Vega.

Head south-west down Garcilasco, the street that leads away from the square directly opposite the road on which you entered the square. Walk one block further down here and you'll reach Plaza San Francisco, with the **Monastery of San Francisco** on the opposite side (see p143). The bottom corner of this square (south) is **Santa Clara** leading to the convent of the same name (see p143), and ultimately the **market** and **railway station** for Machu Picchu. Be careful around here as the area is notorious for muggings and bag slashings.

Return to Plaza de Armas along Santa Clara.

South and east

Start in Plaza **de Armas** and face La Compañía. Walk south-east (downhill) through **Calle Loreto** (see opposite), and turn left at the end when you arrive in Maruri. Visit the **Banco Wiese**, and turn right at the end of the block down Romeritos until you reach a little square where the **Hotel Libertador** is situated. In front of you, slightly to your right, is the **Coricancha and Santo Domingo monastery** (see p142).

From Coricancha, go back up Romeritos to Maruri, then turn right and then left again up San Agustin. The fourth road on your right is **Hatun Rumiyoc** (see opposite), and on the corner is the **Religious Art Museum**.

Turning right, and walking down Hatun Rumiyoc will take you up to **San Blas**, and walking the other way back towards Plaza de Armas leads past the road in which there's the **Convent and Museum of Santa Catalina** (see opposite).

North

Stand in **Plaza de Armas** and face Sacsayhuaman. Walk up the little alley of Procuradores (also known as Gringo Alley or Pizza St) to the north-west. At the end, turn right, then left again and climb up Coricalle. At the end of Coricalle turn right, and you'll soon be on a large paved road.

Walk to the right uphill on the road, and you'll pass the church of **San Cristóbal** (see p146) on your left. Just before the church, turn right and walk downhill, down Resbalosa, savouring the view down towards Cusco. Turn left at the junction of Resbalosa and Waynapata, and continue along to Punacurco (which means 'puma's spine', a reference to the fact that the street plan of Cusco was originally designed to resemble a puma). Soon you'll arrive at a small square, the sides of which are graced by the **House of the Serpents**, **Cabrera's House** and the **Seminary of San Antonio Abad** now a hotel (see p146).

If you turn right, heading back towards Plaza de Armas, you'll walk down a street called Cordoba del Tucumán, past the **Museo Inka** (see p146) and end up back on the plaza.

North of Plaza de Armas

This covers the arc of streets between Plateros and Triunfo, under the shadow of Sacsayhuaman.

● **San Cristóbal Church** (free, no set opening times) stands proudly high above Cusco, its grounds enclosed by a massive Inca wall that is possibly the remains of the palace of the first Inca, Manco Capac. The church was built by the quisling, Inca Paullu, as a demonstration of his Christian faith.

● **Museo Inka (Archaeology)** and **Admiral's Palace**. This is at Cuesta del Almirante 103 (Monday to Friday 8am-5pm, Saturday 9am-5pm, s/5). The museum's collection is well displayed and informative with leaflets in English. They also have some Inca gold though you might have to ask to see it, and some paintings. A particularly gory *Execution of Atahualpa* shows his head being cut off (it wasn't, he was garrotted and then partly burnt). Look out too for the reconstructed burial chamber, or Mallkiwasi. The impressive buildings belonged to Admiral Don Francisco Maldonado.

● **House of the Serpents** Legend has it that this house was owned by the man who stole the golden disc of the Sun from the Coricancha, then gambled it away playing cards. It's called the House of the Serpents because of the carved snakes on its stones, and such ornamentation indicates it's a Spanish construction not an Inca one.

● **Cabrera's House** Cabrera founded Ica on the coast and also Cordoba in Argentina, and his house is an interesting colonial mansion with his coat of arms on the façade, its large salons and spacious interior patio graced with arches. The house is now the **Banco Continental Cultural Centre** (free entrance), the highlight of which is a room devoted to photographs of Cusco dating back to the thirties by the city's most famous photographer, Martín Chambi.

● **Seminary of San Antonio Abad** This is now Hotel Monasterio (see p134), which makes it easy to visit if you put on your clean clothes and are prepared to pay their prices for a beer. The open courtyards are spoilt by glassed-in cloisters, but it's a splendid building.

MOVING ON

Air

The airport is five minutes by taxi from Plaza de Armas, whence you can fly to most major Peruvian towns.

● **Airlines Aerocondor** (☎ 252774), at the airport; **Aero Continente** (☎ 243 031, ▤ 235666), Portal de Carnes 254, and at the airport (☎ 235696); **American Airlines** (☎ 248282), Calle Saphy 848; **Helicusco** (☎ 243555, ▤ 227283) Calle Triunfo 379; **Lanperu/Lanchile** (☎ 255552/3/4, ▤ 255555) Av El Sol 627B; **Lloyd Aereo Boliviano** (☎ 222990, ▤ 229220, ▭ www.labairlines.com), Santa Catalina Angosta 160; **TANS** (☎ 242727, ▤ 251000 and Lima 213 6000, ▭ www.tansperu.com.pe), San Augustin 315-317.

There are seven flights daily to Lima. The cheapest leaves early in the morning and costs around US$58. Later flights cost US$10-20 more.

The helicopter company **Helicusco** will fly you to Machu Picchu and back by 24-seat helicopter for US$170 (US$90 one way Cusco to Machu Picchu, US$100 Machu Picchu to Cusco). The flight takes 25 minutes and leaves Cusco at 8.30am, returning at 3pm.

Bus

All long-distance buses leave from and arrive at the terminal, near the airport. The route to Lima via Abancay and Ayacucho is now open again, and the run takes about 24 hours and costs about US$25. Other destinations include Nazca (check with the South American Explorers' Club about whether this route is safe) which costs US$20, Abancay US$5, Juliaca US$10, 6 hours and Arequipa US$8, 10 hours.

Local buses leave from a variety of departure points but there's a stop near Clorindo Matto de Turner school on Av de la Cultura for the Sacred Valley (take a taxi there), or try Av Grau near Centenario. Tickets to the furthest destination in the Sacred Valley, Ollantaytambo, cost about US$1, and the journey takes half a day.

Rail

The station for the Puno line is **Huanchac** and the station for Machu Picchu is **San Pedro**. Tickets for the Puno line can be bought only at Huanchac. Tickets for Machu Picchu can be brought from either. Check the train timetable, the times when the stations are open to sell tickets and the ticket prices as everything changes often. Those wishing to get to Machu Picchu as cheaply as possible should heed the advice given on p267.

● **Buying tickets** The central reservation office of Perurail can be contacted on ☎ 084-221992. **Huanchac station** is open for tickets from Monday to Friday 7am-5pm, and Saturday to Sunday 7am-12pm. **San Pedro station** is open for tickets Monday to Friday 8am-3pm, Sunday 8am-12.30pm. If you haven't booked in advance, it's worth going along an hour before the train leaves to see if there are any tickets left. For details of times and prices, see p267-8.

Around Cusco

RUINS NEAR CUSCO (DAY HIKE)

There are lots of small but interesting sites within walking distance of Cusco's Plaza de Armas. You could probably cover many in half a day if you wanted to but you'd miss so much; it's worth spending a little time exploring each one, and anyway walking through the rolling grassland around Cusco is a pleasant way to acclimatize to the altitude. Four of the five sights below are included in the Cusco Visitor's Ticket (BTU) – the fifth, Salapunco, is free to enter anyway; or, if you don't have that, you can buy a separate ticket covering just these five sights for s/21 (s/10.50 students).

The route described here is the most commonly walked day hike, and visits Sacsayhuaman, Qenko, Salapunco, Puca Pucara and Tambo Machay – take a packed lunch. If you don't feel like a walk, you can always take a tour (p131; s/20), take the bus (Pisac bus, s/1.5 – ask to be dropped off at Tambo Machay), or hire a horse (s/20-25 per day). Horses are readily available at Sacsayhuaman; just ask around. If your Spanish isn't good enough to do this, one of the tour agencies will be able to sort it out.

Sadly there have been muggings in the ruins close to Cusco and some attempted rapes (at Sacsayhuaman and Qenko). Leave valuables at the hotel, don't go to these places on your own, or at dawn and dusk.

❏ 'This was the greatest and most superb of the edifices that the Incas raised to demonstrate their majesty and power. Its greatness is incredible to those who have not seen it; and those who have seen it, and studied it with attention, will be led not alone to imagine, but to believe, that it was reared by enchantment – by demons, and not by men, because of the number and size of the stones placed in the three walls, which are rather cliffs than walls, and which it is impossible to believe were cut out of quarries, since the Indians had neither iron nor steel wherewith to extract or shape them. And how they were brought together is a thing equally wonderful, since the Indians had neither carts nor oxen nor ropes, wherewith to drag them by main force. Nor were there level road over which to transport them, but, on the contrary, steep mountains and abrupt declivities, to be overcome by the simple force of men. ... It passes the power of imagination to conceive how so many and so great stones could be so accurately fitted together as scarcely to admit the insertion of the point of a knife between them'. **Garcilasco de la Vega**. *Comentarios reales que tratan del origen de los Incas* (1609).

Sacsayhuaman

(7am to 5.30pm, Visitor's Ticket). It takes about 20 to 30 minutes to walk to Sacsayhuaman from Plaza de Armas. There are several routes but the easiest way is to go up one of the streets by the cathedral to Pumacurco, also called Palacio and Herrajes, turn left and walk uphill. After some stairs you'll reach a main, tarred road; at the top of the first bend is the ticket office (make sure you have the right money as they very rarely have any change) and a path leading up the hill along a small gully. Follow the stairs (you can go either way around the large hillock that blocks the way) until you reach the massive stones of Sacsayhuaman on your left.

No one knows for sure what Sacsayhuaman was. It was called 'the Fortress' by the Spanish, but current research suggests that it was more likely to be a temple, and Inca tombs have been discovered in the area. Whether or not it was designed to be a temple, it was certainly used as a fort by the armies of Manco Inca when they attempted to dislodge the Spaniards from Cusco (see p94), and the Spanish chronicler, Pedro Sancho, estimated that it was large enough to hold a garrison of 5000 Spanish soldiers. He went

TIMINGS
YOU COULD WALK FROM SACSAYHUAMAN TO TAMBO MACHAY, VISITING ALL THE SITES IN 2 HOURS BUT THIS WOULD BE A WASTE AS ALL THE SITES ARE SO INTERESTING. ALLOW A HALF-DAY FOR THE WHOLE WALK. FOR A LONGER WALK CONTINUE UP THE VALLEY PAST TAMBO MACHAY AND DISCOVER QUIET GRASS-LANDS AND A GLITTERING STREAM

MOUNTAINS

Tambo Machay

PISAC →

RÍO

THERE IS ANOTHER PATH HEADING OFF TO THE WEST

Day hike from Cusco

Puca Pucara

FOOTBALL FIELD

FENCES

0   1km

0   1/2 mile

TRAILBLAZER

STAY ON THE VALLEY FLOOR

CAREFUL - MARSHY GROUND

CLIFFS

HUT WITH BARRIER ACROSS THE ROAD

STREAM

Sacsayhuaman

RODADERO (THE SLIDING PLACE)

TUNNEL

QOCHA

FIELDS

ROAD Salapunco
A VERY LARGE ROCK IN ROLLING FIELDS.

THE INCA'S THRONE

ESPLA-NADE

Qenko Chico

Qenko

WALL

MUYUMARCA

REMAINS OF SALLAMARCA & PAUNCAMARCA

TICKET OFFICE

Calle Pumacurco

STATUE OF CHRIST

CENTRAL CUSCO

on to say that the widely-travelled Spaniards he was with commented 'that they have never seen a building to compare with this fortress, nor a stronger castle'.

It was topped by three towers and riddled with tunnels in which the historian, Garcilasco de la Vega, remembers playing when he was a child. The towers were called Salla Marca, Paunca Marca and Muyu Marca. The concentric rings of foundations of the last remain, but the stones of the others were pillaged in the days when Cusqueños used Sacsayhuaman as an unofficial quarry. Some tunnels remain in the northern amphitheatre – bring a torch.

The mound opposite the zigzag walls is called the Inca's Throne or the *rodadero* (sliding place). It was probably where a high-ranking person supervised sacred ceremonies, but nowadays the deep polished grooves in the rock are used by children as a slide. The green meadow between the Inca's Throne and the tiered walls is called the Esplanade.

Qenko

From Sacsayhuaman, the path leads to Qenko (7am-5.30pm, Visitor's Ticket), which is further to the east beyond the statue of Christ. If you stand in the Esplanade and look away from Cusco you'll see a path heading uphill towards a barrier (which you can't see from the Esplanade) with a hut beside it. Walk up there, turn right (east) beyond the hut and follow the road past some souvenir sellers into a small wood. The road turns to the left (north), and on your right there is the stone mound of Qenko Chico (little Qenko), at the bottom of which there is a wall containing a block carved with twenty-one angles. A little further on, by a car park on the right-hand side of the road, is Qenko.

Qenko – the name means 'zigzag' or 'labyrinth' – is a huaca (sacred site). Immediately below the car park at the front of the site there is a monolith called the Seated Puma which is enclosed by a niched wall of fine masonry.

There are carvings everywhere, but some are a little indistinct: a llama, a condor, and snakes have all been identified. One recent discovery is a structure that seems to cast a shadow rather like a puma's head when the sun rises on the winter solstice (21 June). You'll probably have already seen a photograph of this on the cover of *The Awakening of the Puma*, sold in every bookshop in Cusco.

Salapunco

At Qenko it's best to ask someone for directions but you should follow the road uphill for about 50 metres; just before it joins the main road there is a path off to the right through the trees towards a village.

Go down the path to a small gully, pass through a gap in the wall and turn left uphill along the side of the gully. Keep the village on your right and just past it you come to a crossroads. Take the diagonal path (east) across the fields to a large rocky outcrop ahead.

This is Salapunco, aka Cusilluchagoc, (always open, admission free) another carved limestone monolith riddled with passages and providing excellent views from the top. It isn't on the tour routes and so is often deserted.

Puca Pucara

If you stand on the top of Salapunco and look away from Cusco, you can see directly below you a clear track. Follow the track to the left (west) for just a few minutes until you come to a junction with a smaller path coming from your left. Follow this path north and down to a small marshy depression and on through boggy ground as it traces the seasonal course of a small stream. After climbing for about half an hour you pass a small village with a football field on your left, and beyond it you should be able to see the road running parallel to you. Shortly after this the path joins the road, and then Puca Pucara (7am-5.30pm, Visitor's Ticket) appears 50 metres away on the right.

Puca Pucara is probably a hunting lodge on one of the Inca's private estates near Cusco. It was originally thought to be a military checkpoint or on a main Inca road. The name can be translated as 'red watchtower' or 'red fort'.

Tambo Machay

You can see the signpost to Tambo Machay from Puca Pucara. Return to the road, walk away from Cusco and turn left (west) at the corner following the signpost to Tambo Machay (7am-5.30pm, Visitor's Ticket). It is about 200 metres away.

Tambo Machay (the name means 'inn cave') is known popularly as Los Baños del Inca, (the Inca's Baths), and was probably a centre of water worship. The whole complex is an architectural frame for a spring which falls from one terrace to another, slips underground, then emerges again in two cascades.

Returning to Cusco

You can either retrace your steps, or catch a bus or taxi on the road by the turning to Tambo Machay.

THE SACRED VALLEY

The fertile valley of the Urubamba river, also called the Vilcanota, snakes its way through the old Inca province of Antisuyu, an area which the Incas valued greatly. There, beside this tributary of the Amazon, they built their retreats, palaces and sacred places: the fortress of Ollantaytambo (clinging to the steep sides of the river's gorge), Pisac with its Inca canal, three kilometres long, its imposing terraces and, of course, the once-lost Machu Picchu.

Urubamba means 'place of the bugs or spiders' but the area is called the Sacred Valley in all today's tourist literature. It's probably so called to attract tourists to the proliferation of ruins in the area, but some suggest the valley is sacred because it was Cusco's granary, and others because it is connected with the sun and sky. (However, there's no doubt it was very important to the Incas, and previously-unknown carvings were uncovered in the valley as recently as March 2000). One Quechua legend says that after the sun sets in the evening it passes through the underworld beneath the Urubamba where it drinks the chill water to refresh itself before emerging at dawn. Another legend says that the

Urubamba is the earthly mirror of the celestial river, the Milky Way, and that water flows from one into the other.

There are many good hikes around the Sacred Valley. Hilary Bradt's *Backpacking and Trekking in Peru and Bolivia* describes some splendid little walks, as does Charles Brod's *Apus & Incas*, although this book is hard to obtain. Regular buses run from Cusco to the towns in the Sacred Valley (see towns below and also p147), and there are many hotels out here where you can stay to escape Cusco's bustle.

Pisac

Viceroy Toledo, who supervised the crushing of the last Incas, built Spanish Pisac on an Inca settlement in the shadow of the great terraces of the Inca ruins known as the Citadel. Many tombs have been found here, and there is a rare Intihuatana – a sacred carving or 'hitching post of the sun', many of which had their tops broken off by the Spanish. The site is open 7am-5.30pm (Visitor's Ticket) and is definitely worth visiting.

The Sacred Valley

TO PUNO

Pisac

Puca Pucara
Salapunco
Qenco

Tambomachay

Sacsayhuaman

Poroy

CUSCO

Calca

Rio Urubamba

Chinchero

Anta

Izcuchaca

Urubamba

Maras

Moray

Zurite

Rio Huarocondo

Ollantaytambo

TO MACHU PICCHU

TO MOLLEPATA

20KM
10
0
APPROXIMATE SCALE

It's a fair climb up to the ruins, and if you're not yet acclimatized you'll need to take your time. The path begins behind (north of) the market, and forks after 10mins: the upper path (signposted 'subida', or 'uphill') is, misleadingly, the gentler, easier path, and follows the narrow Quitamayo stream up to the northernmost ruins of Hanan Pisac; the other, steeper path heads across the river and straight up the hill to the fortress and lookout post overlooking Pisac town.

There are markets in Pisac on Tuesday, Thursday and Sunday mornings at which you can pick up well-made souvenirs. A shop on Plaza de Armas is worth mentioning because it sells fabrics produced by a weavers' collective, and all profits the shop makes go straight back to the weavers.

Pisac is 32km from Cusco. To get here catch a minibus (45 mins, s/2) from Calle Huascar, Calle Puputi 208 or Inticahuarina in Cusco.

Chinchero

There are Inca remains here (7am-5.30pm, Visitor's Ticket) and the church has paintings from the Cusco School. The Sunday market (crafts as well as local produce) is worth coming for, particularly since it attracts fewer tourists than the Pisac markets. Buses from Cusco leave early in the morning, usually from Calle Huascar (s/2).

Urubamba

Urubamba is a largish town, and the centre of the bus network; this is where you change if you're travelling between Cusco and Ollantaytambo. It also has a local market and is the home of a number of the local weavers, ceramicists, potters (Seminario Ceramicas at the Taller Workshop at Calle Berriozabal 111 are a particular favourite), sculptors and artists whose wares fill the souvenir shops in Cusco; you can spend a diverting morning wandering around their studios watching them at work and looking for bargains. Primarily, however, Urubamba is a good base from which to explore other parts of the Sacred Valley.

Two to three hours' walk from Urubamba (or you can catch a Cusco-bound bus, s/1 from Urubamba, and ask to be dropped off on the way) is the site of **Moray**, an Inca experimental farm, where a natural depression has been transformed into circular terraces of different sizes. This strange place was probably used to study the effect of altitude on different plants.

You can walk from Moray (two hours) to the **Maras Salinas**, another bizarre site, where layers of beige and white salt-pans are still used to crystallize salt from water.

Where to stay and eat There are plenty of hotels in Urubamba, which range from the expensive and rather flash English-owned *Hotel Incaland* on Av Ferrocarril (☎ 201071, 🖹 201117, 🖵 www.incalandperu.com) with room rates starting at US$80/90 sgl/dbl in the high season, to the mid-priced *Los Girasoles* (☎ 201390) on the outskirts of town beyond the Torrechayoc Church. Los Girasoles has camping sites, dormitory beds as well as doubles and singles; it's a touch overpriced at US$8 for a dormitory bed, or US$10/20 sgl/dbl, though you can't fault either the pastoral setting, the facilities (including a pizzeria,

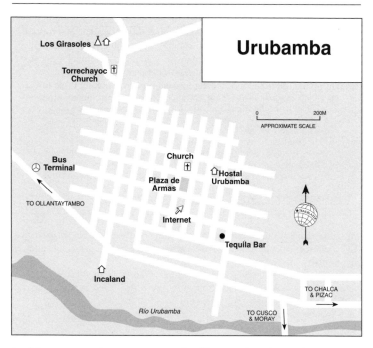

Urubamba

Los Girasoles

Torrechayoc Church

Bus Terminal

TO OLLANTAYTAMBO

Church

Plaza de Armas

Hostal Urubamba

Internet

Tequila Bar

Incaland

Río Urubamba

TO CUSCO & MORAY

TO CHALCA & PIZAC

0   200M
APPROXIMATE SCALE

bar/leisure room and a permanent supply of hot water) or the spacious grounds. There are some cheaper places too, such as ***Hostal Urubamba*** (no phone; s/10 per person per night) on Jirón Bolognesi, one block east of Plaza de Armas. For nightlife, try ***Tequila Pub*** on Av Mariscal Castilla.

Transport Urubamba is a 2¹/₂-hour minibus ride from Cusco (from Calle Huascar or Inticahuarina, s/3). It's 1¹/₂ hours from Pisac and about 50 minutes from Ollantaytambo (s/1.5).

Ollantaytambo

At the end of its flat, verdant plain, the Urubamba river flows faster and enters a gorge which leads down from the Andes to the Amazon. It was in this beautiful, strategic spot, 68 kilometres from Cusco, that the Inca Pachacutec built his fortress of Ollantaytambo. It's a lovely place, green and relaxed, enclosed in hills that hide some of the most impressive ruins in the valley. Stay here if the strains of Cusco are getting you down, or if you want to explore the Sacred Valley or Machu Picchu from closer than Cusco itself.

The fortress temple Myth has it that the name comes from an Inca captain, Ollanta, who fell in love with Pachacutec's daughter. Pachacutec forbade them to marry, at which Ollanta rebelled. Pachacutec himself was killed in the ensu-

---

Ollantaytambo Museum

A burnished plaque on the museum in Ollantaytambo records its opening by none other than HRH Princess Anne. Many people wonder what she was doing out here. The answer is that Catcco, the organization that runs the museum, was set up as a joint project by the Cusichaca Trust (see p87), the University of Cusco, local community groups, and the British Embassy. It's an attempt to harness the tourist dollar to benefit the local people of Ollantaytambo directly, in a way that helps people come away with a greater understanding of campesino life and history. It's a very good museum, and is well worth a visit. It's open Tuesday to Sunday 10am-1pm and 2-4pm; entrance costs s/5, although two students can get in for the price of one. For a fascinating, detailed examination of the Inca stonework here, read *Inca Architecture and Construction at Ollantaytambo* by Jean-Pierre Protzen (1993).

---

ing battle, and Ollanta almost defeated the army of the empire but was betrayed. The new Inca took pity on him because of his great prowess in war and allowed him to marry the princess.

It was to the forbidding fortress temple (7am-5.30pm, Visitor's Ticket), high above the valley floor, that Manco Inca retreated when he was being pursued by the Spanish (p96), and from here that he defeated a raiding party of seventy Spaniards sent to seize him, forcing them to retreat after days of heavy fighting. It was the first time the Spanish had been worsted in open combat against the Incas. It was to be the last time too; a few months later Manco, realizing Ollantaytambo was too near to Cusco to be secure, opted to retreat over the mountains to Vilcabamba.

The steep terraces seem to bar your route up to the fortress, and walls rise from the near-vertical cliff faces – you can see why the Spanish failed to capture this place. At the top lies the unfinished Sun Temple, consisting of massive mortarless slabs perfectly slotted together and stained with orange lichen. The double doorjambs you'll see here are rare in Inca buildings and indicate that this was a very important site.

Old town Below on the valley floor lies the old town of Ollantaytambo – one of the best surviving examples of Inca urban planning. The Incas built their towns in blocks called *canchas,* and one cancha housed several families. In most of Peru these canchas have long since been knocked down and the ancient Inca streets built over, but both remain here. Look out for more double doorjambs which show that this town itself was as important as the ruins that cling to the hills above. This place is one of the most photogenic in the entire Andes.

Where to stay and eat There's the excellent if expensive North American-owned *El Albergue* (☎ 204014; US$15 per person per night), Casilla 784 Cusco (entrance on the platform of the station), and the cheaper but very good *Hostal*

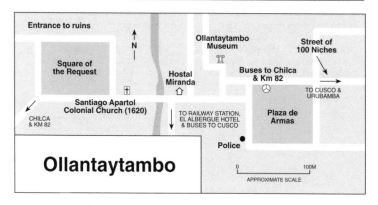

Ollantaytambo

Miranda (☎ 204091; s/20/30 sgl/dbl, but haggle). *La Fortaleza* is a good restaurant on Plaza de Armas, and the food at the Miranda is very tasty and they serve enormous portions.

Transport From Cusco you can get here by the expensive tourist train (about two hours, see p267-8) or by colectivo or minibus. The railway station is about a 10-15 minute walk from the town centre. Colectivos and minibuses from Cusco leave from Calle Huascar or in the side street of Inticahuarina. You will have to change in Urubamba.

From Ollantaytambo, buses and colectivos to Urubamba, Chilca and Km82 leave from the main square, while buses directly to Cusco (s/5) leave from the train station, where they meet the train coming from Aguas Calientes; as such, you'll probably have to fight for a seat with those alighting from the train, and you are probably better off taking a colectivo to Urubamba and changing there.

Aguas Calientes
Also known as Pueblo Machu Picchu, this village is very much the end of the line now that the track that used to run on to Quillabamba has been destroyed. Really just a dormitory town for the ruins themselves, it's an ugly rash in the pristine forest of the Sanctuary.

The trail up the mountain Putucusi starts here (ask at Gringo Bill's), and there are some rather tacky hot springs (s/5) where you can rest your aching bones after you return. Also here, rather surprisingly for this remote place, is a first-class restaurant and the best hotel in the whole valley. For up-to-date information, Agua Calientes now has its own website 🖥 www.machupicchu peru.com.

Where to stay The top hotel is *Machu Picchu Pueblo Hotel* (☎ 211122, 🖷 211124); reservations in Lima (☎ 422 6574, 🖷 422 4701, 🖥 www.inka terra.com.pe), a beautiful place with bungalows set in the enclosing forest.

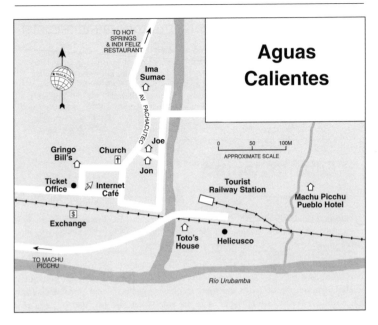

TO HOT
SPRINGS
& INDI FELIZ
RESTAURANT

**Aguas
Calientes**

Ima
Sumac

AV PACHACUTEC

Gringo
Bill's

Church

Joe

Jon

0   50   100M
APPROXIMATE SCALE

Ticket
Office

Internet
Café

Tourist
Railway Station

Machu Picchu
Pueblo Hotel

Exchange

Toto's
House

Helicusco

TO MACHU
PICCHU

Río Urubamba

Singles/doubles with attached bathroom cost US$155/173 plus tax, and not
including breakfast.

Other accommodation includes ***Gringo Bill's*** (☎ 211046, 🖳
gringobill@yahoo.com, www.machupicchuperu.com/gringo.htm), at Pasaje
Ccolla Raymi 104, just off the plaza. Though the eponymous Bill no longer runs
the show, the place still maintains its high standards; though room rates seem
excessive at US$30/40 sgl/dbl, not including breakfast, there's a 10% discount
if you stay for more than one night.

For cheaper accommodation, head up the hill towards the hot springs; this
street, Av Pachacutec, is dotted with places to stay including the efficient and
comfortable ***Ima Sumac*** (☎ 211021; s/20/30 sgl/dbl after bargaining). Cheaper
still, in an alley off Pachacutec are ***Hospedaje Joe*** and ***Hospedaje Jon***, where
rooms can cost as little as s/7 per person per night.

Where to eat The best restaurant is the French-run ***Indi Feliz,*** Calle Lloque
Yupanqui Lt 4. If you walk up to the springs it's on the left just after the school
on Av Pachacutec. Dishes here include freshly-baked quiche lorraine and
Urubamba trout smothered in melted butter. Prices are quite reasonable and portions large. ***Toto's House***, overlooking the river at the eastern end of the village,
offers an 'all-you-can-eat' buffet for US$10, while ***Arriero's***, half way up Av

---

Paddington Bear – an endangered species

Paddington, a small, fat bear with a duffle coat, a love of marmalade sandwiches and an extraordinarily hard stare, came from 'darkest Peru'. For those not familiar with this character, he was the star of a string of books written by Michael Bond. Paddington was found by the Brown family on the platform at London's Paddington station (hence his name), with a note around his neck which read: 'Please look after this bear, thank you'.

The British actor, Stephen Fry, has taken this message as a call for help not just for the Paddington Bear of the books he grew up on but for the species as a whole. *Tremarctos ornatus*, the spectacled bear, is now officially listed as endangered: fewer than 900 remain in the wild. Fry has helped to launch Bear Rescue which has set up a small-scale breeding programme, establishing a sanctuary in the grounds of the Machu Picchu Pueblo Hotel in Aguas Calientes. One bear has been rescued from a private animal collection and another from a circus in Chile.

On an informative and entertaining website – **www.bear-rescue.tv** – Stephen Fry explains the history and future of the project. There's a live webcam, downloadable videos and slideshows.

Pachacutec, serves up some pretty scrumptious pizzas. Cusco's **Chez Maggy** has a branch at Pachacutec 156.

Transport The village boasts two **train stations**: the modern one, surrounded by wire fencing and policed by armed guards, serves the expensive tourist trains, while the local trains (and the 'economic' tourist trains that leave at 6.10 am and 6.10pm) set off from the stretch of tracks running beneath the police station, to the south of the main square. There's no indication that this is a station, for it's little more than a rail track with pizza restaurants either side. All train tickets must be bought from the booth (8.30am-6pm) to the east of the police station. See p267-8 for details and timetables of the train service.

The **bus for Machu Picchu** leaves from the bus 'station', just a patch of concrete where the train tracks pass over a small stream. You can buy tickets at a half-built concrete house near where the bus leaves.

See p258 for more information on transport from Aguas Calientes and Machu Picchu.

PART 6: MINIMUM IMPACT

Minimum impact trekking

There are problems on the Inca Trail. Some are unavoidable: people are attracted to the spot because of its solitude, and when they arrive they turn it from an unvisited oasis to a tourist attraction. Some of the problems, however, can be avoided, such as those of litter and erosion, of pollution and destruction of the ancient Inca sites.

A lot of the damage done by tourists flows from selfish thoughtlessness. They forget that they're not the only people who'll walk in these hills: others, too, will be tempted to light a little cooking fire or camp in the ruins – a knock-on effect that endangers the environment. We who have the privilege of walking in this place must also accept the responsibility of helping to preserve it, at the very least by removing our rubbish.

ENVIRONMENTAL IMPACT

Continue to contaminate your bed, and you will one night suffocate in your own waste. Chief Seattle, taken from *Chief Seattle's Testimony* (Pax Christi and Friends of the Earth, 1976).

We are not entering a wilderness when we come to the Machu Picchu Historical Sanctuary. People, plants and animals have been living here for centuries in harmony. The influx of tourists threatens to ruin this delicate balance and we are part of the problem. By following a few rules, however, we can be part of the solution.

Pack it in, pack it out
If you've carried something into the Sanctuary, carry it out again. Some suggest burying litter but this isn't a solution as there are too many people walking these trails. Put your used packets and empty tins in a large plastic bag and dispose of them in Cusco. The rubbish bins along the trail are usually full to overflowing so it would be helpful if you took away some of the litter left by other people, too.

● **Is it OK if it's biodegradable?** Not really. Of course, things like an apple core will rot away in no time but orange peel takes six months to biodegrade, and clothes will take 15 years.

● **Lavatory paper** Lavatory paper is a vexed subject. Some people keep a lighter in a bag with their loo paper to burn the stuff. I find it difficult to get it

---

Opposite Top: The campesinos won't be the only ones interested in your trekking. (Photo © Richard Danbury). **Bottom:** Arriero with his mules, Mollepata. You should pay a fair price for local services – see p162. (Photo © Henry Stedman).

to catch light so I pack it out along with everything else I've brought in. Put one plastic bag inside another (in case of ruptures), put the used paper inside and seal the top with a piece of wire. When you get to a lavatory (there are five on the trail) you can just flush the paper away. It might be biodegradable but if you leave it on the ground it will flutter around for a long time, a sordid reminder of your passing. Pack out sanitary towels, too.

Bury your excrement
Bring a little trowel to bury excrement. Make sure you do it *well* away from the trail.

Don't pollute water
Don't relieve yourself within 20m (70ft) of a stream or other water supply. People have ignored this rule, and as a result giardia (see p170) has infected the streams in the Sanctuary.

Don't pollute streams with soap. Some people bring a collapsible plastic bucket to collect water to wash in from a stream. Dirty water should be poured away at least 20m from the water source.

Avoid using detergent to clean pans; use a wire scrubber in swiftly flowing water. If you must use detergent, wash up in a collapsible bucket away from the stream. I think 'biodegradable camping detergents' are a con, because all detergents are biodegradable – the problems only start when they've biodegraded.

Erosion
Inca roads were designed for llama hooves and bare human feet, and there wasn't much traffic in those days as no one could travel without a permit. Today the old stones bear the weight of thousands of tramping boots and running porters, and the old paths have become deeply scored into the mountainside.

There have been efforts to deal with the problem, and the section up to Abra de Huarmihuanusca (Dead Woman Pass) has recently been paved. However, you can help things get better by sticking to the paths and camping only where you're supposed to.

Camp-fires
It's a park rule that you're not allowed to have a camp-fire, so don't. This is because the wood you're burning is not unlimited and also there's the danger of camp-fires getting out of control: there were large fires in 1988, 1994 and 1997 that were probably caused by careless tourists or their porters.

Camping in the ruins
Inca ruins that have stood for hundreds of years are being damaged by selfish hikers who want the experience of sleeping in them, and think that it won't do any harm. But it does. Just peek over the other side of Sayacmarca and you'll

Opposite At the colourful market in Pisac (see p152), which takes place on Sunday, Tuesday and Thursday mornings, you can buy anything from a bunch of carrots to an alpaca sweater. (Photo © Melissa Graham).

see a pyramid of turds and a field of paper dropped by people who think that they're the only ones who've ever camped here.

Litter's not the only problem. Camp-fires can cause damage to the ancient walls, and careless campers knock off stones. And there's the more intangible way that people stake ownership with their sweaty bodies and nylon tents to the ruins that should belong to everyone.

Obey the park ruling and don't camp in the ruins, tempting as it might be. Wardens occasionally patrol the ruins to catch people camping illegally.

Don't pick flowers or disturb animals

You will be walking in a UNESCO natural World Heritage Site. It's a sanctuary where plant- and wild-life are supposed to exist without human interference, so don't pick the plants and leave any animals you see in peace.

The authorities may also be responsible for damage to the place, sometimes by accident, at other times on purpose. An example of accidental, well-meaning damage happened at Intipata (see p188). The site was regularly cleared of encroaching plant life until it was discovered that it was a haven for a rare orchid.

ECONOMIC IMPACT

If tourists were more aware of the power of their money and the responsibility that goes with it, they could do a lot of good.

The power you have to do good

Some locals are as guilty of not looking after the Sanctuary as the tourists and authorities. The villains are often cheap tour operators, who drop litter and exploit their porters: porters are often paid very little for the back-breaking work of carrying your bags, and may not be provided with either food or shelter.

● **Pay a fair price for a fair service** If you take a cheap tour, the misery of the porters and the filth that's dropped on the ground is your responsibility –

Machu Picchu cable car

Some threats to the Sanctuary are caused by the desire to improve the locals' standard of living and attract more tourists. The most important is the cable car. First mooted in 1998, then shelved in 2001, and then proposed once more in 2002, this would take up to 400 tourists an hour from the valley floor up to Machu Picchu. I've great doubts about it, both because it could increase the number of tourists tramping around the old stones, and also because it'd detract from the wonderful isolation of the site. Others disagree with me, notably John Hemming, the author of *The Conquest of the Incas*, who points out that it couldn't be much worse than the current set-up: a dreadful road from the valley floor, trafficked by knackered old buses belching filthy black smoke into the pristine mountain air.

you're the one who's saving the price of a trip to the cinema by not giving these people a living wage. Don't encourage this situation. Go for the more up-market tours where the porters are more realistically paid and more effort is made to ensure that litter is removed.

There's nothing worse than the shameful sight of a Westerner bargaining with a porter over what is to him the price of a newspaper and to the porter a square meal. Of course you may need to bargain and you shouldn't allow yourself to get ripped off, but find out from other hikers what the current fair price is, and pay accordingly.

The power you have to do bad
Well-meaning trekkers have created a begging culture amongst the children who live along the trail. In the busier villages, you'll be swamped with little hands and engulfed by children's voices piping: *'Dame dulce'*, *'Dame regalo'* (give me a sweetie/candy, a present). Because of their success with other tourists, little kids now associate gringos with an unlimited supply of money and sweets.

What you do about it is a matter for you. It's hard to resist the plaintive faces and grubby hands. I think that giving makes the situation worse: if they've done something helpful, reward them. Otherwise, sing them a song or make them laugh and they'll begin to see you more as a person, and less as an animated gum-ball machine.

CULTURAL IMPACT

Many campesinos get a pretty odd idea of life outside Peru as all they see of the world is well-dressed, apparently rich, tourists. Explain to them what the cost of living is like back home – how much does a loaf of bread cost, or a pint of milk – and how many hours you worked to earn the money to come to their country. Help them put your holiday into perspective and realize that we're not all millionaires.

Consider the feelings of local people
Some tourists leave their basic tact at home and forget that the locals they meet on holiday can be offended just as easily as they can themselves. It's often simple things caused by thoughtlessness that can really irritate.

● **Photographs** Ask permission before you take a photo and if your subject doesn't want you to take one, don't. Some children dress up and look deliberately cute, and then charge money when you ask to photograph them. Don't rip them off, but if you pay too much it becomes demeaning when they earn the same amount in ten seconds as their parents earn in ten hours.

● **Camping** If you're planning to camp somewhere near a village, ask permission: making contact can also help with safety.

● **Clothing** Although it matters less in Peru than in Islamic countries, wearing inappropriate clothing can still offend.

In churches you should show proper respect by covering normally exposed skin. Don't bathe naked in mountain streams where you could be overlooked.

● **Don't flaunt your wealth** However poor you may be by Western standards, your wealth is way above the wildest dreams of most campesinos so don't flaunt it. Never leave valuable items such as cameras or watches lying about.

● **Be polite** Some campesinos can be offended if they offer you a place to stay the night and you refuse and set up your tent in their fields instead. Not surprisingly, they can also get offended if they offer you food and you turn it down and cook your own. Wouldn't you be? Be aware of this, and try not to step on any toes. Some campesinos are over-friendly in a way that's not helpful; they might point you in a direction you know is wrong, or proffer unwanted help. Keep your patience and just decline pleasantly.

● **Always keep your sense of humour** If things aren't working out as you want don't lose your temper. It's more likely that the person you're talking to does not understand what you want than that they're being deliberately obstructive. A smile costs nothing.

Return hospitality
You'll probably encounter hospitality that will make you swell up with guilt, as someone who can afford nothing gives you much and won't accept repayment. If you find yourself in this position, don't force money on people who don't want it as they have their pride just as you do. Share your food with them, and try and give them something of yourself in return: try and speak Quechua, listen to them (some shepherds are just lonely), and tell them about your home or how much you like their country. Campesinos are as proud and patriotic as anyone.

Safe trekking

SAFETY IN THE HILLS

If you're properly prepared for your trek, you should have no problems, just a wonderful time.

Weather
The weather in the Machu Picchu Historical Sanctuary is very changeable. Expect rain and carry warm clothing, even if the sun's out and it's a beautiful day, because while the valleys are bathed in beautiful sunshine the high passes may be enveloped in cloud. For more information about the climate see p19.

Getting lost
In good weather most of the trails described in this book are clear and easy to follow. I don't believe it's possible to get lost on the stretch from Huayllabamba to Machu Picchu, as it's a heavily beaten path and there'll be many other peo-

ple walking at the same time as you. In bad weather, however, there are points on the more remote trails where the path will disappear, and there are sections of the Mollepata and Vilcabamba treks that are difficult in any weather.

Therefore a **compass** is absolutely essential if you're walking the longer trails. Some people bring a handheld GPS (Global Positioning System), but they really aren't worth it unless you head off into the wilderness.

Tell people where you're going

Before you leave on your trek, it's wise to inform someone at home and to tell your hotel manager or a fellow traveller where you're going and when you plan to be back; they should be aware of what to do if you don't get back, and how long to wait before raising the alarm.

Dogs

Dogs can be dangerous if they're carrying rabies and a nuisance when you're hiking. They'll often bark as you pass, but they seldom attack. If they look threatening, throw stones at them – this is what the locals do. The mere act of bending down to pick one up often scares them off.

A note of caution

Sadly there are some theft problems on the Inca Trail, and you'll hear some scare stories from other travellers but only believe one tenth of what you hear. Remember many thousands of hikers walk these trails each year without meeting any trouble at all.

The problems seem to be centred around the village of **Huayllabamba**; tents were slashed there when I was walking the trails for this book. You can easily reduce the risk of being a target by not camping near Huayllabamba, by travelling in groups, by stuffing your valuables deep down into your rucksack when you walk and by not leaving anything tempting outside your tent when you zip-up for the night. The SAEC (see p129) in Cusco is a good source of information as to the current situation.

Other villages on these trails are usually trouble free, but when you camp near one it's best to ask a local family for permission, partly out of politeness but also to come under their protection.

HEALTH IN THE HILLS

Walking in the Sanctuary is invigorating. It's generally a very healthy place, the blustering winds blow the cobwebs away and the sun warms your heart. When you come down from the high altitude, you'll feel like Superman. Nevertheless, you should be aware of illnesses associated with altitude above 3000m (10,000ft).

AMS – acute mountain sickness

AMS and the medical conditions, High Altitude Pulmonary Oedema (HAPO or HAPE) and High Altitude Cerebral Oedema (HACO or HACE), that can result from it are all entirely preventable if certain precautions are taken.

The important thing to remember is that **it is the speed of ascent not the altitude itself that causes AMS**. The body takes several days to adapt to an increase in altitude. The higher you go above sea-level, the lower the barometric pressure, resulting in less oxygen reaching your lungs with each breath you take. At 2500m/8202ft it's about 25% lower but up to this altitude the effects are rarely felt; at 5000m/16,400ft the pressure is almost 50% lower.

AMS is uncomfortable but not dangerous unless it's a severe case. You'll feel a headache and nausea. In bad cases you may start vomiting. It's a bit like having a hangover, and it usually passes after one to three days. You can take painkillers (but not sleeping tablets) and acetazelomide (see opposite), but the best thing to do is rest, and if it gets worse, descend.

HAPO and HACO are very serious, and potentially life-threatening. You should know both how to recognize them and what to do if you suspect someone's got them, but if you take care you're very unlikely to come across either. **HAPO** occurs when the lungs get waterlogged. Symptoms include not being able to breathe properly and finding it more difficult to exert yourself than usual. It tends to progress from AMS, but it's not common in trekkers. The pulse increases, fluid is coughed up, there's fever, and your extremities go blue (compare fingernail beds with a healthy person). Sometimes there's also chest tightness, and the lungs sound crackly. Once the person descends, recovery is usually quick and complete.

HACO is a build-up of fluid in the brain. Anyone who gets it will suffer from loss of balance, severe lassitude and will eventually fall into a coma. There may also be an altered mental state – hallucinations, weakness or numbness on one side of the body, and an inability to talk or make sense. Headache,

---

SERIOUS AMS SYMPTOMS – IMMEDIATE DESCENT!

- **Persistent, severe headache**
- **Persistent vomiting**
- **Ataxia** – loss of co-ordination, inability to walk in a straight line, making the sufferer look drunk.
- **Losing consciousness** – inability to stay awake or understand instructions.
- **Liquid sounds in the lungs**
- **Very persistent, sometimes watery, cough**
- **Difficulty breathing**
- **Rapid breathing or feeling breathless at rest**
- **Coughing blood, pink phlegm or lots of clear fluid**
- **Severe lethargy**
- **Marked blueness of face and lips**
- **High resting heartbeat – over 130 beats per minute**
- **Mild symptoms rapidly getting worse**

nausea and vomiting are also symptoms. Death occurs quickly if the person remains at altitude, and even if you get them down, there can be long-term neurological damage.

All are caused by the body's response to the lower oxygen pressure in the air, and all can be largely treated by descending promptly.

● **Headache** Headache is an important warning sign of trouble. If you have a headache follow Dr Peter Hackett's headache rule: rest, don't ascend, eat snacks, drink plenty of fluids, take mild pain medicine. If it's not going away or you suspect altitude sickness, don't ascend. If you suffer from severe shortness of breath at rest (you don't get your breath back after 15 minutes) or if you have any of the symptoms listed in the boxed text on the opposite page **descend immediately** – even if it's the middle of the night.

● **Ataxia** Ataxia is altered balance and muscular coordination. You can test for it by drawing a 2m (6ft) line on the ground and walking heel-to-toe along it. If you can't walk in a straight line, then fear the worst and descend.

● **Acetazelomide** Acetazelomide (Diamox) is a drug that can prevent and treat AMS (not HAPO or HACO). It's a diuretic and so will make you urinate more, and it makes your fingertips tingle. It's widely available in Peru. The dose is 125mg twice a day, usually taken before you go to sleep. You can stop taking it after a couple of days at altitude. Some doctors recommend taking the same dose as a treatment for AMS, though by far the best thing is to descend. Don't take acetazelomide if you're allergic to sulpha drugs.

● **Coca leaf** Coca leaf (see p48) has been used for centuries to reduce the effects of AMS. You chew it in a quid in your mouth, with a little *llibita* (a catalyst). Some say it works; all it did for me was turn my shirt green when I spat out the juice and missed the ground.

Injury

An elementary knowledge of First Aid is useful. In an emergency, the basics are ABC: first check the casualty's **airway's clear**, then check **breathing** and **circulation**.

● **A Airway** Make sure the mouth is clear and the tongue is not obstructing the airway. Clean out vomit or anything else that's in the way.

● **B Breathing** Check the casualty's breathing by putting your ear close to his mouth.

● **C Circulation** Check the heart's beating by feeling for a pulse on the wrist, groin or neck, or by feeling the chest. If there's no pulse, then start cardiac massage. Remember to stanch any wounds that are bleeding profusely (if it's arterial blood – red and spurting – press heavily on the bleeding point for 10 minutes, then apply a crepe bandage. Raise the wounded area above the level of the heart).

If the injury is serious and you need trained medical help you'll have to get the casualty out because there are no doctors on the remoter regions of this trail. Strap up suspected broken bones, try to keep the person as immobile and as warm as possible and ask the locals for help.

Animal bites

● **Rabid animals** If you get bitten by a dog, bat or other similar animal, there's a risk of contracting **rabies**, so wash out the wound with copious amounts of soap and water. Use a stiff brush if you have one, and get into the corners of the wound even if it hurts, then disinfect. Seek medical help as quickly as possible – there's a rabies centre in Lima (see p106). Rabies can kill you and since it may lie dormant for months; you must get expert advice even if you feel fine.

● **Snakes** You are very unlikely to get bitten by a snake. If you do, don't try sucking the venom out or cutting into the wound. Keep still, wash the wound and surrounding skin with water to remove any excess venom. It's reassuring to know that many snakes aren't venomous, and many snake bites don't result in venom being injected. Remove any rings, watches or other constrictions because the bitten area may swell.

If you can, capture and kill the snake so it can be identified but make sure it's dead. I read somewhere the story of a paratrooper who was bitten by a snake. His colleagues did all the right things to the victim, caught the snake so that it could be identified by the doctor, beat it to death and stuffed it in a sack. The victim and sack were evacuated by air but in the plane, the 'dead' snake escaped from its sack and bit the pilot.

If a limb's been bitten, splint it, but don't apply a tourniquet unless you know what you're doing. Many limbs are lost through inexpertly applied tourniquets. It's vital not to panic, **keep calm**, reassure yourself that even if you're bitten you're unlikely to die. Gene Savoy, the explorer of Vilcabamba, was bitten by a venomous snake forty years ago and he's still not dead.

Extreme heat and cold

● **Hypothermia** A person gets hypothermic when they are extremely cold, and this can kill them. If someone's hypothermic, they'll stumble, be confused, act oddly and be extremely cold to the touch. They may not notice they are ill, so if someone's acting like this warm them up. The best way to do this is to share bodily warmth, as James Bond said in *The Spy Who Loved Me*: strip the victim naked, get undressed yourself and jump into a sleeping bag together.

● **Sun-stroke and sunburn** The tropical sun in the high Andes burns quickly. **Sunburn** can be avoided by covering exposed skin (wear a long-sleeved cotton or linen shirt rather than a T-shirt) and putting sunblock on your face – especially your nose and ears. Always wear a hat.

When a person's temperature has been driven up dangerously high by the sun (usually above 40°C or 104°F), they've got **sun-stroke**. A sun-stroke patient will be confused and possibly delirious. Breathing and pulse rate will be rapid (over 30 breaths a minute and a pulse of over 100 beats a minute). Reduce temperature by fanning, gradually cooling them by sponging frequently with a cool damp cloth. If the person loses consciousness you must get them to a doctor quickly.

Not dangerous but irritating

● **Blisters** If you feel skin rubbing, put a piece of moleskin on it or some of the new Second Skin (Compeed) you can buy in pharmacies. If you've got a blister you can burst it with a sterilized needle (hold it in a flame for a few seconds) then cover it with a sterile dressing. Alternatively cover the unbroken blister with a build-up of moleskin.

● **Cracked skin and lips** Carry moisturizing cream and lip balm. Some people find the skin painfully pulling back from their nails and cracking – it grows back when you descend to lower altitudes.

Cook it, peel it, wash it or forget it

Many of the bugs that travellers pick up come from dirty water or food that's been prepared by someone with dirty hands. The key to avoiding these diseases is hygiene, but that's not something you're going to have complete control over. If you are doubtful about something you're offered to eat – if it's had flies on it, if it's not piping hot, if it's raw – leave it. The travellers' golden rule is if you can't cook it, peel it, wash it (in purified water) then forget it. Sadly that means that you should avoid ceviche (it's raw fish), which is a shame because it's a wonderful dish. I'm not encouraging you to go against sensible medical advice but it's worth saying that if you leave Peru without eating ceviche, you're missing out. If you do try it, perhaps wait until after you've been trekking.

Water purification

When you're hiking, you should purify your water unless you're getting it from a spring right at the top of a valley, as humans and livestock upstream from you are probably polluting it. There are a number of ways of doing this. You can use iodine tablets or drops, a water filter, or you can do it by boiling.

● **Iodine tablets** If you use tablets, use iodine not chlorine, as bugs like giardia aren't killed by chlorination. However, you shouldn't use iodine at all if you've got a thyroid problem, and it's not good for anyone to use it for long periods of time. It makes the water taste disgusting but you can add Vitamin C tablets or flavoured fruit powders to neutralize the taste. There are a number of brands on the market in the West (eg Potable Aqua and MicroPur). One tablet purifies a litre of water in about ten minutes.

● **Iodine drops** Using a 2% solution (Tincture of Iodine), the dose is 5 drops per litre of clean water which must then stand for 20-30 minutes. If the water is cloudy double the dose. You need a dropper to dispense the correct dose. Wrap the bottle and dropper in more than one plastic bag. An iodine leak in the centre of a pack can be a very messy business.

● **Water filter** This is a portable device that chemically or mechanically removes impurities from water, but they're expensive, and mechanical filters don't clean the water thoroughly enough to be much use.

● **Boiling** Current research shows that water need be brought only to the boil (even at altitude) to kill the bugs in it so drinks made from boiling water are generally safe.

Diseases from other people's filth

● **Diarrhoea** Despite the best precautions, just about everyone gets the 'Inca Two Step' in Peru. It's nothing to worry about. Don't plug yourself up immediately with Imodium: if your body wants to get rid of the contents of your bowels, let it. Drink lots of (uncontaminated) fluids: take a little weak soup or flat soft drinks, have some camomile tea with sugar and if you have re-hydrating powders, use them now. Only block yourself up if you have to travel or are becoming seriously dehydrated; avoid travelling if you can because it's best to rest for a couple of days. Be reassured that most of these attacks pass. However, if you're not better after 2-3 days, or if you get worse, you should try to see a doctor as you could have one of the following:

● **Dysentery** Dysentery is caused by drinking infected water or eating contaminated foods. It feels like diarrhoea with stomach cramps, and you may have blood in your faeces. Dysentery is treatable, but amoebic dysentery can cause difficulties if it's not caught.

● **Giardiasis** Giardiasis (giardia) is caused by eating or drinking giardia parasites that live in dirty water and food. The symptoms are foul-smelling belches and wind and a distended belly. It often goes away on its own, but if it doesn't it's easily treatable by a doctor.

● **Cholera** Transmitted in a similar way, cholera is rare in travellers. It mostly afflicts people who live in poor conditions where there's little fresh water; it's easily treatable.

Things not to worry about
I'm writing this last bit, not because you're in the least likely to come across any of these diseases, but to give you something to read on the bus.

● **Chagas disease** This is a rare, insect-borne disease transmitted by the bite of the assassin bug. The colourfully-named insect lives in the walls and roof of rustic huts, and comes out at night to feed on you. When it bites your skin, it tramples its faeces into the puncture hole and with the faeces go the germ that causes the disease. The bite hurts, so you'll know you've been bitten. If you're unlucky enough to be infected, the bite will swell and become inflamed. If this happens, get a blood test because the symptoms don't begin to appear properly for some years, by which time they're difficult to treat. Interesting fact about Chagas disease: Charles Darwin died from it, aged 73.

● **Leishmaniasis** This disease is transmitted by sandflies, and causes ulcers, most of which heal painlessly – but some don't. Interesting fact about leishmaniasis: this is the disease you can see afflicting some of the subjects of Moche pots who look like Boris Karloff. Obviously the people portrayed in the pots suffered from the unhealing kind of ulcer.

● **Oroya (verruga) fever** This is another rare disease, caused by the bite of the phlebotomus sandfly which lives only on Andean slopes between 800m and 2600m (2625ft and 8525ft). It's easily treatable with antibiotics, but if not caught will cause death by breaking down your red blood cells. The symptoms are bone and muscle pain, and anaemia. Interesting fact about Oroya fever: it's extremely rare, but everyone who gets a touch of fever thinks they've got it.

Using this guide

ROUTE DESCRIPTIONS

In the route descriptions which follow, directions are given as a compass point and an indication of whether to go right or left. An example might read: 'turn north (R)' which means north is to your right, or 'turn left (W)' which means left is a westerly direction.

Direction

On all the trails except three you can walk in the opposite direction to the one given here. The exceptions are that you're not allowed to start at Machu Picchu and walk to Huayllabamba or to Chachabamba (Km104), and it wouldn't be sensible to do the Chilca Circuit in reverse because you'd have to pay the Inca Trail fee without actually walking it.

ROUTE MAPS

(See p22-3 for Route Planning map)

Scale and walking times

These maps are drawn to an approximate scale of 1:50,000 (20mm to one kilometre). Remember that much of the walking is uphill and down, and the mere length of a trail is no indication of how long it's going to take you. Walking time is more important. In the margin of the maps, you'll see the time it takes to get from one '▲' to the next '▲'. Timings usually run in both directions and are approximate: some people are going to walk much faster, and some slower than I did. If you've got a mule or porter to carry your kit, you'll take only about a half to three quarters of the time given.

Note that **the time given refers only to time spent actually walking,** so you will need to add more time to allow for rest stops. This will obviously vary from person to person but as a rough guide add 20-30% to allow for stops.

Up or down?

The trail is shown as a dotted line. Many of the trails are up or down. One arrow indicates a steep slope; two arrows indicate a very steep slope. The arrow points towards the higher part of the trail. If, for example, you were walking from A (at 900m) to B (at 1100m) and the trail between the two were short and very steep, it would be shown like this: A - - - >> - - - B.

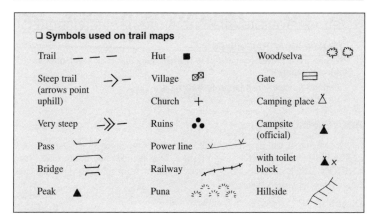

❏ **Symbols used on trail maps**

Trail	_ _ _	Hut	■	Wood/selva	
Steep trail (arrows point uphill)		Village		Gate	
		Church	+	Camping place	△
Very steep		Ruins		Campsite (official)	
Pass		Power line		with toilet block	
Bridge		Railway			
Peak	▲	Puna		Hillside	

Altitudes

The altitudes in this book were taken from GPS and altimeter readings and have an average margin of error of +/- 150m.

Place names

Quechua words can be spelt in a number of different ways. In this section of the guide, places are spelt in the Hispanic way, because it's more familiar and because that's the spelling used on most maps.

Some places have more than one name: for example, Ancascocha is Silque on some maps, Patallacta is sometimes called Llactapata, and Paucarcancha often goes under the name of Inca Raccay ('raccay' means 'ruin' in Quechua, so 'Inca Raccay' indicates any Inca ruins). Where there's a potential cause for confusion I've given all the names.

Practicalities

FOOD AND WATER

Many of the smaller streams shown on the maps are seasonal and may be dry when you walk, so you should carry more water than you think you need. Note that there's **nowhere to buy food on these trails**: you need to carry everything you're going to eat.

TICKETS AND PRICES

If you're going on a tour the price of a ticket for the trail should be included. The Classic Inca trail (Km88) and the trails from Km82, Mollepata, and Chilca

⊡ ⌐⌐ ⌐⌐ ⌐⌐ ⌐⌐ ⌐⌐ ⌐⌐ ⌐⌐ ⌐⌐ ⌐⌐ ⌐⌐ ⌐⌐⊡

THE NEW INCA TRAIL RULES

(See also p11-12 (overview) and p130 (Cusco); note that these regulations are subject to change).

Licensed guides for independent groups

With the implementation of the new rules regarding access to the Inca Trail, everybody passing the wardens' posts at Km82, Km88, Km104 and at Huaylla-bamba will be asked to show that they are part of a tour. The only exception to this rule is that groups of up to 10 trekkers who don't want to use a tour operator will be allowed to walk independently as long as they contract a licensed guide to accompany them, and as long as they do not contract any other persons such as porters or cooks. Unfortunately, nobody seems to know who these 'independent licensed guides' are: extensive enquiries both in Cusco and on the trail failed to turn up a single guide who wasn't working for a tour operator. As the new rules are enforced, these licensed guides should become more visible. The estimated cost of one of these independent guides, incidentally, is US$60 a day.

These rules don't cover the Vilcabamba trek. The sections from Mollepata and Chilca to Huayllabamba can also be done without a licensed guide or organized tour, but this means that once you get to Huayllabamba you won't be able to get any further along the Inca Trail. One way around this is to arrange in advance to meet up with an organized tour at Huayllabamba. All of the agencies in Cusco said they were willing to let trekkers join their tour at Huayllabamba, though you still have to pay the full tour price – even though you would be joining on the tour's second morning, having missed the entire first day. See p130 for information on arranging treks in Cusco and p271-30 for Cusco travel agencies.

Numbers restricted to 500 trekkers per day; other new rules

The authorities have also decided to restrict the numbers walking the trail to a maximum of 500 visitors per day and numbers are likely to be reduced further. Restricting access is a pity but I hope it's for the best; there's no doubt that something had to be done as unlimited access to the trail had caused filth to build up and damage to be caused to the old sites. But you can't help having some reservations as the Peruvian government do tend to see the Inca Trail and Machu Picchu as a cash cow, taking what they can and providing only limited support to locals and the local environment. (In September 2000, the whole site was blockaded by local farm workers, students and teachers protesting about lack of help from central government).

Other new rules include the following: plastic water bottles have thankfully been banned, (though evidence on the trail suggests this has yet to be properly enforced); pets and pack animals are also banned (though llamas can go as far as Huayllabamba!), as are walking poles and sticks because they damage the Inca paths. Finally, porters are now no longer allowed to carry more than 20kg and have to pay an entrance fee of US$15; the days of porters straining along the trail under bags three times their own body weight are thankfully no more.

The trail rules are changing regularly. Before you go, check the latest information with the SAEC (see p106), or on the Internet: ⌨ www.andeantravel web.com or www.peruperu.com/inca-trail.htm.

⊡ ⌐⌐ ⌐⌐ ⌐⌐ ⌐⌐ ⌐⌐ ⌐⌐ ⌐⌐ ⌐⌐ ⌐⌐ ⌐⌐ ⌐⌐⊡

cost US$50 (payable in dollars or soles). The Km104 trail is US$25, as is the walk from Mollepata to Km88. (All half price with ISIC card).

On all trails except the Mollepata and Chilca hikes there's a checkpoint near the start of the trail where you buy your ticket; keep it safe as you'll be asked to produce it when you reach Machu Picchu. On the Mollepata and Chilca trails you buy your ticket at the exit gate of the Trekkers' Hotel (see p188). There is no charge for the Vilcabamba trail.

GETTING TO THE TRAILHEADS

The **train** from Cusco to Machu Picchu leaves regularly each day from San Pedro station (see p147), though the cost can be up to US$35 one way. It stops en route at Chilca, and Kms 82, 88 and 104. See p267-8 for details of times.

Tourist buses are a cheaper option for those travelling to Chilca or Km82; tickets from the travel agents on Plaza de Armas cost between s/12 and s/17, leave at 6-6.30am, and they'll even pick you up from your hotel. The disadvantage of taking these is that they don't arrive at the start of the trail until about midday; furthermore, if you're starting at Km82, because you're travelling with a bus full of other travellers the likelihood is you'll be walking with them too. For this reason, if you have the time I strongly recommend spending a night in Ollantaytambo, and catching a **local bus** or truck to Chilca or Km82 from there. The advantages are threefold: it's far cheaper (s/4.5 from Cusco to Ollantaytambo by local bus, and another s/1.5 to Chilca or Km82); you arrive at the start of your trek much earlier (the first truck or bus leaves Ollantaytambo's main square some time after 6am, taking about 30 minutes to reach Chilca and an hour to Km82); and thus you will start way before anybody else. Ollantaytambo has much to recommend it too (see p155-7).

Buses to Mollepata leave from Cusco's Calle Arcopata at 5am. There is sometimes a later one, though not everyday. Buses to Abancay from the same place can drop you at the bottom of a track that leads up to Mollepata. See p207 for details of why these aren't such a good idea. Both buses charge s/2. The situation changes often, so ask at your hotel for the latest information (don't trust what they tell you at the tourist information office because they often get it wrong).

For details of how to get to the start of the Vilcabamba trail at Huancacalle, see p220-2.

❏ **Walking times on trail maps**
Note that on all the trail maps in this book the times shown alongside each map refer only to **time spent actually walking**. When planning your walking for the day you should add about 20-30% to allow for rest stops.

The classic Inca Trail

Starting through the eucalyptus forest on the banks of the Urubamba river, the trail quickly turns into a steep series of climbs and descents. There are three passes to go over, the highest being 4200m (13,750ft) and it takes three to four days to reach Machu Picchu.

KM88 → HUAYLLABAMBA   [MAP 1, p177]

Km88 to Patallacta

The train stops very briefly at **Km88** – watch the kilometre markers by the side of the railway or ask someone to tell you when it's near so you can be prepared to gather your kit and make your way to the doors. Jump off, pass along the tracks in the direction the train's been going (W) and follow a little path down to the river, where you'll find a **bridge** and a **park warden's booth**. Here you pay the trail fee. Km88 is sometimes known by its Quechua name, Corihuayrachina.

Across the bridge, you can go either left (E) or right (W). To the right there's a detour to the seldom-visited ruins of **Huayna Quente** and **Machu Quente** (see p176), a 20-minute walk away. The path actually continues all the way to Chachabamba, a pleasant and much quieter alternative to the other Inca trails (see box on p196).

The main trail goes off to the left (E), following the southern banks of the Urubamba through a eucalyptus forest. After three quarters of an hour you'll reach the valley of the **Cusichaca river** and the extensive ruins of **Patallacta** (see p178) where you can *camp*. (On some maps Patallacta is shown as Llactapata).

The small round tower on the ridge by the river is called **Pulpituyoc** which means 'containing a pulpit'. The Incas built only round walls when a building was particularly significant, so this was an important place.

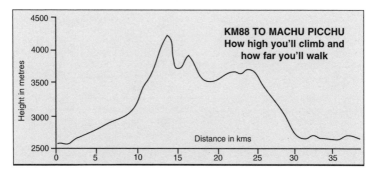

KM88 TO MACHU PICCHU
How high you'll climb and how far you'll walk

Patallacta to Huayllabamba

Passing by the foot of Patallacta, the trail continues south before crossing over the Cusichaca and climbing up the opposite slope. It's a bit steep here, a fore-taste of the rest of the trail. It settles on the eastern bank, and you begin to follow the Cusichaca towards Huayllabamba.

After about an hour of gentle but steady climbing, you'll come to a **bridge** over the river (note that this is the second bridge over the Cusichaca; the first leads over to a small settlement on the river's western banks and should be ignored). Just before this second bridge there are huts from which you can buy soft drinks. Half an hour after the bridge you cross another over a tributary of the Cusichaca, the Llulluchayoc, and arrive at the outskirts of **Huayllabamba**, a village built above Inca terraces.

Huayllabamba is the largest village you'll pass through, and it's the last place where you can buy anything before the Trekkers' Hotel at Huinay Huayna. There is a *campsite* here, but people who've slept here and in other campsites near Huayllabamba have had things stolen (the SAEC – see p106 –

Huayna Quente and Machu Quente

The people who lived by the Urubamba before the coming of the Incas never ven-tured further downriver than the site of Huayna Quente and Machu Quente, and no sign of their settlements has been found beyond these sites. This all changed after the Inca Pachacutec conquered this region (see p79), and the Incas drove roads along both the north and the south banks of the Urubamba river, deep into the Amazon rain forest. Details of a walk along the southern trail of the Urubamba can be found on p217.

Huayna Quente and Machu Quente were two sites along the southern road, and like most of the sites on the Inca Trail were some sort of combination of a tambo (an inn or waystation), a gateway, a religious site and an agricultural station. **Huayna Quente** was the more important and built in a different style from the sites further upstream of Patallacta (see p178) and Huillca Raccay (see p192). Reached by a glorious Inca path leading off the main riverside track, Huayna Quente in some ways resembles Machu Picchu itself, intricately planned and built in fine stonework. Scholars think it dates from the end of Pachacutec's reign, or the begin-ning of the reign of his successor, Tupac Yupanqui (Topa Inca), in the second half of the fifteenth century. The high standard of the stonework suggests that it was pri-marily a small pilgrimage centre on a road to Machu Picchu. Its two stone baths were associated with the ritual worship of water, and its two sacred rocks and a sacred cavern were huacas (sacred spots). Like most of the Inca sites on the trail it was probably self-sufficient agriculturally – it might even have exported some maize – and it's surrounded by extensive terraces and canal systems. Thirty-four thousand square metres of terracing have been uncovered.

Machu Quente is much less interesting, and seems to have been a more utili-tarian agricultural site. There is a large building that could have been a barracks, as well as a curious carved stone, reminiscent of the much larger Nusta España at Huancacalle (see p222) by the bridge over the stream.

THIS AREA IS ALSO KNOWN AS CORIHUAYRACHINA

ALTERNATIVE ROUTE TO MACHU PICCHU VIA CHACHABAMBA (SEE P.217)

Km 88 2500m

OVERLAP WITH MAP 6

PARK WARDEN'S BOOTH

Río Urubamba

KM 88

KM 88

Machu Quente

Huayna Quente

THIS PATH LEADS TO HUAYNA QUENTE & MACHU QUENTE (20 MINS)

Patallacta & Pulpituyoc

TO CHILCA

Huillca Raccay

FORK TO PATALLACTA

FORK TO PATALLACTA

3/4 HR

3/4 HR

THERE APPEAR TO BE TWO PATHS HERE NOW. CHOOSE THE MOST-USED ONE.

1 HR

1 HR

0   1km
0   1/2 mile

VILLAGE

Río Cusichaca

FIRST BRIDGE (DON'T CROSS)

OVERLAP WITH MAP 2

YOU CAN BUY SOFT DRINKS FROM SHACKS ALONG THIS PART OF THE TRAIL BUT YOU'LL BE LUCKY TO FIND ANY MORE AFTER HUAYLLABAMBA

1/2 HR

1/2 HR

Q. Llulluchayoc

Huayllabamba 3000m

TOURIST INFORMATION OFFICE. REGISTER HERE

TRY TO AVOID CAMPING HERE. THERE ARE MANY THIEVES ABOUT.

HUAYLLABAMBA BRIDGE

HUAYLLABAMBA BRIDGE

3/4 HR

3/4 HR

MAP 1

PAUCARCANCHA

PAUCARCANCHA

OVER-LAPS WITH MAPS 11 AND 16

MAP 16

MAP 11

Paucarcancha 3200m

TRAILBLAZER

Patallacta and Pulpituyoc

Patallacta is one of the largest and most important sites in the whole area. It was first discovered by Hiram Bingham in 1911 and, while it was excavated when Bingham returned in 1915, most work on the area has been done since the late 1970s by Dr Ann Kendall and the Cusichaca Trust; you can see the results in the museum at Ollantaytambo.

Patallacta was primarily an agricultural station set amongst extensive terraced land that was used for growing maize, the staple of the Incas, and it supplied Machu Picchu and Ollantaytambo with part of their food. It's also near the high altitude lands up the Cusichaca river where potatoes and other root crops were grown, produce that probably made its way through Patallacta for shipment to other parts of the district. In its buildings lived the labour that tended the fields, both local and *mit'a* workers, and the soldiers who manned the hill fort of Huillca Raccay (see p192). It was probably built around 1450 as it's a classical Inca settlement, and it consists of one hundred and sixteen buildings and five baths, all laid out on a regular pattern. The main canal that fed the town's baths fell into disuse shortly after the Spanish conquest, which suggests that Patallacta was abandoned around 1540.

The other function of Patallacta was strategic. Inca roads run along both the north and the south banks of the Urubamba and up the Cusichaca, and Patallacta was built at this major road junction rather as Birmingham in England grew up at another major transport intersection. Built where it was, Patallacta could provide a reservoir of loyal Incas producing food for the region at this strategically important cross-roads.

Pulpituyoc is the religious or ceremonial complex of Patallacta, and consists of eleven buildings, two baths and a carved rock. Unlike Patallacta, Pulpituyoc was built on virgin ground, uninhabited before the arrival of the Incas. The exact nature of the religion or ceremonies carried out at Pulpituyoc remains a mystery.

---

report a person being attacked in 1997) so it's wise to press on up the trail and camp somewhere else. At the top of the village is a warden's office where you must register.

HUAYLLABAMBA → PACAMAYO CAMP   [MAP 2, opposite]

Huayllabamba to Llulluchapampa campsite

From the bridge over the Llulluchayoc the path leads uphill on the river's left-hand (south-west) bank. It hairpins and gets very steep, and after a pretty exhausting hour you reach the **Yunkachimpa campsite** which has a river running close by. The campsite itself is OK but, alas, the surrounding hills have been used as an *al fresco* toilet by trekkers – don't walk around in the dark in bare feet!

Pass through the campsite and over a **bridge** across a river called the Chaupihuayjo on some maps, Huayruro on others. Then head steeply uphill through a clearing, before following the left-hand (south-west) bank of the

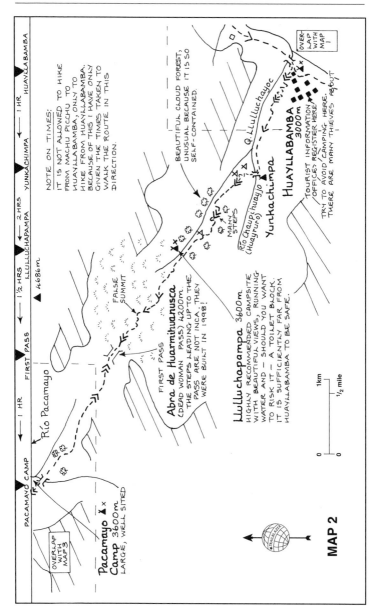

PACAMAYO CAMP ← 1 HR → FIRST PASS ← 1½ HRS → LLULLUCHAPAMPA ← 2 HRS → YUNKACHIMPA ← 1 HR → HUAYLLABAMBA

NOTE ON TIMES:
IT IS NOT ALLOWED TO HIKE FROM MACHU PICCHU TO HUAYLLABAMBA, ONLY TO HIKE FROM HUAYLLABAMBA. BECAUSE OF THIS I HAVE ONLY GIVEN THE TIMES TAKEN TO WALK THE ROUTE IN THIS DIRECTION.

▲ 4686m.

Río Pacamayo

Pacamayo Camp 3600 m.
LARGE, WELL SITED

OVERLAP WITH MAP 3

FALSE SUMMIT

FIRST PASS

Abra de Huarmihuanusca
(DEAD WOMAN PASS) 4200m.
THE STEPS LEADING UP TO THE PASS ARE NOT INCA, THEY WERE BUILT IN 1998!

Llulluchapampa 3600 m.
HIGHLY RECOMMENDED CAMPSITE WITH BEAUTIFUL VIEWS, RUNNING WATER AND — SHOULD YOU WANT TO RISK IT — A TOILET BLOCK. IT IS SUFFICIENTLY FAR FROM HUAYLLABAMBA TO BE SAFE.

BEAUTIFUL CLOUD FOREST, UNUSUAL BECAUSE IT IS SO SELF-CONTAINED.

MANY STEPS

Río Chaupi huayjo (Huayruro)

Yunkachimpa

Q. Llulluchayoc

HUAYLLABAMBA 3000 m.

TOURIST INFORMATION OFFICE: REGISTER HERE!
TRY TO AVOID CAMPING HERE. THERE ARE MANY THIEVES ABOUT.

OVERLAP WITH MAP 1

0 ___ 1km
0 ___ ½ mile

MAP 2

Llulluchayoc as it veers to the west. You'll soon enter a beautiful **cloud forest** or *polylepsis* woodland, rare in the Andes because it's self-contained. The path climbs steeply up an exhaustingly large number of steps, following the river course up through the wood, at times going right down to the river, at times rising up the valley side away from it.

About an hour from Yunkachimpa there are another two *campsites*. The first is just inside the forest, but if you continue upward for another 20 minutes, just beyond the edge of the forest you'll reach another: **Llulluchapampa.** This is a much better place to camp, with running water and wonderful views down the valley. On the top tier of sites there's a toilet block just by the thatched shelter with a cross on top.

Llulluchapampa to Dead Woman Pass/Abra de Huarmihuanusca

You can see the first pass – no one knows who the dead woman was though many guides claim the name arose because the pass looks like a dead woman – from Llulluchapampa. It looks deceptively close but in fact it's a gruelling one and a half hours' walk.

The trail runs parallel to the river and climbs up into the hills above the river's spring, through windy puna, over the newly-laid paving that protects the mountain from erosion.

Dead Woman Pass to Pacamayo camp

Here begins the first of the three tiring descents you'll face on the trail. You'll experience considerable strain on your knees as you go down 800m (2624ft) over about 1 1/4 miles.

At the bottom there's a very large *campsite*, nestling in some trees on the floor of the valley of the river Pacamayo. There's a toilet block here, and it's large so it's a favourite place for tours. It's a good idea to fill your water bottles at the stream here as the water from here to Sayac Marca can be unreliable and brackish.

PACAMAYO CAMP → THE THIRD PASS   [MAP 3, opposite]

Pacamayo camp to the second pass

From the Pacamayo camp the path climbs very steeply up a series of **steps**; you'll be glad to pause every now and then at viewpoints over the valley below. After about an hour, you reach the Inca ruins of **Runcu Raccay** (see p182), a circular structure with a rectangular outbuilding. This was probably a tambo, where chasquis rested, but some think it was a guard post or even, because of the circular walls, a ritual building.

The second pass (sometimes called Abra de Runcu Raccay) is another hour up, and there are a couple of **false summits** to get over first. Just before the real pass there are some **lakes**, beside which you can *camp*. Down by the lakes there's a sign saying 'Deer Area', though if you see any deer these days, you'll be lucky.

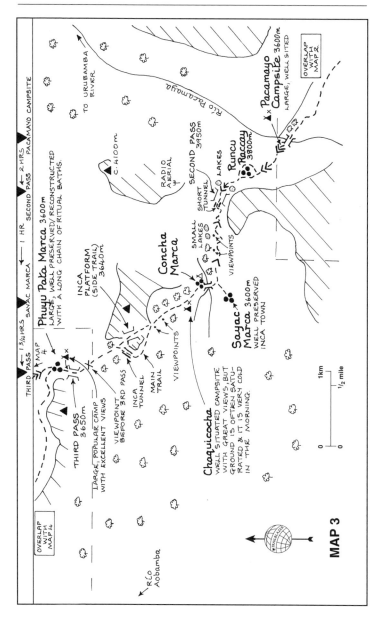

MAP 3

OVERLAP WITH MAP 4

THIRD PASS 3650m

LARGE, POPULAR CAMP WITH EXCELLENT VIEWS.

VIEWPOINT BEFORE 3RD PASS

MAP 4

INCA TUNNEL

MAIN TRAIL

VIEWPOINTS

Chaquicocha
WELL SITUATED CAMPSITE WITH GREAT VIEWS, BUT GROUND IS OFTEN SATURATED & IT IS VERY COLD IN THE MORNING.

Phuyu Pata Marca 3600m
(LARGE, WELL PRESERVED/ RECONSTRUCTED WITH A LONG CHAIN OF RITUAL BATHS.

INCA PLATFORM (SIDE TRAIL) 3640m.

Concha Marca

VIEWPOINTS

Sayac Marca 3600m
WELL PRESERVED INCA TOWN

SMALL LAKES

VIEWPOINTS

SHORT TUNNEL

SECOND PASS 3950m

LAKES

Runcu Raccay 3800m.

C. 4100m.

RADIO AERIAL

Río Pacamayo

TO URUBAMBA RIVER

Pacamayo Campsite 3600m
LARGE, WELL SITED

OVERLAP WITH MAP 2

THIRD PASS ◄— 1 3/4 HRS. SAYAC MARCA ◄— 1 HR. SECOND PASS ◄— 2 HRS. PACAMAYO CAMPSITE

RÍO Aobamba

1km
1/2 mile

0
0

Runcu Raccay

The small, circular site of Runcu Raccay was discovered by Hiram Bingham when he was searching out the entrance roads to Machu Picchu. He considered it to be a fortress, dominating the highway. It was explored in more detail in 1940 by Dr Paul Fejos, who thought it was a tambo, a rest-place for passing travellers. In design it's a transitional building, a bridge between the practical styles of the Cusichaca river and the more elaborate designs of Machu Picchu and the Cedrobamba sites (Cedrobamba is the name given to the areas around Machu Picchu).

It's interesting that the ruins of the Inca Trail were excavated during two periods when the northern nations of the world were embarking on the two most murderous wars in history. Bingham's second expedition was digging quietly in these hills in 1915 while the fields of Flanders were soaked in blood, and Fejos was busy excavating these ruins in 1940.

Runcu Raccay

Niches

Entrance

Niches

Upper Level

Lower Level

Lower Still

DIRECTION OF INCA TRAIL

0   5   10M
APPROXIMATE SCALE

The second pass to Sayac Marca

From the second pass the trail heads generally westwards. It passes through a short tunnel, the first of two on the route, and begins to switchback steeply as it descends to a small viewpoint, after which it continues down more gently. To your right (N), you'll see some lakes and in front (W), clouds permitting, you'll see Sayac Marca. The trail descends quite steeply again, and just before it makes a hairpin bend, there's a staircase going up on the left (south-west). About 50 metres (150ft) up this staircase lies **Sayac Marca** (see opposite and p184).

Sayac Marca

VALLEY

Rock

Bath

Bath

Bath

Round
Walled
Building

TRAILBLAZER

NOT TO SCALE

INCA TRAIL
MAP 3

REMAINS OF
AQUEDUCT

OLD TRAIL

ⵔⵔ ⵔ⎕ⵔ ⵔ⎕ⵔ ⵔ⎕ⵔ ⵔ⎕ⵔ ⵔ⎕ⵔ ⵔ⎕ⵔ ⵔ⎕ⵔ ⵔ⎕ⵔ ⵔ⎕ⵔⵔ

Sayac Marca (see p183) and Concha Marca

Sayac Marca was discovered by Hiram Bingham when he followed an Inca road across the hills from Machu Picchu, but the name Sayac Marca was coined by the Fejos expedition in the 1940s. Bingham's half-Spanish, half-Quechua name for these ruins, Cedrobamba (Cedar Plain), actually refers to the elongated spur on which all the sites close to Machu Picchu are built. Fejos changed the name to Inaccessible Town, a name that describes the position of the ruins perfectly, protected as they are on three sides by a precipice that descends to the dense jungle of the valley of the river Aobamba below.

The dramatic setting of Sayac Marca was no accident as it's built at a fork in the old Inca road. Today's Inca Trail follows one fork to Machu Picchu, but the other fork descends to the bottom of the Aobamba valley. From here it's been traced up the other side of the valley, where it passes through some ruins called Llactapata, and then descends to the Santa Teresa river. Here it climbs again to more ruins, Ochopata, about 15km from Sayac Marca, and then it becomes lost in the jungle. This road is completely overgrown these days, and you shouldn't attempt to follow it without a map, compass and experience in jungle hiking.

There is some very impressive stonework here, indicating that this was an important place. Look for what Bingham called 'eye-bonders', holes drilled in corners of buildings and edges of walls, which were used for securing roofs of thatch (you can see reconstructions of Inca roofs in Machu Picchu). Notice also the characteristic way that the Incas incorporated and emphasized the natural features on which they built – a large outcrop is the unadorned centrepiece of Sayac Marca, and the whole structure is built on and emphasizes a prow of rock.

Bingham thought that Sayac Marca was a fortified outpost of Machu Picchu, but Fejos wasn't so sure, saying that if the Incas wanted to build fortifications they could do a much more impressive job – he takes Sacsayhuaman as an example. Nevertheless it's unlikely that the site was a tambo (as were the nearby buildings of **Concha Marca** with their small terrace system): there isn't enough agricultural land for Sayac Marca to be a farming outpost, nor is the stonework impressive enough for it to be a religious centre. No one has come up with a conclusive answer as to what the ruins were.

While the function of Sayac Marca isn't clear, the date when it was constructed is more certain. The planning of the site is elaborate; the layout is flexible and responds to the terrain, which makes archaeologists think it was built after the classical period of Inca construction, and the ruins are dated to the last half of the 15th century.

ⵔⵔ ⵔ⎕ⵔ ⵔ⎕ⵔ ⵔ⎕ⵔ ⵔ⎕ⵔ ⵔ⎕ⵔ ⵔ⎕ⵔ ⵔ⎕ⵔ ⵔ⎕ⵔ ⵔ⎕ⵔ ⵔ⎕ⵔⵔ

Sayac Marca to the third pass

In the shadow of Sayac Marca, tucked away in a little valley, is the small Inca dwelling of **Concha Marca**. There's a stream nearby, and it's a good place to fill up with water as there are no more streams until the third pass, but in the interests of health make sure you purify your water carefully because there's a small *campsite* here, and the stream could be contaminated.

The section of trail from here to the third pass is very, very beautiful. The paving is for the most part original Inca, and the path crosses high stone embankments as it skirts deep precipices. You're enclosed in a cathedral of forest. If you find yourself walking this part of the trail in the mist, you'd be sensible to camp and wait for the weather to clear: it's such a wonderful view, missing it would be a crime. There's a good *campsite* about 20 minutes' walk from Sayac Marca, called **Chaquicocha**, where there's a toilet block and space for about 15 tents on grassy knolls either side of the path.

Just after Chaquicocha the path heads steeply uphill and passes two **viewpoints**. Near the second viewpoint a side trail leads off the main path to the right (N). This path returns to the main route about a kilometre (half a mile) further on, but it bypasses the main Inca tunnel so few people take it and it's now very overgrown. It leads to a pleasant remote platform before descending again to the main trail.

The main trail skirts a spur, turning from the north-west to the north-east. It descends, going through an impressive **Inca tunnel**, before climbing again to the third pass. A little before the third pass you'll reach a spot from which you can see down to two different river valleys, the Urubamba and the Aobamba. It's a spectacular view. Just after this is a large *campsite*, right on the top of the pass.

THE THIRD PASS → MACHU PICCHU   [MAP 4, p187]

Phuyu Pata Marca

The other side of the pass there's the most impressive Inca site yet: **Phuyu Pata Marca**. Once more, this name comes from the Fejos expedition, and it means 'Cloud-Level Town'. The name's well chosen: you'll often see banks of clouds billow over this pass and you may be engulfed in a field of seamless white. It was once a remote, magical place, but it's surrounded by a large *campsite* now which makes it lose much of its mystery.

Look for the six 'Inca baths' which you'll walk through on your way to the ruins. Despite the name, these are probably not baths, or even public hydrants, which is what Bingham thought they were. More likely they are a feature of ritual worship of water, and there are similar structures at Huinay Huayna, Tambo Machay (see p151) and Machu Picchu itself. The stonework you'll see in Phuyu Pata Marca is by far the most impressive you've come across so far, but it will get even better.

From Phuyu Pata Marca, there are **two options**: the usual route and the less travelled old route.

The usual route

This takes you down the most impressive flight of Inca steps on the entire trail. The Incas turned a 500m (1500ft) hillside into a staircase. Be careful of your knees, which will feel the strain by the end of the day. It will take about three hours to reach the Trekkers' Hotel, and you'll pass through increasingly dense forest as the path twists and turns its way down. This is a lovely walk.

To get to 'the usual route', walk to the other side (W) of Phuyu Pata Marca from the baths. There you'll see **descending stairs**; this is where you start. There's usually a beaten path to this spot around the lower terraces of the ruins.

Phuyu Pata Marca

Phuyu Pata Marca is another site that was discovered by Bingham but fully excavated by Fejos. When Bingham passed by, all he noted were the baths and the tops of some of the walls of the upper-most buildings; everything else was covered by the jungle. When Fejos set about digging he discovered a much larger and much more important site than Bingham had ever imagined existed, and in two months of work he managed only partially to clear the area. He discovered two plazas, four house groups and one intriguing house hidden in a terrace, discoverable only by a door in the terrace wall (it's to the east of the site near the lower road).

Phuyu Pata Marca, like Sayac Marca is built in a late Inca style, when the formalism of classical Inca planning had given way to a more fluid style. Archaeologists think that it was put up late in Pachacutec's reign or early in that of his successor, Tupac Yupanqui (Topa Inca), late in the fifteenth century. The stonework on the upper terrace is particularly fine, with a wall where the stones are almost perfectly slotted together. Towards the bottom of the site, to the north-west, there is a group of caves that have been enlarged and extended by the Incas. When they were discovered the roofs were blackened and the floors were covered with a thick layer of ash, but all this was recent and not related to the Incas. Only a few Inca remains were found, pottery of a plain type used for cooking.

Phuyu Pata Marca's function, like that of Sayac Marca, is unclear but the fountain or baths suggests that the site was associated with the ritual worship of water, and perhaps it was a place for ritual cleansing on the final leg to Machu Picchu. It could also, of course, have been a guard settlement, or a remote hunting lodge.

After about an hour, you'll be able to see the tin roof of the Trekkers' Hotel: a monstrous wart in the virgin forest. This is where the trail is heading. After about 2^1/$_2$ hours, you'll reach a **pylon** just off the trail. A 30-minute shortcut to the hotel descends east (R) from just a few metres before this pylon, switchbacking steeply as it loses a lot of height. This short-cut isn't actually that much quicker and is a lot less pleasant than the normal route, which continues on under the wires to the Inca site of Intipata (see p188), from where a second trail leads off from the bottom terrace back south to the hotel.

The route less travelled

This used to be the route everyone took until the Inca staircase was discovered 20 years ago. It adds another couple of kilometres to the total length of the trail, but you do get a magnificent view of Machu Picchu in the valley a kilometre below.

This path also leaves Phuyu Pata Marca from the west but instead of going downhill it stays on the same level as the ruins. (Fill up with water before you leave; there are no streams along the way.) For the first hundred metres along the path you may be tiptoeing through the turds left by inconsiderate campers. Soon you'll be out into the open puna, skirting a small depression and gazing at stupendous views over the Urubamba a good mile below you. After an hour or so, you arrive at a rustic **gate** and, a little further on, a rustic **hut**.

MAP 4

AGUAS CALIENTES
(MACHU PICCHU PUEBLO)

Templo de La Luna
c 2850m

Huayana Picchu

PUENTE RUINAS STATION

Machu Picchu
2500m

TOURIST HOTEL

Inca Bridge

Cerro Machu Picchu

Intipunku
2700m

Río Urubamba

OVERLAP WITH MAP 7

Intipata

Trekkers' Hotel 2700m

PYLON

[SEE TEXT FOR DIRECTIONS OUT OF TREKKERS' HOTEL FOR MACHU PICCHU]

ISOLATED HUT SELLING DRINKS TO THE TOURISTS.

Huinay Huayna

GATE

USUAL ROUTE WITH 500m OF INCA STEPS

OVERLAP WITH MAP 3

OLD ROUTE

Phuyu Pata Marca
3600m

PASS 3650m

0   1km
0   ½ mile

MACHU PICCHU

45 MINS   INTIPUNKU

USUAL ROUTE   2 HRS

TREKKERS' HOTEL

FROM ISOLATED HUT TO TREKKERS' HOTEL ALLOW 1½ HRS ON THE OLD ROUTE

ISOLATED HUT

3 HRS   OLD ROUTE   1 HR

THIRD PASS

THIRD PASS

From the hut, the Trekkers' Hotel is about an hour further on. Some old maps are confusing here; I got dreadfully lost with one trying to follow the route. You should head down the spur, under the first set of electricity wires, then the path turns right (E) before you come to the second set of wires. Skirt the forest, go under the second wires, then hairpin down. The jungle gets quite close here, but the path is obvious. You're likely to be the only people on it. Half an hour of descent later, you'll come out on a large, paved trail. Left (N) there's **Intipata;** right (S) is the continuation of the usual route from Phuyu Pata Marca. Your best bet is to walk to Intipata, descend to the lowest terrace, and take the path heading south back to the Trekkers' Hotel.

Trekkers' Hotel

The *Trekkers' Hotel* (not to be confused with the expensive, plush Tourists' Hotel, Machu Picchu Sanctuary Lodge (see p244), at Machu Picchu) isn't a pleasant place. It's all concrete-walled tin shacks, and the place has a bad reputation for theft. It's crowded, smelly and cramped, but it's the **last place where you're allowed to camp** before Machu Picchu – hence it's always full. In high season, tours send porters running along the track before dawn to book sites, so you must get here early in the day to get a decent spot to camp.

There's a restaurant here (ridiculously overpriced at s/15 for a main course), some beds (s/20 a night) or you can sleep on the floor for a couple of soles.

Intipata

The site of Intipata is of interest to both historians and naturalists alike. For the latter, there is a very rare breed of orchid that is said to grow amongst the stones of the ancient Inca terraces. So concerned are the authorities to preserve this habitat for the flower, that rumours currently abound that the site is to be left uncleared, thereby allowing the jungle to reclaim the land once more.

This would no doubt disappoint Dr Fejos, who in 1940 spent four months clearing over 40,000 square metres of the forest, discovering and mapping forty-eight of the site's terraces. Despite these four months Dr Fejos didn't feel he'd discovered everything and was sure that there were many more terraces. In his record of the expedition he describes Intipata, almost despairingly, as 'extending indefinitely to the south'. Like Phuyu Pata Marca, three of Intipata's terraces are hollow and hide what Fejos called 'terrace houses'.

The name Intipata was thought up by a member of his expedition, and means Sunny Slope. Not only because of the number of terraces, but also because of the absence of plazas, religious structures or fortifications, there's little doubt that Intipata was primarily an agricultural settlement, but it probably had a strategic function as well. From Intipata you can see across to the lookout platform on the top of Cerro Machu Picchu, and down to the Inca site of Choquesuysuy. Messages could be transmitted to the mountain city of Machu Picchu from the floor of the Urubamba below through the lookout point on the top of Intipata. From the bottom of the terraces a path leads directly back to the Trekkers' Hotel.

There's also piped water (cold showers for s/5), a lavatory block and a mediocre **museum** full of stuffed animals. A 10-minute trail leaves from the southern end of the hotel to the ruins of **Huinay Huayna** (see below), a glorious terraced complex with a flight of 10 baths and some very impressive stonework. If you do come here, don't leave anything valuable in your tent.

Trekkers' Hotel to Machu Picchu

To see the sun rise over Machu Picchu you'll need to get up two hours before dawn to reach **Intipunku** (the gateway of the sun) in time. Machu Picchu is 45

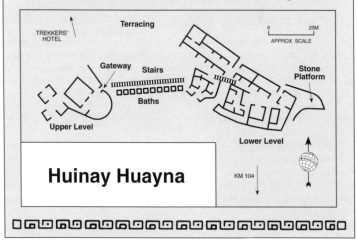

Huinay Huayna (Wiñya Wayna)

The name means 'forever young' in Quechua, and the place is named after a pink orchid of that name that grows here.

The similarities between Huinay Huayna and the nearby Intipata are startling, as both are sites where the Incas terraced the whole side of a mountain. Obviously they both were used for growing food, but Huinay Huayna was more important – there are more buildings, the stonework is higher quality and there is a magnificent sequence of ten baths. All this suggests that the site was a religious centre, probably associated with the ritual worship of water, although some think it was a high-status hunting lodge where the Inca or his highest caste retainers might escape the trials of public life. The upper terrace, which incorporates some of the largest polygonal blocks in the whole area, contains some particularly fine masonry, and all over the site you'll find gabled houses, exterior pegs used for securing thatch and recessed niches. This, coupled with the flexible way the settlement was planned, suggests that it was built after the classical period of Inca architecture, in the latter part of the fifteenth century.

A window at the bottom of the site frames beautifully the nearby waterfall; some say this shows the Incas shared our aesthetic values of what makes a good view.

TREKKERS' HOTEL

Terracing

0   25M
APPROX. SCALE

Gateway Stairs

Stone Platform

Baths

Upper Level

Lower Level

Huinay Huayna

KM 104

minutes further on. **You are not allowed to camp at Intipunku**. Remember to have your flashlight ready, as you'll be packing and walking in the dark.

The gate out of the Trekkers' Hotel opens at 5am, and closes at 2.30pm. If you've come from Mollepata or Chilca and haven't already bought your permit, you must do so here. The only difficult thing about this part of the trail is finding this gate; check before you go to bed to avoid a frantic search in the small hours of the morning. In the lower northern corner of the Trekkers' Hotel site you'll find three doorless privies and a path descending from them. Follow it down to an unimposing wooden gate, the Gateway to Machu Picchu – a gate which looks as though it leads to the rubbish bins not to one of the greatest archaeological sites on the planet.

The trail from this point is mostly flat. It goes up and down a little, passes a couple of apparently impassable sheer rock faces, before climbing about 14 very steep steps to what you think is Intipunku. It's not. Intipunku is just around the corner, up steps with a more gentle gradient. This is an awe-inspiring approach, the architecture reinforcing your sense of anticipation. When you finally reach **Intipunku**, you look down across the wide bend of the Urubamba and can see, sheltering under the sugar loaf mountain of Huayana Picchu, your journey's end, **Machu Picchu** (see Part 8, p243).

Variations on the classic trail

These variations add an extra half-day to a day to the classic trail by starting further up the Urubamba. You won't see much more from starting at Chilca than you would if you started at Km82.

STARTING AT CHILCA   [MAP 5, opposite]

You can reach Chilca by road or by train – the tour companies drive here. Chilca, also known as Km77, is a very small village, but there's more to it than there is to either Km88 or Km82. If taking the train, make sure you're prepared to get out in good time; if taking the bus, warn the driver that you wish to get off at Chilca, otherwise he'll assume your destination is Km82.

The **bridge** across the Urubamba is slightly to the west of where the train stops – travel south through the houses towards the river bank, and you'll see it. Cross the bridge, and turn right (W).

The path to Km82 continues west, following the southern bank of the river. It's a steep descent at first, then the trail heads through a **eucalyptus forest**, before turning north-west.

Shortly before you come to the village of **Rocabamba** where there's a stream, you'll walk through some interesting tree-like **cacti**. The trail and river then both turn west again, and pass through **scrub** before heading towards the Km82 bridge. See below for directions from Km82.

STARTING AT KM82 [MAP 6, opposite]

This is the end of the road for the tourist buses, which pull in at the 'car park' at the top of the town. For train travellers, once again the train stops only briefly at **Km82**, so ask your fellow passengers where to get off and prepare yourself to jump. There are a couple of shops at Km82 with a few basic supplies, and the warden's kiosk where you have to register and buy your ticket. Walk along the tracks (W), and down towards the river where you'll find a new bridge, which you should cross. (There is a dirt road out to Km82 down which the occasional brave truck makes its way but traffic is rare here.)

On the south side of the Urubamba, turn right (W) and follow the trail as it climbs steeply up from the river. Soon it levels out and passes through a football field following the river's south-westerly course. You walk through a graveyard and a small village full of children who will fearlessly pester you for presents and sweets. Just where the river turns due west again, you'll come to the village of **Miskay**.

At the end of the village you'll come to a place where there's a path heading south off the main trail; apparently going through someone's front garden. Turn left (S) here, heading towards a wall of rock where the trail veers to the right (south-west) again.

Follow the path as it goes westward. It soon leads down one side of a deep gully to a stream and then up the other side. Shortly after this you come to the ruins of the Inca hillfort **Huillca Raccay** high above the mouth of the Cusichaca and the extensive site of Patallacta. Huillca Raccay is a very ancient site, and it's been inhabited since 500BC. The Incas, when they conquered the area, took over this place and built a fort here because it commands the entrance to the Cusichaca

Huillca Raccay

Huillca Raccay is one of the most fascinating sites in the whole area, and one of the earliest, and it has been extensively excavated by Dr Ann Kendall. She's discovered that people lived here for many years before the arrival of the Incas, and that it was the first site that the Incas developed when they arrived. They built a fort here, called by some Chuncuchua, and Dr Kendall found a site nearby where the builders of the fort lived when they were working on its construction. Judging from modern experiments and archaeological discoveries, the fort itself was erected in just one season.

It's easy to see why the Incas built here. High up in this eyrie, Inca soldiers had an excellent view up and down the Urubamba river and controlled the mouth of the Cusichaca. And if the area had once been a centre of pre-Inca power, the building of an Inca fort was a visual statement of the arrival of the Inca Empire. Later, when Inca control was secure and Patallacta was built (see p178), Huillca Raccay could protect and control the agricultural settlements below it on the floor of the Urubamba valley.

It's quite a complicated site. Dr Kendall has discovered 37 buildings, including storage lofts, control buildings (gate-houses) and what are possibly barracks, as well as seventy pre-Inca buildings on the tableland behind.

JUNCTION OF PATHS

2 3/4 HRS

WARDEN'S POST.
YOU PAY THE TRAIL
FEE HERE IF YOU
START FROM KM 82
OR KM 77 (CHILCA)

KM 82 2600m.
THE ROAD ENDS HERE AND
THE TRAIN STOPS HERE.

KM 82

CLIFFS

TO CHILCA & KM 77

SCRUBLAND

FOOTBALL FIELD

RIO URUBAMBA

RIO CUSICHACA

VILLAGE WITH PERSISTENT BEGGING CHILDREN

MAP 6

1 1/2 HRS

KM 82

2 1/2 HRS

0   1km
0   1/2 mile

OVERLAP WITH MAP 5

WRONG WAY

HUAYLLA-BAMBA

SOMEONE'S FRONT GARDEN

WALL OF ROCK

KM 82

MISKAY 2650m

QISHUARPACTA

Huilca Raccay

WRONG WAY

HUAYLLABAMBA

Rio Urubamba

Patallacta & Pulpituyoc

OVERLAP WITH MAP 1

Rio Cusichaca

JUNCTION OF PATHS

Beware of the Pishtaco

On your walk in the hills, if you come across a pale gringo wearing a dark robe – beware! He could be a vampire, or as they're known locally, a Pishtaco. These apparitions were first seen about the time of the conquest. They take the form of pale-skinned strangers, and carry with them a bag of dust, the powdered bones of their victims. They'll creep up on you when you're unaware, and blow this magic powder in your face, rendering you completely insensible. Then they'll drag you off to their lair, where they hang you upside down and let your fat drip into large bowls beneath your body. In the old days, it was said that this human fat that they collected was used to make church bells, now the story goes that it's used to power the space shuttle.

The anthropologist, Robert Randall, has pointed out the myth of Pishtacos has a basis in truth, albeit allegorical truth. These pale-skinned strangers who kidnapped locals and used their fat are a symbol of the conquering Spanish, who worked the Incas to the bone and used their sweat to grease the wheels of the Spanish Empire.

valley. You won't see much here today, however, though for some of the trail you'll be walking on a pre-Inca canal (the section of the path flanked by stones).

From here it's simple to descend to the **main trail from Km88 to Huayllabamba**, which follows the eastern bank of the Cusichaca river though there are lots of paths down through the bush and it's easy to think you've got lost. You'll be fine as long you continue generally west and downhill towards the Cusichaca. You'll soon come to a large, heavily-beaten trail heading north-south. This is the path you want, turn left (south) and follow this trail to Huayllabamba. (**Route continues on p178**).

The shorter trails

These trails are useful for those who haven't got time to spare. It's only a day's walk up a grassy hillside from Km104 to the Trekkers' Hotel and a couple of hours further to Machu Picchu along the classic Camino Sagrado del Inca. The alternative route, along the river from Km104 to Trekkers' Hotel, runs via Choquesuysuy and involves a steep climb up the Purification Trail; allow $1^1/_2$-2 days for this route.

KM104 → TREKKERS' HOTEL   [MAP 7, opposite]

The train pulls up at **Km104**, deep in the selva. Km104 is low, my altimeter read 2100m (6888ft), and the heat can get oppressive down here on the valley floor.

The trail up to Huinay Huayna and the Trekkers' Hotel is mainly across the exposed flank of a mountain with **no shade** and the sun burns and dries you out.

The weather is very changeable so bring **rain-gear**. You must take **water**, or you will have a very miserable couple of hours. Fortunately there is a small stream of sweet water at the beginning of the trail where you can fill your bottles. You are also under a little **time pressure**. The best campsites at the Trekkers' Hotel fill up quickly, so if you arrive at sundown you can expect to be left only the grotty spots.

Km104 to Huinay Huayna

As at Km88, the train stops only briefly at Km104, so be prepared to jump out at a moment's notice. The trail leads down to the river to your left (S), but

Chachabamba

Chachabamba sits on the old Inca road along the southern bank of the Urubamba river, most of which is lost in the undergrowth. The ruins have been cleared; they were built in a sophisticated style, a style that's more reminiscent of Machu Picchu than of the earlier site of Patallacta. Archaeologists think it dates from the late 15th century.

There are both open and closed buildings (three-walled and four-walled), a boulder shrine, 14 baths – one of the largest sequence of baths on the Inca Trail – and a circular stone reservoir, all of which suggests that Chachabamba was an important religious site. This may have been combined with a gate-keeping function, with both Chachabamba and the site of Choquesuysuy lower down the Urubamba guarding this entrance to Machu Picchu.

Chachabamba was uncovered by Dr Paul Fejos in 1940. Before he stumbled across it no one knew it was there, although the railway had already been built along the northern bank of the river.

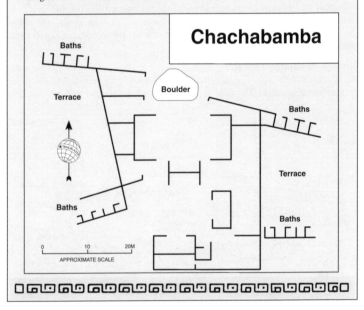

depending where you got off the train you might have to walk a little along the tracks to find the bridge and the warden's post across the river. Here you pay the trail fee.

After crossing the river, the trail heads off to the right (W) towards the ruins of **Chachabamba** (see above). From here you have two choices: continue due west along the river to the ruins of **Choquesuysuy** (see opposite), from where you can take a very steep path up to Huinay Huayna; or head due south away

Choquesuysuy and the Purification Trail

Choquesuysuy is larger and more important than was first thought, and new terraces are still being dug out of the forest. Built at two sides of the Quebrada stream at Km107, the site comprises six complex house groups, a total of 18 buildings and seven fountain baths, as well as some pretty terrific walls and terraces.

Undoubtedly built for some religious purpose, the Choquesuysuy complex also occupied a highly strategic position on the banks of the Urubamba, with paths leading both up to Huinay Huayna and along the valley to Machu Picchu. As such, the site must have had a secondary function as some sort of control post for people travelling up and down the valley. Though today the power station blocks the direct path along the valley to Machu Picchu, the trail up to Huinay Huayna is now open, though it's one heck of a steep climb – less than an hour down but 2-3 hours back up. The route has been dubbed the **Purification Trail**, picking up on the presumed function of Choquesuysuy as a place of ritual cleansing for those approaching Huinay Huayna.

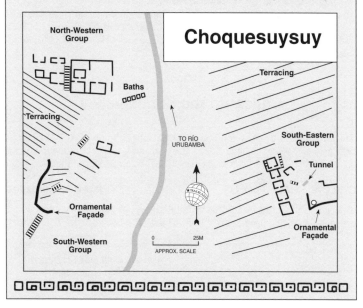

from the river behind the ruins, where the path begins to climb the mountain, entering some pleasant woods and crossing a stream. This is a good place to fill up with water. The path then heads westward and upward, leaving the woods for open grassland, soon passing under electricity pylons. The river itself is now far below you to your right (N). After 1½km (just under a mile) you are treated to a sight of the wart that is the Trekkers' Hotel, with the Intipata in the distance behind it; a little further along the path you pass a shelter that's been built beside

> ❏ **Walking times on trail maps**
> Note that on all the trail maps in this book the times shown alongside each map refer only to **time spent actually walking**. Add about 20-30% to allow for rest stops.

the trail. A little further still and you get your first view of **Huinay Huayna** (see p189), an island of stone enshrouded by the deep green of the surrounding forest. Down to the valley floor there's the significant site of Choquesuysuy.

The path continues as before west and up, past another shelter, then undulates sharply before at last descending into a forest and shade. It rounds a small spur and then reaches a beautiful waterfall and forest. You pass close to Inca walls still lost in the green clutches of the jungle, before stumbling out into clear light at the foot of Huinay Huayna.

Huinay Huayna to the Trekkers' Hotel
To get to the Trekkers' Hotel, pass up the stairway to the urban area of the terraces, follow the stairs off to the right, and then ascend by the series of Inca baths, and turn right (north-west). It's a 10-20 minute walk. See p188 for information about the Trekkers' Hotel.

Chilca up the Silque valley

This beautiful walk takes you up the Silque valley, over a 4700m (15,740ft)-high pass and down the other side to Huayllabamba, taking in fertile low-lying areas and high puna. It takes five to seven days to get to Machu Picchu.

CHILCA → HALF WAY UP   [MAP 8, opposite]
You can reach Chilca by road or by train – most independent travellers go by train but the tour companies drive here. **Chilca** (also known as Km77) is a very

CHILCA TO MACHU PICCHU
How high you'll climb and
how far you'll walk

Height in metres

Distance in kms

small village, but there's more to it than Km88 and Km82, including a rather smart hotel on the edge of town, the *Nustayoc Lodge*, which is popular with tour groups. Make sure you're prepared to get out of the train in good time. Once you get off the trail, look south-east and you'll see the valley of the river Silque. This is where you're heading.

The **bridge** across the Urubamba is slightly to the west of where the train stops. Travel south through the houses towards the river bank, and you'll see it. Cross the bridge, and turn left (E), and you'll shortly come to a fork by a hut; take the right-hand, more southerly, fork. A little later the path hugs a rock wall and heads east, then the wall falls away near some huts, and the path forks again. Take the right (more southerly) fork, and continue up the valley away from the Urubamba. It's a pleasant walk along tractor ruts through the fields.

After about 25 minutes, the valley begins to narrow and the path turns more to the south. After a further 50 minutes, you come to a **bridge** over the river, guarded by a hut and ferocious dogs. You need to cross this bridge and get onto the left (E) side of the river. Carry on walking south past a couple more huts and, on your left, a field with a huge boulder at its centre. Ignore the next bridge you'll see across the river (with an arched gateway at its end) and, an hour after the bridge you crossed over, the path becomes steeper, passes another hut and reaches a third **bridge**. Cross this.

HALFWAY UP → PAST ANCASCOCHA   [MAP 9, opposite]

There's no flat place to camp for the next couple of hours, so if it's getting late you should *camp* around here. The path, now on the right-hand side of the river (W), climbs steeply through scrub and hairpins back and forth, before descending to the river again and passing over to the other side (E). It crosses the river five more times before settling for the west (right-hand) bank. This final **bridge** is just above the confluence of the Silque and another river.

Once on the western bank, the path climbs steeply up the side of the valley – the floor's pretty flat and you can *camp* there. You'll pass an isolated farm set in mountain fields that almost everyone thinks is Ancascocha (a couple of hours further on) but this is actually **Sayllapata**. You'll know you've really arrived in **Ancascocha** because the village nestles in a flat area of puna at the confluence of three rivers. It's a fair-sized place; don't expect to be able to buy any provisions here but it's a good place to *camp* (make contact with the villagers first).

Ancascocha to the fork in the rivers
At the lower end of Ancascocha the path, valley and river all turn to the right (W), and you should cross the river near to some huts – there's a footbridge just by them. The path then ascends gently along the valley floor, and when the river forks you follow the left hand (south-west) river. The other one leads to some beautiful **waterfalls** (which you can see off to the west across the grassy puna), where it's also possible to *camp*.

PAST ANCASCOCHA → VALLEY TURN   [MAP 10, p203]

The fork in the rivers to the pass (Puerto Huyanay)
From the fork in the rivers you head south-west. The path here is unclear, it's just a collection of braiding cattle-tracks, but as long as you keep ascending gently and going south-west, parallel to the river, you're doing fine. After a couple of hours you'll see in front of you a grassy spur which obscures your view – you need to walk up and across this. If the weather's clear, on the other side of the spur you'll see some glorious red mountains to your left and you

FORK IN RIVER ← 20 MINS ANCASCOCHA

AROUND HERE IS THE LAST LARGE FLAT AREA BEFORE THE PUNA OF ANCASCOCHA, ABOUT 3 HOURS AWAY. IF IT'S GETTING DARK IT'S BEST TO CAMP HERE

2ND BRIDGE CROSSED 1 HR

OVERLAP WITH MAP 8

STEEP SLOPES

8TH BRIDGE CROSSED 1 HR | 2ND BRIDGE CROSSED 1 HR

IGNORE PATH

THERE'S A CAVE HERE WHERE YOU CAN SHELTER

Q Cachijata

MAP 9

GULLY WITH STREAM

3470m

RIO SILQUE

SATURATED GROUND

Sayllapata

FIELDS

THE VALLEY FLOOR IS REASONABLY FLAT AND SUITABLE FOR CAMPING

8TH BRIDGE CROSSED 1 3/4 HRS

UNDULATING PATH

1 1/2 HRS →

PUNA GOOD CAMPING

2 1/2 HRS

OVERLAP WITH MAP 10

ANCASCOCHA

RUINED HUTS GOOD CAMPING

ANCASCOCHA (SILQUE ON SOME MAPS) 3900m

SCHOOL

THE PATH HERE IS UNCLEAR. SEE MAP 10.

0 ————— 1km
0 ————— 1/2 mile

FORK IN RIVERS ANCASCOCHA
1 HR → 1/4 HR →

cross a stream that runs from them. You can *camp* here. The path to the pass doesn't go towards the red mountains; it continues across the side of the scree-slope to the left of the waterfall that flows over a cliff ahead of you, feeding the lake below. The path heads in the direction of the waterfall but keeps above it. Soon you'll find yourself overlooking a corrie (cirque), with a small lake on its flat floor. A glacier is poised on the slopes of the mountain that's the other side (N) of the corrie to you. The floor of the corrie makes a lovely *campsite*.

To reach the pass (**Puerto Huyanay**) follow the path as it winds its way up to the head of the corrie – it gets steep and it switchbacks uphill. Just after the head of the corrie you walk across a large scree slope, following a little stream past some tiny lakes. Continue south-west and in just over an hour from the cor-rie you'll come to the pass, marked by an *apachita* (cairn – pile of stones) on a gently sloped puna hillock.

The pass to Inca Raccay
The pass and the area around it is all a bit flat and featureless, and it's easy to get lost up here, especially when the visibility is bad. Use your compass to get the right general direction. The valley you want heads north/north-west from the pass, away from the glacier-clad red mountains to your left. (You need to aim for the far side (W) of the river as you walk downwards and westwards).

There are several trails mostly heading in the right direction but to be on the safe side follow the one that looks most worn, tend to bear left (west) and always go down. You'll know you've got it correct because you'll begin to head south and cross a stream to find what looks like a **derelict hut**, then cross anoth-er stream and head off to the north-west. The derelict hut is actually **Inca Raccay** – see below.

Inca Raccay to the turn in the valley
Continuing downhill and north-west from the hut you'll descend gently and eventually ford another stream. Look back and you can see a high three-tiered

---

Inca Raccay

Inca Raccay is the first Inca ruin on the old direct road from Cusco to Machu Picchu, a road that rises from the plain of Anta up to the peaks of Salcantay, before descending along the Quesca river. The ruins don't look very impressive today, but they were originally a tambo – an inn providing food and shelter to travellers. Remains of watchtowers have also been discovered close by, so it's likely that Inca Raccay was also an outpost which could warn the people in the lush agricultural lands down near the Urubamba river of any danger that came over the pass.

The ruins were constructed to a standardized plan which makes them difficult to date but suggests that they were built before the virtuoso stonework of Machu Picchu and Cedrobamba (the buildings close to Machu Picchu); the first half of the 15th cen-tury seems likely. Originally there were seven houses, including three large, two-door buildings that contained the storage lofts (marcas) where provisions were kept.

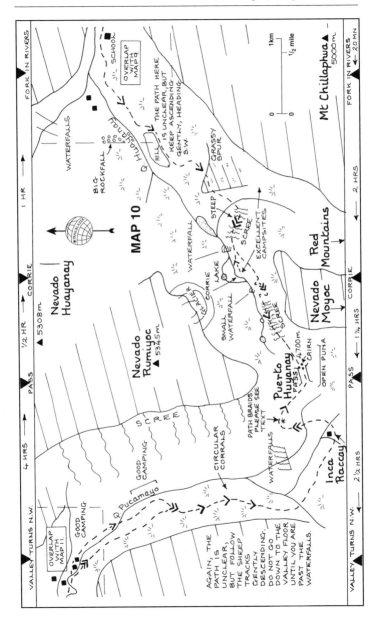

MAP 10

VALLEY TURNS N.W. — 4 HRS — PASS — ½ HR — CORRIE — 1 HR — FORK IN RIVERS

OVERLAP WITH MAP 11

GOOD CAMPING

Q. Pucamayo

GOOD CAMPING

SCREE

CIRCULAR CORRALS

Nevado Rumiyoc ▲ 5345m.

Nevado Huayanay ▲ 5308m.

GLACIER

CORRIE

SMALL WATERFALL

WATERFALL

WATERFALL

WATERFALLS

BIG ROCKFALL

WATERFALLS

SCHOOL

OVERLAP WITH MAP 9

Q. Huaylla

HILL THE PATH HERE IS UNCLEAR, BUT KEEP ASCENDING GENTLY, HEADING S.W.

GRASSY SPUR

STEEP

SCREE

EXCELLENT CAMPSITES

LAKE

Puerto Huayanay PASS 4700m

PATH BRAIDS PLEASE SEE TEXT

CAIRN

OPEN PUNA

SCREE

SCREE

Nevado Moyoc

Red Mountains

Mt Chillaphua ▲ 5000m.

Inca Raccay

AGAIN, THE PATH IS UNCLEAR, BUT FOLLOW THE SHEEP TRACKS GENTLY DESCENDING. DO NOT GO DOWN TO THE VALLEY FLOOR UNTIL YOU ARE PAST THE WATERFALLS.

VALLEY TURNS N.W. — 2½ HRS — PASS — 1¼ HRS — CORRIE — 2 HRS — FORK IN RIVERS — 20 MN

TRAILBLAZER

0   1km
0   ½ mile

waterfall at the head of the valley. Once you can see the waterfall, make your way down to the valley floor over the next couple of kilometres (a mile or so). The path once again is not clear, and the intersecting cattle tracks are confusing. But you need to be on the valley floor by the time you reach the huddle of houses by the **westward bend** in the river. Stand at this turning point and look down the valley and you can see laid out below a much more tropical landscape, dotted with houses and fields and smudged by the smoke of a dozen cooking fires. This is a good place to *camp*.

TURN IN THE VALLEY → PAUCARCANCHA   [MAP 11, opposite]
The turn in the valley to Quesca
After the turn in the valley, the path switches from one bank to the other a couple of times. Another stream joins from the south and soon after a fast-flowing river joins from the east, followed by more rivers and streams until you find yourself walking in the middle of a huge network of waterways.

It is very, very easy to lose the path here: the best tactic is to join the southern (left-hand) side of the valley. If you can't ford the river there are a couple of rickety bridges you can use. The map opposite gives further details. If you're not sure of the path, just hug the riverbank until you arrive at the school at Quesca, about an hour downstream from the bend in the river. This is the largest village in the area, but it's not big. You can usually *camp* here if you get permission.

Quesca to Paucarcancha
Quesca to Paucarcancha is mostly a straightforward, uphill path keeping to the west bank of the widening river, but there's one difficult bit: shortly after you pass the ruins of a tambo called **Incasamana** (just off the trail to the right – north-east), there's a small gully carved out by a stream (coming from a hot spring) that runs through red rock and is coloured red itself. Walk down the stream a little and you'll see the main path heading straight as an arrow through the now dense scrubland towards Paucarcancha. This is the path you want. Looking up on the skyline directly in front (north-west) of you, you can see

---

Incasamana
A half-day's walk from Inca Raccay along the Anta to Machu Picchu road is Incasamana, another tambo for passing travellers. Unlike Inca Raccay just by the pass, Incasamana is surrounded by land that was cultivated – over three hundred square metres have been discovered, and storage lofts have been found here, too.

Incasamana and Inca Raccay (see p202) were built along a similar standardized plan, probably around the same time in the early stages of the Incas' domination of the area (early fifteenth century). Nearby there's a hot spring, and it's easy to imagine a weary Inca traveller soaking his bones in the water after crossing the high passes, knowing that he's only a couple of day's journey from Machu Picchu.

MAP 11

Nevada Huayana 5000 m.

2 HRS TURN IN VALLEY TO NW

TURN IN VALLEY TO NW

QUESCA

QUESCA

1¼ HRS

THE WATER IN THIS STREAM IS COLOURED RED. WALK DOWNHILL ALONG STREAM TO FIND PATH.

NETWORK OF STREAMS AND RIVERS: VERY FAST FLOWING IN THE RAINY SEASON

AT THIS POINT, WHERE THE VALLEY TURNS WESTWARD, THE FLORA BECOMES MUCH MORE TROPICAL

OVERLAP WITH MAP 10.

FOOTBALL FIELD AND SCHOOL

QUESCA 3600 m.

Incasamana

Río Pucamayo

CAMPING IS POSSIBLE HERE. YOU MIGHT BE ABLE TO SLEEP ON THE FLOOR OF THE SCHOOL.

THE FIRST BRIDGE LEADS TO A HOUSE.

IF THIS RIVER IS TOO HIGH TO FORD, THERE IS A BRIDGE UPSTREAM.

Paucarcancha 3200 m.

2½ HRS

PAUCARCANCHA

1¼ HRS

PAUCARCANCHA

OVERLAP WITH MAP 1

MAP 1

1 km
½ mile

0

0

Q. Churamayo

OVERLAP WITH MAP 16

Río Cusichaca

TO SALCANTAY
R. MOLLEPATA

Paucarcancha

Standing on the walls of this reconstructed Inca fort and looking down at the Cusichaca and Quesca rivers, you can see one of the reasons why the Incas chose to build it. Paucarcancha dominates both valleys, valleys along which Inca roads ran. These roads led over the Salcantay watershed to the Apurímac river, a source of danger to Inca stability since the days of the Cancha invasion. Paucarcancha was, therefore, a guarded entry point to Machu Picchu and the Urubamba from the Apurímac to the south.

The archaeologist, Dr Ann Kendall, discovered that a large non-Inca population lived in the areas around Paucarcancha and Huayllabamba. These people were the indigenous inhabitants of the area, and the Incas pretty much let them be but the imposing walls of Paucarcancha must have been a permanent reminder of who was really in control.

Paucarcancha is the first large Inca site that's been discovered on the old Anta to Machu Picchu road and is probably a gateway to the region. It was built quite late in comparison with the tambos of Inca Raccay and Incasamana, after the early constructions in the area around Patallacta, around the mid to late fifteenth century. Within the complex are sixteen buildings, one of which looks a little like a barracks and could have held soldiers or perhaps *mit'a* workers. The people who lived in Paucarcancha had enough fields to grow all their food, and over ten thousand square metres of terracing have been discovered in the hills nearby. It's likely it also functioned as a tambo.

Paucarcancha

TO HUAYLLABAMBA

TO MOLLE PATA

Trapezoidal Windows

Gabled House

TO ANCASCOCHA

RECONSTRUCTED SECTION

RECONSTRUCTED SECTION

Grassy Area

Dead Woman Pass/Abra de Huarmihuanusca (see p180), which is the first pass on the trail from Huayllabamba to Machu Picchu.

One and a half hours out of Quesca is the site of **Paucarcancha** (see opposite). Paucarcancha is built at the junction of three valleys: the valley you've just walked down, the upper Cusichaca leading to Salcantay and Mollepata and the lower Cusichaca leading to Huayllabamba and the Urubamba river. Its position makes it a sensibly-placed fort but it was probably a tambo as well.

OPTIONS FROM PAUCARCANCHA

From Paucarcancha, there are **three options**: the first is to turn left (south) and walk towards Mollepata (see Map 16, p215); the second is to turn right (north) and walk towards Huayllabamba, then turn up the Llulluchayoc towards Machu Picchu (see Map 2, p179); the third option is to walk to Huayllabamba, then down the Cusichaca river to the Urubamba, where you could either pick up the train from Km88, 82 or walk all the way back to Chilca and complete a circuit (see Map 1, p177).

The Mollepata trek

This hike takes six or seven days, and is quite gruelling; the pass is at 5000m (16,400ft) on the shoulder of the mountain Salcantay. However it's a wonderful walk and takes you right from the watershed of the Apurímac to the Urubamba.

MOLLEPATA → ABOVE MARCOCASA   [MAP 12, p209]

Mollepata is a village at the end of a dirt track off the main Cusco to Abancay road. The early bus from Cusco (5am from opposite the western end of Calle Arcopata, s/5) will take you right into the village, but some of the later ones will drop you only at the bottom of the dirt track, down by the Apurímac river in the heat among the biting insects.

MOLLEPATA TO MACHU PICCHU
How high you'll climb and
how far you'll walk

Height in metres · Distance in kms

It's a good few kilometres from the main road to Mollepata, and you *could* walk it but I wouldn't recommend that unless you like desert hiking. You can usually hitch up from the main road to Mollepata, but you should pay the driver s/3 or so.

There are a couple of hostals, the better one (s/10 per night) being one block to the west of the main plaza, on the western side of a small plazoleta, plus a few small stores where you can buy some basic last-minute provisions. There are arrieros for hire in Mollepata – the Pérez family are often recommended and as a result they're a little more expensive than others: s/25-s/30 a day rather than the going rate of s/20-s/25. Be clear whether or not the sum decided includes your providing food. There's also, uniquely as far as I know, a female arriero called Graciela Pinedo living in Mollepata near the Pérez family.

Mollepata to the glade after the bridge

The trail leaves from Mollepata's Plaza de Armas. Take the road that leaves from the plaza's north-west corner, and walk up the cobbles until you arrive at a T junction. Turn right (north-east) and then the path veers around to the north-west.

As you leave the village the houses become more and more infrequent. You're walking along the left (W) side of a valley that's heading just about due north-west. In a short time you'll pass under some power lines, and then a little further on the path will head uphill (W), hairpinning steeply. You then cross a bridge and turn almost back on yourself as you climb up the valley side before coming to a pleasant glade. This is a place to catch your breath and prepare for the difficult bit to come.

The difficult bit

It's easy to get lost after the glade, though the campesinos around here are used to trekkers getting lost and often point out the way.

The main valley to Soray, where you're heading, runs from the north-west to the south-east in what's a straight line if you're a condor. In fact the line of the valley is broken by a large gully which appears as a fork in the valleys when you walk uphill. One valley heads off more to the west, one to the north. You want to take the valley that goes more to the north. There's an isolated hillock between the northern and western valleys that you should avoid.

The best advice for tackling this section comes from trekker Richard Derham:
● Reach a house with three-way pylons and a tin and thatch roof.
● About 100m further on, come to an irrigation channel at the top of the climb.
● Follow the channel for 600m.
● The path then crosses the channel, so the water's now flowing on your right (E).
● Follow this path for 50m past a house, then start to head uphill.
● By a pile of large stones, a cattle track goes to the left round the hill, a dirt road (through a wooden gate) to the right. Go straight up a track that leads uphill to two pylons close together. The trail becomes obvious again.
● The channel is on your right; cross it after 50m, so it runs on your left.

Head straight up the most used path towards a gate, and don't veer off to the left into the valley on the other side of the crest of the hill. After the gate, stick to the main path, ignoring the left fork.

OVERLAP WITH MAP 13

VIEW OF HUMANTAY

THE LEFT FORK LEADS TO AN OLD STONE WATERCOURSE, WHICH IN TURN LEADS TO SORAY PAMPA, A PLEASANT ALTERNATIVE ROUTE.

Río Blanco

MAP 12

LEFT FORK ½ HR

1 HR

MARCOCASA

THE PATH BRAIDS, THEN ASCENDS THROUGH ERODED MUD GULLEYS.

Nadapata
GREAT CAMPING

Marcocasa 3500m
A PLEASANT CAMPSITE IN PASTURE.

THE PATH BRAIDS

DIFFICULT SECTION SEE TEXT

GLADE - NICE VIEWS, A GOOD PLACE TO REST. A STREAM FOLLOWS THE PATH JUST AFTER THIS.

POWER LINES

TO MARCOCASA

MOLLEPATA

MARKET

PEREZ FAMILY

TO HOSTAL

POLICE

CHURCH

PLAZA DE ARMAS

TO CUSCO ROAD

HOUSES BECOME MORE SCARCE.

STREAM

PLAZA DE ARMAS

MOLLEPATA 2800m.
FIND THE PLAZA DE ARMAS AND HEAD UP THE MAIN STREET ON ITS LEFT (WEST) COME TO A T JUNCTION AND TURN RIGHT. HEAD OUT OF THE VILLAGE ALONG THIS TRACK. IF IN DOUBT, ASK!

LEFT FORK

½ HRS

MARCOCASA

3 HRS

MOLLEPATA

2½ HRS

MOLLEPATA

0   1km
0   ½ mile

You should then find yourself at **Marcocasa**, a green, open area which is a good place to *camp*. Marcocasa is $2^1/2$-3 hours from Mollepata. Fill up your water bottles here, as the streams from here to Soray are seasonal and unreliable. Marcocasa offers some superb views of the snow-capped Huarohuirani (to the north behind the hill) and the village of **Qurawasi**, away in the distance to the west.

From Marcocasa, head north and uphill through some deeply-eroded mud gullies and into a wood. The path then winds in a north-westerly direction and settles on the left-hand (W) side of the valley of the Blanco river, where the path finally levels out. (If you find yourself on the right-hand (E) side of a river valley, you've gone the wrong way. Head back down to Marcocasa and try again.) Ahead of you is a glorious view of Mount Humantay, with Llana Urco on its left (east) and Hatun Casa to the south of that.

ABOVE MARCOCASA → SORAY   [MAP 13, opposite]

The path from here to Soray is easy – you're walking in the same direction, along a valley towards an objective, Soray Pampa, that lies at the foot of Mount Humantay. It takes a good $3^1/2$-4 hours to get there. There are two paths: the main one is the lower one, and there's an upper path that follows the route of an ancient Inca watercourse, that starts by the viewpoint. The upper one isn't suitable for mules.

About half an hour after you get your first view of Humantay, you'll come to an open green field with a farm by a stream: the *campsite* of Chacha Cancha (this is my approximation of what I was told it's called). I thought this a good place to camp but the stream is seasonal and not reliable.

After 1-$1^1/2$ hours you reach a gate across the path, next to a hut that's home to some very noisy dogs. You'll then enter some woods – Soray is about another half-hour's walk. You'll pass a large scree slope on your left (W), and after that if you look to your right (E), you'll notice a waterfall as the Blanco river flows over a steep cliff. Soon after, you walk out of the woods and onto some high puna fields – you've reached **Soray pampa**.

The pampa is often latticed with small drainage canals and streams that you'll have to cross (though these disappear in dry years). Keep to the left (W) side of the fields, close to the rock wall if you want to remain dry-booted. At the far (N) end of the pampa there's **Soray** itself, over the other side (N) of a stream – often there's a bridge but you might have to use stepping stones. This is a good place to *camp*.

SORAY → THE PASS   [MAP 14, p213]

You can hire arrieros in Soray. I hired Antonio Huari Huillca, who charged s/20 a day and was reliable, friendly and had sound animals; he'll probably double his rates when he finds out he's in this book.

Mt Humantay
5910m

SORAY
3950m

RUSTIC 'GATE'
BY ROCK
OVERHANG

OVERLAP
WITH
MAP 14

Soray Pampa

EXCELLENT CAMPSITES.
KEEP TO THE NORTH OF
THE PLATEAU. IT IS DRIER.

5189m

WATER-
FALL

FIELDS

STEEP
CLIFF

BEWARE OF
THE DOGS HERE

SCREE

'GATE' INTO THICK
WOODS (WOODEN
BARS ACROSS THE
TRACK).

GULLIES

THERE ARE
MANY GULLIES
AND DRY STREAMS
IN THIS AREA.

Rio Blanco

THIS AREA OF
THE TRAIL IS
SUBJECT TO
LANDSLIDES.

SEASONAL
STREAMS

A GOOD CAMPSITE
I WAS TOLD IT WAS
CALLED CHACHA CANCHA
BUT THIS MIGHT NOT
BE A COMMON NAME
AS IT DOESN'T APPEAR
ON ANY OTHER MAP.

FARM.

TRAILBLAZER

OVERLAP
WITH
MAP 12

0   1km
0   ½ mile

MAP 13

VIEW OF
HUMANTAY

SORAY PAMPA

SORAY PAMPA

1½ HRS

1½ HRS

3 HRS

½ HR ⏴ CAMPSITE

CAMPSITE

LEFT FORK

½ HR

LEFT FORK

Soray to Salcantay pampa

The trail heads up the valley to the north-east, to the right. The path takes the northern (left) side of the little valley and passes through a rustic gate by a rock overhang, then crosses to the right (south-east) bank. Mount Salcantay, the sacred mountain of the Incas, is ahead of you. Descend to a stream and cross to the left-hand side where the path becomes boggy and the track indistinct. As long as you continue following the stream north-east, however, you're doing fine.

You're now underneath a massive wall of scree at the end of this valley – it's the terminal moraine (end debris) of a glacier. The flat ground before the moraine is called Salcantay pampa, and is a great place to *camp*. The path follows the moraine round to the right (E), back across the stream (which is actually three streams now) all the way up to the pass.

Salcantay pampa to the pass

To get to the pass, follow the path which switchbacks steeply up the right-hand (E) hillside that faces the moraine. You'll soon reach a small, flat spot called Quera Machay (aka Isu Pata), which is another good place to *camp*. The path heads north from Quera Machay, then round to the right (E), steeply uphill. Don't go down to the lateral moraine of the glacier, keep the river between you and it. As you climb, the gully gets narrower and narrower, until the path seems to disappear when you reach the top. There's another stream here which you need to keep on your right – it's not the same as the one that runs down by the glacier. You'll know you've got it correct when you can look back over the wall of the lateral moraine and see two lakes.

From here, you should be able to see the pass at the top of a very, very steep path, surrounded by little ridges. Don't be tempted to cut out the pass and go over the watershed by the glacier – there are dangerous holes under the glacier and you could easily slip down into them. The **pass** is the most knife-edged of passes I've ever seen – it's just a metre or so wide. You can look down into the great valley up which you've come, and over into the wide valley where you're now headed.

THE PASS → PAMPA CAHUANA   [MAP 15, p214]

From the pass, head steeply downhill. Go over and have a look at the glacier on your left (N) which is the origin of the river Cusichaca. It's worth stopping and thinking that this is one of the origins of the Amazon, and the melt-water from this mountain flows to the Atlantic Ocean.

The trail from here to Paucarcancha is easy – you just follow the valley down – first east-north-east to Pampa Cahuana, then north-east.

Taking it step by step, the path first heads south-east across puna, then bends round to the north-east and descends quite steeply. Just before a ridge, about an hour and a half beyond the pass, there's a beautiful *campsite*, flat, green and protected from the wind but it's often occupied by tour companies. Down the other side of the ridge, the path crosses a plain of glacial outwash before settling on the northern (L) bank of the river. This area is flat and good for camping too, it's called the **Quebrada Sisay pampa.**

MAP 14

PASS 5000m.
THE FINAL ASCENT
AND DESCENT IS
VERY STEEP. THE PASS
ITSELF IS A KNIFE
EDGE, WHICH WILL MAKE
EVEN THE STRONGEST
STOMACHS A LITTLE
QUEASY.

Mt Salcantay

GLACIER

DON'T GO
NEAR THE
GLACIER
SEE
TEXT

Pampa
Japonés

OVER
LAP
WITH
MAP 15

Quera Machay 4300m.

Mt Rayusqa 5350m.

DIFFICULT BIT

PLEASE
SEE
TEXT

LARGE
ROCK

BOGGY AND
THE PATH IS
INDISTINCT

GLACIAL MORAINE

TERMINAL
MORAINE

Salcantay
Pampa
GOOD CAMPSITES

THE TERMINAL MORAINE
COMPLETELY BLOCKS THE
END OF THE VALLEY

RUSTIC 'GATE' BY
ROCK OVERHANG

OVERLAP
WITH
MAP 13

Soray Pampa

SCREE

▲ Mt Humantay 5910m.

Soray ⊠

0   1km
0   ½ mile

SORAY ½ HR — GATE — 2½ HRS — TURN IN VALLEY — 1½ HRS — PASS

SORAY — ½ HR — GATE — 1¼ HRS — TURN IN VALLEY — ½ HR — PASS

HUTS BY THE TURN TO THE N.E.

OVERLAP WITH MAP 16

THERE IS A PATH ON THIS SIDE OF THE STREAM TOO, AND IT PROVIDES A GOOD VIEW OF THE INCA CANAL BELOW.

Pampa Cahuana 4000m.

HUTS BY THE TURN TO THE N.E.

★ TRAILBLAZER

MAP 15

← 1½ HRS →

Nevados Paljay 5420m.

STEEP

GULLY
GULLY

Q Sisay Pampa

SHEPHERD'S HUT

THE STREAM MEANDERS AND BRAIDS A LOT HERE.

FLAT PUNA, GOOD CAMPING

1km
½ mile

0

0

RUINED HUTS

BOGGY

← 1 HR →

← 2½ HRS BEGINNING OF PUNA →

GLACIAL MORAINE

EXCELLENT CAMPSITE

BEGINNING OF PUNA →

← 3½ HRS

Mt Salcantay 6270m.

GLACIER

OVERLAP WITH MAP 14

PASS 5000m. THE FINAL ASCENT AND DESCENT IS VERY STEEP. THE PASS ITSELF IS A KNIFE EDGE WHICH WILL MAKE THE STRONGEST STOMACHS A LITTLE QUEASY.

◄ PASS

◄ PASS

MAP 16

THIS IS A REASONABLY GENTLE DESCENT THROUGH A VERY BEAUTIFUL VALLEY. YOU CAN FEEL THE WARMTH AS YOU GET LOWER.

Paucarcancha 3200m

OVER-LAP WITH MAP I

OVER-LAP WITH MAP II

PAUCARCANCHA

PAUCARCANCHA

1 ½ HRS

2 ½ HRS

Q. Churomayo

Río Cusichaca

NARROW GORGE

FOOTBALL FIELD

THE STRAIGHT SECTION OF RIVER IS AN INCA-BUILT CANAL. THERE ARE PLENTY OF CAMPSITES ALONG BY THE CANAL.

Pampa Cahuana 4000m

PATH GOES RIGHT THROUGH FARM (WITH NOISY DOGS)

FLAT AREA, GOOD FOR CAMPING.

BRIDGE

BRIDGE

½ HR

½ HR

TURN IN THE VALLEY BY HUTS

TURN IN THE VALLEY BY HUTS

OVERLAP WITH MAP 15

0   1km
0   ½ mile

Keep on this side of the river, and skirt around two gullies with seasonal streams running in them. The land gets very steep. In a short while you'll see on the other side of the river a couple of huts and a large stream coming down from the south – there is a path on this side of the river too, but the main path's on the north. Just after the huts and stream the valley turns north-east and looking down you can see an Inca canal, glistening in the sun (there's a better view from the southern path). This area's called **Pampa Cahuana.**

PAMPA CAHUANA → PAUCARCANCHA   [MAP 16 p215]

The path passes through the centre of a huddle of a number of farms and a football pitch, and then crosses a **bridge** to the right-hand (E) bank of the river. You are crossing over the Inca canal. Then, after a narrow gorge, the river, valley and path all turn northwards. The valley descends gently, and the flora changes from high puna to scrub, bathed in warmth and flourishing with butterflies and insects. One and a half hours after the bridge you arrive at the ruins of **Paucarcancha** (see p207).

OPTIONS FROM PAUCARCANCHA

From Paucarcancha, you have **three options**: walk to Huayllabamba and complete the Inca trail (see Map 1, p177); walk down the Cusichaca where you could either take a train out, walk to Chilca (again, see Map 6), or walk west along the Urubamba to Chachabamba and Machu Picchu; turn up the valley you find on your right (E) and walk up to Puerto Huyanay (see Map 11, p205).

Other trails near Machu Picchu

CHILCA CIRCUIT (5-6 DAYS)

(To follow this route description look at the Route Planning map on p22-3). A Chilca circuit would take you up the Silque valley, down the Cusichaca valley and back around to Chilca along the Urubamba river. It would take about five or six days. Remember that it's not a good idea to do this circuit anti-clockwise because you'd have to pay the Inca Trail fee twice.

THE FULL MOLLEPATA (2 WEEKS)

(See Route Planning map on p22-3). An extended Mollepata hike would take you from Mollepata, over the Salcantay pass, down the Cusichaca to the Urubamba, along to Chilca, then up the Silque valley. At the top of the Silque valley you'd turn right and head up to the pass of Puerto Huyanay. You'd then follow the Quesca valley and down to Paucarcancha and then Huayllabamba where you'd pick up the classic Inca Trail to Machu Picchu. This hike would take you about two weeks.

❏ The Riverside Trail from Km88

An unusual and very pretty alternative to the classic Inca Trail is to follow the Urubamba valley all the way to Chachabamba. The permit for this route costs the same as that for the Inca Trail, namely US$50, or US$25 for students.

The path begins across the bridge from the warden's office: while those following the classic Inca Trail turn left after the bridge, the riverside path splits off to the right, heads due south away from the river for 50m, then leads off west in the shadow of a large stone wall, and continues west along the Río Urubamba for the next 15km.

The walk is, as they say around these parts, 'muy tranquilo', which is its chief attraction: I encountered precisely nobody after the first few hundred metres, and heard nothing but the roar of the river, the occasional birdsong and the sound of my own footfall for that next 15km. The walk's perfect if you want to avoid the crowds, don't want any knee-jarring descents or steep climbs (the longest ascent lasts no longer than 15 minutes), or just want something different – a walk along forest- and grass-clad slopes rather than over mountain passes. It's also shorter than the regular Km88 walk, and you can get all the way to the Trekkers' Hotel in one day if you're in a desperate hurry – though I strongly recommend you spread the walk over two or three very easy, relaxing days.

There are some Inca ruins along the way too, including **Machu** and **Huayna Quente** (see p176) – don't miss the wonderful little carved boulder by the bridge beneath the former – and the impressive **Torontoy** complex on the northern banks of the Urubamba. This is the Inca compound of Raccy Pata, more commonly known as Torontoy after the canyon in which it is built. This site's age and purpose remain in the realms of conjecture, though Ann Kendall has estimated from the fine, classical stonework that it was probably built sometime during the latter part of the reign of Pachacutec, or possibly the early years of his successor, Tupac Inca, during the heyday of the Inca Empire. Kendall has also suggested that at least one of its functions was to serve as upmarket accommodation for the Inca or another member of the travelling élite – the Machu Picchu Pueblo Hotel of its day. A possible temple building has also been identified within the compound. The rope and pulley contraption (*oroya*) strung across the river has not been used since the footbridge at Km88 was built so you'll have to make do with a distant view. If you do manage to get across, look out for the incredible 44-angled stone in one of the walls – a marvel of masonry that puts even the 12-angled stone in Cusco in the shade.

There are other, lesser ruins lying unrestored in the forest, especially near the **Río Pacamayo**. Unimpressive though they may be, some of the runs here are circular in design, suggesting pre-Inca occupation, which is highly unusual for this part of the Urubamba.

The path is fairly well maintained and signposted, but because of the comparative unpopularity of the trail it is sometimes a little overgrown. That said, it's very difficult to get lost, and the path never peters out altogether. **Snakes**, however, are a potential hazard – I came across four while researching this walk, each one basking in the sunshine on the path. But if you give them time to slither away and are careful where you sit and tread, they shouldn't be a problem.

Campsites along the way include the warden's post by the Río Pacamayo, about two hours from Km88, and by the ruins at Chachabamba, three hours further on. From the latter you can either take the standard path up to the Trekkers' Hotel (see p188), or continue along the river all the way to Choquesuysuy, from where the newly-established Purification Trail leads up to Huinay Huayna (see p189).

The Vilcabamba Trail

This is a fascinating walk through the forest between the remote villages of Huancacalle and Chaunquiri via the ruins of Espíritu Pampa, believed to be the remains of Vilcabamba, the last city and capital of the Inca empire. The trail follows what is believed to be the same route taken by Manco Inca as he fled the Spanish in 1537, and also that taken by the Spaniards themselves in their two invasions of Vilcabamba in 1539 and 1572.

In common with the Inca Trail, the best time to attempt this walk is between **May and September**; outside this period the route is often impassable and you probably won't find a guide/arriero willing to take you. It involves approximately the same amount of walking as the Inca Trail, namely three to four days. Unlike the Inca Trail, however, this is no walk in the (national) park. There are no designated campsites here, no rubbish bins, flush toilets or drink sellers. The path is extremely muddy and marshy in places. Depending on how many people have used it in the weeks before you, it may be very overgrown as well, and for some stretches you may find yourself having to hack your way through the forest – at times you'll feel like a true explorer.

The weather can play havoc with the trail: landslips that obliterate the path are common throughout the year, while bridges are often swept away by the raging rivers in the wet season – and in the Vilcabamba region it seems to be nearly always the wet season.

Having overcome all the obstacles and hazards, understandably you may anticipate something really spectacular at the end of the journey. Though the area covered by Vilcabamba La Vieja is large, the ruins don't stand up to such expectations; they bear little comparison with even the lesser monuments on the Inca trail; nevertheless this trek has other attractions which make it a most rewarding and memorable experience. The route itself is a gloriously beautiful hike through virtually every kind of vegetation zone found in Peru; as a crash course in the variegated ecology of this country, this trail is hard to beat. Then there are the ruins along the way, many of which are off the path and covered in vegetation. While none could be described as breathtaking, for those who feel that the ruins on the Inca trail have been over-restored, and thus seem a touch artificial, here's a chance to see some in their pristine, untouched state. The path itself is also of Inca origin, and here and there you'll find the distinctive giant paving slabs. Nor must you forget the terrific sense of achievement one feels when reaching these ruins; for those who found the Inca Trail a bit of a cinch, this provides a much tougher challenge.

But perhaps the best feature of this trek is its remoteness. This is one walk where you can be sure, (or 95% sure), that you won't meet other tourists. And for anybody who has found themselves shuffling along the Inca Trail in the high season as part of an endless human queue, that is another good reason to recommend this walk.

PREPARATIONS

There's no reason why anybody with a little stamina and a decent pair of calf muscles can't complete this trek, though some preparation is necessary.

You'll need a tent and food; there are no hotels or designated campsites but good camping spots have been marked on the maps in this section. Then you need to engage an **arriero**, which can be done in Huancacalle: see p222.

Other than a machete, which your arriero should have (check this before you leave), the walk needs no special **equipment**, though a bottle or two of insect repellent would come in useful, and keeping everything wrapped in plastic bags is even more necessary here than on other treks because of the extremely wet weather you're bound to encounter. This is a malarial area so don't forget your anti-malarials.

Finally, there is one more piece of preparation to be made before you head off to Vilcabamba: read about the place (see p31 for a list of books).

TIMING AND GETTING TO THE TRAILHEAD

This trail takes you from Huancacalle and Chaunquiri via Espíritu Pampa. To reach Huancacalle you need to take a bus from Cusco to Quillabamba (9 hours), then another bus or a truck from Quillabamba to Huancacalle (4-5 hours).

It takes only 3-4 days to walk from Huancacalle to Chaunquiri but the **timing of your walk** is very important. As buses from Chaunquiri (at the end of the trek) tend to leave only after the weekly market on Saturdays and Sundays, you'd be well advised to aim to finish your walk at a weekend to avoid being stranded in the village. Remember to take into account the time it takes to travel to the Vilcabamba region, plus any time you may wish to spend before your trek in Quillabamba or Huancacalle, both of which are worth a day at least. Those in a hurry can jump out before Quillabamba at Chaullay and from there look for a bus or lift to Huancacalle: by bypassing Quillabamba it might just be possible to reach the start of the trail in one day from Cusco.

Taking all the above into consideration, however, it's best to allow about **nine days** for the whole trek.

Cusco to Quillabamba

Buses to Quillabamba leave throughout the day from the Paso Santiago Terminal in the north-west of Cusco. It's a spectacular journey that takes you over the **Pass of the Eagle**, with awesome views of the Veronica range; don't

❏ **Chaullay**
Chaullay was once the site of Chuquichaca, one of the Inca's famous rope bridges. As the main entrance into the Vilcabamba valley, the bridge became strategically crucial in the defence of the Inca's territory and was cut down if an invasion was anticipated. It was also here that the envoy Atilana de Anayo was murdered by Inca troops protecting the bridge, an event that led to the final invasion of Vilcabamba in 1572.

take a night bus or you'll miss it all. The journey takes about nine hours and costs s/15; Trans Tur seems one of the better companies. Ninety minutes before Quillabamba lies **Chaullay**, where those in a hurry can alight and try to catch a lift straight to Huancacalle.

Quillabamba

Built at the confluence of the Chuyapi and Urubamba (Vilcanota) rivers, **Quillabamba** is a friendly little jungle town with a large food market at its centre where you can buy provisions for the trek.

There's a variety of accommodation options in town, ranging from the cheap but clean *Urusayhua Hostal* (☎ 281426; s/10/15 sgl/dbl) Pasaje Lima 114, to the much smarter *Quillabamba Hotel* (☎ 281369; s/40/65/80 sgl/dbl/tpl) on Av Grau, which has its own pool, and the equally comfortable *Don Carlos Hotel* (☎ 281150; s/45/65/85 sgl/dbl/tpl), just to the west of Plaza de Armas, which has Internet facilities (s/5 per hour).

For food, try one of the chicken restaurants on San Martín, or *Venecia Pizzeria* on Plaza de Armas. For snacks, *Chemo's Panadería and Pastelería* does a fair empanada. The **Internet café** Cibermaster is at Av Bolognesi 403.

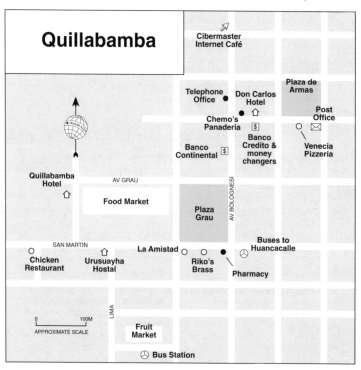

Quillabamba to Huancacalle

From Quillabamba, it's four to five hours to Huancacalle (s/8), taking the road back down to Chaullay, then up the Vilcabamba valley. At the moment there are three buses daily, at 9am, 11am and 1pm.

Just a few minutes before Huancacalle lies **Pucyura**, one of the older and larger villages in the valley. In years gone by all visitors had to register with the police here, though recently, as the threat from the Sendero Luminoso (see p43) has all but vanished, this rule seems to have been relaxed. Pucyura was also the location of the first church in the valley, built by Friar Diego Ortiz following the peace treaty between the Spaniards and Titu Cusi in 1568; the modern church you see today stands on the site of the original.

Huancacalle

Built in the prettiest part of the Vilcabamba valley, **Huancacalle** is a typical Andean village, the kind of place where the people smile and greet you as you walk past and where the pigs and chickens roam free and the donkeys and dogs are untethered. Huancacalle is also the traditional starting point of the walk to the ruins of Vilcabamba and is fairly used to catering for trekkers. While there are no camping shops or pizza restaurants, this is the place where mules and guides can be hired and last-minute provisions acquired.

There is a hostal in Huancacalle, the *Sixpac Manco Hostal* at the very end of the village, sponsored by the author and Vilcabamba expert Vincent Lee (see p31) and run by the Cobos family, the best-known guides in the village. They charge s/15 per night for a comfortable room, and s/3 per meal. As alternatives there are a couple of gloomy **cafés** in town, where s/2 will get you a plate of rubbery meat and potatoes.

HUANCACALLE → UTUTO
[MAP 18, p226; MAP 19, p227; MAP 20, p228]

The trek kicks off with a lengthy but not particularly arduous uphill tramp of about two and a half hours, most of it along a snaking dirt road from the centre of Huancacalle (3181m/10,434ft) to the Abra Ccolpa Casa ('Salty Pass'; 3900m/12,792ft). To follow every twist and turn in the road would be time-consuming but, by taking the short cuts marked on the map you would have a more direct route to the pass.

A short way out of Huancacalle take the right fork in the road and leave it to follow the trail. After a zigzagging bend the path rejoins the road, leaving it

---

❏ **Walking times on Maps 18-27 (Vilcabamba Trail)**
Note that on all the trail maps in this book the times shown alongside each map refer only to **time spent actually walking**. For the trail times in the Vilcabamba section (Maps 18-27) you may find the pace a little faster than for the Inca Trail timings. When planning your walking for the day you should add about 30-50% to allow for rest stops.

❑ The Vitcos walk [MAP 17, p224]

The ruins of Vitcos lie between the Río Vilcabamba and Las Andenes stream and you can spend a delightful **half day** exploring these and neighbouring monuments. The caretaker of the ruins lives in Huancacalle in the house underneath the 'Welcome' sign, and officially you should register with him before setting off. The paths are clearly marked and it's difficult to get lost.

The trail begins across the two rivers from Sixpac Manco Hostal, from where it heads north via the ruins of an old **Spanish mill** up to the crest of the hill known as **Rosaspata** (3050m/10,004ft). At the northern end of the crest, overlooking the town of Pucyura, are the ruins of **Vitcos**, Manco's first capital in Vilcabamba, and another of Hiram Bingham's discoveries.

Manco established his palace here in 1537, before abandoning it just days later following a raid by Diego de Almagro's faithful commander, Orgóñez. Manco returned to Vitcos regularly, however, largely because its climate had more in common with the Inca's old home in Cusco (being only 600m lower than the former capital) than the sweaty humidity of the jungle. Indeed, Manco was eventually assassinated here in 1544 by a group of seven Spaniards to whom he had given refuge, supporters of the defeated Almagrist cause in the civil war against the Pizarrists (see p97). The fugitives hoped that the murder of Manco would curry favour with the conquering Pizarrists. The murder was recorded by his young son, Titu Cusi, one of the great chroniclers of post-conquest life and a future Inca himself:

'One day with much good fellowship they were playing at quoits with him: only them, my father, and me, who was then a little boy . . . Then just as my father was raising the quoit to throw, they all rushed upon him with knives, daggers and some swords . . . .he fell to the ground covered with wounds, and they left him for dead. I being a little boy, and seeing my father treated in this manner, wanted to rush over to help him. But they turned furiously on me and threw a lance which only just failed to kill me too.'

Manco survived for another three days, long enough to learn that his assailants had all been captured and suffered horrible deaths at the hands of his supporters. The heads of the seven renegades were still on display at Vitcos 21 years later.

Although Titu Cusi survived this assault he too met his death at Vitcos, after a violent illness. In the eyes of the Inca's followers this illness was the result of poisoning. The Spanish were once again implicated: Friar Diego Ortiz, one of the priests allowed into Vilcabamba as part of the peace treaty between Titu Cusi and the Spanish, was renowned for his knowledge of medicine, and relations between the Inca and his priest had been strained for some time prior to Titu Cusi's death. If anything, the poor friar's fate was even more gruesome than that of the seven renegades who had killed Manco (see p234). Today the entire hill of Rosaspata is dotted with Inca foundations and ruins, though only those on the northern spur have been cleared of vegetation. While the palace has yet to be restored and lacks the day-to-day care lavished on other Inca monuments, its **marble lintels** abutting the plaza and a small, finely carved stone **throne** are still *in situ* today; it's a pleasant spot for a rest.

From Vitcos, a second path heads south along the eastern slopes of the hill and down to a series of smart Inca terraces, or *andenes*, adorned here and there with gigantic carved boulders clearly the work of Inca craftsmen. Continue around Rosaspata and at the foot of its southern slopes you'll find the ruins of the Inca temple of **Nusta España**, also known as Yurac-Rumi ('White Stone'), an impressive set of stone chairs, large sacred rocks, foundations and water channels. *(cont'd over)*

❑ The Vitcos walk   (cont'd from p223)

At its centre lies a huge boulder over seven metres high and carved with a series of small protrusions, steps, platforms and other decorations; this is a **huaca**, or sacred site. The working of the stone is reminiscent of Qenko (see p150). According to one contemporary Spanish account 'There was a devil, captain of a legion of devils, inside the white stone called Yurac-Rumi,' and that devil was 'visible on various occasions'. Today sightings of the devil are rare, particularly since the temple was exorcized and burnt by Friar Diego Ortiz. The locals in Huancacalle tell of another former use for Yurac-Rumi. According to legend, in Inca times it was traditional for girls to urinate at the top of the pale grey channel running along the top of the boulder in order to prove their virtue: if the urine followed precisely the channel's course, so legend has it, then the girl had successfully proved her virginity.

To return to Huancacalle, continue heading west from Nusta España then down the steep hill to the river.

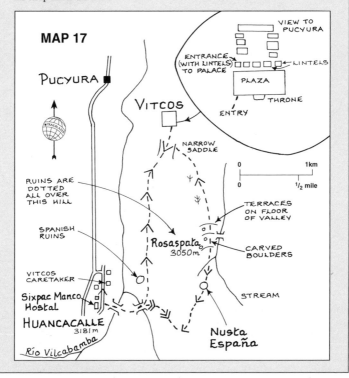

MAP 17

VIEW TO PUCYURA

ENTRANCE (WITH LINTELS) TO PALACE — LINTELS

PLAZA

THRONE

ENTRY

PUCYURA

VITCOS

NARROW SADDLE

RUINS ARE DOTTED ALL OVER THIS HILL

SPANISH RUINS

VITCOS CARETAKER

Sixpac Manco Hostal

HUANCACALLE 3181m

Río Vilcabamba

Rosaspata 3050m

TERRACES ON FLOOR OF VALLEY

CARVED BOULDERS

STREAM

Nusta España

0 ____ 1km
0 ____ ½ mile

Opposite Top left: Waterfall near Huinay Huayna (see p189). (Photo © Richard Danbury).
Top right: Sixteenth century bell-tower at Vilcabamba La Nueva (see p225).
Bottom: Eromboni Pampa (see p239) at Espíritu Pampa. (Photos © Henry Stedman).

just before a bridge near the Seventh Station of the Cross. Go over the next bridge, then continue with the Río Vilcabamba on your right. You will pass the Eighth and Ninth Stations of the Cross, rejoining the road once and crossing it twice before joining it again near the Eleventh Station of the Cross, to pass through the village of San Francisco de la Vitoria de Vilcabamba, often referred to just as Vilcabamba, or as **Vilcabamba La Nueva** to distinguish it from Manco's capital.

This was the first Spanish settlement founded in the Spanish province of Vilcabamba and was its first capital. It was moved in the late sixteenth century from its original site near Vitcos to its current location near the source of the Río Vilcabamba to service a now-exhausted silver mine that lies nearby. The central feature of Vilcabamba is the large Italian Catholic mission and its adjoining church, a modern construction embellished with a door portraying the life of San Francisco. The church is built on the site of the original sixteenth-century edifice, whose ancient bell-tower still stands. There is no accommodation in Vilcabamba, though you should have no trouble obtaining permission to camp. There are also two small shops here, the last you'll see for a couple of days.

From Vilcabamba, the road wends its way northwards and upwards before petering out about 20 minutes before **Abra Ccolpa Casa** (the pass). At the pass, the dividing line between the low Andes and the Amazon basin is a little, modern shrine to Santa Rosa de Lima, built at the northern end of a small, flat grassy plateau – the overgrown remains of an Inca plaza. There are even the remains of a little Inca shrine here on the plateau's south-eastern corner, though now it's not much more than a heap of mossy stones.

From Ccolpa Casa the path continues north-west past possibly the highest school in the world (recognizable by its one green and one red door) and across undulating puna to **Mollipunku**, an ancient Inca crossroads where paths from both left (to Chalca) and right merge with yours; Inca paving slabs and steps still protect the pathway here.

About twenty-five minutes later you reach and cross the Río Chalca on Puente Antiguo (Mankechaca), where the trail splits. The upper and more obvious path climbs to **Pampaconas** (3340m/10,955ft), a windswept and rather chilly village with a little group of ruins including another Inca platform nearby. Be warned: just before Pampaconas is a deep bog into which some of the Spanish invaders of 1572, Bingham in 1911 and countless others have plunged. Indeed, the bog is so renowned around here that unusually it even has its own name, **Oncoy Cacha**.

The alternative to the Pampaconas route is to walk on the lower and more direct path, the start of which, though not immediately obvious from the Puente Antiguo, lies just two minutes away and is not difficult to find: just walk through the grassy field along the riverbank below the main path and you'll soon see it leading off to the north, along the valley towards **Ututo** where it rejoins the trail

---

Opposite Top: Approaching Salcantay Pass (see p212) on the Mollepata trek. (Photo © Henry Stedman). **Bottom:** Huinay Huayna (see p189). (Photo © Richard Danbury).

MAP 18

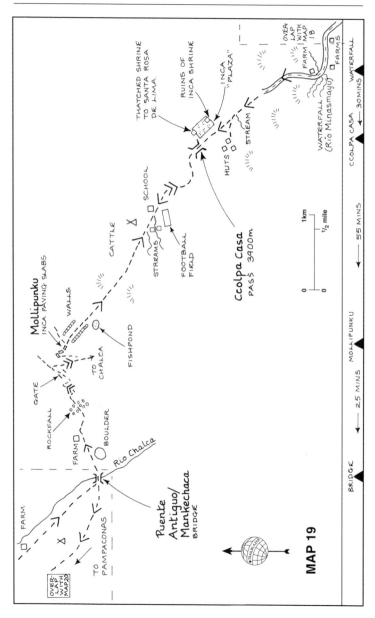

MAP 19

FARM

TO PAMPACONAS

Puente Antiguo/Mankechaca
BRIDGE

Rio Chalca

FARM

BOULDER

ROCKFALL

GATE

TO CHALCA

FISHPOND

WALLS

Mollipunku
INCA PAVING SLABS

CATTLE

STREAMS

SCHOOL

FOOTBALL FIELD

Ccolpa Casa
PASS 3900m.

HUTS

STREAM

INCA "PLAZA"

RUINS OF INCA SHRINE

THATCHED SHRINE
TO SANTA ROSA
DE LIMA

FARM

OVER LAP WITH MAP 18

FARMS

WATERFALL

WATERFALL
(Río Minasmayo)

OVER-
LAP
WITH
MAP 20

| BRIDGE | ◀ | ⟵ 25 MINS ⟶ | MOLLIPUNKU | ◀ | ⟵ 55 MINS ⟶ | CCOLPA CASA | ◀ | ⟵ 30 MINS ⟶ | WATERFALL | ◀ |

0   1km
0   ½ mile

OVER-
LAP
WITH MAP21

PUENTE ANTIGUO

1km

1/2 mile

0

40 MINS

PATH UNCLEAR
AT BEGINNING.
JUST FOLLOW
COURSE OF
RIVER THROUGH
GRASSY FIELD.

OVER-
LAP
WITH MAP19

PUENTE ANTIGUO

FOREST BEGINNING
TO APPEAR ON
OPPOSITE BANK.

1 HR 15 MINS CHANCARA

LARGE ORANGE
CONCRETE BRIDGE

Río Kolpac'asa

GATE   FARM   TO
PAMPACONAS

IGNORE ALL OTHER
BRIDGES ACROSS
STREAM

ISLAND IN
MIDDLE OF
RIVER

WALLS

SMALL BUSHES
LINE THE PATH

Puente Antiguo/
Markechaca

1 HR

Río
Pampaconas

FIELD/
PASTURE

Río Pampaconas

HUT
(CHANCARA)

PAMPACONAS
3340m

Oncoy Cacha
A DEEP BOG –
BEWARE!

UTUTO

PATH TO
PAMPACONAS

Río Pampaconas

INCA
STEPS

REMAINS OF
INCA PLAZA WITH
WELL-STRUCTURED
ANDENES

PAMPACONAS

1 HR 15 MINS

ROCKY CLEARING.
CAN SEE THE
CONTINUATION
OF OUR PATH ON
THE OTHER SIDE
OF THE RIVER

Río Pampaconas

UTUTO
2450m

BOGGY
GROUND

THERE ARE LOTS OF STREAMS
BEFORE UTUTO, SOME WITH
BRIDGES, SOME WITHOUT. IT
IS ALSO EXTREMELY MUDDY
AND BOGGY ROUND HERE.

INCA
PATH

SLIPPERY WOODEN
BRIDGE OVER STREAM

MAP 20

UTUTO

Pampaconas

Pampaconas features regularly in sixteenth-century records. It was to this spot that a wife and sister of Manco, Cura Ocllo, was taken by the Spaniards following their destruction of Vilcabamba in 1539. To prevent the Spaniards raping her, Cura covered herself in excrement and 'filthy matter' so that 'the men who were trying to rape her would be nauseated'. The tactic provided only a temporary reprieve, however, for Cura was killed in anger by the Spaniards shortly afterwards following yet another rejection of a peace treaty by Manco.

Pampaconas was also a centre for worship. Not only did the Incas hold various sun-worshipping ceremonies on the grassy plateau but Titu Cusi also gave permission for the Spanish to erect the first Christian cross in Vilcabamba here, under which missionaries were allowed to preach to the heathen locals. During the invasions in 1539 and 1572, the Spaniards were forced to leave their horses behind here, the path beyond being too forested. Bingham had to do the same in 1911, though today the path ahead is open to horses all the way to Espíritu Pampa.

from Pampaconas. Take note that there's some extremely boggy ground around Ututo, one of the largest settlements in the Pampaconas valley, though if you can find a dry patch of ground it's an excellent place to pitch a tent for the night.

UTUTO → URPIPATA
[MAP 21, p230; MAP 22, p231, MAP 23, p233]

This is perhaps the most pleasant and certainly the easiest stage of the walk, an undemanding and largely downhill march through increasingly dense but always gorgeous cloud forest.

The forest begins as soon as you cross the large concrete bridge at Ututo. This first stretch on the Pampaconas' eastern banks is very pretty indeed, a sun-dappled, mossy path adorned with the occasional Inca stairway and punctuated by a few clearings where cows and horses look on and graze.

According to Vincent Lee, the Spaniards were unaware of this particular trail, and instead tried to carve out a path along the cliffs and through the forest on the opposite bank: this explains why they took eight days to reach Vilcabamba from Pampaconas, while walkers today can do it in just over two.

After the Puente de Cedru, (Cedruchaca in Quechua) there follows an uphill climb before the path bends to the west towards the tiny clearing of **Tambocarahuina**. Whilst the clearing itself is unremarkable, it does provide an excellent view of the slender ridge above the scattered farms of **Tambo**, a little way to the north. Lee has identified this ridge as the site of the Inca bastion known as **Huayna Pucará**, or the new fort (see box p232).

At the end of elongated Tambo, the path descends along a series of switchbacks to the Río Zapatero and the one-hut settlement of the same name, before continuing to the village of **San Fernando**. Then you come to three rivers –

the Sucsu Chincana, Ounay and Vista Alegre – quite close together. The bridges across each are very slippery and some trekkers prefer to wade through the rivers instead; those who do decide to tackle the bridges are advised to do so on all fours. Immediately after the second river is the small but aptly named settlement of **Vista Alegre** ('Happy View'). If it's getting late you may wish to stop here for the night, as the Spanish did in 1572; the next place to camp is at **San Cristobal**, just over an hour further on.

40 MIN
TO TAMBOCARAHUINA

CEDROCHACA

1 HR 15 MIN

BRIDGE

Río Urumbay

OVERLAP
WITH
MAP 22

Río Pampaconas

SMALL
LANDSLIDE

NUMEROUS
WILD FLOWERS
IN MARCH/
APRIL

MAP 21

Puente de Cedro/
Cedrochaca

INCA
STEPS

STREAM

ROCKY CLEARING.
CAN SEE THE CONTINUATION
OF OUR PATH ON THE OTHER SIDE
OF THE RIVER.

OVER-
LAP
WITH
MAP 20

0   1km

0   ½ mile

BRIDGE AT
UTUTO.

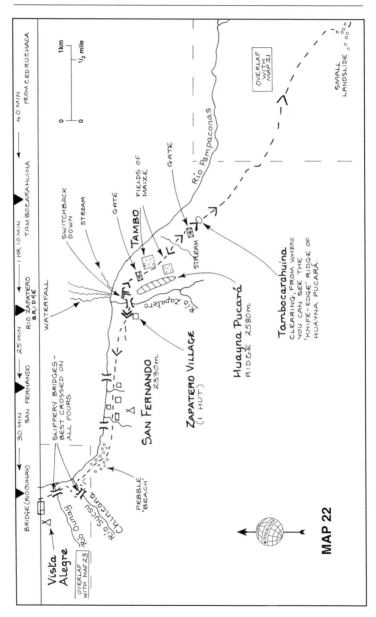

MAP 22

Huayna Pucará

According to accounts of the Spanish invasion of 1572, it was at Huayna Pucará that the Incas planned to launch a major assault on the advancing Spanish army. Boulders were lined up along the crest of the ridge above the path, ready to topple down onto unsuspecting Spanish heads as they passed along the path beneath the fort, while archers were positioned on the other side of the river, ready to kill off any who survived this initial onslaught.

Unfortunately for the Incas, one of their number defected to the Spanish side just before the ambush, and told them of the trap that had been set. Under cover of darkness, troops climbed stealthily up the hillside; now it was the Spaniards who had the element of surprise on their side. As dawn broke, the Incas awoke to find Spanish troops in position above their fort. Realizing they'd been rumbled, they put up a rearguard action before eventually retreating in despair, leaving the huge boulders perched and primed directly above the path – where, if you scramble up the slopes to the top of the ridge above Tambo, you can still find them today. After this defeat, the Inca army put up no further resistance.

After negotiating these three rivers you'll again find yourself heading due north on an undulating path following the natural contours of the valley walls. The forest begins to press ever closer on both sides now and if nobody has walked this way for a few weeks you may find you have to resort to the machete in places. But having gradually climbed away from the river after about two hours you'll come upon the settlement of **Urpipata** lying just beneath the crest of the hill – an ideal spot to camp for the night. Lee has identified Urpipata as the site of **Machu Pucará** (the Old Fort). Near to Urpipata, to the right of the trail are a few walls that might have once formed part of the fort's defences, though this is mere conjecture. If you're interested, ask your guide or one of the villagers to show you the site.

Machu Pucará

According to Titu Cusi, the Incas launched their first concerted attack against the advancing Spaniards in 1539 at Machu Pucará, and enjoyed their greatest success here too. From their hideout above the path they ambushed the invading army, dropping boulders onto them from a great height and killing anywhere between 13 Spaniards (according to the Spaniards) and 36 (according to the Incas). Ten days later, however, Pedro Pizarro climbed the hill with 100 soldiers, and forced the Incas into retreat. In the second invasion of 1572, however, the Spaniards encountered no such trouble and found the place abandoned.

OVERLAP WITH MAP 24

LOG PATH: SLIPPERY!

FENCES

TO RIO TUNQUI MAYA 45 MINS

FARMS

Río Urpipata JUST A SMALL STREAM

RIO URPIPATA

Urpipata 2000m

GATE: - START OF URPIPATA

COFFEE PLANTATION

NOW NEAR TOP OF CREST OF HILL, ABOVE TREES ON OPEN GROUND

FARM

KURCOMOYO (FARM)

50 MINS

MAP 23

★ TRAILBLAZER

FAIRLY DENSE FOREST NOW. FOLLOW RIVER NORTH ON UNDULATING PATH, FOLLOWING CONTOURS OF CLIFF FACE

San Cristobal

SMALL, GRASSY CLEARING BEFORE RIVER. A GOOD PLACE FOR A REST. ABOVE THE PATH IS THE FARM OF SAN CRISTOBAL, WHERE YOU MAY BE ABLE TO CAMP FOR THE NIGHT.

SAN CRISTOBAL

Río Pampaconas

0   1km
0   ½ mile

WIDE, STONY RIVERBED

1 HR 5 MIN

Río Vista Alegre

NARROW PATH HERE - WATCH FOR "TRAFFIC" COMING THE OTHER WAY.

Vista Alegre

OVERLAP WITH MAP 22

Río Dunay

Río Sucsu Chincana

SLIPPERY BRIDGES— BEST CROSSED ON ALL FOURS.

RIO SUCSU CHINCANU

URPIPATA → ESPIRITU PAMPA   [MAP 24, opposite; MAP 25, p236]

This stage begins much as the previous one finished, with a walk through thick forest and over rivers as you hug the western banks of the valley. Immediately after the bridge over the first river, the **Tunqul Mayu**, there's a particularly well-camouflaged bog, so use a stick to test the ground ahead of you before taking each step. At the time of writing, the bridge over the second river, the **Lucu Mayu**, had disappeared altogether, though a replacement should have been built by the time you read this. A fairly steep climb then ensues up to the now abandoned settlement of **Cedro Casa**. Now reclaimed by the forest, you may well miss it altogether – look for a bend west in the path by a tree that is obvious (at least in March/April) from its glorious orange blossom.

One hour further on and you should find yourself traversing the giant outcrop known as La Roca, from where you can see the village of **Consevidayoc** (1470m/4822ft) a further hour to the north. The imprint of man's hand is all around this village, from the fields of maize and coffee to the recently denuded hills and as a consequence the occasional landslip. In Vincent Lee's opinion Consevidayoc, a fairly large place by the standards of Vilcabamba with its own football field and school, is built on the site of ancient Marcanay, the last resting place of Friar Diego Ortiz. The Spanish destroyed Marcanay utterly when they found out about the horrors inflicted on Ortiz (see below), which goes some way to explaining why there are only a few scattered stone ruins here today; they are east of the village by the football field.

The Martyrdom of Friar Diego Ortiz

The Inca Titu Cusi fell ill and his friar, Diego Ortiz, gave him medicine. The Inca then died. The chronicler, Sarmiento de Gamboa takes up the story:

'When his chiefpeople and captains saw that the Inca Don Felipe Titu Cusi Yupanqui was dead, and that the prayers and sacrifices of the said Father Friar Diego Ortiz were of no avail, an Indian named Quispi, who is still living, came to the said Friar, and asked him why his God had not cured the Inca if he was so powerful? And without giving the father time to answer, the Indian struck him. Our Lord permitted that his hand and his arm up to the shoulder should wither. It is dried up to this day, and the Indian knew his sin. The Friar went down on his knees, and turned the other cheek to the smiter. He received another blow and they tied his hands behind his back and dragged him along. They opened a place under the beard with a kind of knife called a *tumi* and fastened a rope in his mouth by which they dragged him, making him suffer an unheard of martyrdom'. (*Historia de los Incas*, Pedro Sarmiento de Gamboa, 1572, trans. Sir Clements Markham).

Ortiz was dragged before the new Inca, Tupac Amaru, who refused to see him, and the friar was killed. His body was buried upside down, to prevent divine vengeance.

For many years, it seemed as if the martyrdom of Diego Ortiz would ensure his canonisation, but he was not to become a saint. Nevertheless, his bones were hallowed and he was venerated.

OVERLAP WITH MAP 25

VIEW NORTH TO CONSEVIDAYOC

La Roca

SMALL ROCKY WATERFALL

RÍO

0   1km

0   ½ mile

Río Diablo

PATH UNDULATES QUITE SEVERELY IN THIS SECTION, FOLLOWING THE SAME REPETITIVE PATTERN: WEST AND DOWN TO STREAM, THEN UP AND EAST AFTERWARDS.

STREAM WITH SLIPPERY BOULDERS

Cedro Casa
EASY TO MISS AS ABANDONED AND BEING RECLAIMED BY FOREST.

SWITCHBACKS STEEP UP

Río Lucu Mayu

LANDSLIDE

Huaynapata
SMALL CLEARING IN FOREST

BOG! CHECK GROUND WITH STICK BEFORE ADVANCING

Río Tunqui Mayu

FARMS

Río Pampaconas

MAP 24

LOVELY CLEARING

LOG PATH - SLIPPERY!

OVERLAP WITH MAP 23

FENCES

1 HR. TO CONSEVIDAYOC

FIRST SIGHT OF CONSEVIDAYOC FROM LA ROCA

1 HR

CEDRO CASA

1 HR

RÍO TUNQUI MAYU

45 MINS

FROM URPIPATU

STEPS — THE INCA'S
GRAND CEREMONIAL
ENTRANCE

1570 m

TO MAP 26

ESPÍRITU
PAMPA

TO THE
RUINS

TOP OF HILL

40 MINS

Río Consevidayoc

LOW FERNS

STEPS THROUGH
WATERFALL

TO
CHUNTABAMBA

GATE

PATH FORKS

30 MINS

YUCCA
PLANTATION

POULTRY
FARM

HUTS

Río Consevidayoc

CONSEVIDAYOC
1470 m

SCHOOL

TRAILBLAZER

MAP 25

CONSEVIDAYOC

COFFEE

1 HR.

0   1 km
0   ½ mile

MAIZE

SMALL
LANDSLIDE

DENUDED
SLOPES

SMALL
STREAM

La Roca

FIRST VIEW OF
CONSEVIDAYOC
FROM LA ROCA

OVERLAP
WITH
MAP 24

After Consevidayoc, the path climbs up past a fork in the path: veer left; the right-hand trail leads to Chuntabamba, bypassing Espíritu Pampa altogether.

Slowly the vegetation flanking the path changes from forest to fern; this hill seems to receive little rain in April, the path becomes an arrow-straight line of baked, cracked orange clay. At last the trail turns westwards over the crest of the hill, and one minute later the lush valley of **Espíritu Pampa** moves into view.

The descent to the 'Plain of the Spirits', which is what 'Espíritu Pampa' means, is certainly a dramatic one, down a steep, wide ceremonial stairway. At the bottom, cross two streams and you arrive at a large farm by a small church-cum-school. Below the farm there is an excellent spot for camping, the perfect base for exploring the ruins.

The ruins of Espíritu Pampa

The map below depicts the central area of the site only, where the most impressive ruins lie. If you have your own machete it's a lot of fun searching among the undergrowth for some of the other buildings here; there are said to be over 400 ruins. Watch out for snakes. Please, though, be very careful not to disturb any of the stones of the ruins as Vilcabamba has not been fully investigated by archaeologists.

If you'd like a more complete picture of the pampa, check out the maps and drawings by Vincent Lee at the back of his books, *Forgotten Vilcabamba* and *Sixpac Manco*.

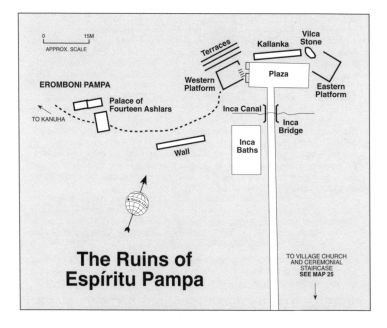

The Ruins of Espíritu Pampa

▯ ▱▱ ▱▱ ▱▱ ▱▱ ▱▱ ▱▱ ▱▱ ▱▱ ▱▱ ▱▱ ▱▱

The Inca's last capital?

At first sight, the ruins at Vilcabamba seem unimpressive. There's a distinct lack of majesty about the place and the few ruined buildings that survive appear rather mundane and unworthy of a capital city. This lack of grandeur has prevented many scholars down the years – Hiram Bingham included – from believing that this really was the city founded by Manco Inca in the sixteenth century.

Most visitors to Espíritu Pampa today are similarly underwhelmed. Yet there are enough clues in even these crumbling walls to put up a pretty good case for this being Vilcabamba. For a start, one must remember that the Incas were now living in severely reduced circumstances, their empire gone, their wealth appropriated and, presumably, many of their finest stonemasons and craftsmen gone. This would explain why the ruins cannot compare with those in Cusco or Machu Picchu. Secondly, capital or not, there is little doubt that the masonry on show is Inca in origin. The lintels, the fine ashlars, the baths and canals all seem distinctly Inca in concept and design. Ironically, perhaps the most persuasive evidence that these are Inca ruins is provided by the one monument that is almost completely free of any Inca embellishments: the Vilca stone in the south-east corner of the plaza is so reminiscent of Nusta España and the Sacred Rock at Machu Picchu that it seems only logical to assume that the same people were behind the construction of all three sites: Espíritu Pampa, therefore, must be of Inca origin.

But is it Manco's capital? The fact that the ruins are spread over such a wide area and are so numerous suggests that this settlement was certainly large enough to be the capital. Then there is the grand ceremonial stairway that even now, almost 500 years later, never fails to impress visitors. It is a typically majestic piece of Inca work, albeit one tempered by the reality of their reduced circumstances; though Manco had relinquished most of his empire and had been forced to flee into inhospitable jungle, it seems he couldn't resist making this one defiant gesture. Then there are the terracotta roof tiles, imitations of the Spanish tiles the Incas would have seen in Cusco, discovered by Bingham and others at Espíritu Pampa. This helps to date the town, for if it were a town built before the conquest the builders would not have used tiles, but straw or turf. Gene Savoy argues in his book, *Antisuyu*, that the presence of the tiles suggests that this is an Inca town built after the conquest and that it's Manco's jungle capital, Vilcabamba.

If the ruins at Espíritu Pampa fail to convince, perhaps the walk you have taken to get here will. By comparing contemporary accounts of the Spaniards' march to Vilcabamba with the – admittedly meagre – ruins you find along the path today, it is possible to tally one with the other. Perhaps the most convincing of these ruins en route is Huayna Pucará, where one finds a number of boulders lined up by the Incas for dropping on the enemy below, as described in contemporary accounts of the battle. Then there is Pampaconas, which not only has ruins of its own but unusually has even retained the same name as that used by Spanish chroniclers.

Of course some doubts do remain: the village of Marcanay, mentioned frequently in contemporary accounts, may or may not have been on the site of modern Consevidayoc – the ruins there are not conclusive – while those of Machu Pucará, or the Old Fort are negligible and maybe not even of Inca origin. Nevertheless, as John Hemming says in the conclusion of *Conquest of the Incas*:

'Unless someone can discover another ruin that so exactly fulfils the geographical and topographical details known about Vilcabamba, and that also contains imitation Spanish roofing tiles, the lost city of Vilcabamba has finally been located at Espíritu Pampa.'

▯ ▱▱ ▱▱ ▱▱ ▱▱ ▱▱ ▱▱ ▱▱ ▱▱ ▱▱ ▱▱ ▱▱

Although the ruins are not particularly spectacular, this abandoned city does exude a certain amount of charm, particularly the way the jungle has gradually encroached and reclaimed the area. The building blocks are green with moss, vines and creepers grasp the ruins while trees now grow through them, their roots like flying buttresses emerging from the stones.

However you decide to explore the site, don't miss the following: the carefully carved **baths** and the bridge over the Inca-built **canal** on the way into the city; the football-field sized **plaza** with the large **Vilca stone** in its north-eastern corner; the intact and rather impressive green mossy wall a couple of minutes to the south of the plaza and, further on, the **Eromboni Pampa**, home of the Palace of Fourteen Ashlars.

With such scant remains, it's quite difficult to imagine what life was like for the inhabitants of Vilcabamba. But it cannot have been easy. Most of the city's residents were used to living at altitudes some 2000m higher than Espíritu Pampa, and the low altitude and humid climate must have left many feeling unwell. The diseases, poisonous snakes and spiders of the forest constituted a constant threat, as did the Spanish just a few days' march away. Furthermore, the uneven terrain, though easy to defend, was difficult to farm.

Yet the city must have had its advantages too. According to some reports there was enough pasture for grazing, and the tropical forest provided its own crops, including coca, cotton, sugar, honey, cassava, sweet potatoes and maize, as well as rabbits, turkeys, pheasants and other fowl. Also the city was built to a comfortingly familiar Inca blueprint and so many natives still felt a strong sense of loyalty towards Manco combined with deep mistrust of the Spanish, and you can see why a few thousand chose to remain at Vilcabamba under Manco and his successors. Indeed, as the Spanish historian Martin de Murúa reports:

'The Incas enjoyed scarcely less of the luxuries, greatness and splendour of Cuzco in that distant land of exile. For the Indians brought with them whatever they could get from outside for their contentment and pleasure. And so for that time they enjoyed the good life there.'

ESPIRITU PAMPA → CHAUNQUIRI   [MAP 26, p240; MAP 27, p241]

This is the shortest stage, but also one of the more exhausting. Not only are the climbs and descents steeper and more frequent, but the steaming jungle heat quickly saps the strength too.

From in front of the church/school a path leads down to a sturdy new bridge over the Río Espíritu Pampa and on to the smaller **Río Chuntabamba** and a junction with the path from Consevidayoc. The first concrete buildings since Vilcabamba Nueva, a two-storey house and a *posta de salud* (health station), lie an hour outside Espíritu Pampa to the left of the path. About an hour later, having passed through numerous plantations of coffee, oranges and maize, you'll reach a fork in the trail. Though both paths lead eventually to Chaunquiri, the upper path is much more dangerous and a number of locals have died on that route in the past few years. You should take the lower path down to the Consevidayoc, cross the bridge, and clamber up the other side of the valley.

GOOD CONCRETE
BRIDGE

OVERLAP
WITH
MAP 27

Río
Villacarmen

GATE

GATE

COFFEE
PLANTATIONS

HOUSES

Río Consevidayoc

TRAILBLAZER

POSTA DE
SALUD

HOUSE

GATE

MAP 26

Río Chuntabamba

HUT

PATH FROM
CONSEVIDAYOC

GATE

Río Espíritu Pampa

CHURCH

TO
MAP
25

ESPÍRITU
PAMPA

TO BRIDGE
OVER CONSEVIDAYOC
30 MIN

30 MINS

POSTA DE SALUD

25 MINS

BRIDGE

35 MINS

ESPÍRITU
PAMPA

0   1km

0   1/2 mile

The path on this side rises and falls with tiresome regularity on its way north; however, by way of encouragement, just 45 minutes after the bridge the tin roofs of Chaunquiri appear glinting in the sunlight ahead. To get there you first have to descend rather rapidly down the southern walls of the **San Miguel valley** to the river of the same name. From there it's a further 45 minutes, much of it uphill, to your final destination.

Chaunquiri

Litter-strewn, untidy and built round a muddy football pitch, ramshackle **Chaunquiri** would rarely, under normal circumstances, appeal to tourists. After four days of climbing, staggering and wading through jungle, however, to most walkers this place is akin to Paradise. There's no accommodation here, though there is running water in the **toilet block** (in the pink building by the secondary school). It's in the south-eastern corner of the square; ask for the key from the teacher). There are two cheap **cafés**, open on market days only. Though there's no accommodation, nor any pizzas or cold beer, the great bonus is that it does have transport to villages and towns where these things exist in abundance.

Vilcabamba's giant rats

In the early part of 2000 a remarkable discovery was made in the forests around Vilcabamba by the North American zoologist, Dr Louise Emmons. As she was walking through the undergrowth she scared a tree weasel, which dropped its lunch in her lap. Lunch turned out to be a completely new genus of mammal, never before known to science. It's a rat the size of a cat that lives in trees, and has been called *Cuscomys ashaninka*, after Cusco and the Ashanika, the local people. It's heartening to know that there are still secrets waiting to be discovered in the forests of Peru.

● **Leaving Chaunquiri** You may be able to hitch a lift to **Kiteni** on one of the delivery trucks that occasionally call into the village, usually on a Friday. These don't turn up every week, however, and your best bet is to wait until Saturday afternoon, when trucks start to leave the market for **Kiteni** (s/5), 34km and two hours away. (Kiteni, incidentally, is where they say Tupac Amaru, see p98, was captured.) From there you can catch a bus or truck to Quillabamba (7-9 hours, s/10). There may even be some direct trucks from Chaunquiri to Quillabamba (s/12, 12 hours), especially on a Sunday.

For those who get stuck in Kiteni there's a hostal at the southern end of town, the imaginatively named *Kiteni Hostal*, where rooms go for just s/10 per night. It is possible to walk to Kiteni from Chaunquiri, of course, though this is a dreary, tiring, full-day's walk along a hot and winding jungle road. Another option is to walk to Yuveni, 9km from Chaunquiri, where your chances of catching a lift are slightly – but only slightly – improved.

PART 8: MACHU PICCHU

The Lost City?

I felt infinitely small in the centre of that navel of rocks, the navel of a deserted world, proud, towering high, to which I somehow belonged. I felt that my own hands had laboured there at some remote point in time, digging furrows, polishing rocks. **Pablo Neruda**, *Memoirs.*

For many people, the words Machu Picchu conjure up an image of a lost Inca city, swathed in the green creepers of an encroaching jungle, hidden behind the years, waiting to be discovered by intrepid explorers armed with machetes and attended by armies of porters. It was like this, there's no doubt – all you have to do is look at the photographs of the Hiram Bingham expedition to be reminded of Indiana Jones from the film *Raiders of the Lost Ark* – but today, sadly, some of the mystique has gone. You can now make a day trip to the site by train or helicopter, and if you want to spend the night near the ruins there is a reasonable hotel close to the old stones.

In high season around 2000 people a day visit this 'lost' city , and with these people come inevitable problems: overcrowding, garbage and hotels built like concrete bunkers. But Machu Picchu hasn't been ruined – it would take the most insensitive of philistines not to be impressed by the sight of the sun rising over the rim of the mountains that enclose this awe-inspiring place. This *is* still a Lost City and still a place of magic especially when you come upon it after three days hiking in the wilderness.

Practicalities

Machu Picchu is 2400m (7800ft) above sea level, and it nestles on a ridge between Machu Picchu mountain and the sugar loaf of Huayna Picchu. When the sun's out it burns, so bring sun barrier cream and a hat. It can also get cold up here when the sun's not out, and it sometimes rains unpredictably, so bring a jumper and a waterproof. Insect repellant's a good idea too.

ARRIVAL

You've either come off the trail or come up by bus from the valley below. If and when the cable car (see p162) is built, this will be another way of getting here. If you're going back to Cusco in the afternoon, check the train timetable as it changes often. They normally have the times at the reception desk in the hotel. See p268 for the timetable at the time of writing.

ORIENTATION

If you've just come off the Inca trail, to the right of the path at the top of the ruins is a zig-zag path down to the entrance booth. Here you must leave your kit at a left-luggage store (no charge) because you won't be allowed in the ruins with it (some people claim this is to stop base jumpers from sneaking their parachutes in and launching themselves off into the valley below). The large ugly bungalow you can see by the entrance is the restaurant and hotel. If you've come up by bus from Aguas Calientes you'll be dropped off in the car park in front of the hotel. The entrance to the ruins is just up some stairs to the right of a map of Machu Picchu.

Passing through the entrance booth and around a shoulder of rock, you'll reach an open area. Straight ahead are a couple of thatched cottages between which most visitors enter the site. Before this there is a path uphill, indicated by little white arrows painted on stones. If you follow these (back up the little hill you just climbed down if you've come along the trail) you'll get to a place just below a thatched hut on the top of a promontory. This is the Watchman's hut, the best place to start your tour – see 'A guide to the ruins' (see p249).

OPENING TIMES AND TICKETS

The ruins are open 7am-5pm daily, and entrance costs US$20, (US$10 for students). There is no longer a discount for those who are returning for a second day. If you've walked the trail the price of one day's entrance is included in your trail fee, which you should have paid already.

WHERE TO STAY

You can't camp in the ruins – so don't try. I'm told there's a *shed* where you can occasionally put up your tent, 20 yards down the road to Aguas Calientes on the right (S), with a water pipe outside and a strip-light inside, and a restaurant ten minutes further on where they allow trekkers to sleep on the floor.

The only other place is the free *campsite* at the foot of the hill: cross over the Urubamba, and it's to the right (E) of the bridge. It's filthy; don't leave kit unattended here or you'll lose it.

Machu Picchu Sanctuary Lodge (aka The Tourists' Hotel, ☎ 246419, ▤ 246983, 🖥 www.orient-express.com), which at US$255/275 (sgl/dbl, att) plus tax is overpriced is the only hotel so close to these legendary ruins, therefore they can charge what they want – at the moment. I'm not sure there should be a hotel here at all, but if you haven't got qualms about its being so close to what should be a pristine site, it's an adequate enough place. You can make bookings for Machu Picchu Sanctuary Lodge at Hotel Monasterio in Cusco (see p134).

There is a much wider selection of places in Aguas Calientes (see p157).

WHERE TO EAT

You can have an excellent buffet breakfast and an overpriced canteen lunch at *Machu Picchu Sanctuary Lodge*. The 'all you can eat' breakfast is expensive but worth it at s/65. Lunch, too, is expensive at s/65 and isn't worth it; pick up an overpriced hot dog or burger instead from the *café* above the lavatories. There's also a cheapish *restaurant* a ten-minute walk down the road in a building on your left.

History

People have been arguing about what Machu Picchu was and why it was built almost from the moment Hiram Bingham rediscovered it in 1911. It all seems a bit clearer now, since a lot of light was thrown into this dark corner of history by an old copy of a sixteenth-century document found by the scholars Luis Miguel Glave, María Remy and John Rowe in the library of a Cusco monastery.

MACHU PICCHU REVEALED TO THE WORLD

A young graduate from Yale University named Hiram Bingham had been bewitched by the stories of lost Inca cities ever since visiting a pre-Hispanic ruin called Choqquequirau. (Bingham was originally an expert on Bolívar, not an archaeologist, and he was rather at a loss for what to do when he made it to his first ruin. In the best tradition of the amateur he did his best, helped by a book published by the Royal Geographical Society with the quaint title *Hints to Travellers*.) Bingham raised enough money to lead a seven-man expedition to Peru under the auspices of Yale University and the National Geographic Society. In 1911 he and his team started to explore the uncharted hills around the ancient Inca capital, Cusco.

Uncharted is not the right word: these hills weren't completely unknown territory. The mountain Machu Picchu appears on a map in the 1910 edition of a book on the Incas written by the English historian, Clements Markham, and Bingham himself used a map of the area prepared by Antonio Raimondi. There had even been some reports of ruins around the lower Urubamba. Bingham describes both the failure of a Frenchman, Charles Wiener, to find them in 1875, and what he rather unfairly referred to as the 'treasure hunting' of a Peruvian called Lizárraga.

So in July 1911, Bingham and his team headed out of Cusco down the Urubamba, and almost immediately they discovered a major Inca site which they named Patallacta (it's the site on the corner where the Cusichaca river meets the Urubamba, see p178). After walking a little up the Cusichaca, the team also discovered Huayllabamba and Paucarcancha. Bingham and his companions then travelled on.

On July 23, just a week into the expedition, they camped off the trail at Mandorpampa. A local man, one Melchor Artega, was suspicious of these foreigners, and came over to see what was going on. When they explained that they were looking for ruins, Artega told them that there were some fine ones up in the hills above their camp.

The next day it rained. No one else in the expedition wanted to climb up the steep side of the Urubamba canyon, so Bingham went on his own, accompanied by the expedition's guard, Sergeant Carrasco, and Artega. After an unpleasant crossing of the Urubamba on a flimsy log bridge and a perilous climb through snake-infested forest, he reached a grass-covered hut. There he was welcomed by two men, Richarte and Alvarez, who had been living up on the hillside for four years to escape the army and taxes. They gave Bingham water and fed him, and he describes not really wanting to have a look at the ruins because he was tired, the water was cool and the heat of the day was great. But he did have a look. And the rest, as they say, is history.

WHAT BINGHAM FOUND IN THE JUNGLE

Bingham named the ruins Machu Picchu because that was the name of the mountain on which they were found. Machu means old or big, and Picchu is the name of the area. The sugar loaf mountain that overlooks the ruins is called Huayna Picchu (small Picchu).

Keeper of the royal bridge
FELIPE HUAMÁN POMA DE AYALA (c1590)

Bingham believed that he'd stumbled upon the rebel Incas' stronghold, Vilcabamba (see p237), the site of the last independent Incan state and their place of final refuge in the days when the Spanish were hunting them down. For a number of reasons it's now thought that these ruins aren't Vilcabamba, not least because the routes the Spanish took to get to Vilcabamba don't match the routes you'd need to take to get to Machu Picchu, and the descriptions of the site of Vilcabamba don't fit with the geography around Machu Picchu.

But what Bingham did find is no less impressive: he'd discovered not only a lost city of the Incas but a whole lost province that the Incas had miraculously concealed from the Spanish conquistadors. (No one knows how they managed to pull this off). Within the mountains now enclosed by the Machu Picchu Historical Sanctuary are numerous Inca roads and ruins, towns, cities, forts and outposts – everything from humble mud-and-rock structures to castles of magnificent dressed stone – which have only survived the centuries because no one knew they were there.

It's now thought that Vilcabamba is much further into the jungle at a place known as Espíritu Pampa; a description of the Vilcabamba trail to Espíritu Pampa begins on p218. Bingham would not really mind if he knew this as he also rediscovered Espíritu Pampa.

MACHU PICCHU AS PACHACUTEC'S ROYAL FRONTIER

According to the old papers found by Rowe and his colleagues, the lower Urubamba valley was conquered by the Inca Pachacutec in his expansionist wars of the fifteenth century. It's likely, then, that Pachacutec built the hilltop city of Machu Picchu to celebrate his greatness; he decorated the banks of the Urubamba with Ollantaytambo for the same reason. Machu Picchu was the royal estate at the end of the line, also perhaps a religious centre, the capital of a frontier province, and an impregnable watchtower that guarded the route from Antisuyu to the civilized uplands of Cusco.

The Urubamba route to Antisuyu became less important in later years. All traffic for the *cejas de la selva* (the eyebrows of the jungle) headed down the Lucumayo, and Machu Picchu became a backwater rather than a frontier. By the time of the conquest, it's probable that Machu Picchu was already just an abandoned shell, and when the archaeologists arrived there wasn't much they could dig up.

It's not clear why the city was quite so thoroughly deserted. Perhaps the water ran out – there were hardly enough springs to provide water for Bingham's expedition, so water must have been very scarce when the city was fully inhabited. Perhaps the Incas evacuated the place to create an uninhabited buffer zone between their rebel capital of Vilcabamba and the Spaniard's base in Cusco.

At any rate, Rowe's document says that by the time of the conquest, part of the area was used for growing coca. It was given to Hernando Pizarro when the Spanish carved up the old empire, and it passed from him to the encomienda of a man called Arias Maldonado.

OTHER THEORIES

Tour guides give explanations as to Machu Picchu's past, varying from the plausible to those which have now been disproved by research, and on to the absurd. But it's not just a case of guides making it up to impress the tourists: not everyone agrees on the interpretation of Rowe's document, and it's likely archaeologists will come up with other tenable theories.

Incorrect

The idea that Machu Picchu was a convent of acllas (Inca nuns) was based on evidence that 80% of the bones that Bingham dug up were those of women. This has been disproved by recent re-examination of the bones which showed that the sexes were equally represented.

Alternatively, you might read that Machu Picchu is laid out to resemble both a condor and a cayman (South American crocodile) and that Huayna Picchu is carved into the shape of a large puma. You can believe that if you want to, but I don't. If the Incas had wanted to make Machu Picchu look like a condor or a puma they'd have done a much better job.

Unlikely

An interesting theory of Bingham's suggests that Machu Picchu was between eight hundred and a thousand years old by the time of the Spanish invasion.

According to legend, the Incas had their origin in a sacred cave called Tambo-toqo (see p78), and the mythical first Inca, Manco Capac, built a three-windowed temple on this site to celebrate its significance. Bingham suggested – quite sensibly – that the Temple of the Three Windows in Machu Picchu (see p253) commemorated Manco Capac's temple. However, he went on to suggest that the structure in Machu Picchu was, in fact, the actual one built by Manco Capac, and that Machu Picchu is therefore the primeval home of the Incas. There is little evidence to support this theory and much against it: few pre-Inca objects have been found, the style of the Temple of the Three Windows is fifteenth-century Inca (not fifth century), and anyway Machu Picchu is completely the wrong side of Cusco to be Tambo-toqo.

Plausible

Some say that Machu Picchu was an **agricultural outpost** of the Incas. It was used, they say, to maximize the rare and valuable growing zone between the jungle and the high valleys of Cusco, a suggestion backed by the large tracts of land in the district that have been irrigated and terraced for agriculture. Other people expand on this, suggesting that the area around Machu Picchu was a place where sacred plants were grown by priests.

There are theories that Machu Picchu is a big **observatory**. It's recently been discovered that at dawn on the winter solstice (21 June) the sun shines right through the middle of the window in the Torreon (see opposite p257), casting a shadow. This isn't the only building that was built with an eye on the heavens. The Temple of the Moon, on the far side of the sugar loaf mountain that dominates Machu Picchu, was built to face the Pleiades (also worshipped by the Incas), and some say the Intihuatana (see p254) is a place where the sun could be ceremonially tied and prevented from falling lower in the sky in winter.

Johan Reinhard, a respected anthropologist, suggests an interesting idea in his short book *The Sacred Centre*. Reinhard thinks Machu Picchu was the focal point of a constellation of sacred geographical features: the city is built on a spur of one of the Inca's most important mountains, Salcantay; it perches above the sacred river Urubamba and it is on a sighting line from other important mountains Pumasillo and Veronica. Machu Picchu is, like Cusco, the focus of religion. The city should not be looked at as a citadel but as a religious symbol, a sacred centre. This theory links in with what we know about the Inca religion – the sacredness of certain spots (huacas) and the sacred lines (ceques) which joined them to other spots. It's true, too, that there is a large amount of ornate

Inca architecture in these hills. If Reinhard is right, this means that the Inca Trail is more than just a road – it's a sacred route of pilgrimage.

Of course, these theories aren't necessarily contradictory. It's possible that Machu Picchu was a citadel built to the glory of Pachacutec, on a place found to be sacred in Inca religion, designed in a way so that the heavens could be observed, accessible only after a ritual journey.

A guide to the ruins

This was the habitation, this is the site:
here the fat grains of maize grew high
to fall again like red hail.

The fleece of the vicuña was carded here
to clothe men's loves in gold, their tombs and mothers,
the king, the prayers, the warriors.

Up here men's feet found rest at night
near eagles' talons in the high
meat-stuffed eyries.
Pablo Neruda, from *The Heights of Machu Picchu.*

This walking tour covers the main buildings at the site and summarizes what's known about (or guessed about) each one. The rest is up to your imagination. The best place to start is up at the Watchman's hut – for directions from the entrance booth, see 'Orientation' p244.

AROUND THE WATCHMAN'S HUT AND FUNERARY STONE

This lone hut gives such a perfect view over Machu Picchu that it has been called the **Watchman's Hut**. It guards any entrance to the site from the road to Intipunku (p190), the trail up Machu Picchu mountain, or the road to the Inca Bridge (see p252). It's unlikely that this was a hut for a mere gatekeeper as the stonework's too good.The oddly shaped rock nearby is known as the **Funerary Stone**, but it's probably a sacrificial altar. The Incas often sacrificed llamas, and sometimes even humans. In the festival of Inti Raymi (see p56), there's a llama sacrificed (allegedly – it still looked pretty alive to me), and the remains of the occasional human sacrifice have been found in such places as the volcano of El Misti near Arequipa. Note the strange carvings in the stone of a ring and something a bit like a staircase: no one knows what they're for, but there's one of these rings carved in a rock in Vilcabamba and the Incas often carved their huacas with stair-like designs, Qenko (see p150), for example.

The rock was named the Funerary Stone because Bingham found and excavated many tombs near here, which leads some to think that this stone was the place where the privileged dead were laid out for embalming – a Funerary Stone. Because of these finds, the area around here is often called the upper cemetery.

TO HUAYNA PICCHU AND
THE TEMPLE OF THE MOON
(50 MINS WALK)

Three Door
District

The
Sacred
Rock

Sunken
Square

Main Square
and
Snake Rock

Intihuatana

Temple of the
Three Windows

Ornament
Chamber

Sacred
Plaza

Principal
Temple

Machu Picchu

Lower
Cemetery

Residential
Sector

0   50   100M
APPROXIMATE SCALE

Intimachay

The Mortar
District

Condor Temple
or Jails

TRAILBL

FOUNTAIN
CARETAKER'S
HUT   TREE

TO MAIN TOURIST
ENTRANCE

Cascade of
Fountains

TERRACES

House of the Princess
or Sacristy

Quarry

ENTRANCE
PATH

Royal
Group

Temple of the
Sun (Torreon)
WITH TOMB
OF PRINCESS
UNDERNEATH

TERRACES

Old City
Gate

TO CERRO MACHU
PICCHU
INTIPUNKU

WATCHMAN'S
HUT

TO INCA
BRIDGE

Funerary
Stone

Machu Picchu's districts

Looking out over the city you can see the division of the land into terraces (an agricultural zone) and buildings (an urban zone). The terraces in the agricultural area were primarily for growing foodstuffs, and there are many more at nearby Choquesuysuy and Huinay Huayna (p189). Dr Ann Kendall thinks that there were about 677 hectares (1670 acres) of land under cultivation in the Sanctuary, and that there was a four-fold over-capacity. In other words, the Machu Picchu area was a breadbasket.

There are other suggestions as to what the terracing was for. Some have suggested that they were a defence measure against potential attackers, and others have suggested they were for decoration: the Chronicles say that the terraces at Ollantaytambo were used for growing flowers.

From the terracing you can clearly see another division of the city; the division into Hanan and Hurin districts to the left and right of the main plaza. The Incas often divided their towns into these two sections, which were probably inhabited by different clan groups. There's an interesting theory that every feature in one district (Sun Temple, etc) has a mirror image in the other district.

This is the ideal place from which to take a picture of Machu Picchu.

The Inca Bridge and Machu Picchu mountain

If you're looking down at the town, the path for the **Inca Bridge** goes off from your left, snaking around the top of the amphitheatre of terraces. The path leads along a sheer rock face to an abyss. In Inca times, there was a wooden drawbridge across this void that could be drawn up in times of trouble. The bridge is gone now, but you can walk up to where it was and see the dramatic continuation of path carved into sheer cliff face.

The path for **Machu Picchu mountain** (cerro Machu Picchu) is on the right if you head back up towards Intipunku. It takes about an hour to get to the top and it's a tiring climb.

THE MOAT AND GATE

You can see from the Watchman's Hut a moat and long stairway that divides the agricultural terraces from the buildings. Walk along the path in front of the Hut to the top of the **moat**. According to Bingham, there are 150 steps in the main staircase in the moat and about 3000 in the whole city. Because this is the main route along which an army could approach Machu Picchu, it's thought by many that the moat was a defence feature. Precipices and rock walls guarded the city's other flanks. However, those who prefer to regard Machu Picchu as a sacred rather than a military city see it as an architectural way of excluding the outside profane world from the inside sacred city.

The **Old City Gate** is at the top of the moat, and is an impressive trapezoidal arch with a vast lintel. When Bingham discovered this doorway it was in the process of collapse, so what you see has been repaired. If you stand in the gateway, there is a large wall to your left that overlooks you, which may be to protect the door from attackers. If you were standing here with a battering ram, there'd be nowhere to hide from any rocks and arrows thrown at you. Go through the door and look up at the big ring above the lintel and at the bars sunk in the doorposts to the left and right. These probably provided a method of securing the door.

Bingham found the remains of 41 containers of liquid refreshment in this place and thought that the chicha sellers of the old city were stationed here, selling drink to tired travellers.

THE QUARRY

Walk on through the gateway and along the street and you'll see in front of you a place where there are large boulders lying around. Go down some steps to get there. Bingham found tombs around here and thought this was a cemetery, but it's now thought that this place was the **quarry** for the stones used to build the city. You can see some rocks that are in the process of being split: tiny stones have been fed into small cracks. These stones kept the cracks open, which were then worked apart until eventually the rock was split. This 'Inca work-in-progress' is eagerly pointed out to tourists by guides, but it was in fact an experiment conducted by a modern researcher, Dr Manuel Chavez Ballon.

THE SACRED PLAZA GROUP

Walk on through the quarry and straight ahead rising above the rest of the city, you'll see a mound on top of which is the Intihuatana. You're about to walk into the Sacred Plaza at its base.

The sacred plaza was named by Bingham because Machu Picchu's finest buildings are set around it. On one side the **Principal Temple**, on another the **Temple of the Three Windows**, and looming above it the **Intihuatana** itself.

Bingham's archaeologists dug up the floor of the sacred plaza as a good place to look for artefacts but found nothing. They did, however, find an enormous amount of smashed pottery on the ground outside, beneath the Temple of The Three Windows, which leads many to think that pots were ritually broken here and thrown out of the window as part of some ceremony.

The three-windowed temple is a very important place – Bingham used it as the centrepiece in his theory that Machu Picchu was about a thousand years older than anyone else thought (see p248). The three windows refer to the creation myths of the Incas.

An enormous amount of effort has gone into the building of this place: look downwards out of one of the windows and you'll see that the terrace on which this place was built has been clad in massive, beautifully carved rocks. If you can't quite see from this angle, look back at it when you're walking along the other side of the city.

The principal temple was thus called because it is so impressively built. The ranks of regular bricks have slipped a bit in the years as a result of subsidence. (Some researchers believe there's a serious risk of landslide in the area). In front of them there's a large altar.

Walk to the left of this temple and along a path. You'll see on your right the doorway of the **Ornament Chamber**. Put your head in and have a look at the corners of this room – they're not built from stone blocks but carved from rock – one of these stones has 32 angles in three dimensions. This isn't building, it's sculpture.

THE INTIHUATANA

Continue walking past the ornament chamber and you'll start to climb the stairs up to the **Intihuatana** (see photo opposite p256). The importance of this place is emphasized by its architecture: you have to climb to reach it, and you can't go straight there, you have to turn corners. You get almost the same sense of awed anticipation as you do climbing to Intipunku to get a first sight of Machu Picchu.

Inti means sun and *hata* means to tie, and 'intihuatana' has been translated as 'hitching post of the sun'. The word doesn't appear in the ancient vocabularies of Quechua; it seems it was first noted by the nineteenth century North American traveller, George Squier. Squier came across an Intihuatana in Pisac and thought that it might be a place where the sun was ritually stopped, perhaps when it reached its lowest point in the winter skies, and encouraged to rise higher once more.

Spanish priests, when they came across these sacred rocks of the Incas, used to lop the tops off them or ritually exorcize them, and it's rare for one to survive relatively intact. I say relatively, because in September 2000 the Intihuatana was damaged by a crane. The US publicity firm, J Walter Thompson, was filming an advertisement for Cusqueña beer, when a crane they were using chipped a chunk out of the old stone. There's a rich symbolism in the fact that this ancient monument, which survived the Spanish invasion and centuries lost in the jungle, has now been damaged by the forces of modern capitalism.

Unlike the Torreon (see p257), no one has yet found a precise astrological function for the Intihuatana – the various edges and angles are carved into the mother rock with considerable exactitude but no one knows why. Some archaeologists don't think of it as a ritual hitching post; it's been renamed simply as a gnomon (a carved block), although a gnomon is also the name for the arm on a sundial.

AROUND THE SACRED ROCK

Pass through the space around the Intihuatana, and go down the other side. As you're walking, look down at the minute terraces on your left, apparently too small to be purely for agriculture, yet on such a steep slope that it's doubtful whether they were either necessary or effective for defence purposes.

In front of you to the left is the **Sunken Square**. This area has been carefully terraced to make a little enclosed square apart from the main plaza, and in one corner there are the remains of what looks like a tomb under a large rock. It's often overgrown, and by looking at it you can get an idea of what Machu Picchu must have looked like when Bingham first stumbled up here – that is, unless they've cut the plants back again.

The **Sacred Rock** is to your right, tucked away under the shadow of Huayna Picchu, across the main square. There's a path that leads to it. This rock's called 'sacred' because it has been exposed in such a way that its shape is emphasized, fronted by a plaza and enclosed on two sides with well-built Inca houses. Why it's been exposed like this isn't clear, and you'll hear some bizarre theories: that the rock is a statue of Pachamama, the earth goddess, that it's a puma or that it's a guinea pig. The most likely theory is that the shape of this rock mimics the mountains around it. The plaza makes you want to look at the rock from one side, and you'll notice that it's a good representation of the mountain Putucusi that looms behind. Some, however, have pointed out that the rock's an even better copy of Pumasillo (Puma's Claw), a mountain many miles away on the opposite horizon behind you.

HUAYNA PICCHU

The path for Huayna Picchu leaves from the caretaker's little hut to the left of the Sacred Rock. It's about a 45-minute climb to the top, and in places the path takes you up near-vertical faces with ropes and steps driven into the rock. Tiny terraces cover the top of Huayna Picchu, and the view of the sunrise from up here is even better than that from Intipunku.

A side path on Huayna Picchu leads to the **Temple of the Moon** which is around the other side of the mountain, about 50 minutes' detour down a very steep path (with the occasional ladder). The Temple of the Moon has very high-quality Inca stonework and was orientated to face the Pleiades, who were worshipped by the Incas. Fire damaged the whole mountain in 1997, and it was out of bounds until late 1998.

The trail opens early, at 7am, closes at 1pm. Everybody must be off the mountain by 3pm, and it's best to get up here before the crowds arrive at around 10am.

> ❏ *From the narrow saddleback on which the ruined city stands, the precipices plunge headlong into the raging brown river, fifteen hundred feet below. Looking up makes you even giddier than looking down, for all around the valley are black snow-streaked mountains, looming over you through the driving clouds, and right ahead, at the end of the ridge, towers an appalling berg of rock, like the fragment of a fallen moon. This is called Huayna Picchu. The Incas, who must have been able to climb like flies, built a watchtower on top of it, to guard the approach to the citadel.*
> **Christopher Isherwood** *The Condor and the Cows*, 1949.

THE THREE DOOR DISTRICT AND LOWER CEMETERY

Turn right from the Sacred Rock and walk behind a large boulder. You'll come to a flat rock that hangs a little over the precipice leading down to the Urubamba below. There's an unforgettable view from the edge of it.

Continue walking and follow some little white arrows painted on rocks, and the path will take you to the **Three Door District** (so named because it's got three main doors). This is a clan group area of Machu Picchu, and the houses are arranged in a small labyrinth. Note the pillars sticking out of the building's gables, and also the little carved projecting holes that run along the edge. To these the Incas tied the thatch that made up their roofs – you can see reconstructions of this in the Watchman's Hut, the huts around the sacred rock and the storehouses on the way out.

Looking downhill you can see a terraced area connected to the three-door district by tiny paths and stairways. This is the **lower cemetery**, another area where Bingham found many tombs, but it's very steep – you should only visit it if you have a head for heights and are sure-footed.

THE MORTAR DISTRICT

Back up in the main housing district, the next clan group to the south (straight on) is the **Mortar District**. It got its name because Bingham found some interesting solid stone circles carved into rocks set into the floor of one of these houses, which he thought were mortars used for crushing maize in the house of an important chief. They don't bear much relation to the mortars commonly used by local people today so this theory isn't believed any more, but what they are actually for, no one knows. This district's sometimes called the Industrial Sector.

THE CONDOR TEMPLE OR JAILS

Leave the Mortar District, and go down a flight of stairs bordering the main plaza. Look back across at the marvellous stonework of the Temple of the Three Windows, if you haven't already. At the bottom of the stairs, turn left, and then right. This is the district that Bingham thought contained the **jails** of the city. He noticed the small alcoves with tying places bored into the niche frames at about the height for manacling a prisoner to the rock. People no longer think these were jails; it seems that death was a punishment for many crimes against Inca laws, and there would be no need of jails. It's thought by some that these niches used to contain something sacred and holy: mummies, perhaps, guarded by a taboo stick tied onto the rings.

On the floor further around the corner is a rock that looks a little like a condor with a white ruff, which gives this area its other name: **the Condor Temple**. There's also an altar in a natural fissure in the rock here, a bit like the one in Qenko (see p150). The condor was a sacred bird, sometimes a messenger or an embodiment of the huacas, especially of the apus (mountain spirits). Different birds could represent different things, the smallest bird representing a small mountain and the largest – condors – the sacred mountains of Salcantay, Veronica and Pumasillo. However, not every bird was a messenger – some were just birds, and it took an expert to be able to tell the difference.

Opposite: The Intihuatana (see p254), the Hitching Post of the Sun. (Photo © Bryn Thomas).

THE FOUNTAINS AND THE ROYAL GROUP

Come out of the Condor Temple group, and make your way up the large flight of stairs to a **cascade of fountains**. These little square structures with water flowing through them are probably something to do with the ritual worship of water: there are similar structures in Phuyu Pata Marca, Sayac Marca and Tambo Machay. Bingham again thought them something different, believing that they were the main water supply for the city. The spring that used to feed these now feeds the hotel, and rather prosaically they can be switched on and off like a tap.

At the head of the cascade is the most carefully worked fountain. Uphill from this is the **Fountain Caretaker's Hut**, which, like the Watchman's Hut, is too ornate to be that of a mere caretaker. It is likely to be a place associated with water worship like the fountains it oversees. There are niches and stone pegs inside for hanging things, and there's a theory that it's where a priest supervised the rituals of water worship. It's good to sit in the place and absorb the atmosphere.

On the right (looking from below) of the caretaker's hut is **The Royal Group**. This is an area of particularly fine buildings, which Bingham took to be the place where the most important person lived. The stone is nicely carved, but what draws most attention is the massive lintel over the main door. It weighs about three tons and was probably placed where it is by being dragged up an earth mound, which was then swept away. There's also an enclosed area in this group, possibly a garden, which the historian, Garcilasco de la Vega, describes as being common in the dwellings of people of high status, and often filled with golden statues.

THE TORREON OR SUN TEMPLE GROUP

The circular tower to the left of the Fountain Caretaker's Hut (if you're looking uphill) is the **Torreon** (see opposite p256).

The Torreon was probably a Sun Temple but it does not have the six chambers you normally find in a sun temple. Reminding you of the Serpent Window in the Coricancha in Cusco is a window with holes drilled in the frame. These holes were probably for fixing shadow-casters or aids to astronomy, but some have suggested they concealed snakes – hence the name. It's recently been noted that at dawn on the winter solstice (21 June) the sun shines through the window in the circular wall highlighting the rock in the middle of the temple (see photo opposite). You can't enter the temple as it's been roped off.

Beneath the Torreon is a wonderful place, where the rocks have been carved in three-dimensional asymmetry so that they look as if they're made of putty. This is called the **Tomb of the Princess,** or the Royal Tomb, but that's misleading because no bodies were found here. All the same it's likely that this was an important place for the Incas, judging from the work involved in enlarging and shaping this fissure. Just around the corner from the Tomb there is a flight of eight stairs carved from the living rock, leading to a beautiful double-framed door. There are two of these doors in Ollantaytambo, and they are very impressive, indicating an important dwelling. Note the bars recessed deeply into both door frames, similar to the ones in the Old City Gate.

To the right of the stairs is an entrance into a particularly fine walled building called **The Sacristy** or **House of the Princess**. The walls of Inca buildings are especially remarkable and here both the internal and external walls are amazing pieces of workmanship, especially when you consider that the Incas didn't have iron, only small brass crowbars. Bingham described it as 'the most beautiful wall in all America'.

THE WAY OUT

If you stand at the top of the cascade of fountains facing out into the void, you can see two or three thatched huts away to your right, at the same level as you are. A path leads there. This is the way out to Machu Picchu Sanctuary Lodge (The Tourists' Hotel, see p244), the car park and the buses back to the valley floor.

Moving on

HELICOPTER TO CUSCO

For the adventurous and rich, there's usually a daily helicopter flight which generally leaves at 3pm; there may be more flights if there are enough people. There's often someone selling helicopter tickets, normally from under an umbrella on the wall leading to the entrance booth. The 25-minute ride back to Cusco costs US$100. If there's no one selling tickets, try in Aguas Calientes at Av Imperio de los Incas 123 (☎ 211019 – there's a public phone outside Machu Picchu Sanctuary Lodge).

MACHU PICCHU TO AGUAS CALIENTES (see p157)

Transport for Cusco leaves from Aguas Calientes in the valley below Machu Picchu. The **walk** down there takes one and a half hours (follow the *Camino Peotonal* signpost on the edge of the car park), or you can take the **bus**. The bus ticket office is by the left luggage store; buses leave approximately every half hour, and the fare is s/18.

AGUAS CALIENTES TO CUSCO

From Aguas Calientes the only way back to Cusco is by **train**. The timetable depends on the class of train and upon the vagaries of the Peruvian railway system. See p267-8 for details of times and prices. If you're trying to save yourself some money, catch the train as far as Ollantaytambo (which is half the Cusco fare) and take a local bus from there.

APPENDIX A: QUECHA AND SPANISH

QUECHUA

There are very few readily-available Quechua-English dictionaries or phrasebooks except for Ronald Wright's *Quechua Phrasebook* (Lonely Planet Publications). If you've access to a large library, however, have a look at the *Tri-lingual Dictionary: Quechua of Cusco/English/Spanish* by Esteban Hornberger S and Nancy H Hornberger (three volumes, Quechua Community Ministry 1977). This is a good book, but it sometimes goes over the top with religious vocabulary and doesn't translate words such as 'chicha'!

There are many different ways of spelling Quechua. In most of this book I've followed Dr Ann Kendall and used the Hispanic spelling because many maps use it, but in this section I've tried to use the version which is easiest for English speakers to pronounce (which also happens to be the accepted standard alphabet). Pronunciation of Quechua words is difficult, as the language includes glottal stops, aspirations and plosives not found in most European languages. Stress, as in Spanish, almost always falls on the second last syllable. Letters to watch out for are Q, Q', Qu, Qh, K, K' (glottalizations).

SPANISH

Peruvian Spanish differs from Castilian (Spanish Spanish) in pronunciation and vocabulary but is basically the same language.

The letters for an English speaker to watch out for are the LL (pronounced as an English Y), C (pronounced as an 'S' when followed by E and I, otherwise 'K'), H (silent), HU (pronounced a bit like W), Ñ (the '~' puts an 'I' noise after the N), Q (pronounced K). Unlike Castilian, the S is pronounced as an S not a TH, and the V is usually a V not a B. The rule of thumb about stress is that it goes on the penultimate syllable, unless there's an accent, in which case it goes where the accent indicates.

ENGLISH	QUECHUA	SPANISH
Hello and goodbye		
Greeting!	*Napaykullayki!*	*¡Buenos días!*
How are you?	*Allillanchu?*	*¿Cómo está usted?*
See you later	*Ratukama*	*Hasta luego*
Goodbye (final)	*Kacharpari*	*Aiós*
sir	*tayta*	*señor*
madam	*mama*	*señora*
Excuse me (polite)	*Munayniykimanta*	*Con permiso*
oi!	*yaw!*	*¡oiga!*
Politeness		
Please	*Ama hiinachu kay, allichu*	*Por favor*
Thanks	*Añáy*	*Gracias*
Can I stay here? (spend the night)	*Puñupayukuykimanchu*	*¿Puerdo pasar la noche aqui?*
Yes and no		
yes	*arí, riki* (certainly!)	*sí*
no	*mana, ama* (don't!)	*no*
impossible	*mana atina*	*imposible*
that's good	*allinmi*	*está bien*
that's bad	*manan allinchu*	*no está bien*

ENGLISH	QUECHUA	SPANISH

Directions

Where is…?	*maypin …?*	*¿donde está…?*
…the river	*…mayu*	*…el río*
…the village	*..llaqta, marka*	*…el pueblo*
…the path	*…ñan*	*…el camino, el sendero*
…the pass	*…q'asa*	*…la abra*
…the bus/truck	*…omnibus /karro*	*…el bus/el camión*
…the railway	*…ferrocarril*	*…el ferrocarril*
…the toilet	*…bañu*	*…los baños*
…the hotel	*…qorpa wasi*	*…el hotel*
…the house	*…wasi*	*…la casa*
…water	*…unu*	*…agua*
…food	*…mikuna*	*…la comida*
here	*kaypi*	*aqui*
there	*chaypi*	*allí, allá*
over there	*haqay*	*por ahí*
up	*wichay*	*arriba*
down	*uray*	*abajo*
left	*lloq'e*	*izquierda*
right	*paña*	*derecho*
near	*sispa*	*cerca*
far (far off)	*karu*	*lejos*
straight ahead	*dirichu*	*derecho*
everywhere, nowhere, anywhere	*maypipas*	*en todos partes, en ninguna, dondequiera*

When?

When?	*hayk'aq?*	*¿cuándo?*
now (soon)	*kunan*	*pronto*
right now	*kunallan, kunanpacha!*	*ahora mismo*
later	*qhepata*	*más tarde*
never	*manan hayk'aqpas*	*nunca*

Weather

heat of the sun	*ruphay*	*calor del sol*
rain	*para*	*lluvia*
wind	*wayra*	*viento*
freezing wind	*qasa*	*viento helado*
snow	*rit'i*	*nieve*

How much?

How much is…?	*hayk'atan kubrawanki…?*	*¿cuanto cuesta…?*
..that one	*…haqay, chay*	*…eso/a*
..it to hire a guide	*…pusawasqaykimanta*	*…arrendar un guía?*
it to hire a horse	*…caballoykikunamanta*	*…arrendar un caballo?*
it to hire a llama	*…llamaykikunamanta*	*…arrendar una llama?*
it for a week	*…sapa semanan*	*…por semana*
it for a day	*…sapa p'unchay*	*…por día*
Will you sell me…?	*icha … ta bendiwankiman?*	*¿me vende …?*
…money	*…qolqe*	*…dinero*

ENGLISH	QUECHUA	SPANISH

Food and drink (see pp57-9)

ENGLISH	QUECHUA	SPANISH
meat (dried meat)	*aycha, (ch'arki)*	*carne (charqui)*
fish	*challwa*	*pescado*
chicken	*wallpa*	*pollo*
egg	*runtu*	*huevo*
bread	*t'anta*	*pan*
soup	*chupi*	*sopa*
maize (corn)	*choqllo, sara*	*maíz, choclo*
potato	*papa*	*papa*
fruit	*ruru, añawi*	*fruta*
roast	*kanka*	*asado*
boil	*t'impuy*	*hervir*
fry	*theqtichiy*	*freír*
raw	*hanku*	*crudo*
cooked	*chayasqa*	*cocido*
coca	*kuka*	*coca*
beer	*sirwisa*	*cerveza*
fizzy drink		*bebida gaseosa*
hot (temperature)	*q'oñi*	*caliente*
spicy	*haya*	*picante*
cold	*chiri, khutu*	*frío*
cold food	*kharmu*	*comida fría*

Quantity

ENGLISH	QUECHUA	SPANISH
more	*aswan*	*más*
less	*aswan pisi*	*menos*
a little	*chika, pisi*	*un poco, poquito*
big, large	*hatun*	*grande*
small, little	*huch'uy*	*pequeño/a*
normal sized	*tinku*	*tamaño normal*

Numerals

ENGLISH	QUECHUA	SPANISH
1	*huk*	*uno*
2	*iskay*	*dos*
3	*kinsa*	*tres*
4	*tawa*	*cuartro*
5	*pisqa*	*cinco*
6	*soqta*	*seis*
7	*qanchis*	*siete*
8	*pusaq*	*ocho*
9	*isqon*	*nueve*
10	*chunka*	*diez*
20	*iskay chunka*	*viente*
30	*kinsa chunka*	*trienta*
100	*pachak*	*ciento*
200	*iskay pachak*	*dos cientos*
1000	*waranqa*	*mil*
2000	*iskay waranqa*	*dos mil*

ENGLISH	QUECHUA	SPANISH
Help!		
Help me!	*yanapaway!*	*¡socorro!*
Take me to a hospital	*uspitalman pusaway*	*ilévame al hospital*
Ouch!	*achakáw!*	*¡ay!*
It hurts	*nanan*	*me duole*
I'm cold	*chiriwashan*	*tengo frío*
I'm hungry	*yarqawashan*	*tengo hambre*
I'm thirsty	*ch'akiwashan*	*tengo sed*
I'm tired	*sayk'usqa kan*	*estoy cansado*
Tie up your dog	*atahay alqoykita*	*ate su perro*

APPENDIX B: GLOSSARY

AMS	acute mountain sickness
abra	mountain pass
aclla	Inca nun
acllahuasi	convent
alpaca	type of llama bred for its wool
altiplano	high plateau
amauta	keeper of Inca oral history
andene	terrace
anticucho	beef heart kebabs
Antis	Inca word for the tribes of the rainforest
Antisuyu	the forested eastern district of the Inca Empire
apachita	cairn; pile of stones
apu	mountain spirit
arriero	muleteer, donkey man
audiencia	a seat of government of Spanish South America
awaska	everyday cloth worn by the majority of people
ayllu	Inca kinship group
cabildos	town councils
cacique	Spanish word for a local leader in the time of the Incas
calle	street
cambista	money-changer
campesino	Peruvian peasant
cancha	block of houses in an Inca town
caudillos	the military leaders at the time of Peruvian independence
cejas de la Selva	'eyebrows of the jungle' (the eastern slopes of the Andes, covered by the edge of the rainforest
ceques	sacred lines radiating from the centre of the Sun Temple
cerro	mountain
ceviche	traditional Peruvian dish of marinated raw fish.
cevicherías	seafood restaurants selling ceviche
chacos	Royal Hunts
chasqui	relay-running message carrier

chicha	drink of fermented maize
Chinchaysuyu	the northern quarter of the Inca Empire
chullo	locally-knitted hat
chuño	type of traditional freeze-dried potato
ciadadela	Enclosure surrounded by a large wall, inside which there are labyrinths of storage rooms, a large platform (which doubles as a burial place) and audience rooms called *audiencias*
colectivo	South American form of transport, half-taxi, half-bus
Collasuyu	the far southern quarter of the Inca Empire
Convención (La)	the district further into the jungle beyond Machu Picchu
conquistadors	the Spanish conquerors of Peru
Coricancha	Inca Sun Temple
Corregidors	Crown agents
correo	post office
Coya	the Inca's sister and his official wife
Cuntisuyu	the south-western quarter of the Inca Empire
Curaca	Inca name for local noble
cuy	guinea pig
Encomendero	man who owns an encomienda
encomienda	plot of land governed by a Spaniard
guanaco	type of wild llama
HACO/HAPO	very serious forms of mountain sickness
Hanan	Inca clan division, also a part of an Inca town, the opposite of Hurin
huaca	sacred spot
huayna	small or young
Hurin	an Inca clan division, also a part of an Inca town, the opposite of Hanan
Inca	(see Sapa Inca)
Inti	the sun, the Sun God
Intihuatana	the 'hitching post of the sun', an Inca ceremonial stone
Inti Raymi	a re-creation of the Inca festival of the winter solstice
jirón	street
llama	a South American relative of the camel
llipta	A mixture of lime or quinoa and potash chewed with a quid of coca leaves
machay	cave
machu	old, big
mamacona	mother superior in an Inca convent
mercado	a purpose-built indoor market
mestizo	mixed blood
mit'a	Inca tax, often paid in labour
mitimaes	Inca settlers
nevado	snow-capped peak
orejones	'big-ears', the Spanish name for Inca nobles
Pachamama	an earth goddess
pampa	plain
panaca	the tradition of preserving the estate of a dead person
parillada	plate of grilled meat
pirka	basic method of Inca construction
posta de salud	health station
pucara	Inca fort
pueblos jóvenes	shanty towns
puna	high grassland

Punchao	a sacred idol of the sun from Cusco's Sun Temple, now lost
Qenko	sacred spot near Cusco
qollqa	Inca storehouse
qompi	fine fabric woven for the Inca
Quechua	a name for the Inca language; the Incas' descendants currently living in Peru
quinoa	an Andean grain
quipus	strings and knots used by the Incas for record-keeping
raccay	ruins
Runasimi	the Quechua word for their language
Sapa Inca	the ruler of the Incas (also just 'Inca')
suyu	a division of the Inca Empire
Tahuantinsuyu	Inca name for the Inca Empire
tambo	an inn, way-station or rest-house
tarjeta telefónica	telephone card
taxista	taxi driver
Tiahuanaco	a pre-Inca Peruvian culture
tumi	an Andean knife
urpu	the characteristic pot form ie a fat belly, a curved base and long spout
usno	raised ceremonial square in Inca city
vicuña	rare wild relative of the llama with beautiful wool
Villac Umu	chief of the caste of priests in the Inca state religion
Viracocha	the creator of the Incas, also the name of one of the early Incas

APPENDIX C: PERUVIAN EMBASSIES

Argentina
Av Del Libertador No 1720
1425 Capital Federal
Buenos Aires
(☎ 011-4802 2000, 📠 011-802 5887)

Australia
40 Brisbane Avenue Suite 8,
Ground Floor Barton Act 2600
Canberra
PO Box 106 Red Hill
(☎ 02-6273 8752, 📠 02-6273 8754)

Australia (Sydney consulate)
Level 3, 30 Clarence Street
New South Wales 2000
(☎ 02-9262 6464, 📠 02-9290 2939)

Austria
Gottfried-Keller-Gasse 2/8-35
1030 Vienna
(☎ 01-713 4377, 📠 01-712 7704)

Belgium
Avenue de Tervuren 179
1150 Bruxelles
(☎ 02-733 3185, 🖹 02-733 4819)

Bolivia
Calle Fernando Guachalla Cdra.3
Sopocachi, La Paz
(☎ 02-353550, 🖹 02-367640

Brazil
SES Av das Nacoes, Lote 43
70428-900, Brasilia DF
(☎ 061-242 9933, 🖹 061-244 9344)

Canada
130 Albert Street, Suite 1901
Ottawa, Ontario, K1P 5GA
(☎ 613-238-1777, 🖹 613-232-3062)

Chile
Av Andres Bello 1751
Providencia, Santiago
(☎ 02-235 6451, 🖹 02-235 8139)

Colombia
Carrera 10 No 93-48
Bogota
(☎ 01-218 9212, 🖹 01-623 5102)

Denmark
Rosenvaengets Alle 20, 2nd TV
2100 Copenhagen
(☎ 035-265848, 🖹 035-268406)

Ecuador
Av Republica de El Salvador 495 e Irlanda
Quito
(☎ 02-468410, 🖹 02-252560)

France
50, Avenue Kleber
75116 Paris
(☎ 01-53 70 42 00, 🖹 01-47 04 32 55)

Germany
Godesberger Allee 125
53175 Bonn
(☎ 0228-373045, 🖹 0228-379475)

Israel
37 Rehov Ha-Marganit
Shinkun Vatikim
52584 Ramat Gan
(☎ 03-613 5591, 🖹 03-751 2286)

Japan
4-4-27 Higashi
Shibuya-ku
Tokyo 150-0011
(☎ 03-3406 4243, 🖹 03-3409 7589)

Netherlands
Nassauplein 4
2585 EA
La Hague
(☎ 070-365 3500, 🖹 070-365 1929)

New Zealand
Level 8 Cigna House
40 Mercer St
Wellington, PO 2566
(☎ 04-499 8087, 🖹 04-499 8057)

South Africa
Infotech Building Suite 202
1090 Arcadia St
0083 Hatfield, Pretoria
(☎ 012-342 2390, 🖹 012-342 4944)

Spain
C/Principe de Vergara No 36
5 to Derecha
28001 Madrid
(☎ 091-431 4242, 🖹 091-431 2493)

Switzerland
Thunstrasse 36
3005 Berma
(☎ 031-351 8555, 🖹 031-351 8570)

UK
52 Sloane St
London SW1X 9SP
(☎ 020-7235 1917, 🖹 020-7235 4463)

USA (Washington consulate)
1700 Massachusetts Ave NW
Washington DC 20036
(☎ 202-833-9860, 🖹 202-659-8124)

USA (Miami consulate)
444 Brickell Ave
Suite M-135
Miami, Florida 33131
(☎ 305-374-1305, 🖹 305-374-8935)

USA (New York consulate)
215 Lexington Ave 21st Floor
New York, NY 10016
(☎ 212-481-7410, 🖹 212-481-8606

APPENDIX D: TRAIN TIMETABLES

Until recently, trains were the cheapest form of transport between the major destinations in Peru. All that changed, however, with the privatization of the rail network in 1999, for while the trains remain the most pleasant and safest form of transport, they are certainly no longer the cheapest. Though some dirt-cheap 'local' trains still ply the main routes, the new owners of the rail network, Peru Rail, now forbid non-locals from taking them. It is not just foreigners who are no longer permitted to take these cheaper trains: even Peruvians from outside the local area are barred.

Fortunately, buses provide a cheap alternative to the trains on almost every major route. Unfortunately, the one place where the buses cannot go, and where you are left with virtually no other option but to take the train is, of course, Aguas Calientes, the village below Machu Picchu. Return fares between here and Cusco can be as high as US$70.

There are, however, two ways you can make it cheaper: the first is, rather than travelling all the way between Aguas Calientes and Cusco by train, stop off in Ollantaytambo instead, and complete the rest of your journey by bus (train fares between Ollantaytambo and Aguas Calientes, or Ollantaytambo and Cusco, tend to be half that between Cusco and Aguas Calientes). Buses to and from Cusco pull in and leave from the train station at Ollantaytambo. Secondly, there are two 'Economic trains' that are considerably cheaper: the **Cerrojo Social**, at 6.10am (US$10), which goes to Ollantaytambo only, and the **Social** at 6.10pm (US$15) that goes all the way to Cusco. Note that these two leave from the 'local' train station in Aguas Calientes (see p159), and also that they might not be running when you read this. Check with the SAEC (p106) or 🖥 www.perurail.com.

Fail to get a ticket for either of these, and the only alternative is to buy a ticket on the helicopter (see p146-7), or sit back in the comfy seats of one of the more luxurious trains, enjoy the free soft drink they provide, gaze at the gorgeous scenery and remember that, whilst extortionate by Peruvian standards, these fares are no more than you'd expect to pay in Europe and America for a similar journey.

Please note that the following timetables are subject to change at very short notice and should be used as an approximate guide at best. For a more up-to-date schedule, call in at the train stations or try visiting Peru Rail's **website** at 🖥 www.perurail.com. You can also book online at 🖥 reservas@perurail.com.

Between Cusco and Puno
Trains leave Cusco for Puno on Mondays, Wednesdays, Fridays and Saturdays at 8am, arriving Juliaca at 4.35pm, departing 4.45pm, and get to Puno at 6pm.

Trains leave Puno on Mondays, Wednesdays, Thursdays and Saturdays at 8am, arriving Juliaca at 9.10am, departing 9.15am, and get to Cusco at 6pm.

There are two classes: First Class costs US$60 (this includes a meal) one way, and Turismo (Tourist Class) costs US$12.

Between Puno and Arequipa
This route may be discontinued, so check if it's still running at 🖥 www.perurail.com. The following times are for guidance only.

Trains leave Arequipa on Sundays at 9pm (arrive Puno at 7.35am on Monday), at 7am on Wednesdays (arrive 5.40pm) and 8am on Saturdays (arrive 6.40pm). From Puno trains leave on Mondays at 9.35am (arrive 8pm), and Thursdays and Sundays at 7am (arrive 5.30pm). The Inka (First) class costs US$30, Turismo s/25.

❏ **Stop Press – see update information on p276**

Between Cusco and Machu Picchu

Services are daily, but often the cheaper trains don't run on Sunday.

Service	Cusco	Ollantaytambo		Aguas Calientes		Ollantaytambo		Cusco
	Dep	Arr	Dep	Arr	Dep	Arr	Dep	Arr
Vistadome	6am	8.05am	8.15am	9.30am	3pm	4.25pm	4.30pm	6.50pm
Inka	6.15am	8.30am	8.35am	10am	3.25pm	4.55pm	5pm	7.25pm
Cerrojo Social	8.25am	9.50pm	6.10am	7.45am				
Backpacker	6.30am	8.55am	9am	10.30am	4.10pm	5.50pm	5.55pm	8.30pm
Social	7.50am		11.50am	6.10pm		10.25pm		

	Uru-bamba	Ollantaytambo		Aguas Calientes		Ollantaytambo		Uru-bamba
	Dep	Arr	Dep	Arr	Dep	Arr	Dep	Arr
Vistadome	6am	6.50am	7am	8.10am	8.25am	9.52am		
Vistadome			10.10am	11.18am	1.30pm	2.44pm		
Vistadome			3.10pm	4.30pm	5pm	6.15pm	6.25pm	7.15pm

APPENDIX E: BIBLIOGRAPHY

Some contemporary sources

Comentarios reales que tratan del origen de los Incas, Garcilaso de la Vega 1609 trans Livermore, Texas 1966, trans CR Markham 1869

The Discovery and Conquest of Peru, Pedro De Cieza de Léon, Duke University Press, 1998, trans Alexandra & Noble Cook.

History of the Incas, Pedro Sarmiento de Gamboa, Dover/Constable and Co, London 1999 (reprint of 1907 Hakluyt Markham translation)

Historia del descumbriento y conquista del Peru, Agustín de Zarate, 1555, trans JM Cohen, Harmonsworth, 1968

Historia del Nuevo Mundo, Bernabé Cobo, 1653, trans Ronald Hamilton, *History of the Inca Empire* and *Inca Religion and Customs,* Univ of Texas, Austin 1979 and 1990

Instrucción del Inga Don Diego de Castro Tito Cussi Yupangui, Titu Cusi 1570, in *En el encuentro de dos mundos: los Incas de Vilcabamba,* María del Carmen, Martín Rubio, ed, Madrid 1988

Letter to a King (El Primera Coronice y Buen Gobierno), Felipe Huamán Poma de Ayala 1613, facsimile edition, *Travaux et mémoires de l'institut de'ethnologie,*Paris 1936, vol 23

Relación del descumbriento y conquista de los reinos del Péru, Pedro Pizarro, 1571, trans PA Means, *Relation of the Discovery and Conquest of the Kingdom of Peru,* Cortes Society, New York, 1921

Verdadera relacion de la conquista del Perú, Francisco de Xerex (Pizarro's scribe), July 1534, trans CR Markham, *Reports on the Discovery of Peru,* Hakluyt Society, first series 47, 1872

Modern historians of the Incas

Conquest of Peru, William Prescott, New York, 1847

Conquest of the Incas, John Hemming, Macmillan 1970, Penguin 1983, Papermac 1993

Everyday life of the Incas, Ann Kendall, BT Batsford, 1973
The Incas of Peru, Clements Markham, Smith Elder & Co, 1910
Realm of the Incas, Max Milligan, HarperCollins, October 2001

Inca studies
Inca Architecture and Construction at Ollantaytambo, Jean-Pierre Protzen, OUP, 1993
Inca Road Systems, John Hyslop, Academic Press New York, 1984
Inca Architecture, Louise Margolies & Graziano Gasparini, Univ of Indiana, Bloomington, 1984
Inca Settlement Planning, John Hyslop, University of Texas Press Austin, 1990
Monuments of the Incas Edward Ranney and John Hemming, New York Graphic Society, New York, 1982
Discovering the Inca Ice Maiden, Johan Reinhard, National Geographic, Washington 1998
The Social Life of Numbers, Gary Urton, University of Texas, Austin 1997
Rain of the Moon: Silver in Ancient Peru, Heidi King, Metropolitan Museum of Art, New York 2000
Mathematics of the Incas, Code of the Quipu, Marcia and Robert Ascher, Dover Publications, New York 1981
The Incas, Terence D'Altroy, Blackwell, Oxford 2002

Machu Picchu and the Inca sites around it
An introduction to the Archaeology of Cusco, John H Rowe, Papers of the Peabody Museum of American Archaeology, Harvard University vol 22, No 2, 1944
Archaeological Explorations in the Cordillera Vilcabamba, Paul Fejos, Publications in Anthropology No 3, The Werner Gren Foundation, 1944
Archaeological Investigations of Late Intermediate Period and Late Horizon Period at Cusichaca, Peru, Ann Kendall, in *Current Archaeological Projects in the Central Andes*, edited by Ann Kendall, BAR Int Series 210, 1984
Exploring Cuzco, Peter Frost, Nuevas Imágenes, 2000
Inca Planning North of Cuzco between Anta and Machu Picchu and along the Urubamba Valley, Dr Ann Kendall, BAR Int Series, 421, Oxford, 1988
Lost City of the Incas, Hiram Bingham, Duell, Sloan and Pearce, 1948
Lost City of the Incas, Hiram Bingham, Weidenfeld & Nicholson, 2002, a reprint with photos
Machu Picchu, John Hemming. Readers' Digest, 1981
Machupicchu, Devenir Histórico y Cultural, Efrain Chevarria Huarcaya, UNSAAC, 1992
Machu Picchu Historical Sanctuary, Jim Bartle and Peter Frost, Nuevas Imágenes, 1995
The Sacred Centre Johan Reinhard, Nuevas Imágenes, 1995
Machu Picchu – A Civil Engineering Marvel, Kenneth R Wright and Alfredo Valencia Zegarra, American Society of Civil Engineers, 2000
The Machu Picchu Guidebook, Ruth Wright and Alfredo Zegarra, Johnson Books, Boulder, 2001
The Ancient Incas, Chronicles from National Geographic, Arthur Schlesinger, Chelsea House, Philadelphia, 1999
Inca Architecture and Construction at Ollantaytambo, Jean-Pierre Proetzen, OUP, 1993

Vilcabamba
Forgotten Vilcabamba – Final Stronghold of the Incas, Vincent R Lee, Sixpac Manco Publications 2000.
Sixpac Manco: travels among the Incas, Vincent R Lee, Sixpac Manco publications, 1985
Antisuyu, Gene Savoy, Simon and Schuster, 1970

Books on ancient Peru
Art of the Andes, Rebecca Stone-Miller, Thames and Hudson, 1995
Chavín and the Origins of Andean Civilisation Richard Burger, Thames and Hudson 1992
Peruvian Prehistory Keatinge (ed), CUP, 1988

The Ancient Civilisations of Peru J Alden Mason, Penguin 1957
The Ancient Kingdoms of Peru, Nigel Davies, Penguin, 1997
The Cities of the Ancient Andes, Adriana von Hagen and Craig Morris, Thames and Hudson 1998
The Incas and their Ancestors, Michael Moseley, Thames and Hudson, 1992
The Pre-Hispanic Cultures of Peru, Justo Caceres Macedo, Lima 1998

Modern Peru
A Fish in the Water, Mario Vargas Llosa, Faber and Faber, 1994
Fujimori's Peru, John Crabtree and Jim Thomas (ed), Institute of Latin American Studies 1998
Shining Path, Simon Strong, Harper Collins, 1992
The Peru Reader, University of Wisconsin Press Duke University Press, 1995
The Mystery of Capital, Hernando de Soto, Bantam, London 2000

Latin America
A History of Latin America, George Pendle, Penguin 1963
Ancient South America, Karen Bruhns, CUP, 1994
The Penguin History of Latin America, Edwin Williamson, Penguin, 1992

Quechua
Quechua Phrasebook, Lonely Planet Publications 1989
Tri-Lingual Dictionary: Quechua/English/Spanish Esteban Hornberger S, Nancy H Hornberger, Quechua Community Ministry, 1977

Travel narratives
Cut Stones and Crossroads, Ronald Wright, Penguin 1984
Cuzco: A Journey to the Ancient Capital of Peru, Clements Markham, 1856
Inca Cola, Matthew Paris, George Weidenfeld & Nicholson, 1990
Inca Land, Hirham Bingham, London Constable & Co, 1922
Memoirs, General William Miller, London, 1828
Peregrinations of a Pariah Flora Tristan, Folio 1986 (trans)
Peru. Travel and Exploration in the Land of the Incas, E George Squier, New York, 1877
The Condor and the Cows Christopher Isherwood, Random House, 1948
Voyage a Travers L'Amerique du Sud, Paul Marcoy (Laurent Sant-Criq) Paris 1869

Other books
Death in the Andes, Mario Vargas Llosa, trans Faber and Faber 1996
Royal Hunt of the Sun, Peter Shaffer
The Bridge of San Luis Rey, Thornton Wilder
Canto General, Pablo Neruda (trans Jack Schmitt), Univ of California Press, Berkley 1991
The Dancer Upstairs, Nicholas Shakespeare, Harvill 1995, Picador 1997
To the Last City, Colin Thubron, Chatto & Windus 2002

Health and medicine
Altitude Illness: Prevention & Treatment by Stephen Bezruchka MD, Cordee 1994
Bugs, Bites and Bowels Dr Jane Wilson Howarth, Cadogan 1995
Medical Handbook for Mountaineers Peter Steele, Constable 1988
Medicine for Mountaineering Ed James Wilkerson MD, The Mountaineers 1985

Flora and fauna
Annotated Checklist of Peruvian Birds, Theodore Parker III and others, Buteo Books, 1982
Birds of the High Andes by Jon Fjeldsa and Niels Krabbe, Apollo Books, 1990
Orquídeas del Perú, Moisés Cavero and others, Centro de Datos para la Conservación del Perú, Lima 1991

APPENDIX F: LICENSED TOUR OPERATORS

Note that some companies are officially licensed, but have no listings. I've included them because they may be more active by the time you read this. If any contact details below are no longer correct, it's worth looking at the Andean Travel Website ▣ www.andeantravel web.com for more information about official tour operators based in Cusco.

Amazonas Explorer
PO Box 722 Cusco
☎ 227137 mob: ☎ 084-653366/653400
▣ sales@amazonas-explorer.com
▣ www.amazonas-explorer.com

Andean Adventures
Urb Lucrepata E-13
☎ 263498/232687
▤ 236201
▣ andean@correo.dnet.com.pe

Andean Life
Plateros 372
☎ 221491
▣ www.andeanlife.com

Andes Nature Tours
Calle Garcilazo 210, Ofc.217
☎ 223886/245961
▤ 242522
▣ ant@terra.com.pe

Andina Travel
Plazoleta Santa Catalina
☎ 251892
▣ www.andinatravel.com

Apumayo Expediciones
Garcilaso 265, Ofc 3
☎ 242030/246018

Base Camp
Herrajes 148
☎/▤ 223260/650246

Big Foot
Calle Triunfo 392
Centro Commercial 2nd Level
☎/▤ 222123/238568
▣ www.bigfootcusco.com

Camping Tours
Procuradores 378
No phone listed

Condor Travel
Saphi 848A, Cusco, or
Armando Blondet 249
Lima 27 (☎ 1-615 3000)
☎ 225961/231161/247849
▣ www.condortravel.com/pe

Continental Tours
Calle Plateros 329
▤ 236919/231152
▣ Contitur@telser.com.pe

Culturas Peru Viajes Y Servicio
Calle Triunfo 393
☎ 243629
▣ www.culturasperu.com

Eco Andes Adventure
Urb Magisterial 1ra Etapa pza amauta 219
☎/▤ 247933/228103

Enigma
Calle Garcilaso 132
☎ 222155
▣ www.enigmaperu.com

Eric Adventures
Calle Plateros 324
☎ 228475/234242
▣ cusco@eric.adventures.com

Explorandes
Portal de Panes 236
or San Fernando 287, Miraflores
Lima 18 (☎ 01-445 0532)
☎ 244308
▣ www.explorandes.com

Inca Explorer
Suecia 339
⌨ www.incaexplorers.com

Inkaways
Santa Ursula C19
Suite B1, Wanchaq
☎ 223865
⌨ www.inkaways.com

Inka Wasi Travel Service
Calle San Augustin 409
(also at Lima Airport)
☎ 260380
⌨ www.inkawasitravel.com

Inti Kuntur
265 Portal de Confituria
☎ 246235
⌨ geocities.com/intikunturpe/cusco.htm

Loreto Tours
Calle Medio 111
☎ 228264

Manu Expeditions
Av Pardo 895
☎ 226671/236706/239974
⌨ adventure@manuexpeditions.com

Mayuc Cusco
Portal Confituria 211
☎ 232666
⌨ chando@mayuc.com

Peru Field Guides
Plateros 362
☎ 243475
⌨ www.peruvianfieldguides.com

Peru Treks
Calle Garcilaso 265
Ofc 13, 2nd Floor
☎ 805863
⌨ www.perutreks.com

Peruvian Andean Treks
Av Pardo 705
☎ 225701, 📄 238911
⌨ www.andeantreks.com

Peruvian Odyssey
Pasaje Pumacchupan 831
☎ 222105/238971, 📄 224167
⌨ posacus+@qenqo.rcp.net.pe

Purishunchis
Av El Sol s/n
☎ 222118/262235

Q'ente Tours
Garcilaso 210, Ofc 210B
☎ 238245, 📄 222535
⌨ www.qente.com

Sky Viajes Y Turismo
Calle Sta Catalina A 366C3
☎ 261818, 261414, 📄 240141
⌨ www.skyperu.com

South American Sites (SAS)
Portal de Panes 143
☎ 237292, 📄 225757
⌨ www.sastravel.com

Tambo Trek
Atocsayccuchi 589 San Blas
(PO Box 912)
☎ 237718, 📄 236229
⌨ tambotrx@terra.com.pe

Top Vacations
Portal de Panes 109, Ofc 06
☎ 263278
⌨ www.hikingperu.com

TrekPeru
Jiron Ricardo Palma N9 Santa Monica
☎ 252899/261501, 📄 238591
⌨ trekperu@terra.com.pe

United Mice
Plateros 351
☎ 221139

Vida Tours
Hotel Arqueologo – Interior 204
Calle Ladrillos 425
☎ 227750, 📄 235126
⌨ www.vidatours.com (French)

Particular thanks to the South American Explorers' Club of Cusco (see p106) and to Lorenz Wiest of Germany for help in the preparation of this update. I've organized this section to mirror the main part of the book and so that you can find your way around it both by using the headings and the page numbers.

To contact me with any further updates, recommendations or comments write c/o Trailblazer (address on p2) or email me at richard.danbury@trailblazer-guides.com. A free copy of the next edition or imprint will be sent for the most useful letters.

Page 11: With a group or on your own?
Guided tours now cost from US$180 up to US$500 for the four-day trip (though the cheaper tours aren't the bargain they seem: see p130).

Page 28: General equipment – walking sticks
Walking sticks have been banned on the Inca Trail between Huayllabamba and Machu Picchu since they damage the path but sometimes sticks with rubber bungs on the ends are permitted.

Page 32: Other books
Colin Thubron's novel, *To the Last City* (Chatto & Windus, 2002), follows five travellers on the Vilcabamba Trail (see p218), brilliantly evoking this challenging hike.

Page 43: Terrorism in Peru (box)
Though considerably less powerful than they were, the Shining Path are not completely defeated. In March 2002, ten people were killed when the American Embassy in Lima was bombed, probably by the Shining Path. In June 2003, 71 people working on a gas pipeline in the Apurimac region were kidnapped. They were released shortly afterwards. In July 2003, a patrol of marines was ambushed near Ayacucho and seven people died. In December 2003, the British Embassy in Lima was closed as a result of a security threat. That said, the terrorists are not the threat they were. In the dark decades of the 1980s and 1990s they numbered in the thousands; today there are only a couple of hundred.

The Peruvian authorities have ordered a retrial in a civilian court for Abimael Guzmán, as his first trial in front of hooded military judges was considered potentially unjust. Nicholas Shakespeare's novel, *The Dancer Upstairs*, has been made into a film.

In another development in 2003, the soldiers who'd stormed the Japanese Embassy were tried for executing the terrorists in cold blood. Forensic evidence showed that eight of the rebels had been shot in the back of their necks and a Japanese diplomat said that he'd seen three captured alive. The soldiers were acquitted on the basis that they'd been involved in a military confrontation.

Page 45: Toledo comes to power
Toledo has become unpopular; 2003 started with a series of crippling strikes and massive street protests – in June ten thousand people took to the streets of Lima which made Toledo declare a state of emergency. The underlying problem is that Toledo wasn't able to deliver on his election promises because Peru's economy wasn't as strong as he'd hoped.

Despite this, Toledo has tried hard to maintain his popularity; for example by reducing his salary three times and repeatedly relaunching his administration but it hasn't helped. At the end of 2003 he sacked his third Prime Minister, Beatriz Merino. Merino was dogged by allegations of corruption (and lesbianism) which she denied, but some commentators think the real reason for her dismissal was the fact that she was vastly more popular than Toledo: 60% of the population supported her as opposed to Toledo's rating of 11%. Even the disgraced former President Fujimori managed 31%. Merino has been replaced by Carlos Ferrero, a former Speaker of Congress and a man with a promising reputation as a peacemaker.

Page 45: Clearing up the mess

Peru officially petitioned Japan for Fujimori's extradition in July 2003. Interpol had made the same request in March but as Japan has no extradition treaty with Peru it's very unlikely the former President will return to Peru. The main charges that Fujimori faces relate to a death squad called the Grupo Colina, who were responsible for the killing of 15 alleged rebels in Lima in 1991, and the kidnapping and murder of students from a university in 1992. Fujimori's also alleged to have paid Montesinos US$15m when his spy chief lost his job. Fujimori denies the charges.

Montesinos was convicted in 2003 of various relatively minor offences and was sentenced to nine years' imprisonment. He is still awaiting trial on charges relating to allegations that he was involved in the death-squad killings. He's also currently (February 2004) being tried on allegations that he was involved in the smuggling of 10,000 rifles from Jordan to the Colombian rebel group, the FARC. The prosecution say he had CIA support. Montesinos denies the charges.

Page 47: Human Rights

In August 2003 the Human Rights Commission reported. It made grim reading: 69,000 Peruvians died or disappeared during the civil war, making it one of the worst in Latin America's history. The killing was centred around Ayacucho and three-quarters of the victims were campesinos. Both the government and the Sendero Luminoso were responsible. The Sendero killed and tortured to encourage villagers to support them, the government killed and tortured to persuade villagers not to. Toledo has urged reconciliation and promised to spend US$820m helping those most affected by the tragedy.

The issue of forced sterilizations of Campesina women is now the subject of a Parliamentary Commission. It's estimated that as many as 300,000 sterilizations were carried out between 1995 and 2000.

Page 48: Coca and cocaine (box)

Coca growing in Peru is intimately bound up with the evils of narco-terrorism and sadly that problem's increasing. In 2003 coca production in Peru grew and now the country produces more than any country except Columbia. The Peruvian Government is optimistic that it can reverse this trend but the key problem is the economics of coca production. Coca growers can get up to US$6 for a kilo of coca leaf. They get a fifth of that for a kilo of coffee. The UN suggests the answer is to open the West's markets to the rest of Peru's agricultural exports.

Page 49: Continuing economic problems

Toledo's presidency has been met with street protests and dissent, primarily caused by Peru's economic problems. Despite the economy having grown by 5.3% in 2002, the fastest rate in the region, Toledo hasn't been able to deliver on promises he made on his election such as the pledge to double teachers' pay. And the increasing Sendero activity has meant the army and police have needed more money, so Toledo's had trouble balancing his books. He's had to raise taxes, a move that's been deeply unpopular with both the people and with business. But tax rises may not help Toledo as much as he would like as a large proportion of Peru's economy is informal, so many people don't pay taxes. All in all, growth fell to 1.8% for the first half of 2003 and unemployment – and more particularly underemployment – has remained a problem.

Page 49: The environment

Despite pleas by Hollywood celebrities and pop stars, it currently (February 2004) looks as if the Camisea project is going ahead, led by Argentinian and North American companies. The Inter-American Development Bank (IADB) approved US$135m in funding in late

2003 and more than two-thirds of two 800km gas pipes have already been built. The pipes end at a gas terminal on the coast near Paracas. This creates other concerns, as the seas around Paracas are a marine reserve.

Camisea is not the only point where industrialization is causing friction. In December 2003 a mining company wanted to open a gold mine in the northern town of Tambogrande, near the Ecuadorian border. Despite offering to be sensitive to local people's concerns and offering to re-house them with electricity and water, the townspeople are set against the development. They believe that mining will damage their communities and the environment.

Another significant environmental development over the past thirty years has been the shrinking of the Peruvian glaciers. Central to the culture of both the Incas and the modern Quechua (see p46 describing the festival of Qoyllor Riti) and to tourism (one of the treks in this book skirts a high glacier on Salcantay see p212), glaciers are under threat; they have lost a quarter of their area. This is because they are melting in the dry season more quickly than they can be replenished in the wet – probably as a result of global warming. This makes people worried. In the short term the concern is that large chunks of glaciers may break off and drop into glacial lakes, causing them to flood. This happened in Huarez in 1941 and the resulting flood killed 5000. In the longer term, people are concerned about the opposite, desertification. In the dry season, Peru's rivers are fed predominantly by glaciers melting. If the glaciers continue to shrink, at some point they'll disappear. And with them will go many of Peru's rivers.

Page 51: Media
When Fujimori was toppled as president (see p44), many scandals were revealed, particularly relating to the activities of his former spy-master, Montesinos. Montesinos was taped apparently handing bribes to the owners of two of Peru's most popular television stations, America TV and Panamerica TV to secure the support of the stations for Fujimori.

There are four main radio stations: Radio Nacional is the state-run national broadcaster, and there are three Lima-based shows: Radio Programas de Peru, a talk station; Radio Panamericana, a music station; and Radio Americana, a news and music station. There are also other, smaller radio stations, including Radio Miraflores which broadcasts an hour-long show every Saturday starring none other than the disgraced former president Alberto Fujimori, who records his show from his current home in Japan.

Page 52: Rates of exchange
Rates as at 3 February 2004 are: **Aus$1=s/2.73**, **Can$1=s/2.69**, **Euro€1=s/4.48**, **NZ$1=s/2.43**, **UK£1=s/6.56**, **US$1=s/3.6**.

Page 53: Other forms of money
Euros are not really understood in Peru yet. It's best to take US dollars if you're taking any hard currency into the country.

Page 56: Holidays
10 December National day of reconciliation for the civil war. It's not clear whether this will be an annual holiday or not.

Page 59: Chicha box
The 'champagne of the Incas' – more accurately described by John Hemming as a murky cider – is still widely drunk today.

Page 66: In the beginning
An alternative theory, called Dissimilation theory, is gaining adherents. Dissimilationists believe that civilization arose in one place – perhaps Egypt, perhaps Atlantis or perhaps some unnamed proto-civilization – and then spread throughout the world. Thor Heyerdahl (p89) had a similar view. Attractive though this theory may be, the archaeological evidence doesn't support it.

Page 115: Lima cafés and bars

In late 2003 Starbucks opened two cafés in Lima. A deep irony. Not only because a tall latte costs two-thirds of the average Peruvian's daily wage, and not only because there's a touch of 'coals to Newcastle' about the move, coffee being one of Peru's main cash crops and exports. But mainly because most people in Peru don't drink coffee. And if they do, they drink instant.

Page 119: Lima – Moving on (Lima to Huancayo train)

The Lima to Huancayo train is now running but on an extremely infrequent schedule: once a month between April and October. Contact ⌨ www.perurail.com for more information.

Page 130: Tour agencies

Prices now range from US$180 up to US$500 for a tour on the trail. Beware of the cheaper end tours as they can be dreadful and exploitative.

Page 162: Environmental impact

In 2003, 400,000 people visited Machu Picchu. UNESCO says that this is too many. The Peruvian authorities (INC) said it's an exaggeration to say that there is a problem

Illegal animal smuggling is an increasing problem in South America. It's prompted by the high prices live Amazonian beasts can fetch in the markets in the US and Europe. The police are attempting to clamp down on this trade. In January 2004, a German man was arrested with 400 live toads and insects in his luggage. He said he was taking them to a private zoo in Frankfurt.

Page 267: Train timetables – Between Cusco and Puno

Cusco	Juliaca		Puno	Puno	Juliaca		Cusco
Dep	Arr	Dep	Arr	Dep	Arr	Dep	Arr
8am	3.45pm	4pm	4.45pm	8am	9am	9.15am	4.45pm

Trains leave Cusco for Puno on Monday, Wednesday, Friday and Saturday.
Trains leave Puno for Cusco on Monday, Wednesday, Thursday and Saturday.
Ticket prices: Inka (1st) Class costs US$30 and Turismo US$19.

Page 267: Train timetables – Between Puno and Arequipa

Despite numerous rumours, the train from Arequipa to Puno hasn't yet been discontinued though it's still under threat. At the time of writing the timetable was as follows.

	Arequipa	Sumbay	Juliaca	Puno	Juliaca	Sumbay	Arequipa
Sunday	9pm	00.30am					
Monday			6am	7am			
				9.30am	10.30am	4pm	7.30pm
Wednesday	7am	10.30am	4pm	5pm			
Thursday				7am	8am	1.30pm	5.30pm
Saturday	8am	11.30am		6pm			
Sunday				7am		1.30pm	5pm

Ticket prices: Inka (1st) Class: Arequipa–Puno US$30; Arequipa–Sumbay US$25; Arequipa–Sumbay–Arequipa US$30; Turismo: Arequipa–Puno or vice versa S/25.

Page 267: New luxury rail service to Machu Picchu

A pricey new rail service – **The Hiram Bingham** – now operates between Cusco and Machu Picchu. Leaving from Poroy station (Cusco) at 9am it reaches Machu Picchu at 12.30pm for a tour of the ruins. For the return journey, during which cocktails and dinner are served, it departs at 6.30pm reaching Poroy at 10pm.

Between November and March it runs on Monday, Wednesday, Friday and Saturday; from April to October the service is daily except Tuesday. Including all meals, tickets cost US$416.50 according to the website: check ⌨ www.perurail.com for more details.

INDEX

Abancay 119
Abra de Huarmihuanusca, pass 180, 204
Abra Ccolpa Casa 222, 225
acclimatization 34, 124
accommodation 18, 54-5
  Aguas Calientes 157
  Cusco 130-4
  Huancacalle 222
  Lima 107, 110-12
  Machu Picchu 244
  Ollantaytambo 156
  Quillabamba 221
  Urubamba 154
acute mountain sickness (AMS) 166
Aguas Calientes 157-9, 258
air services 54
  Cusco 146
  Lima 102, 118, 119
  to Peru 16-17
airport tax 52
alcoholic drinks 58
Almagro, Diego de 91-2, 95, 99
alpaca fabrics 59, 139
alpacas 62
altitude and altitude sickness 33-4
ambulances, Lima 105
Ancascocha 200
Andes 36
animal bites 168
Aobamba valley 185
APRA 41, 42
Apurímac river and valley 24, 95
architecture, Inca 86-8
Arequipa route 120
arrieros 15-16, 220
Artega, Melchor 246
Aspero, site 68
Atacama desert 35, 67, 70, 71, 84
Atahualpa, Inca 38, 92-4
Australia to Peru 17
Ayacucho 119
ayllus (clan groups) 82-3
Aymara people and language 45, 46, 76

backpacks 26
Balta, President 40
banks 53
  Cusco 125
  Lima 104
Bashford-Snell, John 74

Batan Grande 77
Beatriz, Inca princess 142
beer 58
Belaúnde Terry, Fernando 42
bibliography 29-32, 65, 268-71
Bingham, Hiram 20, 25, 30, 31, 178,
  182, 184, 185, 186, 225, 229, 238
  245-58 *passim*
birds 63-4
blisters 168
Boleto Turístico Unico (BTU) 140, 147
Bolívar, Simon 40, 104, 124
Bolivia 18, 40, 41
bookshops
  Cusco 125
  Lima 105
boots 25
Brazil 18
budgeting 18, 55
buses 18, 53, 54, 174, 258
  Aguas Calientes 159
  Cusco 124, 147, 220
  Lima 102, 103
  Lima to Cusco 118-20
bus companies 120
Bustamente, President 42

Caballero Muerto 70
cable car (Machu Picchu) 162
Cajamarca 92
Callao 37, 39, 104, 116
Camisea Project 49
camp-fires 161
camping 161-2, 163
Canada to Peru 17
canals, Inca 87
Caral, site 67
cars and car hire 54
  Cusco 125
  Lima 104
cash machines 53
Cave of the Owls 69
Ccolpa Casa 222, 225
Cedro Casa 234
Cedrochaca 229
ceramics
  pre-Inca 69, 72, 74, Inca 88
Cerro Baul, Huari fort 75, 76
Cerro Sechín, site 70
Chacha Cancha 210

Chachabamba, site (Km 104) 21, 196
Chagas, disease 170
Chalca, río 225
Chambi, Martín, photographer 50
Chan-Chan 77
Chancay people 76
Chaquicocha 185
Chaullay 220, 221
Chaunquiri 24, 220, 239, 241
Chavín civilization 66, 70-1, 117
Chavín de Huantar 70, 71
chicha (maize wine) 58, 59
Chilca (Km77) 21, 24, 172, 190, 198, 216
Chile 18, 40, 41
Chimú people 76-8, 81
Chinchero, town and site 154
Chinchorro people 67
cholera 170
Choquesuysuy 21, 196, 197
Chuncuchua 192
Chuntabamba 234
churches, religious buildings
  Cusco
  Cathedral 141-2
  Compañia (Jesuits' church) 142
  Convent of Santa Catalina 144
  El Triunfo 141
  Jesús María 141
  La Merced 143
  San Blas 144
  San Cristobal 146
  San Francisco 143
  Santa Clara 143
  Santa Teresa 144
  Santo Domingo, monastery 143
  Seminary of San Antonio Abad 146
  Lima
  Cathedral 115
  La Merced 116
  San Francisco 116
cinema 50
Classic Inca Trail 20, 172, 175-90
climate 36-7, 164
clothes 25-6
cloud forests 65
coca and cocaine 48, 58, 167, 247
Colca Canyon 120
compasses 28, 165
Concha Marca, site 184
condor eagles 63
Condorcanqui, José Gabriel 39, 124
Consevidayoc 234

consulates
  Cusco 129
  Lima 105
cooking equipment 27, 128
Coricancha, Sun Temple, Cusco 85,
  86, 123, 142-3
Corihuayrachina see Km 88
costa 35, 37
credit cards 53
Creoles 39
culture, Peruvian 50-1
Cupisnique people 69
Cuquipalta, huaca 85
currency 52
Cusco 122-47
  accommodation 130-4
  air services 146
  banks 125
  bars & clubs 137
  bookshops 125
  buses 124, 146
  Cabrera's House 146
  car hire 125
  cathedral and churches 141-6
  Coricancha 142-3
  embassies and consulates 129
  equipment rental and provisions 128
  history 122-4
  Inca walls 142, 144
  language courses 129
  laundry 129
  map 126-7
  market 138
  medical services 128
  museums 142, 144, 146
  orientation 125
  Plaza de Armas 140-1
  police 128
  post office 128
  restaurants 134-7
  shopping 138-9
  sights 140-6
  supermarket 128
  taxis 124
  telecommunications 128
  tour agencies and information 129,
    130, 131
  trains 124, 147
  visas 129
  Visitor's Ticket 140
  walking tours 145
Cusco school of painting 50, 144

Cusicacha valley and river 175, 176, 194, 207, 212
Cusilluchagoc 150

dance 50-1
Darien Gap 17
Darwin, Charles 101
Dead Woman Pass 180, 204
diarrhoea and dysentery 169-70
diphtheria 32
doctors
  Cusco 128
  Lima 105
documentation for tourists 52
dogs 33, 165, 168
doughnuts 58
Drake, Sir Francis 101
drinks and drinking 58-9, 115, 137
drugs 61, 70

economy, Peruvian 47-9
Ecuador 18, 41
education 45-6
El Dorado 91
El Misti, volcano 120, 249
El Niño 36
El Paraíso, site 68
El Señor de Sípan, hoard 73
electricity 55
Emails 56
  Cusco 128
  Lima 105
Embarkation and Disembarkation card 52
embassies and consulates
  Cusco 129
  Lima 105
embassies, Peruvian 264-6
employment 49
encomiendas 38
environment 49
environment & trekkers 160-2
equipment 26-8
  hire of (Cusco) 128
Espíritu Pampa 24, 218, 234, 237-9, 247

fabrics 59
faxes 56
  Cusco 128
  Lima 105
Fejos, Dr Paul 20, 182, 186, 188, 196
ferries 18

festivals 56
fish dishes 57
flora and fauna 62-5
food 18, 28-9, 57-8, 172
  Cusco 134-7
  Lima 114-15
football 51
Fujimori, President Alberto 43-5, 48

Gamarra, President 40
Garcia, President 43, 44
Garcilaso de la Vega, Inca writer 50, 78, 144
  burial place 141
gas cylinders 27, 128
Gateway God 75-6
geographical background, Peru 35-7
giardiasis 170
gold
  Inca 88, 93, 117, 122
  museum, Lima 117
  pre-Inca 69
government, Inca 83-5
guanacos 62
guano 40
guides 15-16
guinea pigs 57
Guitarrero cave 66-7

HACO 166-7
HAPO 166
Haya de la Torre, Victor Raúl 41, 42
health 32-4, 58, 165-70
helicopters 54, 258
Hemming, John 30
hepatitis 32
Heyerdahl, Thor 89
hiking maps, Lima 106

historical background
  Cusco 122-4
  Incas 78-99
  Lima 100-2
  Machu Picchu 245-9
  Peru 37-45
hitch-hiking 53
holidays 56
hospitals
  Cusco 128
  Lima 106
Huaca de los Reyes, site 70
Huaca del Sol 72, 75

Huaca Prieta, site 68
huacas 85
Huamán, Melchor, sculptor 141
Huamán Poma, Inca writer 50
Huancacalle 24, 220, 222
Huancayo 119
Huari civilization 66, 74, 76, 122
Huarpa people 72
Huascar 90, 94
Huayllabamba 20, 21, 24, 165, 176, 178, 245
Huayna-Capac, Inca 81, 90
Huayna Picchu, mountain 246, 255
Huayna Pucará 229, 232, 238
Huayna Quente, site 175, 176, 217
Huillca Raccay, site 192
Huinay Huayna, site 21, 185, 189, 197
Humantay, Mt 210
Humboldt current 35
Humboldt, Baron von 39
hummingbirds 63
hunting, Inca 88-9
hypothermia 168

Ica people 76
Ichma people 76
Inca, The 79, 84
Inca Bridge 252
Inca civilization 78-99
  architecture 86-8
  bibliography 30
  canals 87
  ceramics 88
  civil war 90
  class and clans 81-2
  empire 83-4
  gold 88, 93, 117, 122
  government 82-3
  hunts 88-9
  Machu Picchu 243-58
  metalwork 88
  mythology 78-9
  oral history 79-81
  record keeping 83-4
  religion 84-6
  roads 84
  siege of Cusco 96
  Spanish invasion and rule 91-9
  technology 87
  textiles 88
  Vilcabamba 96-8, 237-9, 246
  warfare 89-90

Inca Museum, Cusco 146
Inca Raccay, site 21, 202
Inca Trail, classic 20, 172, 175-90
Inca Trail tours 130, 131, 173
Incasamana, site 204
independence, Peru 40
independent trekking 11
Initial Period 68-70
injuries 167
inoculations 32-3
insurance 34
Internet sites 31, 56
Inti 84
Intipata, site 188
Intipunku 189, 190
iodine 168
Isherwood, Christopher 50, 122, 255
Isu Pata 212

Juliaca 120

Kendall, Dr Ann 87, 178, 192, 206, 217, 252
Killke people 76, 79, 122
Kiteni 241-2
Km 77 see Chilca
Km 82 21, 172, 190, 192
Km 88 20, 21, 172, 175, 217
Km 104 21, 172, 194, 195
Km 113 20
Kotosh, site 68, 69

La Florida 69
La Oroya 119
languages 46
language courses, Cusco 129
Lee, Vincent 31, 222, 237
Leguía, President Augusto 41, 102
Leishmaniasis 170
Leyenda Negra 38
Lima 37, 41, 100-120
  accommodation 107, 110-12
  air services 102, 118, 119
  Archbishop's Palace 116
  banks and cambios 104
  Barranco 104, 116
  books 105
  Bridge of Sighs 116
  buses 102, 103, 119-20
  cafés and bars 115
  Callao 104, 116
  car hire 104

Lima (*cont'd*)
  Castle of Real Felipe 116
  churches 116
  districts - map 103
  embassies and consulates 105
  emergencies 105
  history 100-2
  laundry 106
  Lima Centro 104, 107-11, 115-16
  medical services 105, 106
  Miraflores 104, 111-13, 116-17
  museums 116-18
  orientation 104
  Parque Kennedy 117
  Plaza de Armas 115
  police 106
  post office 105
  restaurants 114-15
  SAEC 106
  San Miguel 104, 117
  shopping 118
  sights 115-18
  taxis 102, 103
  telecommunications 105
  Torre Tagle 116
  tourist information and tours 103, 106
  trains 119, 120
  visas 107
  zoo, San Miguel 117
literature 50
llamas 62
Llulluchapampa 178, 180
Llulluchayoc river 176, 178
local transport 54
  see also buses, cars, taxis, trains
Loyola, Martín Garcia de 142
Lucu Mayu 234

Machu Picchu 20, 21, 86, 243-58
  bibliography 30
  Condor Temple 256
  districts 252
  Fountain Caretaker's House 257
  fountains 257
  Funerary Stone 249
  history 245-9
  House of the Princess 258
  Inca Bridge 252
  Intihuatana 253, 254
  Jails 256
  lower cemetery 256
  moat 252

Machu Picchu (*cont'd*)
  Mortar District 256
  museum model, Lima 117
  Old City Gate 252
  Ornament Chamber 254
  Principal Temple 253
  Quarry 253
  Royal Group 257
  Sacred Rock 255
  Sacred Plaza group 253-4
  Sacristy 258
  Sunken Square 254
  Temple of the Moon 255
  Temple of the Three Windows 253
  Three Door District 255
  Tomb of the Princess 257
  Torreon 248, 257
  Watchman's Hut 249
Machu Picchu mountain 252
Machu Pucará 232, 238
Machu Quente, site 175, 176, 217
malaria 32
Manco Capac, Inca 78-9, 248
Manco Inca 94, 95, 96, 97, 218, 223, 238
Mankechaca 225
maps 29, 106
Maras, salt-ponds 154
Marcanay 234, 238
Marcocasa 210
maté de coca 58
meat 57
medical kit 29
medical services
  Cusco 128
  Lima 105
medicinal plants 65
metalwork, Inca 88
Mina Perdida, site 69
Minchancamon 78
minimum impact trekking 160-70
Miraflores (Lima) 104, 111-13, 116-17
Miskay 192
Moche people 72-3, 75
Mollepata trek 24, 172, 207-16
Mollipunku 225
money 52-3
Montesinos, Vladimiro 44, 45
Moray, Inca farm 154
mountain viscachas 62
Moxeke, site 69
MRTA 43
muleteers and mules 15-16

mummies
  Chinchorro 67
  Inca 85
  in museums 117, 144
museums
  Cusco
  Coricancha Museum 143
  Museo Inka 146
  Museum of Natural History 142
  Museum of Santa Catalina 144
  Regional History Museum 144
  Cusco
  Religious Art Museum 144
  Visitor's Ticket 140
  Lima
  Military Museum 116
  Museo de la Nación 117
  Museo Nacional de Antropología y
    Arqueología 117
  Museo de Oro del Peru 117
  Museo del Tribunal de la Santa
    Inquisición 118
  museum tours 103
  Naval Museum 116
  Natural History Museum 117
  Ollantaytambo
  Ollantaytambo Museum 156
music and musical instruments 50-1
mythology, Inca 78-9

Nazca 119
Nazca people 73-4, 144
Neruda, Pablo 243
newspapers 51
New Zealand, travel from 17
Nusta Espana, Inca ruins 223-4

Ollantaytambo, town and site 155-7, 247
Omo 75
Oncoy Cacha 225
Orroya (verruga) fever 170
Ortiz, Friar Diego 222, 224, 234
Ounay, river 229
  overland to Peru 17-18

Pacamayo, camp and river 180, 217
Pachacamac 72, 85, 100, 118
Pachacutec, Inca 79, 81, 85, 123, 155, 247
Pachamama 84, 86
Pacopama 69
Pampa Cahuana 212, 216
    ˙paconas 225, 229

Paracas 70, 117
Pass of the Eagle 220
Patallacta, site 20, 175, 176, 178, 245
Paucarcancha, site 204, 207, 216, 245
Paullu Inca, Don Cristóbal 83
peoples of Peru 45-6
Perez de Cuellar, Javier 44
Peruvian crafts 60
Peruvian embassies 264-6
Peruvian Paso 62
Pezet, President 41
pharmacies
  Cusco 128
  Lima 106
photography 28, 128
Phuyu Pata Marca, site 185, 186
pigmy deer (pudú) 62
Pisac, town and site 152, 154
Pisco 119
Pisco (drink) 58
Pishtacos 194
Pizarro, Francisco 90-5, 100, 101, 123
  burial place 116
Pizarro, Gonzalo 96, 97, 143
Pizarro, Juan 96, 143
Pizarro, Pedro 232
Pleiades 84
police
  Cusco 128
  Lima 106
polio 32
politics 47-8
porters 15-16
postal services 57
  Cusco 128
  Lima 105
potatoes 57-8
Potosí, silver mines 37, 38
pottery
  pre-Inca 69, 72, 74
  Inca 88
Prado, President 41
Pre-Inca civilizations 66-78
Puca Pucara, site 151
Pucyura 222
Puente Antiguo 225
Puente de Cedru 229
Puerto Huyanay 200, 202
Pulpituyoc 175, 178
Pumacurco 148
Punchao, sacred idol 98, 99
Puno 120

Purification Trail 21, 197
Putucusi mountain 157

Qenko, site 150
Qosqo *see* Cusco
Qoyllor Riti 46
Quebrada Sisay pampa 212
Quechua language 46
Quechua people 45, 85
Quechua words & phrases 259-64, 270
Quera Machay 212
Quesca 204
Quillabamba 20, 24, 220, 221
quipus 83-4
Quizo Yupanqui, Inca general 101
Qurawasi 210

rabies 33, 106, 168
Raccy Pata 217
radio 51
rail services *see* trains
Raimondi stela 71, 117
Ramón Castilla, President 40
rates of exchange 52
record keeping, Inca 83-4
Recuay people 72
Reiche, Maria 73
Reinhard, Johan 248-9
religions 46
  Inca 84-6
restaurants
  Aguas Calientes 157
  Cusco 134-7
  Lima 114-15
  Machu Picchu 245
  Ollantaytambo 156
  Quillabamba 221
  Urubamba 154
Rímac, river 100
Riverside Trail 21, 217
roads, Inca 84
Rocabamba 190
Rodriguez, Edgar 20
Roman Catholicism 46
Rosaspata 223
route maps 171-2
routes 20-4
Rowe, John 78, 79, 245, 247
Runcu Raccay, site 180, 182
rucksacks 26

sacred lines (ceques) 85
sacred places (huacas) 85
Sacred Valley 151-9
sacred women 86
Sacsayhuaman, site 86, 96, 148, 150
safe trekking 164-70
safety 60-1, 124
Sairi Tupac, Inca 97, 143
Salapunco, site 150
Salcantay, Mt 24, 212
Salcantay Pampa 212
San Cristobal 230
San Fernando 229
San Marcos, University 101
San Martín, José de 40, 101, 104
San Miguel, valley and river 239
Sayac Marca, site 182, 184
Sayllapata 200
Sayri Tupac, Inca 97, 143
Sedru Casa 234
Sedruchaca 229
selva 36, 37
Sendero Luminosa (Shining Path) 43
Shaffer, Peter 32
shopping and souvenirs 59-60
  Cusco 138-9
  Lima 118
  Pisac 154
Sican people 77
Sicuani 120
sierra 36, 37
Silque Valley 21, 198, 200
Sixpac Manco Hostal 222, 223
sleeping bags and mats 26-7
snakes 62, 168, 217, 237
Soray 208, 210
Soto, Hernando de 49, 95
South American Explorers' Club
  (SAEC) 106
Spanish Inquisition 101
  headquarters 118
Spanish invasion and rule 37-41, 91-9
Spanish language 46
Spanish words & phrases 259-64
sports 51
Squier, George, traveller 254
Sucsu Chincana, river 230
sunburn and sun-stroke 168

Tahuantinsuyu 82
Tambo 229

Tambocarahuina 229
Tambo Machay, site 151, 185
Tambo-toqo 248
taxis 54
  Cusco 124
  Lima 102, 103
telephones 55
  Cusco 128
  Lima 105
tents 27
tetanus 32
textiles, Inca 88
Tiahuanaco people 74-6
time 55
tipping 59
Titu Cusi, Inca 78, 97-8, 223, 229
Toledo, Alejandro 45
Toledo, Francisco de 98
Topa Inca 81
Torres, Martin 141
Torontoy 217
tour groups (Inca trail) 173
tourist information
  Cusco 129
  Lima 106
Tourist Police 61
tourist visas 52
tours and trekking agencies 11-15
  Cusco 130, 131
  licensed tour operators 271-3
  Lima 103
trains and rail services 53-4
  Aguas Calientes 159, 258
  Cusco 124, 147
  Lima 119-20
  Ollantaytambo 157
  timetables 267-8
trailheads, getting to 174, 220
travel clinics 33
travellers' cheques 53
travelogues 31
Trekkers' Hotel 185, 186, 188, 189, 190, 198
trekking season 19, 218
Trujillo 42
tuberculosis 32
Tullumayo, river 123
Tumbes 91
Tunqul Mayu, river 234
Tupac Amaru, Inca 98, 242
  grave 143
Tupac Amaru II 39, 124

Tupac Amaru Revolutionary
  Movement 43
Tupac Huallpa, Inca 94
Tupac Yupanqui, Inca 81
TV 51
typhoid 32

Urpipata 232, 234
Urubamba, town 154-5
Urubamba valley and river 21, 24,
  151-9, 185, 199, 217, 221
USA to Peru 17
Ututo 225, 229

Vallejo, César 50
valuables 60
Vargas Llosa, Mario 44, 50
vicuñas 62
vicuña fabrics 59-60
Vilcabamba, ruins 96-8, 237-9, 246
Vilcabamba La Nueva 225
Vilcabamba trail 24, 218-42
Vilcanota see Urubamba
Viracocha, 74, 84
Viracocha, Inca 79
visas 52
  Cusco 129
  Lima 107
visitor's ticket (sites and museums)
  Cusco 140, 147
Vista Alegre 230
Vista Alegre, river 229
visual arts 50
Vitcos, walk and ruins 223-4

Wakwaya 69
water and water purification 58, 59, 169, 172
waterfowl 64
weather 36-7, 164
white-tailed deer 62
wildlife 62-4
wine 58
Wiñya Wayna see Huinay Huayna
writing and writers 50

yellow fever 32
Yunkachimpa 178
Yurac-Rumi 223-4
Yuveni 242

Zapatero, river and hut 229

❏ TRAILBLAZER GUIDES

Adventure Cycling Handbook	1st edn late 2004
Adventure Motorcycling Handbook	4th edn out now
Australia by Rail	4th edn out now
Azerbaijan	3rd edn mid 2004
The Blues Highway – New Orleans to Chicago	2nd edn out now
China by Rail	2nd edn Mar 2004
Coast to Coast (British Walking Guide)	1st edn early 2004
Cornwall Coast Path (British Walking Guide)	1st edn out now
Good Honeymoon Guide	2nd edn out now
Inca Trail, Cusco & Machu Picchu	2nd edn out now
Japan by Rail	1st edn out now
Kilimanjaro – a trekking guide to Africa's highest mountain	1st edn out now
Land's End to John O'Groats	1st edn late 2004
The Med Guide	1st edn mid 2004
Nepal Mountaineering Guide	1st edn mid 2004
New Zealand – Great Walks	1st edn out now
Norway's Arctic Highway	1st edn out now
Offa's Dyke Path (British Walking Guide)	1st edn Jan 2004
Pembrokeshire Coast Path (British Walking Guide)	1st edn out now
Pennine Way (British Walking Guide)	1st edn early 2004
Siberian BAM Guide – rail, rivers & road	2nd edn out now
The Silk Roads – a route and planning guide	1st end out now
Sahara Overland – a route and planning guide	1st edn out now
Sahara Abenteuerhandbuch (German edition)	1st edn out now
Ski Canada – where to ski and snowboard	1st edn out now
South Downs Way (British Walking Guide)	1st edn early 2004
South-East Asia – The Graphic Guide	1st edn out now
Tibet Overland – mountain biking & jeep touring	1st edn out now
Trans-Canada Rail Guide	3rd edn out now
Trans-Siberian Handbook	6th edn out now
Trekking in the Annapurna Region	4th edn Mar 2004
Trekking in the Everest Region	4th edn out now
Trekking in Corsica	1st edn out now
Trekking in the Dolomites	1st edn out now
Trekking in Ladakh	3rd edn mid 2004
Trekking in Langtang, Gosainkund & Helambu	1st edn out now
Trekking in the Moroccan Atlas	1st edn out now
Trekking in the Pyrenees	2nd edn out now
Tuva and Southern Siberia	1st edn late 2004
Vietnam by Rail	1st edn out now
West Highland Way (British Walking Guide)	1st edn out now

For more information about Trailblazer and our expanding range of guides,
for where to find your nearest stockist, for guidebook updates
or for credit card mail order sales (post-free worldwide) visit our web site:

www.trailblazer-guides.com

ROUTE GUIDES FOR THE ADVENTUROUS TRAVELLER

Europe
Trekking in Corsica
Trekking in the Dolomites
Trekking in the Pyrenees
(and the British Walking Series)

South America
Inca Trail, Cusco & Machu Picchu

Australasia
New Zealand – Great Walks

Africa
Kilimanjaro
Trekking in the Moroccan Atlas

Asia
Trekking in the Annapurna Region
Trekking in the Everest Region
Trekking in Ladakh
Trekking in Langtang
Nepal Mountaineering Guide

New Zealand – The Great Walks *Alexander Stewart*
1st edn, 272pp, 60 maps, 40 colour photos
ISBN 1 873756 78 X, £11.99, Can$28.95, US$19.95
New Zealand is a wilderness paradise of incredibly beautiful landscapes. There is no better way to experience it than on one of the nine designated Great Walks, the country's premier walking tracks which provide outstanding hiking opportunities for people at all levels of fitness and proficiency. Also includes detailed guides to Auckland, Wellington, National Park Village, Taumaranui, Nelson, Queenstown, Te Anau and Oban.

Kilimanjaro: a trekking guide to Africa's highest mountain
Henry Stedman, 1st edition, 240pp, 40 maps, 30 photos
ISBN 1 873756 65 8, £9.99, Can$22.95, US$17.95
At 19,340ft the world's tallest freestanding mountain, Kilimanjaro is one of the most popular destinations for hikers visiting Africa. It's possible to walk up to the summit: no technical skills are required. This new guide includes town guides to Nairobi and Dar-Es-Salaam, excursions in the region and a detailed colour guide to flora and fauna.

Trekking in the Everest Region *Jamie McGuinness*
4th edn, 304pp, 38 maps, 52 village plans, 30 colour photos
ISBN 1 873756 60 7, £10.99, Can$27.95, US$17.95
Popular guide to the world's most famous trekking region. Includes detailed walking maps, where to stay/eat along the way plus information on trek preparation and getting to Nepal. Written by a professional trek leader. '*The pick of the guides to the area*' **Adventure Travel**

Trekking in Corsica *David Abram*
1st edition, 320pp, 74 maps, 48 colour photos
ISBN 1 873756 63 1, £11.99, Can$26.95, US$18.95
A mountain range rising straight from the sea, Corsica holds the most arrestingly beautiful and diverse landscapes in the Mediterranean. Among the many trails that penetrate its remotest corners, the GR20, which wriggles across the island's watershed, has gained an international reputation. This guide also covers the best of the other routes. '*Excellent guide*'. **The Sunday Times**

Cornwall Coast Path *Edith Schofield*
1st edition, 192pp, 81 maps & town plans, 40 colour photos
ISBN 1 873756 55 0, £9.99, Can$22.95, US$16.95
A 163-mile National Trail around the western tip of Britain with some of the best coastal walking in Europe. The footpath takes in secluded coves, tiny fishing villages, rocky headlands, bustling resorts, wooded estuaries and golden surf-washed beaches.

Trans-Siberian Handbook *Bryn Thomas*
6th edition, 448pp, 65 maps, 40 colour photos
ISBN 1 873756 70 4, £12.99, Can$26.95 US$15.95
First edition short-listed for the **Thomas Cook Guidebook Awards**.
New sixth edition of the most popular guide to the world's longest rail
journey. How to arrange a trip, plus a km-by-km guide to the routes.
Updated and expanded to include extra information on travelling
independently in Russia. New mapping.
'*Definitive guide*' **Condé Nast Traveler**

Trans-Canada Rail Guide *Melissa Graham*
3rd edition, 240pp, 32 maps, 30 colour photos
ISBN 1 873756 69 0, £10.99, Can$24.95, US$16.95
Expanded 3rd edition now includes Calgary city guide. Comprehensive guide to Canada's trans-continental railroad. Covers the entire
route from coast to coast. What to see and where to stay in the cities
along the line, with information for all budgets.

Sahara Overland – a route & planning guide *Chris Scott*
1st edition, 544 pages, 24 colour & 150 B&W photos
ISBN 1 873756 26 7 £19.99, Can$44.95 US$29.95
Covers all aspects Saharan, from acquiring documentation to vehicle
choice and preparation; from descriptions of the prehistoric art sites of
the Libyan Fezzan to the ancient caravan cities of southern Mauritania.
How to 'read' sand surfaces, using GPS – it's all here along with 35
detailed off-road itineraries covering over 16,000kms in nine countries.
'*THE essential desert companion for anyone planning a Saharan trip on
either two wheels or four.*' **Trailbike Magazine**

Tibet Overland – a route & planning guide *Kym McConnell*
1st edition, 224pp, 16pp colour maps
ISBN 1 873756 41 0, £12.99, Can$29.95, US$19.95
Featuring 16pp of full colour mapping based on satellite photographs, this is a
guide for mountain bikers and other road users in Tibet. Includes detailed information on over 9000km of overland routes across the world's highest and
largest plateau. Includes Lhasa-Kathmandu route and the route to
Everest North Base Camp. '*..a wealth of advice...*' **HH The Dalai Lama**

The Silk Roads *Paul Wilson & Dominic Streatfeild-James*
1st edition, 336pp, 50 maps, 30 colour photos
ISBN 1 873756 53 4, £12.99, Can$29.95, US$18.95
The Silk Road was never a single thread but an intricate web of trade
routes linking Asia and Europe. This new guide follows all the routes
with sections on Turkey, Syria, Iran, Turkmenistan, Uzbekistan,
Kyrgyzstan, Pakistan and China.

The Blues Highway New Orleans to Chicago
A travel and music guide *Richard Knight*
2nd edition, 304pp, 50 maps, 30 colour photos
ISBN 1 873756 66 6, £12.99, Can$29.95, US$19.95
New edition of the first travel guide to explore the roots of jazz and
blues in the USA. ❑ Detailed city guides with 40 maps ❑ Where to
stay, where to eat ❑ The best music clubs and bars ❑ Who's who
of jazz and blues ❑ Historic landmarks ❑ Music festivals and events
❑ Exclusive interviews with music legends Wilson Pickett, Ike Turner,
Little Milton, Honeyboy Edwards and many more.
'*Fascinating*' – **Time Out**

Cusco
Machu Picchu
Vilcabamba